PRINCE2®

Managing Successful Projects with PRINCE2®

AXELOS
GLOBAL BEST PRACTICE

part of Williams Lea Tag

Published by TSO (The Stationery Office), part of Williams Lea Tag,
and available from:

Online
www.tsoshop.co.uk

Mail, Telephone, Fax & E-mail
TSO
PO Box 29, Norwich, NR3 1GN
Telephone orders/General enquiries: 0333 202 5070
Fax orders: 0333 202 5080
E-mail: customer.services@tso.co.uk
Textphone 0333 202 5077

TSO@Blackwell and other Accredited Agents

Cover image © Getty/buildingblock

Chp 1 © Getty/fotandy; Chp 2 © Getty/Jim_Pintar; Chp 3 © Getty/DrPAS; Chp 4 © Getty/Norman Posselt; Chp 5 © Getty/ DrPAS; Chp 6 © Getty/fotandy; Chp 7 © Getty/TeodoraDjordjevic; Chp 8 © Getty/dzika_mrowka; Chp 9 © Getty/DAJ; Chp 10 © Getty/Tom Cockrem; Chp 11 © Getty/DrPAS; Chp 12 © Getty/dogayusufdokdok; Chp 13 © Getty/NCBlanora; Chp 14 © Getty/NCBlanora; Chp 15 © Getty/Lukasz Szczepanski; Chp 16 © Getty/ Darrell Gulin; Chp 17 © Getty/Knaupe; Chp 18 © Getty/Knaupe; Chp 19 © Getty/Wlad74; Chp20 © Getty/Matteo Chinellato; Chp 21 © Getty/NCBlanora

First edition Crown copyright 1996
Second edition Crown copyright 1998
Third edition Crown copyright 2002
Fourth edition Crown copyright 2005
Fifth edition Crown copyright 2009
Sixth edition AXELOS Limited copyright 2017

Second impression 2018

ISBN 9780113315338

Printed in the United Kingdom for The Stationery Office.
Material is FSC certified and produced using ECF pulp, sourced from fully sustainable forests.

Contents

List of figures

List of tables

Foreword

PRINCE2® is widely considered the leading project management method. There are now people qualified in PRINCE2 in the majority of countries around the world. Many companies and governmental organizations are using the method to deliver change and develop new products or services. PRINCE2 provides a tried and tested method from which organizations can benefit.

The updated guidance will help organizations understand how the fundamental principles of PRINCE2 provide the basis of good project management. It also emphasizes how the method can be tailored to give an appropriate fit to a multitude of project sizes, types and environments. This latest evolution of PRINCE2 has been developed through consultation with project professionals to reflect their real-life experiences; something it shares with the previous iterations. It brings this experience together to provide practical guidance on managing projects in a wide variety of environments including those using agile approaches.

This new edition retains the familiar PRINCE2 approach to project management with its overall structure of principles, themes and processes. The theme chapters have been restructured to improve the flow and readability and accommodate the new material on tailoring. We have clarified the minimum requirements for running a project using PRINCE2 and differentiated these from the recommended approaches and techniques that can be used with PRINCE2. To reinforce this message we have also made changes to the qualification syllabus and examination design so that tailoring is explicitly tested in the practitioner exam.

Many projects today involve collaboration across organizational or even national boundaries. PRINCE2 provides a universal language that unites the project team with external suppliers and colleagues in other countries. In such environments a common understanding of what the project is trying to achieve, why the project is being undertaken and the benefits to be delivered, who is responsible for doing what, and what the project timescales are, are crucial to project success. These are all aspects where PRINCE2 can help organizations to better manage their projects.

The changes in this edition are all designed to make the method easier for individuals to use and for organizations adopting PRINCE2.

Good luck with your projects: whatever your delivery environment might be, there will be something in this publication to help you.

Peter Hepworth
CEO
AXELOS Global Best Practice

About AXELOS

AXELOS is a joint venture company co-owned by the UK Government's Cabinet Office and Capita plc. It is responsible for developing, enhancing and promoting a number of best-practice methodologies used globally by professionals working primarily in project, programme and portfolio management, IT service management and cyber resilience.

The methodologies, including ITIL®, PRINCE2®, MSP® and the new collection of cyber resilience best-practice products, RESILIA™, are adopted in more than 150 countries to improve employees' skills, knowledge and competence in order to make both individuals and organizations work more effectively.

In addition to globally recognized qualifications, AXELOS equips professionals with a wide range of content, templates and toolkits through its membership scheme, its professional development programme and its online community of practitioners and experts.

Visit www.axelos.com for the latest news about how AXELOS is making organizations more effective and registration details to join the AXELOS online community. If you have specific queries or requests, or would like to be added to the AXELOS mailing list, please contact ask@axelos.com.

Publications

AXELOS publishes a comprehensive range of guidance, including:

- *PRINCE2 Agile®*
- *Integrating PRINCE2®*
- *Directing Successful Projects with PRINCE2®*
- *Management of Portfolios (MoP®)*
- *Managing Successful Programmes (MSP®)*
- *Management of Risk: Guidance for Practitioners (M_o_R®)*
- *Portfolio, Programme and Project Offices (P3O®)*
- Portfolio, Programme and Project Management Maturity Model (P3M3®)
- *Management of Value (MoV®)*
- *RESILIA™: Cyber Resilience Best Practice*
- *ITIL® Practitioner Guidance*
- *ITIL® Continual Service Improvement*
- *ITIL® Service Design*
- *ITIL® Service Operation*
- *ITIL® Service Strategy*
- *ITIL® Service Transition.*

Full details of the range of materials published under the AXELOS Global Best Practice banner, including *Managing Successful Projects with PRINCE2*, can be found at:

https://www.axelos.com/best-practice-solutions

If you would like to inform AXELOS of any changes that may be required to *Managing Successful Projects with PRINCE2* or any other AXELOS publication, please log them at:

https://www.axelos.com/best-practice-feedback

Contact information

Full details on how to contact AXELOS can be found at:

https://www.axelos.com

For further information on qualifications and training accreditation, please visit:

https://www.axelos.com/qualifications

https://www.axelos.com/training-organization-benefits

For all other enquiries, please email:

ask@axelos.com

Acknowledgements

AXELOS Limited is grateful to everyone who has contributed to the development of this guidance and in particular would like to thank the following:

Authoring team

Nigel Bennett

Nigel was a member of the authoring team for *Managing Successful Projects with PRINCE2* 2009 edition and has recently been a member of the team developing P3M3 version 3. As a consulting director at RSM UK Consulting LLP, Nigel helps UK and international organizations become more capable of delivering their projects, programmes and portfolios effectively and efficiently, assesses and develops project management competency, develops and embeds bespoke frameworks, coaches senior client personnel, and offers bespoke project management-related training. He has also been instrumental in developing innovative online best-practice guidance. Nigel has many years' experience of managing bids and IT projects both at home in the UK and internationally, and has led a project management practice and PMO across emerging markets.

Robert Buttrick

Robert is an international authority on business-led, programme and project management with a successful track record for building project management capability in a wide variety of blue-chip companies, most recently as BT's Programme and Project Management Method director. He wrote *The Project Workout* (Buttrick, 2009) and is an active contributor to project management methods, best practice, professional journals and conferences. Robert received a distinguished service certificate from the British Standards Institution for services to national and international project management standards. He is also a member of the Chartered Institute of Marketing, a chartered engineer and an honorary fellow of the Association for Project Management (APM). He currently works as a consultant and is a visiting teaching fellow at the University of Warwick.

Phil Stanton

Phil is an independent consultant who helps organizations to improve their capability to deliver change. He has more than 25 years' experience of leading and delivering projects and programmes across financial services, infrastructure, government and telecoms. Over the past 15 years, he has helped a variety of organizations to make significant improvements in the cost, speed and reliability of their change delivery. This includes making significant contributions to the design, implementation and embedment of large-scale tailored versions of PRINCE2 at Network Rail (GRIP), Highways Agency (PCF) and Transport for London (PMF and Pathway). Phil also specializes in project and programme assurance and has created assurance frameworks for a number of large organizations.

Mentoring team

Andy Murray

Andy is a chartered director and management consultant specializing in portfolio, programme and project management (PPM), with more than 20 years of varied experience (public sector/private sector, SME/corporate, domestic/international).

Andy has a focus on project/programme governance and the treatment of inherent project/programme complexity. He has worked with AXELOS, HM Treasury, Cabinet Office and the APM in developing guidance on delivering successful projects/programmes, such as IUK Project Initiation Routemap, Directing Change, Co-Directing Change, PRINCE2 and P3M3.

Andy is a partner in RSM UK, responsible for the project and programme service line, and is also RSM's head of infrastructure.

Keith Richards

Keith is the founder and director of agileKRC, a company that specializes in bringing the benefits of agile and lean to organizations of any size.

With more than 30 years' experience in IT and project management, his roles have included being the technical director of the DSDM Consortium, the lead author for DSDM Atern (now more commonly known as AgilePM®) and the lead author for *PRINCE2 Agile*.

He has been a PRINCE2 trainer, an International Accreditation Forum (IAF) accredited facilitator and authored the book *Agile Project Management: Running PRINCE2 projects with DSDM Atern*. He has also been awarded the 'most valuable agile player' at the UK Agile Awards.

Michelle Rowland

Michelle has been PRINCE2 and P3O chief examiner on behalf of AXELOS Limited since 2014. She is an experienced project and programme manager who has, for more than 15 years, been providing a business-led focus to large change initiatives in a variety of organizations and environments.

She is an accredited PRINCE2, MSP, P3O, MoP, M_o_R, PRINCE2 Agile, APMP (now PMQ), agile project management, managing benefits and change management trainer. In addition, Michelle is an APMP marker for the APM.

Project team

Mike Acaster	PPM portfolio manager
Adrian Crago-Graham	Programme manager
Neil Glover	Commissioning editor
Kaimar Karu	Head of product development ITIL
Frances Scarff	Chief adviser to the CEO
Allan Thomson	PPM future product lead

Reference group

The AXELOS project team are grateful to the following members of the PRINCE2 reference group for their help in developing the requirements for the update and reviewing the drafts:

Steve Boronski, ILX Group plc; Paul Bradley, SPOCE; Sue Childs, UX R&D Ltd; Ian Clarkson, QA; Terry Dailey, Deliverables LLP; Steven Deneir, be.Projectized; Patrick Heymann, Office for National Statistics; John Howarth, Tanner James; Nader K. Rad, Management Plaza; Sheila Roberts, CUPE International Ltd; Sue Taylor, ETJ Solutions; Graham Williams, GSW Consultancy Ltd.

Global review group

Appreciation is due to the following for the time and effort put into reviewers' drafts of the publication:

Harminder Ahluwalia, Consulting 2U Ltd; Derek Arbuckle, Leggero Ltd; Nick Ashcroft, MoD; Carol Bartlett, Amicar Consulting Ltd; Brian Baverstock, Sarisbury Consulting Ltd; Brad Bigelow, SHAPE J6; Amanda Bisseker, QinetiQ; Johann Bleeker, Rabobank; Annamarie Boddy, Loose Lid Solutions; Eddie Borup, IBP Solutions Ltd; Alessandro Cagliesi, freelance; Andreas Chlumsky, CONSENSUS Consulting GmbH; Markus Chua Chye Heng, Sapience Consulting Pte Ltd; Tracey Copland, PM-Partners group; Alistair Cranmer, Oppidum BV; Jesús Feliciano Cruz-Franco, Panta Rhei Desarrollo; Danie de Waal, KPMG Services (Pty) Ltd; Eckhard Dechau, Tata Consultancy Services; John Edmonds, Imparo Ltd; Darilyn Evans, ALC Group; Elissa Farrow, About Your Transition; Chris Ferguson, Novare Consulting Ltd; John Fisher, UnconfuseU Ltd; Jeroen Geurtsen, Zestgroup; Simon Harris, Logical Model; Leeanne Hart; Wil Hendrickx, Lagant Management Consultants; Martin Hetland, Laerdal Medical; Carina Höyheim, Metier AB; Detleff Huss, prowum; Peter Johnson, Peter Johnson PJ Ltd; Nikki Kelly, APM Group; Rajiv Khanna, Raj Khanna Associates Ltd; Mark Kouwenhoven, nThen!; Wolfgang Ksoll, self-employed consultant; Richard Lampitt, SPOCE; Markus Lichtner, Konica Minolta; Joerg Lobbes, BPUG – Deutschland; Sean Low, Pink Elephant; John Moore, Newton Software Ltd; Maciej Mordaka, ATOS IT Services; Joseph Nduhiu, Mwasuki Technologies Ltd; Tomasz Nędzi, skills sp. z o. o.; Stefan Ondek, POTIFOB; Ruth Phillips, The Project Hub Ltd; Henny Portman, Hedeman Consulting; Steve Power, Goodstall Consulting Ltd; Wolf Reinhardt, ACT IT-Consulting & Services AG; Lizz Robb, Yellowhouse; Ian Rosser, Hybrid Consulting Ltd; Terje Sagstad, DIVI Learning; Ian Santry, Home Office; Mike Saville, ILX Group plc; Erik Scholten, Scheidt & Bachmann; Marcus Seelis, Konica Minolta; Dennis Sheehan, ILX Group plc; Innocent Shumba, KIM Consulting Group; Jay Siegelaub, Impact Strategies LLC; Hardeep Singh, Project Management Centre; Gerard Snakenborg, AIS BV; Alan Summerfield, Aspire Europe Ltd; Mark Sutton, Yireh Ltd; Karen Swanston, ILX Group plc; Eralp Tezcan, Management Plaza; H.J.P.(Bert) Vliex MSc, Vliex4U; Andy White, training consultant; Stephen Wierzbicki, ABSC Solutions Ltd; Paul Wigzel, Paul Wigzel Training and Consultancy; Mark Woodward, British Council; Greg Wynne, independent consultant; Dr Sami Zahran, ICT Ltd.

Contents summary

This manual provides the definitive explanation of PRINCE2. AXELOS examinations relating to PRINCE2 are based on this manual.

Managing Successful Projects with PRINCE2 comprises:

- **Chapter 1 Introduction** Introduces the structure of the method, its applicability and the structure of the guide. It describes what makes a project a PRINCE2 project and what PRINCE2 does not provide.

- **Chapter 2 Project management with PRINCE2** Explains the key concepts of project, project management and project managers, and introduces some sample project contexts.

- **Chapter 3 Principles** The principles that any project must follow to be a PRINCE2 project.

- **Chapter 4 Tailoring and adopting PRINCE2** How to use the inherent flexibility of PRINCE2 to tailor it for any project and build an organizational PRINCE2-based project management method. This includes common situations that the project manager may encounter.

- **Chapter 5 Introduction to PRINCE2 themes** Identifies and describes those aspects of project management that need to be addressed throughout the life of a project: the themes.

- **Chapter 6 Business case** Describes how a business case supports the continued business justification for a project and the PRINCE2 requirements for the business case theme. It provides guidance for effective business case management.

- **Chapter 7 Organization** How to choose the right roles to make an effective project management team and to work with other stakeholders. It describes what PRINCE2 requires for the organization theme and provides guidance for effective project organizations: there are no mandated techniques.

- **Chapter 8 Quality** Defines the role and importance of quality and quality management in PRINCE2, which is a product-focused project management method. It includes what PRINCE2 requires for the quality theme and guidance for effective quality management.

- **Chapter 9 Plans** Describes the value of planning for effective project management and the types of plan used in PRINCE2. It describes what PRINCE2 requires for the plans theme and provides guidance for effective planning.

- **Chapter 10 Risk** Proposes an approach to managing the inevitable uncertainties that affect projects, both in terms of the threats they can pose and the opportunities they may bring. It includes the PRINCE2 requirements for the risk theme and guidance for effective risk management.

- **Chapter 11 Change** Provides guidance for managing the different types of change that inevitably occur during the life of a project. The PRINCE2 approach to the change theme is described along with guidance for effective change control.

- **Chapter 12 Progress** Explains the importance of measuring progress to the achievement of a project's objectives and provides guidance for effective progress management. It includes the PRINCE2 requirements for managing progress and guidance for effective progress management.

- **Chapter 13 Introduction to processes** Provides an outline of a PRINCE2 project lifecycle described both in project stages and by using the PRINCE2 process model.

- **Chapter 14 Starting up a project** Describes the first activities for starting a project: check the justification; create the project management team; define the project management approach; and plan project initiation, including capturing previous lessons. Guidelines are included for tailoring the process.

- **Chapter 15 Directing a project** Covers the activities that the project board undertakes for decision-making throughout the project lifecycle to remain accountable for the success of the project. Also includes tailoring guidelines for directing a project.

- **Chapter 16 Initiating a project** How to get ready to start work on the project: agree the project management approaches and controls; confirm the plan; prepare the benefits management approach; and assemble the project initiation documentation. It includes tailoring guidelines for the initiating a project process.

- **Chapter 17 Controlling a stage** Describes how to set up work for a stage, monitor progress, manage change (including taking corrective action), and deal with any issues that may impact the stage plan. Also includes tailoring guidelines for the controlling a stage process.

- **Chapter 18 Managing product delivery** Explains how product delivery is controlled by the project and team managers, setting criteria for the execution, delivery and acceptance of work packages. It includes tailoring guidelines for the managing product delivery process.

- **Chapter 19 Managing a stage boundary** Provides the project board with the information it needs to review the current stage and updated business case, and approve the plan for the next stage. Guidelines are provided for tailoring the managing a stage boundary process.

- **Chapter 20 Closing a project** Describes how to close a project on delivery of its products (or agreed variations to them) or prematurely because there is no longer a business justification to continue. It includes tailoring guidelines for the closing a project process.

- **Chapter 21 Considerations for organizational adoption** Provides more detailed guidance for organizations that want to create and embed their own PRINCE2-based project management method. Examples are provided of how organizations have tailored PRINCE2.

- **Appendices and glossary** The appendices provide further supporting information, including role and product descriptions, an example of product-based planning, and a health check. The glossary gives a list of the definitions of specialized terms used in the guide.

Conventions used in this manual

Processes, activities, themes, principles and management documents will always be referred to using the same key words or phrases, and are not otherwise distinguished, as they should be evident from their context.

The term 'corporate, programme management or the customer' is used throughout to refer to the organization that commissions a project. This organization can either be corporate management, programme management or the customer, but we have used this shortened form to aid readability.

Examples are highlighted in tinted boxes.

Abbreviations and acronyms have largely been avoided, and the few that are used are given in full at their first mention and listed below:

APM: Association for Project Management

KPI: key performance indicator

PID: project initiation documentation

PMI®: Project Management Institute

Introduction

This chapter covers:

- the applicability of PRINCE2 to any project
- the structure of PRINCE2: principles, themes, processes and the project environment
- what PRINCE2 is and what it is not
- what defines a PRINCE2 project
- the purpose of the manual

1 Introduction

PRINCE2 (PRojects IN Controlled Environments) is one of the most widely used methods for managing **project**s in the world. It is a structured project management method based on experience drawn from thousands of projects and from the contributions of countless project **sponsor**s, **project manager**s, project teams, academics, trainers and consultants.

PRINCE2 has been designed to be generic so that it can be applied to any project regardless of project scale, type, organization, geography or culture. It achieves this by:

- separating the management of project work from the specialist contributions, such as design or construction. The specialist aspects of any type of project are easily integrated with the PRINCE2 method and, used alongside PRINCE2, provide a secure overall framework for the project work
- focusing on describing what needs to be done, rather than prescribing how everything is done.

PRINCE2:

- is based on established and proven best practice and **governance** for **project management**
- can be tailored to meet the specific needs of the organization and scaled to the size and complexity of different projects
- can be applied to any type of project and can easily be implemented alongside specialist, industry-specific models (e.g. 'engineering models' or 'development lifecycles')
- is widely recognized and understood and provides a common vocabulary for all project participants. In doing so it promotes consistency of project work and the ability to reuse project **asset**s. It also facilitates staff mobility and reduces the impact of personnel changes or **handover**s
- ensures that participants focus on the viability of the project in relation to its **business case** objectives, rather than simply seeing the completion of the project as an end in itself. It ensures that **stakeholder**s (including sponsors and resource providers) are properly represented in planning and decision-making
- promotes learning from project experience and continual improvement in organizations
- is supported by a worldwide network of examination institutes, accredited training and consultancy organizations, and AXELOS consulting partners, who can supply expert support for **PRINCE2 project**s or for organizations planning to adopt PRINCE2.

Because PRINCE2 is generic and based on proven principles, organizations adopting the method as a standard can substantially improve their organizational capability and **maturity** across multiple areas of business activity, such as business change, construction, IT, mergers and acquisitions, research and product development.

1.1 The structure of PRINCE2

The PRINCE2 method addresses project management with four integrated elements of principles, **theme**s, **process**es and the project environment (Figure 1.1):

● **PRINCE2 principles** The principles are the guiding obligations and good practices which determine whether the project is genuinely being managed using PRINCE2. There are seven principles and unless all of them are applied, it is not a PRINCE2 project.

The **PRINCE2 principles** are explained in Chapter 3.

PRINCE2 is a flexible method and one of the principles is that it should be tailored to suit the type and size of project. Chapter 4 describes how to tailor PRINCE2 to make it appropriate to the project.

● **PRINCE2 themes** The themes describe aspects of project management that must be addressed continually and in parallel throughout the project. The seven themes explain the specific treatment required by PRINCE2 for various project management disciplines and why they are necessary.

The PRINCE2 themes are provided in Chapters 5 to 12.

● **PRINCE2 processes** The seven processes describe a progression from the pre-project **activity** of getting started, through the **stage**s of the **project lifecycle**, to the final act of project closure. Each process has checklists of recommended activities, **product**s and related responsibilities.

The PRINCE2 processes are provided in Chapters 13 to 20.

● **The project environment** Organizations often want a consistent approach to managing projects and tailor PRINCE2 to create their own project management method. This method is then embedded into the organization's way of working.

Chapter 21 provides advice and examples on how to tailor and adopt PRINCE2 in an organization.

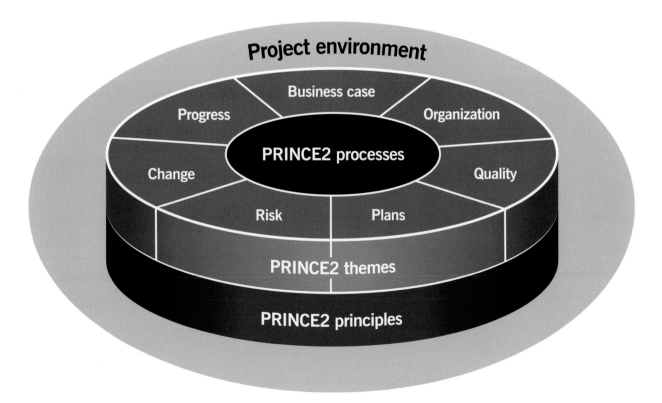

Figure 1.1 The structure of PRINCE2

1.2 What PRINCE2 does not provide

It is not intended (or possible) for PRINCE2 to cover every aspect of project management. There are three broad topic categories which are deliberately considered to be outside the scope of PRINCE2:

- **Specialist aspects** PRINCE2's strength is in its wide applicability. It is entirely generic and excludes industry-specific or type-specific activity. Engineering models, project lifecycles, **agile methods** or specific techniques (such as organizational change management or procurement) can readily be used alongside PRINCE2. PRINCE2 categorizes all these aspects of project work as 'specialist' in contrast to '**management products**' which relate to those required to manage the project. This means that the **specialist product**s concerned need to be identified and included within project **scope** and **plan**s.

- **Detailed techniques** There are many proven planning and control techniques that can be used in support of the PRINCE2 themes; for example, critical path analysis (in planning) and earned value analysis (in progress control). Such techniques are well documented elsewhere. Techniques are only described in detail where PRINCE2 specifically recommends that approach is used, or the approach is unique to PRINCE2, such as the **quality review technique**. Even when PRINCE2 recommends a specific technique, alternative yet equivalent techniques can be substituted as long as they meet the requirements set out in the manual.

- **Leadership capability** Leadership, motivational skills and other interpersonal skills are immensely important in project management but impossible to codify in a method. Leadership styles vary considerably and a style that works in one situation may be entirely inappropriate in another. The fact that it is easy to think of successful leaders who have adopted very different styles, from autocratic to consensus-based, bears this out. For this reason, PRINCE2 cannot address this aspect of project management in detail although creation of an effective project team is discussed in section 7.3.8. There are many leadership models and interpersonal skills training programmes that cover leadership capability.

1.3 What makes a project a 'PRINCE2 project'?

The flexibility about how PRINCE2 can be applied creates the **risk** that a project that is claimed to be following PRINCE2 may be doing so in name only. PRINCE2 therefore sets out some criteria about what makes a project a 'PRINCE2 project'.

 Key message

For a project to be following PRINCE2, as a minimum it must be possible to demonstrate that the project:

- is applying PRINCE2's principles
- is meeting the minimum requirements set out in the PRINCE2 themes
- has project processes that satisfy the purpose and objectives of the PRINCE2 processes
- is either using PRINCE2's recommended techniques or using alternative, equivalent techniques.

Beyond these requirements, users of PRINCE2 have freedom to tailor PRINCE2 to their needs as described in Chapter 4 and throughout the rest of the manual.

1.4 The purpose of this manual

This manual is intended for anyone who will work on a PRINCE2 project and is designed:

- for entry-level project management personnel wishing to learn about project management generally and the PRINCE2 method in particular
- for experienced project managers and anyone who wishes to learn about the PRINCE2 method
- as a detailed reference source for PRINCE2 practitioners
- as a source of information on PRINCE2 for managers considering whether to adopt the method.

The manual helps address the questions frequently asked by people involved in project management and support roles. These questions include:

- What is expected of me?
- What does the project manager do?
- What do I do if things do not go to plan?
- What decisions am I expected to make?
- What information do I need or must I supply?
- Who should I look to for support? For direction?
- How can I tailor the use of PRINCE2 for my project?

2

Project management with PRINCE2

This chapter covers:

- projects, project management and project managers
- project variables
- different project contexts
- project management standards
- applying PRINCE2

2 Project management with PRINCE2

2.1 What is a project?

A key challenge for organizations in today's world is to succeed in balancing two parallel, competing imperatives. These are to:

- maintain current business operations (i.e. maintain profitability, service **quality**, **customer** relationships, brand loyalty, productivity, market confidence, etc.). This is what we would term 'business as usual'
- transform business operations in order to survive and compete in the future (i.e. looking forward and deciding how business change can be introduced to best effect for the organization).

As the pace of change (technology, business, social, regulatory, etc.) accelerates, and the penalties of failing to adapt to change become more evident, the focus of management attention is inevitably moving to achieve a balance between business as usual and business change.

Projects are the means by which we introduce change and, although many of the skills required are the same, there are some crucial differences between managing business as usual and managing project work.

 Definition: Project

A temporary organization that is created for the purpose of delivering one or more business products according to an agreed business case.

There are a number of characteristics of project work that distinguish it from business as usual:

- **Change** Projects are the means by which we introduce change.
- **Temporary** As the definition of a project states, projects are temporary in nature. When the desired change has been implemented, business as usual resumes (in its new form) and the need for the project is removed. Projects should have a defined start and a defined end.
- **Cross-functional** A project involves a team of people with different skills working together (on a temporary basis) to introduce a change that will impact others outside the team. Projects often cross the normal functional divisions within an organization and sometimes span entirely different organizations. This frequently causes stresses and strains both within organizations and between them (for example, between customers and **supplier**s). Each has a different perspective and motivation for getting involved in the change.
- **Unique** Every project is unique. An organization may undertake many similar projects, and establish a familiar, proven pattern of project activity, but each one will be unique in some way: a different team, a different customer, a different location, a different time. All these factors combine to make every project unique.

● **Uncertainty** The characteristics already listed will introduce **threat**s and opportunities over and above those we typically encounter in the course of business as usual. Projects are more risky.

Projects come in all shapes and sizes. An organization may be undertaking an IT project to deliver improved systems required to manage its business; another organization may be undertaking a clinical research project in order to bring a new drug to market; and a third organization may be managing an event.

Furthermore, the environment within which the project is being managed may influence how it is started up, delivered, assured and closed. There may be factors external to the project itself, such as embedded corporate standards, the maturity of the organization, and regulatory frameworks and factors specific to the individual project such as the industry sector, the geographical location and the project's risks.

2.2 What is project management?

Project management is the planning, delegating, monitoring and control of all aspects of the project, and the motivation of those involved, to achieve the project objectives within the expected **performance target**s for time, cost, quality, scope, **benefit**s and risk.

For example, a new house is completed by creating drawings, foundations, floors, walls, windows, a roof, plumbing, wiring and connected services. None of this is project management, so why do we need project management at all? The purpose of project management is to keep control over the specialist work required to create the project product or, to continue with the house analogy, to make sure the roofing contractor does not arrive before the walls are built.

Additionally, given that projects are how we introduce a change, and that project work entails a higher degree of risk than many other business activities, it follows that implementing a secure, consistent, well-proven approach to project management is a valuable business investment.

2.3 What is it we wish to control?

There are six variables involved in any project, and therefore six aspects of project performance to be managed. These are:

● **Costs** The project has to be affordable and, though we may start out with a particular budget in mind, there will be many factors which can lead to overspending and, perhaps, some opportunities to cut costs.

● **Timescales** Closely linked to costs, and probably one of the questions project managers are most frequently asked, is: When will it be finished?

● **Quality** Finishing on time and within budget is not much consolation if the result of the project does not work. In PRINCE2 terms, the project product must be fit for purpose.

● **Scope** Exactly what will the project deliver? Without knowing it, the various parties involved in a project can very often be talking at cross-purposes about this. The customer may assume that, for instance, a fitted kitchen and/or bathroom is included in the price of the house, whereas the supplier views these as 'extras'. On large-scale projects, scope definition is much more subtle and complex. There must be agreement on the project's scope and the project manager needs to have a sufficient understanding of what is and what is not within the scope. The project manager should take care not to deliver beyond the scope as this is a common source of delays, overspends and uncontrolled change ('scope creep').

- **Benefits** Perhaps most often overlooked is the question: Why are we doing this? It is not enough to build the house successfully on time, within budget and to quality specifications if, in the end, we cannot sell or rent it at a profit or live in it happily. The project manager has to have a clear understanding of the purpose of the project as an investment and make sure that what the project delivers is consistent with achieving the desired return.

- **Risk** All projects entail risks but exactly how much risk are we prepared to accept? Should we build the house near the site of a disused mine, which may be prone to subsidence? If we decide to go ahead, is there something we can do about the risk? Maybe insure against it, enhance (underpin) the house foundations or simply monitor with ongoing surveys?

PRINCE2 is an integrated method of principles, themes and processes that addresses the planning, delegation, monitoring and control of all these six aspects of project performance (see Figure 2.1).

2.4 What does a project manager do?

In order to achieve control over anything, there must be a plan. It is the project manager who is **responsible** for planning the sequence of activities to build the house (e.g. working out when the bricklayers will be required).

It may be possible to build the house yourself, but being a project manager implies that you will delegate some or all of the work to others. The ability to delegate is important in any form of management but particularly so in project management, because of the cross-functionality and risks.

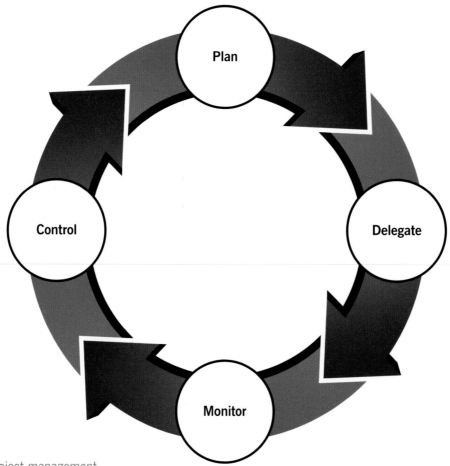

Figure 2.1 Project management

With the delegated work under way, the aim is that it should 'go according to plan', but we cannot rely on this always being the case. It is the project manager's responsibility to monitor how well the work in progress matches the plan.

Of course, if work does not go according to plan, the project manager has to do something about it (i.e. exert control). Even if the work is going well, the project manager may identify an opportunity to speed it up or reduce costs.

 Key message

One aim of PRINCE2 is to make the right information available at the right time for the right people to make the right decisions about the project. Those decisions include whether to take **corrective action** or implement measures to improve performance.

2.5 Projects in context

PRINCE2 assumes that there will be a customer who will specify the desired result and (usually) pay for the project, and a supplier who will provide the resources and skills to deliver that result.

PRINCE2 refers to the organization that commissions a project as 'corporate, programme management or the customer' (by 'corporate, programme management' we mean corporate or programme management). This organization is responsible for providing the project's mandate, governing the project, and for realizing any benefits that the project might deliver or enable (for projects in **programme** and **portfolio** contexts, see sections 2.5.2 and 2.5.3).

PRINCE2 refers to a supplier as the person, group or groups responsible for the supply of the project's specialist products.

Projects can exist within many contexts; they may be stand-alone (with their own business case and justification) or they may be part of a programme or wider portfolio. Figure 2.2 shows how projects may fit within a programme and portfolio context. In addition, projects may be wholly managed within the commissioning organization or be part of a commercial relationship.

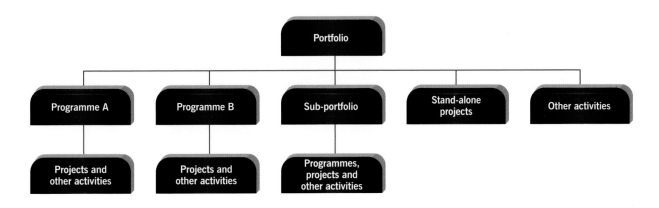

Figure 2.2 Projects in the context of portfolios and programmes

2.5.1 Stand-alone projects

Projects can exist as stand-alone entities within an organization and outside the governance structures introduced by programmes or portfolios, or where an organization has been set up solely for the purpose of undertaking the project.

2.5.2 Projects within programmes

Definition: Programme

A temporary, flexible organization structure created to coordinate, direct and oversee the implementation of a set of related projects and activities in order to deliver **outcome**s and benefits related to the organization's strategic objectives. A programme is likely to have a life that spans several years.

A project may be part of a programme, and the programme manager may commission a project to enable or deliver products or **output**s that contribute to some of the programme's expected outcomes. The project will be impacted by the programme's approach to governance, its structure and its reporting requirements.

Tip

PRINCE2 defines the term 'sponsor' as the role that is the main driving force behind a programme or project. The guidance uses the term 'commission' for the activity or **authority** to request the project. The organization commissioning the project will usually provide the project sponsor.

2.5.3 Projects within a portfolio

Definition: Portfolio

The totality of an organization's investment (or segment thereof) in the changes required to achieve its strategic objectives.

Corporate organizational structures can vary from 'traditional' functional structures to project-focused corporate organizations. In the 'traditional' functional structure, staff are organized by type of work (e.g. marketing, finance and sales) and there are clear reporting lines. In contrast, the standard practice in project-focused corporate organizations is to work with project teams.

Organizations may have corporate structures in which projects are commissioned to deliver products or outputs that contribute to the strategic objectives of the organization, and are managed within portfolios. A portfolio may comprise programmes, projects and other work that may not necessarily be interdependent or directly related but must all contribute to achieving the strategic objectives.

2.5.4 Projects in a commercial environment

If the project is being run to deliver to a specific set of customer requirements, the customer may have entered into a commercial relationship with a supplier following a formal tender. The organization delivering the project (the supplier) will do so in order to satisfy a particular need identified by the customer. The contract between the parties sets out how the customer and supplier will work together to deliver the project but the rights and duties covered by the agreement may constrain how a project manager manages the project.

The customer may break the work down into one or more elements. The number of elements is that which is necessary to deliver the customer's business case. Some of those elements may then be used to procure suppliers to deliver that work, while others may form the basis of work to be delivered by the customer itself. For a supplier, the work to be delivered may be the subject of a legally binding contract resulting from the procurement process. In order to deliver this work, the supplier may itself procure subcontractors by further breaking down its work into additional elements.

In a commercial environment, sometimes there may be hierarchies of commercial relationships between suppliers. Rather than a simple customer/supplier relationship involving two organizations, projects often involve multiple organizations constrained by multiple contracts. There may be a primary commissioning organization (or one prime contractor), but there may be several customers and/or several supplier organizations, each of which may have its own business case for undertaking the project. Examples include:

- joint ventures
- collaborative research
- intergovernmental projects
- interagency projects (e.g. for the United Nations Development Programme)
- bidding consortium and alliance contracting
- partnerships.

When managing projects in a commercial environment, consider that there may be multiple sets of:

- reasons for undertaking the project (business case)
- management systems (including project management methods)
- governance (possibly requiring disclosure of different sorts of project data at different points in the project's life)
- organization structures
- **delivery approach**es (see section 2.6.3)
- corporate cultures (e.g. behaviours, cultures, **risk appetite**).

Further advice and guidance related to **tailoring** PRINCE2 in a commercial environment can be found throughout this manual.

2.6 Applying PRINCE2

2.6.1 PRINCE2, international standards and bodies of knowledge

A standard provides rules, guidelines or characteristics that can be used consistently to ensure that materials, products, processes and services are fit for their purpose; it does not, however, state how activities should be carried out to achieve this.

A method, such as PRINCE2, provides not only a set of activities to be done, together with roles, but also techniques for undertaking these activities.

A body of knowledge looks at what a competent project manager should know and focuses on what and how to do it.

The PRINCE2 method exists within the context of a number of such standards and bodies of knowledge including:

- *ISO 21500:2012 Guidance on Project Management* (International Organization for Standardization, 2012)
- *BS 6079–1:2010 Project Management. Principles and Guidelines for the Management of Projects* (British Standards Institution, 2010)
- *A Guide to the Project Management Body of Knowledge (PMBOK® Guide)* (Project Management Institute, 2013)
- *APM Body of Knowledge* (Association for Project Management, 2012)
- The IPMA *Individual Competence Baseline for Project, Programme & Portfolio Management* (4th version, ICB4): an inventory of competences for individuals to use in career development, certification, training, education, consulting, research and more (International Project Management Association, 2015).

When designing and **embedding** a project management method based on PRINCE2 (see Chapter 4), an organization needs to be aware of these standards and bodies of knowledge, and should apply them in a manner appropriate to its business.

For more information about PRINCE2 and international standards, see Appendix B.

2.6.2 PRINCE2 and commissioning organization standards

An organization will typically develop values, principles, policies, standards and processes that are fit for purpose, including those required to govern, manage and support programmes and projects.

A programme defines its strategies in a plan which must ensure that the programme's vision and goals align with those of the organization. Projects commissioned by a programme will typically inherit programme strategies which may be used to replace the project's approach to **quality management**, **risk management** etc., tailoring them as appropriate.

If the project is commissioned by a customer from outside the project organization, then the mandate may require the use of some or all of the customer's standards or methods. Examples may include the use of the customer's issue management process and specific reporting requirements.

The project manager may need to tailor the project (see section 4.3) to meet standards and process requirements, but within the guidelines of the organization's method. This will be recorded in the **project initiation documentation** (PID).

Tip

Varied uses of terminology can be particularly confusing where multiple best-practice methods are employed within the same organization, and care must be taken to map or integrate the methods.

2.6.3 PRINCE2 and delivery approaches

The **project approach** is the way in which the work of the project is to be delivered. It may rely on one or more delivery approaches, which are the specialist approaches used by **work package**s to create the products. Typical approaches include:

- a waterfall approach where each of the **delivery step**s to create the products takes place in sequence (e.g. in a construction project where requirements gathering and design take place before building begins) and the product is made available during or at the end of the project
- an agile approach often, but not exclusively, for software development where requirements gathering, design, coding and testing all take place iteratively through the project.

There are typically a number of delivery steps within the delivery approach (e.g. the **sprint**s within an agile approach or steps such as study, design, build, test, etc. within a waterfall approach).

The application of PRINCE2 can be very different depending on which delivery approach is used. For further guidance, see sections 9.3 and 16.5.

Key message

PRINCE2 Agile regards agile as a family of behaviours, concepts, frameworks and techniques. For more information about using agile and PRINCE2 together, see *PRINCE2 Agile* (AXELOS, 2015).

2.6.4 Measures of success

The traditional approach to measuring time, cost and quality may still have its place but it does not necessarily tell the whole story. The best way to summarize the project status at a point in time is to identify **key performance indicator**s (KPIs).

When designing KPIs, a balance should be struck between qualitative and quantitative measures, leading and lagging indicators, and project inputs and outputs. The number of KPIs should be balanced to create only information that is necessary and sufficient.

Key message

Objectives are what the project needs to achieve, whereas KPIs are the measures that indicate whether or not progress is being made towards achieving the objectives.

What are lagging and leading indicators?

Lagging indicators

Measure performance that follows events, and allow management to track how well actual performance matches that which was expected. An example could be the number of unexpected errors reported after a particular software **release**.

Leading indicators

Measure progress towards events, and allow management to track whether it is on course to achieve the expected performance. An example would be the persistent failure of a supplier to meet quality requirements early in the project.

The KPIs should be aligned with the quality expectations and **acceptance criteria** defined in the **project product description**, and the project **tolerance**s (time, cost, quality, scope, benefits and risk) defined in the PID.

One way to show project progress is through a project dashboard that uses graphical representations such as pie charts and histograms to display the status and trends of performance indicators. These can show the status for quantitative KPIs and are easy to understand by relevant stakeholders at all levels.

2.6.5 PRINCE2 and organizational capability

It is generally recognized that organizations which demonstrate higher levels of project management capability can also demonstrate increases in business performance through the effective use of project management methods such as PRINCE2. **Maturity model**s such as AXELOS Limited's Portfolio, Programme and Project Management Maturity Model (P3M3) provide a way of baselining organizational capability against a maturity scale, diagnosing weaknesses and planning for improvements.

P3M3 characterizes an organization's maturity using the following 5-point scale:

- Level 1: Awareness of process
- Level 2: Repeatable process
- Level 3: Defined process
- Level 4: Managed process
- Level 5: Optimized process.

An organization assessed at level 3 would typically ensure that a project management method such as PRINCE2 is consistently deployed and used by all projects (see Chapter 21). The organization's embedded version of PRINCE2 may need to take account of the types and scale of project being delivered, the environment within which the organization operates (e.g. regulatory or commercial), commissioning organization standards and the delivery approach(es) used. The method may also allow for tailoring (see Chapters 4 and 21), perhaps within specific rules or guidelines, in order to recognize the differences specific to individual projects.

Principles

This chapter covers:

- why PRINCE2 is based on principles
- the flexibility of a principle-based approach
- the seven PRINCE2 principles

3 Principles

PRINCE2 is designed so that it can be applied to any type of project, taking account of its scale, organization, geography and culture. It is designed to contribute to the success of a project without burdening it with bureaucracy. The themes, processes and **product description**s describe what should be done but, in general, not how.

PRINCE2 is principle-based rather than prescriptive; the principles are:

- universal in that they apply to every project
- self-validating in that they have been proven in practice over many years
- empowering because they give practitioners of the method added confidence and ability to influence and shape how the project will be managed.

The PRINCE2 principles provide a framework of good practice for people involved in a project and were developed from lessons taken from both successful and failed projects.

The seven PRINCE2 principles are:

- continued business justification
- learn from experience
- defined roles and responsibilities
- manage by stages
- manage by **exception**
- focus on products
- tailor to suit the project.

To be following PRINCE2, these principles must be adopted when managing a project. Minimum requirements set out in the themes and processes chapters must also be satisfied. These minimum requirements describe what has to be done, rather than how it is done.

The principles are described in more detail in the following sections, 3.1 to 3.7.

3.1 Continued business justification

 Key message

A PRINCE2 project has continued business justification.

PRINCE2 requires that for all projects:

- there is a justifiable reason for starting the project
- that justification is recorded and approved
- the justification remains valid, and is revalidated, throughout the life of the project.

In most organizations the business justification is usually documented in some form of business case. Some organizations may use business plans or similar as the business justification during the early stages of the project, although these plans may not satisfy the requirements of a business case. The format and formality of documentation might vary, depending on organizational standards, needs and circumstances.

The business justification drives decision-making to ensure that the project remains aligned with the benefits being sought that contribute to the business objectives. Organizations that lack rigour in business justification may find that projects proceed even when there are few real benefits or when a project has only tentative associations with the corporate, programme management or customer strategies. Poor alignment with corporate, programme management or customer strategies can also result in organizations having a portfolio of projects that have mutually inconsistent or duplicated objectives.

Projects driven by legislation or regulation, which are compulsory, should be supported by a business justification to demonstrate that the chosen option represents the best value for money.

Although the justification should remain valid, it may change. It is therefore important that the project and evolving justification remain consistent. If a project can no longer be justified then it should be stopped. Stopping a project in these circumstances is a positive contribution to an organization as its funds and resources can be reinvested in other more worthwhile projects.

3.2 Learn from experience

Key message

PRINCE2 project teams learn from experience: lessons are sought, recorded and acted upon throughout the life of the project.

Projects involve a temporary organization for a finite timescale for a specific business purpose. A common characteristic is that the project includes an element of uniqueness such that it cannot be managed by existing line management or functional units. It is this element of uniqueness that makes projects challenging as the temporary team may not have experience of a project like the one being undertaken.

Learning from experience takes place throughout PRINCE2:

- **When starting a project** Previous or similar projects should be reviewed to see if lessons could be applied. If the project is a 'first' for the people within the organization, then it is even more important to learn from others and the project should consider seeking external experience.
- **As the project progresses** The project should continue to learn. Lessons should be included in relevant **reports** and reviews. The goal is to seek opportunities to implement improvements during the life of the project.

● **As the project closes** The project should pass on lessons. Unless lessons provoke change, they are only lessons identified (not learned).

It is the responsibility of everyone involved with the project to look for lessons rather than wait for someone else to provide them.

3.3 Defined roles and responsibilities

 Key message

A PRINCE2 project has defined and agreed roles and responsibilities within an organization structure that engages the business, **user** and supplier stakeholder interests.

Projects involve people. No amount of scheduling or control will help if the wrong people are involved, if the right people are not involved, or if people involved do not know what is expected of them or what to expect of others.

A project is typically cross-functional, may involve more than one organization, and may involve a mix of full-time and part-time resources. The management structures of the parties involved in the project are likely to be different with different priorities, objectives and interests to protect. The day-to-day line management structures may not be designed for, or suited to, project work.

To be successful, projects must have an explicit **project management team structure** consisting of defined and agreed roles and responsibilities for the people involved in the project and a means for effective communication between them.

All projects have the following primary stakeholders:

● 'business' sponsors who endorse the objectives and ensure that the business investment provides value for money

● 'users' who, after the project is completed, will use the products to enable the organization to gain the expected benefits

● 'suppliers' who provide the resources and expertise required by the project (these may be internal or external).

Therefore, all three stakeholder interests need to be represented effectively in the **project management team**; two out of three is not enough. If the project costs outweigh the benefits, the project will be seen as a failure. Equally, if the outcome of the project does not meet the users' or operational needs, or cannot feasibly be delivered by the suppliers, failure is inevitable. The stakeholder interests are represented on the project board (see section 7.2.1.1).

The defined project management team structure unites the various parties in the common aims of the project. For all those people involved, a defined project management team structure provides the answer to the question: What is expected of me?

3.4 Manage by stages

Key message

A PRINCE2 project is planned, monitored and controlled, management stage by management stage.

PRINCE2 breaks the project down into discrete, sequential sections, called **management stage**s.

Definition: Management stage

The section of a project that the project manager is managing on behalf of the project board at any one time, at the end of which the project board will wish to review progress to date, the state of the **project plan**, the business case and risks and the next **stage plan**, in order to decide whether to continue with the project.

The choice of appropriate management stages for a project will depend on a number of factors, including:

- the size and complexity of the project (e.g. shorter management stages offer more control, whereas longer management stages reduce the burden on senior management)
- significant decisions and control points required during the project's lifecycle; these will often be linked to key investment, business or technical decisions
- organizational policies and standards.

In PRINCE2, a project must have at least two management stages:

- an **initiation stage**
- at least one further management stage. The more complex and risky a project is, the more management stages will be required.

The focus on managing by stages ensures that the project is properly initiated before work starts on delivery of the project's outputs. It also:

- provides review and decision points, giving the project board the opportunity to assess the project's viability at defined intervals, rather than let it run on in an uncontrolled manner
- gives the ability to ensure that key decisions are made prior to the detailed work needed to implement them
- allows clarification of what the impact will be of an identified external influence, such as the corporate budget-setting process or the finalization of legislation
- facilitates the manage by exception principle by delegating authority to the project manager management stage by management stage.

The project board authorizes one management stage of the project at a time. Towards the end of each management stage (other than the final one) the project manager will review the business case and project plan, update the project documentation with the results of the stage, and create an **end stage report** and stage plan to request **authorization** to commence the next management stage. The end stage report, together with the stage plan for the next management stage, should contain all the information necessary to enable the project board to conduct an **end stage assessment** and make a decision as to whether to proceed.

The project board only authorizes the next management stage if there is sufficient business justification to continue. If the project no longer has a valid business case, and the project board has been delegated the appropriate authority, it will prematurely close the project. Without this authority, the project board will escalate its recommendation for closure to the corporate, programme management or customer decision makers.

 Key message

The project board delegates the authority for day-to-day control of a management stage, within agreed tolerances, to the project manager.

As long as the management stage is forecast to remain within tolerance, the project manager has discretion to make adjustments as required. This allows the project board to manage by exception, retaining the level of control it requires while reducing the administrative overhead of being involved.

3.5 Manage by exception

 Key message

A PRINCE2 project has defined tolerances for each project objective, to establish limits of delegated authority.

PRINCE2 enables appropriate governance by defining distinct responsibilities for directing, managing and delivering the project and clearly defining accountability at each level. Accountability is established by:

- Delegating authority from one management level to the next by setting tolerances against six aspects of performance for the respective level of the plan:
  - Cost The degree of permissible overspend or underspend against an agreed budget
  - Time The degree to which a project is permitted to deliver later or earlier than an agreed target completion date
  - Quality How much something can vary from agreed **quality criteria**. For example, a project to produce a new sports watch might have a target that the watch should work under water to a depth of 50 metres, with a permissible tolerance of plus or minus 5 metres

- **Scope** Permissible variation of the plan's products. For example, a project might be required to deliver all of the must do, 'mandatory' requirements but be permitted to deliver only 50 per cent or more of its should do, 'desirable' requirements

- **Benefits** The degree to which it is permissible to under-deliver or over-deliver benefits (realized or estimated). For example, the business case for a sales improvement project might have been modelled with a plus or minus 2 per cent range of increased income generation

- **Risk** Limits on the plan's aggregated risks. For example, a tolerance might be set that the cost of aggregated threats must remain less than 10 per cent of the budget and that the cost of any single threat must be no more than 5 per cent of the agreed budget.

- Setting up controls so that if those tolerances are forecast to be exceeded, they are described as being in exception and immediately escalated to the next management level for a decision on how to proceed.

- Putting an **assurance** mechanism in place so that each management level can be confident that such controls are effective.

This implementation of 'manage by exception' provides for very efficient use of senior management time as it reduces senior managers' time burden without removing their control by ensuring decisions are made at the right level in the organization.

3.6 Focus on products

Key message

A PRINCE2 project focuses on the definition and delivery of products, in particular their quality requirements.

Projects that focus on what the project needs to produce are generally more successful than projects whose primary focus is the work activity. This is because the purpose of a project is to fulfil stakeholder expectations in accordance with the business justification, and to do this there must be a common understanding of the products required and the quality expectations for them. The purpose of a project can be interpreted in many different ways unless there is an explicit understanding of the products to be produced and the criteria against which they will be individually approved.

Under the principle of focus on products, PRINCE2 requires projects to be output oriented rather than work oriented. PRINCE2 calls these outputs 'products'.

Definition: Product

An input or output, whether tangible or intangible, that can be described in advance, created and tested. PRINCE2 has two types of products: management products and specialist products.

An output-oriented project is one that agrees and defines the project product prior to undertaking the activities required to produce it. The set of agreed products defines the scope of a project and provides the basis for planning and control.

 Key message

The guidance uses the terms 'output' and '**deliverable**' synonymously with the term 'product'. 'Project product' is used to describe the output from the project, including its component products, as defined in the project product description (see section A.21). The term 'project's products' refers to the specialist and management products created during the project.

This focus on products:

● ensures that the project only carries out work that directly contributes to the delivery of a product; that is, the project does no more work than it needs to deliver its agreed products

● helps manage uncontrolled change ('scope creep') by ensuring that all changes are agreed in terms of how they will impact **project product**s and the business justification for the project

● **reduce**s the risk of user dissatisfaction and **acceptance** disputes by agreeing, at the start, what will be produced by the project.

A PRINCE2 project uses product descriptions to provide such clarity by defining each product's purpose, composition, derivation, format, quality criteria and quality method. They provide the means to determine effort estimates, resource requirements, dependencies and activity **schedule**s.

 Tip

Projects using an agile delivery approach will initially focus on the purpose, derivation and quality criteria of the project product to deliver the initial features. More detail about the composition and format will emerge as the product evolves and progresses to its final state.

The focus on products supports almost every aspect of PRINCE2: planning, responsibilities, status reporting, quality, **change control**, scope, product acceptance and risk management.

3.7 Tailor to suit the project

Key message

PRINCE2 is tailored to suit the project environment, size, complexity, importance, team capability and risk.

The value of PRINCE2 is that it is a universal project management method that can be applied to take account of the project's environment, size, complexity, importance, team capability and risk, and can be used for any project type, geography or culture. It can be used on any project because the method is designed to be tailored to suit each project's specific needs and context.

The purpose of tailoring is to ensure that:

- the project management method used is appropriate to the project (e.g. aligning the method with the business processes that may govern and support the project, such as human resources, finance and procurement)
- project controls are appropriate to the project's scale, complexity, importance, team capability and risk (e.g. the frequency and formality of reports and reviews).

Tailoring requires the project board and the project manager to make proactive choices and decisions on how PRINCE2 will be applied. When tailoring PRINCE2, it is important to remember that effective project management requires information (not necessarily documents) and decisions (not necessarily meetings).

The PID should describe how PRINCE2 has been tailored for that particular project so that all those involved on the project understand how PRINCE2 is to be used and how to carry out their particular responsibilities.

If PRINCE2 is not tailored, it is unlikely that the project management effort and approach would be appropriate for the needs of the project. This can lead to 'mechanistic' project management at one extreme (a method is followed without question) or 'heroic' project management at the other extreme (a method is not followed at all).

4

Tailoring and adopting PRINCE2

This chapter covers:

- what you can and cannot tailor
- who is responsible for tailoring and documenting
- examples of different project environments
- tailoring and embedding PRINCE2 in an organization

4 Tailoring and adopting PRINCE2

4.1 Tailoring PRINCE2

Definition: Tailoring

Adapting a method or process to suit the situation in which it will be used.

The seventh PRINCE2 principle states that PRINCE2 should be tailored for a project's particular circumstances (see section 3.7). The goal is to apply a level of project management that does not overburden the project management team but provides an appropriate level of governance and control, at an acceptable level of risk. Tailoring can be done in two ways:

● If an organization does not have its own project management method, tailoring will be done directly from this manual.

● If an organization has its own PRINCE2-based project management method, this will be tailored to suit the project.

Section 4.3 provides advice on tailoring the guidance given in this manual; this is also applicable for tailoring an organization's PRINCE2-based project management method, bearing in mind that the organization may place limits on the extent of tailoring permitted or required.

4.2 Adopting PRINCE2

Organizations adopt PRINCE2 by tailoring it to their needs, often creating their own PRINCE2-based method and then embedding its use within their working practices.

Definition: Embedding

The act of making something an integral part of a bigger whole. Embedding is what an organization needs to do to adopt PRINCE2 as its corporate project management method and encourage its widespread use.

Section 4.4 discusses adopting PRINCE2 for use within an organization, including what to consider when tailoring PRINCE2 at an organizational level and different approaches for embedding its widespread use. Chapter 21 deals with this topic in more detail.

4.3 Tailoring PRINCE2 to suit different projects

4.3.1 What can be tailored?

Key message

Tailoring can be applied to processes, themes, roles, management products and terminology.

Tailoring is concerned with the appropriate use of PRINCE2 on any given project, ensuring that there is the right amount of governance, planning and control, in accordance with PRINCE2's principles. The following aspects of PRINCE2 may be tailored:

● Processes may be combined or adapted (e.g. by adding or combining activities).

● Themes can be applied using techniques that are appropriate to the project.

● Roles may be combined or split, provided that accountability is maintained and there are no conflicts of interest. See section 7.2.1.10 for restrictions.

● Management products may be combined or split into any number of documents or data sources. They will often take the form of formal documents, but can equally be slide decks, wall charts or data held on IT systems if more appropriate to the project and its environment.

● Terminology may be changed to suit other standards or policies, provided it is applied consistently.

Key message

Tailoring, as a PRINCE2 principle, is mandatory (as are all principles), so if the organization does not consider tailoring, it is not using PRINCE2.

PRINCE2's principles should not be tailored as they are universal and always apply.

Effective tailoring requires skill, experience and judgement. There is no single 'right' tailoring solution for a project. People in organizations with a high level of project management capability or maturity (see section 2.6.5) are likely to find tailoring easier than those working in less mature organizations. They are also likely to take a different approach to tailoring, which reflects the higher level of skills and competencies in the organization.

Tailoring does not mean excluding any of PRINCE2's processes or themes. PRINCE2 is a web of interlinking parts: themes are used in processes; techniques bring themes to life; individuals fulfil project roles and create management products. If the practitioner omits any part, project management may be weakened and hence the likelihood of project success decreased.

Each theme and process chapter in this manual contains guidance which may be used to help decide on the level of tailoring that is appropriate.

PRINCE2 provides product description outlines in Appendix A for those management products that fulfil a particular purpose, supporting the themes and processes. Tailoring allows these to be split or combined into as many documents or information sources as needed. Each product description includes quality criteria which have been designed to meet the needs of a wide variety of projects, but are unlikely to be appropriate for all projects; hence they need to be tailored to suit the project's circumstances. Appendix A includes general tailoring advice in its introduction and each outline product description suggests a range of possible formats for each product.

A project manager may need to use specific product naming terminology (e.g. to reflect customer needs or practice within their own organization). Examples include:

● the use of PMI's 'project management plan' instead of PRINCE2's 'PID'

● the use of 'project closure report' instead of **'end project report'**.

Care should be taken when changing management product names to ensure that they still reflect the intended PRINCE2 purpose.

Project lifecycles can comprise as many management stages as necessary to manage the risk associated with the project. PRINCE2 does not prescribe the names of any of the management stages nor the number required, except that the lifecycle must contain at least two (referred to as the initiation stage and a delivery stage in this manual). Section 9.3.1 provides more guidance on management stages.

Tips

● Ensure any tailoring of PRINCE2 adds value. One of the advantages of using PRINCE2 is that it comprises roles, terminology and processes that people become familiar with and so clarifies project governance and facilitates team working and cross-organization cooperation; too much tailoring may negate these advantages.

● When tailoring individual elements of PRINCE2, check the impact on any other elements to ensure they are all consistent.

4.3.2 Who is responsible and where is tailoring documented?

The project manager is responsible for identifying and documenting the level of tailoring for the project. Tailoring affects how a project is managed and so it is documented as part of the PID, which is reviewed by the appropriate stakeholders and approved by the project board. Both the project board and the project manager may be advised by **project assurance**, **project support** roles or a **centre of excellence** (if one exists).

Key message

Management products comprise information that supports decision-making. All parts of a product should add value, otherwise they should not be included in the product's composition ... but this decision should not be taken until the needs of the project are truly understood.

Conversely, if the circumstances of the project require additional information, this should be added to the management product's composition.

Amend the quality criteria accordingly.

Team managers (see section 7.2.1.8) may suggest to the project manager any tailoring which would help them manage their work packages more effectively.

4.3.3 Tailoring is constrained and influenced by context

Figure 4.1 shows the environmental and project factors which constrain and influence how a project should be tailored.

The project processes and **procedure**s should, when necessary, draw on the organization's own internal policies, processes, methods, standards and practices.

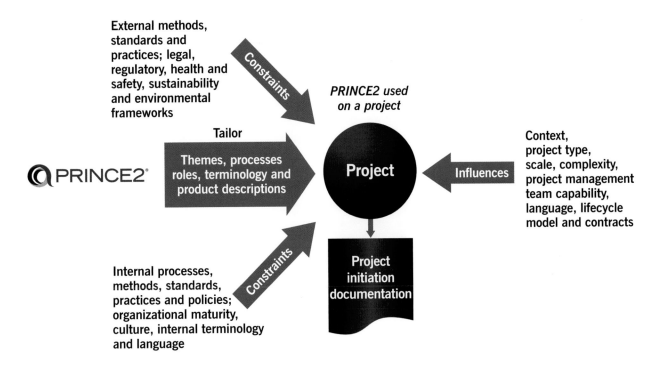

Figure 4.1 **Constraints** and influences on tailoring a project

Tip

Create a glossary of terms if adopting some of the organization's own terminology, providing commonly used alternatives, to help communication. Use the defined terms consistently in all documents and communications, whether written or verbal.

Tailoring may need to take into account standards, policies, laws or regulations from outside the organization, including those relating to health, safety, sustainability and environment. In some regulated industries, such as rail or aerospace, mandatory certification points may determine the most appropriate project lifecycle and management stages to use.

The nature of the project itself influences how PRINCE2 should be tailored. The competence of those working on the project (how familiar they are with project management practices) often drives the level of detailed guidance needed. Contracts with customers or suppliers need to be taken into account when considering tailoring. The specialist products also have an influence, as specialists usually have their own working practices (such as for agile delivery). The project manager's job is to integrate these so that the project's outputs and outcomes will be delivered and benefits realized.

The project's immediate context is relevant; for example, if it is part of a programme or a portfolio, the higher-level manager may provide processes, procedures, techniques or approaches for the project manager to follow. For good governance, it is vital that the chain of accountability from any higher level (organization, portfolio or programme) to the project level is clear.

Key message

The tailoring guidance provided in this manual is not exhaustive, as the application of PRINCE2 is limitless. Guidance is provided to illustrate things to consider and some example tactics that can be applied. Such guidance should not be interpreted as the definitive approach to tailoring as it is not specific to a particular project. The practitioner should consider the pros and cons of the tailoring choices as they relate to their specific project circumstances and ensure that:

- tailoring complies with the PRINCE2 principles and any overriding corporate standards or policy
- tailoring does not increase the risk of failing to meet the project's objectives
- the reasons for the tailoring choices are documented in the PID.

4.3.4 Some common situations

4.3.4.1 Simple projects

The perceived complexity or scale of a project is relative to the organization and context; a 'small' project in a large multinational enterprise is likely to dwarf a large project in a local company.

It is usually more helpful to think in terms of 'simple' projects, rather than 'small'. A simple project is one that the organization perceives as straightforward and of low risk.

Simple projects must adhere to the seven PRINCE2 principles (see Chapter 3); however, the degree of formality for managing the project may be relaxed provided the resultant risk is acceptable.

> ## Tailoring example for a simple, two-stage project
>
> On a simple project, the **project mandate** comprised a short email outlining the business need and expectations together with costs and timescales for the initiation stage of the project. This was used to approve the start of the project; no **project brief** was produced. The project management team used the project mandate to produce a simple PID, which included:
>
> - the justification for the project
> - a basic project plan with several product descriptions
> - the details of all the controls to be applied.
>
> A **daily log** was used to record risks, **issue**s, lessons and quality results.
>
> Following **approval** of the PID there was just one more management stage. The project manager held regular **checkpoint**s, with verbal reporting, which enabled the production of **highlight report**s to the project board.
>
> At the end of that management stage (and hence the project), an end project report was produced which also included the information for a lessons report, **follow-on action recommendations** and a **benefits management approach**. No stage plans, work packages, **team plan**s, end of stage reports or **issue report**s were needed, as they were incorporated in other products in sufficient detail.

4.3.4.2 Projects using an agile approach

Agile has a very strong focus on principles. The Agile Manifesto (2001) and most of the agile frameworks and methods all promote a set of principles in some form. PRINCE2 principles align with these principles and are complementary to the agile way of working. Some of the PRINCE2 principles are 'very much agile', such as continued business justification, learn from experience, focus on products, manage by stages, and manage by exception; the last being synonymous with giving people autonomy and empowerment.

PRINCE2 management stages can be aligned with a series of sprints or releases, introducing management control points to support a fail fast and learn fast environment. In situations that have a higher risk or higher uncertainty, the management stages can be of a much shorter duration.

> ## What do 'fail fast' and 'learn fast' mean?
>
> Using **timebox**es/sprints in agile delivery enables fast detection of possible failure of products. The fail fast effect reduces waste of resources and is a useful learning experience.

PRINCE2's manage by exception principle should be implemented correctly and should be at the heart of empowering people to self-organize and stay in control. Tolerances are set around quality criteria so that everything that is delivered must be delivered to at least the minimum acceptable level of quality.

Product descriptions (sometimes written as **epic**s or user stories), quality criteria and **quality tolerance**s can be prioritized and decomposed to provide flexibility in what is being delivered. This makes it easier to stay in control and focus on the delivery of value (or benefit) in a timely manner without compromising quality.

 Tip

In a PRINCE2 project, if all or part of the project's specialist products are delivered using agile, make sure the project manager understands the agile way of working and that the agile team understand the project manager's need for reliable information.

For further information about the relationship between the project manager and an agile delivery team, see *PRINCE2 Agile* (AXELOS, 2015).

4.3.4.3 Projects involving a commercial customer and supplier relationship

PRINCE2 is based on there being a customer/supplier environment. It assumes that there will be a customer who will specify the desired result and (usually) pay for the project, and a supplier who will provide the resources and skills to deliver that result. As discussed in section 2.5.4, additional considerations apply if the relationship between the customer and the supplier(s) is a commercial one. The contract between the parties acts as a constraint on a project manager's or team manager's degree of freedom when managing the project or work package. For this reason, it is good practice to ensure that contracts reflect and promote good working relations rather than inhibit them and that any tailoring to PRINCE2 respects the parties' contract obligations.

Taking a project from a supplier's perspective, the project lifecycle should be defined to take into account pre-contract activities, such as qualification, designing and costing the solution, bidding and negotiation. It may also take into account activities at the end of the project, such as warranty and maintenance periods.

 Tip

The PID and contract fulfil different purposes. One aspect of a contract is to describe who is liable if either party fails to fulfil its contractual obligations. The content of the PID should focus on practical management arrangements to make sure that each party can fulfil its obligations: the PID must reflect the contract conditions. Try to avoid including the PID as part of the contract documentation, as it may limit the project manager's ability to adapt it if the PID has to go through a formal contractual review for each change.

4.3.4.4 Projects involving multiple owning organizations

The guidance for tailoring PRINCE2 in a multi-owned project is similar to that for the commercial customer/supplier context, but in multi-organization projects tailoring can become extremely complicated. Project boards may have more members than can practically make effective decisions. If the parties have equal authority, a consensus has to be built on each decision, which can be time-consuming. As a result, project managers may begin to take decisions that are beyond their remit, in order to maintain momentum. For complicated situations, consideration should be given to adopting programme management as a more effective means of governance.

There is guidance on programme governance in *Managing Successful Programmes* (MSP) (Cabinet Office, 2011).

 Tip

When the project is being sponsored by a number of separate organizations, ensure governance is unambiguously defined, especially with respect to who can make which decisions, how risk is allocated and what happens in the case of non-performance.

4.3.4.5 Projects within programmes

If the project is part of a programme, people undertaking programme management roles may also define, influence or constrain tailoring. As a project within a programme may have different contexts, including any combination of simple project, agile and commercial, all the guidance for those situations may apply to the project.

 Tip

If a project is part of a programme, take care to ensure that the management products and other documentation are clearly labelled to identify the project, so that readers are not confused as to whether it is a programme-level document or which project within the programme it relates to.

4.4 Adopting PRINCE2 in an organizational environment

4.4.1 Effective use of PRINCE2 in an organization

Few organizations undertake only one project; in large organizations there can be hundreds or even thousands of projects running concurrently. Requiring each project manager to work directly from PRINCE2 to create a management approach and controls for each project is wasteful, not only in terms of the time needed to tailor PRINCE2, but also in terms of senior management, stakeholders and the project management teams having to learn new approaches for each project they work on.

Furthermore:

- the lessons from one project cannot easily be exploited on other projects; teams will continually invent different ways of doing the same thing
- building common information support systems is problematic if there is no common approach
- training is likely to be generic, rather than focused on particular challenges, and hence less effective.

For this reason, many organizations find it more effective and efficient to develop their own project management method, based on PRINCE2 and tailored to suit their needs and circumstances.

The increase in business performance through the effective use of project management methods across organizations has been demonstrated through the use of maturity assessments: the higher the maturity an organization attains, the more effective it is in business terms (see sections 2.6.5 and 21.1.1.3).

Adopting PRINCE2 in an organization involves two key activities:

- tailoring PRINCE2 to create the organization's own project management method
- embedding the tailored method by ensuring that people in the organization understand and use it appropriately.

These activities are introduced in the following sections and covered in more detail in Chapter 21.

4.4.2 Tailoring PRINCE2 to create an organization's project management method

An organization's project management method should form a seamless part of the organization's overall governance and management system. Section 4.3 describes how PRINCE2 can be tailored for an individual project; the same concepts are applicable when creating an organization's project management method based on PRINCE2. In addition, rather than consider the circumstances of just an individual project, all the projects that the organization typically undertakes need to be considered, together with any other organizational, or externally adopted, policies, processes and practices (see Figure 4.2).

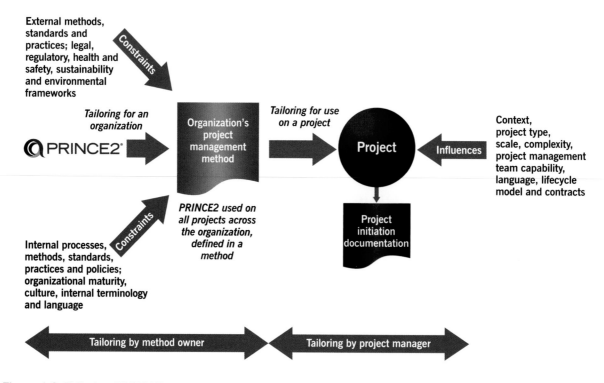

Figure 4.2 Tailoring PRINCE2 to create an organization's project management method

Tip

The way a method is drafted influences the extent to which it will be used. A method which has a consistent look and feel with a logical structure is likely to promote more confidence in its users than one which is documented in a variety of formats, styles and media. Make sure the content is consistent, especially the terminology, whether in information systems, documents, posters, videos, presentations or web sites. The greater the consistency between the parts, the easier it will be for people to understand.

Tailoring PRINCE2 to create such a method would be undertaken by the owner of the project management method. A project manager would normally only have to deal with those aspects which are unique to the project being managed, as shown on the right of Figure 4.2.

For information about the role of a centre of excellence in managing an organization's methods, see *Portfolio, Programme and Project Offices* (Cabinet Office, 2013).

4.4.3 Embedding PRINCE2 in an organization

Encouraging the widespread use of PRINCE2 in an organization involves more than publishing a project management method. The method has to be consistently deployed, effectively introduced and used in practice. This requires changing the way the people in an organization work so that the outcome (in this case, widespread use of the project management method) can be realized. Such change cannot usually be accomplished in a single project, and managing the development and introduction of a project management method is often better undertaken as a programme.

The management of change is a specialist activity which refers to any approach to transition individuals, teams and organizations from their current way of working to a new way of working. The objective is for an organization to gain benefits by transforming the way it operates.

What is the difference between changing and transforming?

Transformation is a term, common to programme management, used to describe a distinct change to the way an organization conducts all or part of its business.

Tip

Do not confuse the 'management of change', as discussed here, with PRINCE2's change theme (Chapter 11). Different organizations, standards and methods often use the terms 'change management', 'management of change' and 'change control' interchangeably, so check the intended meaning in whatever context you are working.

There are many models for managing change; however, at the heart of them all is gaining the support of the individuals who are required to change their way of working. This involves:

● understanding the current situation (current state)

● designing how the organization will work when the transformation is completed (future state)

● identifying what changes are needed to move from the current state to the future state

● developing the necessary capabilities to meet the organization's needs (roles, processes, systems, behaviours)

● engaging those affected by the change and winning their support or, at least, consent.

In order to ensure that the project management method continues to be used effectively, the method must be managed on a day-to-day basis, with improvements being introduced, based both on experience in using it and to reflect any changes in the organization's context and operations.

See section 21.2 for more detail on embedding PRINCE2 in the organization.

Introduction to PRINCE2 themes

This chapter covers:

- what themes are and why they matter
- the seven PRINCE2 themes
- basic concepts about tailoring the themes
- the structure of the themes chapters

5 Introduction to PRINCE2 themes

The PRINCE2 themes describe aspects of project management that must be addressed continually as the project progresses through its lifecycle. For example, the business justification for the project will need to be updated and revalidated throughout the project lifecycle, change will take place and risks will need to be managed.

However, the strength of PRINCE2 is the way in which the seven themes are integrated, and this is achieved because of the specific PRINCE2 treatment of each theme (i.e. they are carefully designed to link together effectively).

The PRINCE2 processes (see Chapters 13 to 20) address the chronological flow of the project, with actions relating to different themes mixed together. Here, in the theme chapters, the logical thread that runs through each theme is highlighted and more detailed guidance is provided in order to amplify the process activities. Table 5.1 lists the seven PRINCE2 themes and the chapters in which they are described in more detail.

Table 5.1 The seven PRINCE2 themes

Theme	Description	Answers the question	Chapter
Business case	The project starts with an idea which is considered to have potential value for the organization concerned. This theme addresses how the idea is developed into a viable investment proposition for the organization and how project management maintains the focus on the organization's objectives throughout the project.	Why?	6
Organization	The organization commissioning the project needs to allocate the work to managers who will be responsible for it and steer it through to completion. Projects are cross-functional so the normal line function structures are not suitable. This theme describes the roles and responsibilities in the temporary PRINCE2 project management team required to manage the project effectively.	Who?	7
Quality	The initial idea will only be understood as a broad outline. This theme explains how the outline is developed so that all participants understand the quality attributes of the products to be delivered and then how project management will ensure that these requirements are subsequently delivered.	What?	8
Plans	PRINCE2 projects proceed on the basis of a series of approved plans. This theme complements the quality theme by describing the steps required to develop plans and the PRINCE2 techniques that should be applied. In PRINCE2, the plans are matched to the needs of the personnel at the various levels of the organization. They are the focus for communication and control throughout the project.	How? How much? When?	9
Risk	Projects typically entail more risk than stable operational activity. This theme addresses how project management manages uncertainty.	What if?	10
Change	This theme describes how project management assesses and acts upon issues which have a potential **impact** on any of the **baseline** aspects of the project (its plans and completed products). Issues may be unanticipated general **problem**s, requests for change or instances of a product not meeting its specification.	What is the impact?	11
Progress	This theme addresses the ongoing viability of the plans. The theme explains the decision-making process for approving plans, the monitoring of actual performance and the escalation process if events do not go according to plan. Ultimately, the progress theme determines whether and how the project should proceed.	Where are we now? Where are we going? Should we carry on?	12

5.1 Tailoring the themes

How the themes are applied can be influenced by tailoring. This may range from being rigid and prescriptive through to allowing the project management team a large degree of freedom as to how they implement each theme.

All seven themes must be applied in a project but they should be tailored according to the risk, scale, nature, complexity or simplicity of the project concerned, always ensuring that any minimum requirements specified in a theme are satisfied.

A tailored PRINCE2 theme should reflect any tailoring of the processes and terminology. Tailoring a theme does not necessarily mean rewriting a PRINCE2 theme itself. In most cases, the themes are implemented through the project's risk, quality, change control and **communication management approach**es. These should contain procedures regarding how the themes are implemented in practice for that particular project. The level of control required will influence the degree of formality and frequency of monitoring, reviewing and reporting. When applying the themes, take account of risk and any relevant external factors, such as corporate, portfolio, programme and customer policies and standards, and capture them in the project's management approaches, as shown in Figure 4.1.

Many of the themes imply that procedures may need to be developed: PRINCE2 does not prescribe how these should be documented or published. They can range from being a simple set of activities to a fully developed procedure with a flow chart.

PRINCE2 provides a table of responsibilities relating to each theme; these may be reassigned provided they do not introduce any conflict of interest, particularly between the roles associated with directing a project, as opposed to managing a project.

Each theme in this manual contains suggestions for different tailoring options for implementing the theme in practice, together with ideas on how to deal with some common situations.

 Key message

Tailoring allows the PRINCE2 themes to be adapted to create appropriate procedures and controls, provided that:

- the PRINCE2 principles are upheld
- the minimum requirements in each theme are satisfied
- the purpose of each theme is not compromised.

Tip

The processes, procedures and controls through which themes are implemented can become overly complex and prescriptive. This often creates an unnecessary burden on projects and seldom provides greater control.

It is usually better to keep processes and procedures as simple as possible and ensure the project management team really knows how to use them. The more knowledgeable the team, the lighter the processes, procedures and control can be. It is better to coach people in using a process or procedure than to keep adding more detail in the hope they will understand it better.

5.2 Format of the theme chapters

Each theme chapter is structured as follows:

- **The theme** Why the theme is important to the successful delivery of a project and the core concepts necessary to understand PRINCE2's requirements for the theme.
- **PRINCE2's requirements for the theme** What is required, as a minimum, to be following PRINCE2.
- **Guidance for the effective use of the theme** How to practically apply the theme to different organizations, environments and delivery approaches.
- **Techniques** Techniques that can be used for the theme.

Business case

This chapter covers:

- creating and maintaining the business justification
- the relationship between outputs, outcomes and benefits
- developing and managing a business case
- PRINCE2's requirements for the business case theme
- investment appraisal techniques

6 Business case

6.1 The business case theme

Key message

The purpose of the business case theme is to establish mechanisms to judge whether the project is (and remains) desirable, viable and achievable as a means to support decision-making in its (continued) investment.

Organizations undertake projects because they want to make measurable improvements in one or more aspects of their business. These measurable improvements are called benefits.

Tip

Measurable improvements (benefits) also apply to projects that deliver outputs to satisfy regulatory requirements. Not delivering the output could have a detrimental effect on the organization and a measurable cost.

PRINCE2 projects deliver outputs in the form of products, the use of which results in changes in the business. These changes create outcomes. The outcomes allow the business to realize the benefits that are set out in the business justification for the project. Outcomes that are perceived as negative by one or more stakeholders are called **dis-benefit**s.

Examples of output, outcome and benefits

- **Output** New sales system
- **Outcome** Sales orders are processed more quickly and accurately
- **Benefits** Costs are reduced by 10 per cent, volume of sales orders increased by 15 per cent and revenue increased by 10 per cent annually.

Figure 6.1 shows the relationship between outputs, outcomes and benefits.

In PRINCE2, all projects must have a documented business justification. This sets out not only the reason for the project, but also confirms whether the project is:

- desirable: the balance of costs, benefits and risks
- viable: able to deliver the products
- achievable: whether use of the products is likely to result in envisaged outcomes and resulting benefits.

The business justification is usually documented in a business case.

The **senior user**(s) is responsible for specifying the benefits and subsequently realizing the benefits through the use of the products provided by the project. The **executive** is responsible for ensuring that those benefits specified by the senior user(s) represent value for money, are aligned with corporate, programme management or customer objectives, and can be realized. See section 7.2.1 for information about these roles and the project board.

It is a PRINCE2 principle that a project must have continued business justification. This requires that the business justification is not just developed at the beginning of the project, but that it is kept under regular review and updated in response to decisions and events that might impact the desirability, viability or achievability of the project.

If the business justification ceases to be valid then the executive must stop or change the project following review by the project board.

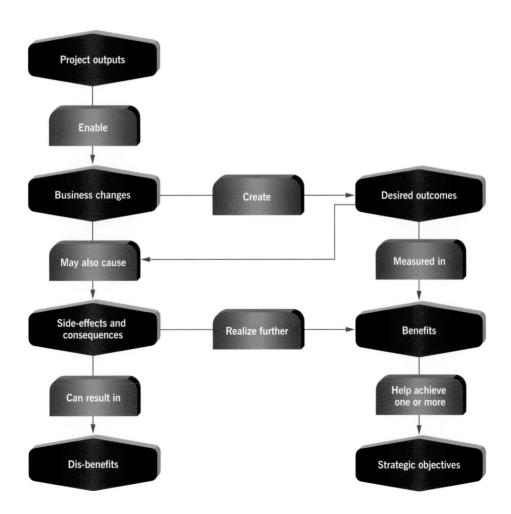

Figure 6.1 Relationship between outputs, outcomes and benefits

6.2 PRINCE2's requirements for the business case theme

To be following PRINCE2, a project must, as a minimum:

- create and maintain a business justification for the project; usually a business case (PRINCE2's continued business justification principle)
- review and update the business justification in response to decisions and events that might impact desirability, viability or achievability of the project (PRINCE2's continued business justification principle)
- define the management actions that will be put in place to ensure that the project's outcomes are achieved and confirm that the project's benefits are realized (PRINCE2's continued business justification principle)
- define and document the roles and responsibilities for the business case and benefits management (PRINCE2's defined roles and responsibilities principle).

PRINCE2 requires that two products are produced and maintained for the business case theme:

- Business case Provides the costs, benefits, expected dis-benefits, risks and timescales against which viability is justified and continuing viability is tested. It is acceptable to use an alternative document such as a corporate business plan to replace the business case for part of the project lifecycle.
- Benefits management approach Defines the management actions that will be put in place to ensure that the project's outcomes are achieved and confirm that the project's benefits are realized.

In PRINCE2 the business case is developed at the beginning of the project. Throughout the life of the project the business case is reviewed and updated as it develops and evolves (see Figure 6.2). It is formally verified by the project board at each key decision point, such as at stage boundaries, and confirmed throughout the period that benefits accrue.

Tip

The business case theme is central to PRINCE2 projects as it is at the heart of why a project is being done. PRINCE2 does not define what techniques to use to demonstrate or prove that a project is viable, only that it should be done. Such techniques are often prescribed within organizations, either formally or through custom and practice.

Appendix A, section A.2, provides a product description and suggested content for the business case.

In the context of Figure 6.2:

- Develop Means getting the right information upon which decisions can be made
- Verify Means assessing whether the project is (still) worthwhile
- Maintain Means keeping the business justification updated with actual costs and benefits and with current forecasts for costs and benefits
- Confirm Means assessing whether the intended benefits have been (or will be) realized. Confirming benefits will mostly take place post-project, although benefits may be realized during the project.

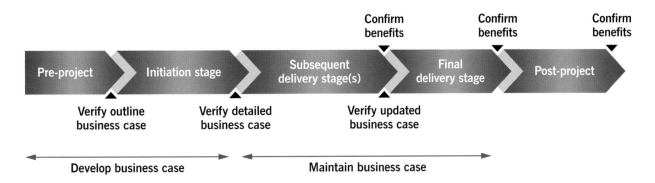

Figure 6.2 The development path of the business case

The business case is at the centre of any impact assessment of risks, issues and changes by asking the question: How will this risk, issue or change affect the viability of the business case and the business objectives and benefits being sought?

6.2.1 Developing the business justification

In PRINCE2 the executive is **accountable** for ensuring that the business justification is produced and approved. Development of the business justification may be delegated (for example, to the project manager).

If the project is part of a programme then an approved business justification may be provided as part of the project brief. Whoever is given the task of developing the business justification, it is important to ensure that they have the appropriate business skills required (e.g. understanding the difference between a cash-flow forecast, a profit-and-loss account and a balance sheet).

An initial **version** of the business justification should be derived from the project mandate as part of the starting up a project process if it is not provided by some other pre-project processes. Typically, this will be documented in a formal business case, although some organizations may use other documents, such as business plans. The initial business justification has to be approved by the project board in the directing a project process to initiate the project.

In most cases the project costs, timescale, products and risks will not be sufficiently understood to provide a robust justification of the project and this initial version will need further development and refinement as the project progresses. The initial version of the business justification is referred to as the 'outline business case' in the rest of this manual.

Typically, a more detailed business case will be developed from the outline business case during the initiating a project process. It might be that the business case will undergo further refinement across management stages as project costs, timescale, products and risks are further understood. This manual uses the term 'detailed business case' to describe this business case and its refinements; other approaches may use the term 'full business case'.

 Key message

The business justification for a project should include not only the costs of developing the products produced by the project but also any changes to operational costs post-project. Most organizations have policies that define how these costs should be accounted for in business justifications.

6.2.2 Verifying and maintaining the business justification

Continued business justification drives all decision-making by ensuring that the business objectives and benefits being sought can be realized. The business justification must be reviewed and verified:

- at the end of the starting up a project process by the project board, to authorize project initiation based on a reasonable justification
- at the end of the initiating a project process by the project board, to authorize the project
- as part of any impact assessment by the project manager of any new or revised issues or risks
- in tandem with an **exception plan** by the project board, to authorize the revised management stage and the continuation of the project
- at the end of each management stage by the project manager, to determine whether any of the costs, timescales, risks or benefits need to be updated
- at the end of each management stage by the project board, to authorize the next management stage and the continuation of the project
- during the final management stage by the project manager, to assess the project's performance against its requirements and the likelihood that the outcomes will provide the expected benefits
- as part of the benefits reviews (possibly by corporate, programme management or the customer), to determine the success of the project outcomes in realizing their benefits.

It is the responsibility of the executive to assure the project's stakeholders that the project remains desirable, viable and achievable at all times.

6.2.3 Ensuring and confirming that benefits are realized

As shown in Figure 6.1, projects deliver outputs, the use of which results in outcomes in the business that provide benefits to the organization. The principle of this linkage is straightforward; however, reality is often much more difficult. In order for the benefits to be realized, the outcomes have to be achieved, which means that the outputs from the project actually have to be used and used in the way intended.

Many organizations will be able to identify projects that have produced products that were never fully utilized, organizational changes that were never fully implemented and IT systems that were never fully used. There are many reasons why this might be the case, including:

- The scope of the project explicitly excludes benefits realization. This will commonly be the case where the project is part of a larger programme and the project only delivers some of the products required to achieve the outcomes from the programme or project.
- Failure of the project team to fully understand everything that needs to be done to help the organization use the project product. For example, it is a common failure that project teams provide an IT system and training, but no post-training or ongoing support to ensure that any post-training issues are addressed.
- Commitment to the changes introduced by the project is either overtaken by more pressing business-as-usual priorities, or simply just fades.
- Parts of the organization were never fully committed to the changes.

In practice, benefits are seldom realized unless they, and the prerequisite business changes, are proactively managed during the life of the project, even if the outcomes and benefits realization are not within the project's scope. If the project management team does not understand the benefits the project is to realize and the business changes (outcomes) needed, it is unlikely to be able to develop the right outputs and also unlikely to be able to build and sustain the commitment to and confidence in the changes during the project's lifespan.

The senior user, who is responsible for specifying the benefits from the project, is also accountable for confirming that the forecast benefits are realized. This may involve a commitment beyond the life of the project as it is likely that many benefits will not be realized until after the project has closed. For this reason, it is usually advisable that the senior user comes from an area of the business impacted by the change.

This poses a dilemma because, when the project closes, the 'temporary organization' is disbanded along with the framework (and in particular the funding and resources) to carry out any measurement activities.

The benefits management approach defines the management actions that will be put in place to ensure that the project's outcomes are achieved and to confirm that the project's benefits are realized. It is first created by the project manager in the initiating a project process during the initiation stage and is submitted to the project board for approval when seeking project authorization. If corporate, programme management or the customer are to manage or participate in the benefits reviews, the project board may need to seek their approval.

The benefits management approach should be updated during each management stage with actual benefits achieved and any updates for benefits management activities or benefits reviews (whether within or beyond the life of the project).

The benefits management approach may be managed by the project, by corporate, programme management or by the customer, and is likely to be managed beyond the life of the project. PRINCE2 recommends that it is kept separate from the project plan and stage plans.

Any benefits that can be measured during the life of a project should be confirmed by the senior user for formal reporting by the project manager in the end stage report(s) and project closure report. When benefits can be reviewed during the life of the project, the benefits management approach should include appropriate mid-project benefits reviews. Any residual benefits should be re-examined and their forecast updated as part of the managing a stage boundary process.

Post-project benefits review(s) will involve corporate, programme management or the customer holding the senior user(s) to account by asking them to provide evidence of how the individual benefits allocated to them have been gained in comparison with those benefits promised to justify the cost and risk of the project when it was authorized. The post-project benefits review(s) will also review the performance of the project product in operational use and identify whether there have been any side-effects (beneficial or adverse) that may provide useful lessons for other projects.

By default, the executive is responsible for ensuring that benefits reviews are planned and executed, but there are circumstances where this may not always be the case.

For projects in a programme environment, the project's benefits management approach may be produced and executed by the programme, as one of the roles of the programme is to coordinate the realization of the benefits of its projects.

For post-project measurement activities, the responsibility for benefits reviews will transfer from the executive to corporate, programme management or the customer as the project closes (as the reviews will need to be funded and resourced).

6.2.4 Business case responsibilities in PRINCE2

Responsibilities for managing the business case in PRINCE2 are set out in Table 6.1. As described in Chapter 7, if roles are combined then all the responsibilities in this table must still be undertaken (see section 7.2.1.10).

Table 6.1 Responsibilities relevant to the business case

Role	Responsibilities
Corporate, programme management or the customer	Provide the project mandate and define any standards to which the business case needs to be developed.
	Hold the senior user(s) to account for realizing the post-project benefits enabled by the project product.
	Accountable for the benefits management approach (post-project).
Executive	Accountable for the business case for the duration of the project.
	Accountable for the benefits management approach (for the duration of the project) unless being managed by corporate, programme management or the customer.
	Oversee the development of a viable business case, ensuring that the project is aligned with corporate, programme management or customer strategies, and secure the funding for the project.
Senior user(s)	Accountable for specifying the benefits upon which the business case is approved.
	Ensure the desired outcome of the project is specified.
	Ensure that the project produces products that deliver the desired outcomes and that those outcomes will generate the desired benefits.
	Ensure that the expected benefits (derived from the project's outcomes) are realized.
	Provide statements of actual benefit achievements versus forecast benefits at benefits reviews.
Senior supplier(s)	Accountable for the supplier business case(s) (if they exist); see section 6.3.3.
	Confirm that the products required can be delivered within the expected costs and are viable.
Project manager	Responsible for development of the business case and benefits management approach as delegated by the executive.
	Review impact of issues and risks on the continued viability of the business case.
	Assess and update the business case and benefits management approach at the end of each management stage.
	Assess and report on project performance at project closure.

Table 6.1 *continues*

Table 6.1 *continued*

Role	Responsibilities
Project assurance	Verify and monitor the business case against external events and project progress.
	Ensure the project fits with the overall corporate, programme management or customer strategies.
	Monitor project finance on behalf of corporate, programme management or the customer.
	Ensure the value-for-money solution is constantly reassessed.
	Monitor changes to the project plan to identify any impact on the needs of the business or the business case.
	Review the impact assessment of potential changes on the business case and project plan.
	Verify and monitor the benefits management approach for alignment with corporate, programme management or the customer.
Project support	The business case and benefits management approach should have a baseline and therefore be under change control. Project support should advise the project manager of any proposed or actual changes to products that affect the business case.

6.3 Guidance for effective business case management

6.3.1 Business justifications can take many forms

The business case itself, whether outline (from the starting up a project process) or detailed (from the initiating a project process or managing a stage boundary process), need not be a distinct document nor have that label.

The structure, contents and format of a business justification will often depend on the maturity of the organization, the type of project and the delivery approach used. For example:

- Organizations with mature project management will often have annual (or similar) business plans, with an entry in the business plan constituting the initial business justification for the project. Typically, a detailed business case would only be developed when the project has been fully scoped.

- Some projects may need to deliver incrementally in order to fund subsequent stages/phases/deliveries of the project. This is where an agile approach may be particularly beneficial as, without it, the business case would not be justified.

- In some cases it might be more effective and efficient to present the business justification as a slide deck than it is to create a lengthy document.

In organizations with mature project management it will usually be the case that the structure, contents and format of the business justification will be mandated at some corporate level and aligned with the preferences of the governance body that authorizes investment in the project. For example, the finance function in the organization may own and mandate the structure, contents and format of a business case. Even very simple projects need some form of explicit business justification, no matter how this is documented or expressed.

6.3.2 PRINCE2 products need to be used, not just delivered

A problem that commonly occurs is that projects are often successful from a delivery perspective, but fail from an investment perspective.

Although one of PRINCE2's principles is a focus on products, it is important to remember that the benefits underpinning the business justification of the project are delivered through the use of the products produced by the project, not just their delivery. As the project's outcomes and benefits are often only realized after the project has closed, it is easy for project teams to become focused solely on creating products (the outputs).

The link from the project's outputs to outcomes and benefits needs to be clearly identified and made visible to those involved in the project, otherwise there is a danger that the original purpose of the project can get lost and benefits will not be realized.

6.3.3 Customers and suppliers will usually need their own business cases

The business case for a customer's project is separate from a supplier's business case for bidding for and working on that customer's project. The customer needs to ensure that its project is viable and risks are acceptable, bearing in mind the suppliers chosen. A supplier would have to ensure that it will benefit from the work it undertakes on the project. In other words, the project will be profitable from the supplier's perspective.

6.3.4 Projects within programmes

If the project is part of a programme, the programme will typically define both the approach to business case development and provide an outline business case for the project.

The project's business case will typically be aggregated into the overall programme business case and is likely to be reduced in content. It may comprise just the details of the budget and timescales, a list of benefits (and the **benefits tolerance**), and a statement of what the project contributes to the programme outcomes. The justification aspects of the project business case should be in the programme business case.

Benefits will usually be defined, tracked and managed by the programme management team, and the project's benefits management approach may be part of the programme's benefits realization plan.

6.3.5 Projects using an agile approach

An agile approach may require more information (and possibly emphasis) on the tolerances around benefits with respect to priorities, timescales and how much of the scope will be delivered in the product. One way to present a business case is to show the best case, expected case and worst case of the amount of the project product requirement that will be delivered given a fixed cost and time.

When creating a business case, it is important to understand how incremental delivery of a product, and the value associated with it, could impact project viability (positively or negatively) and also the ability to achieve the early realization of some benefits. If there is a high level of uncertainty, the business case should be developed very quickly and the **assumption**s tested quickly.

6.4 Techniques: investment appraisal

There are many investment appraisal techniques, and organizations will often have preferences on which to adopt for specific projects. The selection of technique may be influenced by the type of organization (e.g. public sector accounting rules) or the organization's own standards.

Examples of investment appraisal techniques

- **Whole-life costs** Analysing the total cost of implementation and any incremental transitional, operational and maintenance costs.

- **Net benefits** Analysing the total value of the benefits less the cost of implementation, transition and ongoing operation, calculated over a defined period.

- **Return on investment (ROI)** Profits or savings resulting from investments expressed as a percentage of the initial investment.

- **Payback period** A calculation of the period of time required for the ROI to repay the sum of the original investment.

- **Discounted cash flow** A means of expressing future benefits based on the current value of money. Sometimes discounted cash flows include risk adjustments as the business may not be confident that all the benefits will materialize.

- **Net present value** The total value of discounted future cash inflows less the initial investment. For example, if the discount rate is 6 per cent, the value of money halves approximately every 12 years. If a project is forecasting a £500 000 benefit to materialize in year 12, then it is only worth £250 000 in today's money.

- **Sensitivity analysis** Business cases are based on uncertain forecasts. In order to identify how robust the business case is, it is useful to understand the relationship between input factors (e.g. project costs, timescale, quality, scope, project risks) and output (e.g. operations and maintenance costs, business benefits and business risks). Sensitivity analysis involves adjusting the input factors to model the point at which the output factors no longer justify the investment. For example, a project might be worthwhile if it can be done in 4 months, but ceases to be worthwhile if it were to take 6 months.

Chapter 6 – Business case

Organization

This chapter covers:

- the key roles for an effective organization
- the four levels of project management
- the difference between PRINCE2 roles and job titles
- the importance of stakeholders and communication
- PRINCE2's requirements for the organization theme
- guidance for effective project organization

7 Organization

7.1 The organization theme

Key message

The purpose of the organization theme is to define and establish the project's structure of accountability and responsibilities (the who?).

Every project needs effective direction, management, control and communication. Establishing an effective project management team structure and approach for communication at the beginning of a project, and maintaining these throughout the project's life, are essential elements of a project's success.

For this reason, one of PRINCE2's principles is that projects must have defined and agreed roles and responsibilities within an organization structure that engages the business, user and supplier stakeholder interests.

Definition: Stakeholder

Any individual, group or organization that can affect, be affected by, or perceive itself to be affected by, an initiative (i.e. a programme, project, activity or risk).

In order to be flexible and meet the needs of different environments and different project sizes, PRINCE2 defines a set of roles that need to be undertaken, together with the responsibilities of each of those roles. PRINCE2 does not define jobs to be allocated to people on a one-to-one basis. Roles can be shared or combined according to the project's needs, but the responsibilities must always be allocated.

PRINCE2 identifies three principal categories of project stakeholders (business, user and supplier; see Figure 7.1), although there may be a wide range of other stakeholders with an interest in the project (e.g. government, regulator or unions). Each of the three principal categories of stakeholders has a specific interest in, or viewpoint on, the project, and each category of stakeholders also has specific roles on the project in order to ensure that their interests are met, as detailed below:

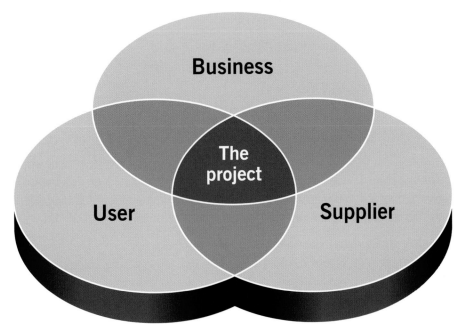

Figure 7.1 The three principal project interests

- **Business** The products of the project should meet a business need that justifies the investment in the project. The project should also provide value for money. The business viewpoint therefore should be represented to ensure that these two **prerequisites** exist before a project commences and remain in existence throughout the project.

  PRINCE2 defines an executive role to represent business interests on the project.

- **User** PRINCE2 makes a distinction between the business interests and the requirements of those who will use the project's outputs. The user viewpoint represents those individuals or groups for whom some or all of the following will apply:
  - they will use the outputs of the project to realize the benefits
  - they will operate, maintain or support the project's outputs
  - the outputs of the project will impact them.

  The user presence is needed to specify the desired outputs and ensure that the project delivers them through the supplier.

  PRINCE2 defines a senior user(s) role to represent user interests on the project.

- **Supplier** The creation of the project's outputs will need resources with certain skills. The supplier viewpoint should represent those who will provide the necessary skills and produce the project product.

  The supplier needs to have an understanding of all the relevant standards with which the output (product) needs to comply, and the project may need to use both in-house and external supplier teams to construct the project product.

  PRINCE2 defines a senior supplier(s) role to represent supplier interest on the project.

In PRINCE2, the business, user and supplier interests are brought together on the project board, which is accountable for the success of the project (see section 7.2.1.1).

A successful project management team should:

- have business, user and supplier stakeholder representation
- ensure appropriate governance by defining responsibilities for directing, managing and delivering the project and clearly defining accountability at each level
- review the project roles throughout the project to ensure that they continue to be effective
- have an effective approach to manage communication flows to and from stakeholders.

Managers at the level required to make decisions and commitments may be too busy to be involved on a day-to-day basis with the project. However, projects need day-to-day management if they are to be successful. PRINCE2 separates the direction and management of the project from the delivery of the project's outputs, concentrating on the former and using the principle of manage by exception.

The project management structure has four levels, three of which represent the project management team and a fourth that sits outside the project. Figure 7.2 illustrates these four levels of management.

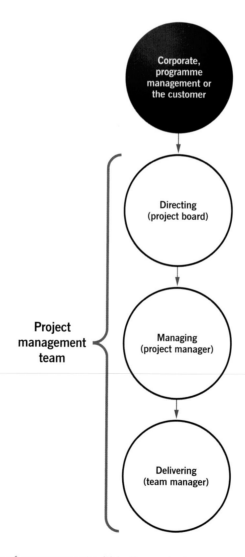

Figure 7.2 The four levels of management within the project management structure

The four levels of management are:

- **Corporate, programme management or the customer** This level sits above the project management team but will be responsible for commissioning the project, including identifying the executive and defining the project-level tolerances within which the project board will work. This information should, if possible, be recorded in the project mandate.

- **Directing** The project board is responsible for the overall direction and management of the project within the constraints set out by corporate, programme management or the customer. The project board is accountable for the success of the project (see section 7.2). As part of directing the project, the project board will:
  - approve all major plans and resources
  - authorize any deviation that exceeds or is forecast to exceed stage tolerances
  - approve the completion of each management stage and authorize the start of the next management stage
  - communicate with other stakeholders.

- **Managing** The project manager is responsible for the day-to-day management of the project within the constraints set out by the project board. The project manager's prime responsibility is to ensure that the project produces the required products in accordance with the time, cost, quality, scope, benefits and risk performance goals (see section C.5).

- **Delivering** Although the project manager is responsible for the day-to-day management of the project, team members are responsible for delivering the project product and its components to an appropriate quality within a specified timescale and cost. Depending on the size and complexity of the project, the authority and responsibility for planning the creation of certain products and managing a team of specialists to produce those products may be delegated to a team manager, who is accountable to the project manager (see section C.6).

There will be a wider range of stakeholders which may affect, or be affected by, the project. These stakeholders may be internal or external to the corporate, programme management or customer organization and may:

- support or oppose the project
- gain or lose as a result of project delivery
- see the project as a threat or enhancement to their position
- become active supporters or blockers of the project and its progress.

It is important to analyse who these stakeholders are and to engage with them appropriately. Effective engagement with these stakeholders is key to a project's success (see section 7.3.9).

Example of stakeholder identification

Stakeholder analysis identified the following stakeholders for a project to relocate a chemical factory:

- a number of unions
- an environmental pressure group
- an industry regulator
- a number of corporate, programme management or customer functions (e.g. internal audit, finance, legal)
- the external contractor
- some members of the public affected by the project.

Note that some of these were external to the project management team but internal to the corporate, programme management or customer organization.

7.2 PRINCE2's requirements for the organization theme

To be following PRINCE2, a project must, as a minimum:

- define its organization structure and roles. This must minimally ensure that all of the responsibilities in PRINCE2's role descriptions are fulfilled (PRINCE2's defined roles and responsibilities principle)
- document the rules for delegating **change authority** responsibilities, if required
- define its approach to communicating and engaging with stakeholders.

PRINCE2 requires that two products are produced and maintained for the organization theme:

- PID In the context of the organization theme, this provides the single source of reference for how the project is to be managed. The PID sets out the project management team structure and roles.
- Communication management approach This describes the means and frequency of communication to stakeholders both internal and external to the project.

Both these products should be created during the initiating a project process.

Appendix A (sections A.5 and A.20) provides product descriptions and suggested content for these products.

7.2.1 PRINCE2's mandated project management team roles

PRINCE2 mandates that certain project roles are fulfilled on every project. As noted below, the roles may be combined within certain limits.

Figure 7.3 shows the mandated roles within an illustrative project team structure. Even though the project roles are mandated, the structure is not and is provided only as an example.

Appendix C provides details of these roles and their associated responsibilities. For a specific project these role descriptions should be tailored and supplemented to include information that specifies the responsibilities, goals, limits of authority, relationships, skills, knowledge and experience required. PRINCE2 uses the term 'project team' to cover the project management team and everyone else working on the project.

7.2.1.1 Project board

All PRINCE2 projects must have a project board. The project board has authority and responsibility for the project within the instructions (initially contained in the project mandate) set by corporate, programme management or the customer.

The roles and responsibilities of the project board are described in Appendix C, section C.1. They include:

- being accountable to the business, user and supplier interests for the success or failure of the project
- providing unified direction to the project
- delegating, using the PRINCE2 organizational structure and controls designed for this purpose
- facilitating integration of the project management team with the functional units of the participating corporate, programme management or customer organizations
- providing the resources and authorizing the funds necessary for the successful completion of the project
- effective decision-making
- providing visible and sustained support for the project manager
- ensuring effective communication both within the project team and with external stakeholders.

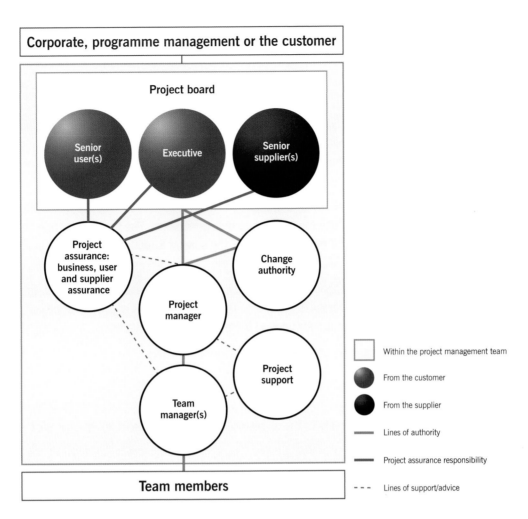

Figure 7.3 PRINCE2 project management team roles

PRINCE2 requires that the project board always represents business, user and supplier interests. This is usually done through the executive, senior user and senior supplier, although PRINCE2 does not require three people on every project board. On smaller/simpler projects some of the roles may be combined.

7.2.1.2 Executive

Although the project board has collective responsibility for the project, the executive, supported by the senior user(s) and senior supplier(s), is ultimately accountable for the project's success and is the key decision maker. The project board is not a democracy controlled by votes.

The executive's role is to ensure that the project is focused throughout its life on achieving its objectives and delivering a product that will achieve the forecasted benefits. The executive has to ensure that the project gives value for money, ensuring a cost-conscious approach to the project, balancing the demands of the business, user and supplier.

The executive is appointed by corporate, programme management or the customer during the pre-project process of starting up a project. The role of the executive is vested in one individual, so that there is a single point of accountability for the project. The executive will then be responsible for designing and appointing the rest of the project management team, including the other members of the project board. If the project is part of a programme then corporate, programme management or the customer may appoint some or all of the project board members.

The executive secures funding for the project and is responsible for the business case and continued business justification of the project.

7.2.1.3 Senior user

The senior user is responsible for specifying the needs of those (including operations and maintenance services) who will use the project product for user liaison with the project management team and for monitoring that the solution will meet those needs within the constraints of the business case in terms of quality, functionality and ease of use.

The role represents the interests of all those who will use the project product, those for whom the product will achieve an objective, or those who will use the product to deliver benefits. The senior user role commits user resources and monitors products against requirements. For the sake of effectiveness the role should not be split between too many people.

The senior user(s) specifies the benefits and is held to account by demonstrating to corporate, programme management or the customer that the forecasted benefits that were the basis of project approval are in fact realized. This is likely to involve a commitment beyond the end of the project's life.

If necessary, more than one person may be required to represent the users.

7.2.1.4 Senior supplier

The senior supplier represents the interests of those designing, developing, facilitating, procuring and implementing the project product.

This role is accountable for the quality of products delivered by the supplier(s) and is responsible for the technical integrity of the project. This role will include providing supplier resources to the project and ensuring that proposals for designing and developing the products are feasible and realistic.

In many cases, the senior supplier also represents the interests of those who will provide the maintenance services for the specialist products after closure of the project (e.g. engineering maintenance and support). Exceptions to this do occur, however (e.g. when the maintenance services are provided by the customer organization, such as an internal IT department, or are outsourced to a different supplier). In this instance the operations and maintenance interests are more likely to be represented by a senior user. In fact, the distinction is not really important; what matters is that operations, service and support interests are represented appropriately from the outset.

If necessary, more than one person may be required to represent the suppliers.

7.2.1.5 Project assurance

The project board is responsible, via its project assurance role, for monitoring all aspects of the project's performance and products independently of the project manager.

Project board members are responsible for the aspects of the project assurance role aligned with their respective areas of concern (business, user or supplier). If they have sufficient time available, and the appropriate level of skills and knowledge, they may conduct their own project assurance tasks; otherwise they may appoint separate individuals to perform these.

The project board may also make use of other members of the corporate, programme management or customer organization to take on specific project assurance roles, such as appointing the corporate quality manager to monitor the quality aspects of the project. Project board members are accountable for the project assurance actions aligned with their area of interest, even if they delegate these to separate individuals.

Project assurance is not just an independent check, however. Personnel involved in project assurance are also responsible for supporting the project manager, by giving advice and guidance on issues such as the use of corporate standards or the correct personnel to be involved in different aspects of the project (e.g. **quality inspection**s or reviews).

When project assurance tasks are shared between project board members and other individuals, it is important to clarify each person's responsibilities. Anyone appointed to a project assurance role reports to the project board member overseeing the relevant area of interest, and must be independent of the project manager. The project board should not assign any project assurance roles to the project manager or project support.

As part of its function to monitor all aspects of the project's performance and products independently of the project manager, project assurance should be involved in all the PRINCE2 processes.

7.2.1.6 Change authority

One consideration at project initiation should be who is permitted to authorize requests for change or **off-specification**s. It is the project board's responsibility to agree to each potential change before it is implemented. In a project where few changes are envisaged, it may be reasonable to leave this authority in the hands of the project board. But projects may be in a dynamic environment, where there are likely to be, for example, many requests to change the initial agreed scope of the project. Technical knowledge may also be needed to evaluate potential changes.

If it has not already been determined within starting up a project, the project board needs to decide, before the project moves out of the initiating a project process, if it wishes to delegate some authority for approving or rejecting requests for change or off-specifications. These delegated authorities must be written into the appropriate role descriptions. For projects that exist within a programme, the programme management should define the level of authority that the project board will have in order to be able to approve changes.

The project manager and/or the people with delegated project assurance responsibilities may act as the change authority. Refer to Chapter 11 for more information on change.

7.2.1.7 Project manager

The project manager is the single focus for day-to-day management of a project. This person has the authority to run the project on behalf of the project board within the constraints laid down by the project board. The role of the project manager must not be shared.

The project manager will usually come from the corporate, programme management or customer organization, but there may be projects where the project manager comes from the supplier. Refer to section 7.3.4 for more information on roles in the context of customer/supplier relationships.

The project manager is responsible for the work in all the PRINCE2 processes except for the directing a project process, and appointing the executive and the project manager in the pre-project process of starting up a project. The project manager also delegates responsibility for the managing product delivery process to the team manager(s).

The project manager manages the team managers and project support, and is responsible for liaison with project assurance and the project board. In projects with no separate individual allocated to a team manager role, the project manager will be responsible for managing work directly with the team members involved. In projects with no separate project support role, the support tasks also fall to the project manager, although they may be shared with team members.

As the single focus for the day-to-day management of a project, there are many different aspects to the project manager role, some of which are shown in Figure 7.4.

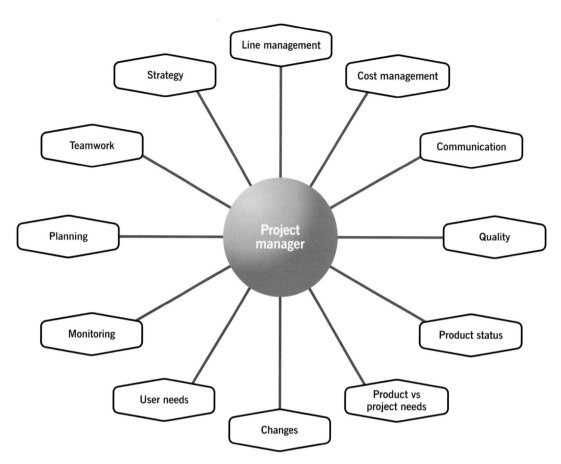

Figure 7.4 The many facets of the project manager role

7.2.1.8 Team manager

The team manager's primary responsibility is to ensure production of those products allocated by the project manager. The team manager reports to, and takes direction from, the project manager.

The team manager role may be assigned to the project manager or a separate person. There are many reasons why the project manager may decide to appoint other people to be team managers rather than undertake the role themselves. Among these are the size of the project, the particular specialist skills or knowledge needed for certain products, geographical location of some team members and the preferences of the project board. The project manager should discuss the need for separate individuals as team managers with the project board and, if required, should plan the role at the start of the project during the starting up a project process, or for each management stage in the preceding managing a stage boundary process.

The project manager uses work packages to allocate work to team managers or team members. They can be used formally or informally depending on the needs of the project. Defining the deliverables at the appropriate level will assist new team managers in becoming more effective as it is clear what has to be produced and, with the definition of reporting frequency and method, the feedback from the team manager can be clearly controlled.

If the team manager comes from the supplier organization, there could be a reporting line to a senior supplier. It is vital that any such links are understood to avoid conflicts of interest and any undermining of the project manager's authority.

The structure of the project management team does not necessarily reflect line function or seniority but represents roles on the project. A team manager, for example, may be more senior in the corporate, programme management or customer organization than the project manager, or may be a senior representative from an external supplier. In the context of the project, however, the team manager reports to, and takes direction from, the project manager.

7.2.1.9 Project support

Project support is the responsibility of the project manager. If required, the project manager can delegate some of this work to a project support role: this may include providing administrative services or advice and guidance on the use of project management tools. It could also provide specialist functions to a project such as planning or risk management. Unless performed by a corporate, programme management or customer function, project support is typically responsible for administering change control.

The role of project support is not optional, but the allocation of a separate individual or group to carry out the required tasks is. The role defaults to the project manager if it is not otherwise allocated.

Key message

Project support and project assurance roles must be kept separate in order to maintain the independence of project assurance.

Some corporate, programme management or customer organizations may have a **project office** (a temporary office set up to support the delivery of a specific project) or a similar structure, which can fulfil some, or all, of the project support role. For more information on the use of a project office, see *Portfolio, Programme and Project Offices* (Cabinet Office, 2013).

7.2.1.10 Combining roles

PRINCE2 allows the above roles to be combined within the following constraints:

- the executive and project manager roles cannot be combined
- there cannot be more than one executive or project manager
- the executive's accountability for project success cannot be delegated
- the project board should not assign any project assurance roles to the project manager, team manager or project support.

When combining roles, the project board should consider any conflicts of responsibilities, whether one person has the capacity to undertake the combined responsibilities, and whether any bottlenecks might be created as a result. Also, it is not recommended to combine the roles of senior user and senior supplier as this can create conflicts of interest for an individual.

PRINCE2 provides role description outlines in Appendix C, and they should be tailored to the needs of the specific project and each specific appointment. In addition, each theme chapter provides the responsibilities relevant to that theme.

7.2.2 The communication management approach

The communication management approach contains a description of the means and frequency of communication to parties both internal and external to the project. It facilitates engagement with stakeholders through the establishment of a controlled and bidirectional flow of information. Where the project is part of a programme, the communication management approach should align with the programme's approach to stakeholder communication and engagement.

The project manager is responsible for documenting the communication management approach during the initiating a project process. It is also important to review and possibly update the communication management approach at each management stage boundary in order to ensure that it still includes all the key stakeholders. When planning the final management stage of the project it is also important to review the communication management approach to ensure it includes all the parties who need to be advised that the project is closing.

During a project, corporate management, programme management or the customer retains control by receiving project information as defined in the communication management approach and taking decisions on project-level exceptions escalated by the project board.

7.2.3 Organization responsibilities in PRINCE2

Responsibilities for organization in PRINCE2 are set out in Table 7.1. If roles are combined then all the responsibilities in this table must still be undertaken.

Table 7.1 Responsibilities relevant to the organization theme

Role[a]	Responsibilities
Corporate, programme management or the customer	Appoint the executive and (possibly) the project manager.
	Provide information to the project as defined in the communication management approach.
Executive	Appoint the project manager (if not done by corporate, programme management or the customer).
	Confirm the appointments to, and structure of, the project management team.
	Approve the communication management approach.
Senior user	Provide user resources.
	Define and verify user requirements and expectations.
Senior supplier	Provide supplier resources.
	Advise on the technical aspects of the proposed products.
Project manager	Prepare and update the communication management approach.
	Design, review and update the project management team structure.
	Plan and undertake stakeholder engagement.
	Prepare role descriptions.
Team manager	Manage project team members.
	Advise on project team members and stakeholder engagement for their part in the project.
Project assurance	Advise on selection of project team members.
	Advise on stakeholder engagement.
	Ensure that the communication management approach is appropriate and that planned communication activities actually take place.
Project support	Provide administrative support for the project team.

a Note that change authority is an optional role and has not been included in this table.

7.3 Guidance for effective project organization

7.3.1 General considerations

Ensure that the organizational structure of the project team is suitable for the size, scale and complexity of the project.

'Organization' is the PRINCE2 theme most affected by project size, scale and complexity. The right people with the right experience need to be in the right roles, in the right numbers and at the right time.

Roles and responsibilities need to be carefully considered for all projects. Standard role description outlines will need to be tailored to match each individual's actual capability and authority in the context of the project role they will be undertaking.

For smaller, simpler projects, the primary concern often is how to ensure that all PRINCE2 responsibilities are fulfilled by a relatively small set of people. Some points to consider include:

- Scaling the project management team is primarily about consolidating role and function. Roles can be combined but should not be eliminated.
- As the executive and senior user roles are both from the customer environment, these can often be combined.
- As the project manager is likely to be much closer to the project board than on larger, more complex projects, members of the project board are often in a better position to carry out their own project assurance rather than appointing another individual to fulfil this role.
- For small teams it may not be necessary to appoint team managers. The project manager of a simple project can carry out those responsibilities.

Typically, on a larger, more complex project, responsibilities will be distributed among a larger set of people, with some roles and responsibilities being shared. For example, there may be multiple senior users. In such circumstances, the primary concern is ensuring that individual accountabilities, limits of delegation and authority, and governance are absolutely clear.

7.3.2 Project organization in an organizational environment

Whether or not a project forms part of a programme or portfolio, it will always exist within both an organizational environment and a wider context. Corporate organizational structures can range from 'traditional' functional structures to project-focused corporate organizations and variations in between. In the 'traditional' functional structure, staff are organized by type of work (e.g. marketing, finance and sales) and there are clear reporting lines. In contrast, the standard practice in project-focused corporate organizations is to work with project teams.

The level of overlap between the interests of the business, user and supplier stakeholders will change according to the type of corporate, programme management or customer organization and project. For example, there are likely to be more overlapping interests between the business and an in-house supplier than an external supplier.

7.3.3 Projects within a programme

A project can be run as a stand-alone entity or can be part of a programme of related projects (see section 2.5.2). A project which forms part of a programme may be impacted by the programme structure and its various reporting requirements.

The programme and project management team structures and roles need to be integrated such that:

- there are clear lines of responsibility and accountability from top to bottom, and duplication is avoided
- reports and reviews are efficient (e.g. projects within a programme that have common project board members could align stage boundaries, and meet collectively to conduct end stage assessments for all the projects as part of a programme review).

The integration of roles may involve the following:

- The programme manager may be the executive for one or more of the projects.
- Within a programme, there may be multiple project boards, a single body directing several projects (effectively replacing multiple project boards) or a combination of the two.
- A business change manager from the programme may fulfil the project role of senior user (or have input into the appointment of the senior user) for one or more of the projects, or be the executive for one or more of the projects.
- The programme's design authority (if used) may fulfil the project role of change authority or project assurance for one or more of the projects. The purpose of a design authority at a programme level is to ensure that there is appropriate alignment and control when changes are being planned and implemented.
- A single programme office may take project support responsibilities for all projects.

Programme manager, business change manager and design authority are defined in *Managing Successful Programmes* (Cabinet Office, 2011) and fulfil programme-level requirements.

What are the roles of business change manager and design authority?

The business change manager is responsible for benefits management from identification through to realization, and for ensuring that the implementation and embedding of the new capabilities are delivered by the projects. The business change manager is a senior role drawn from the area of the business affected by the programme.

The design authority provides expert advice about, and may have responsibility for, some corporate function, service, standard or strategy that will be affected by the programme.

The choice of project structure and appointments will depend on the needs, complexity and scale of the programme. It is the programme manager's responsibility to assess the pros and cons of the choice of organization structure, and appointments need to be evaluated along with their consequences.

The project's communication management approach should be aligned with the programme's stakeholder engagement strategy, with communications being controlled and scheduled as part of the programme communications plan. Stakeholder analysis for the project may be performed by the programme, or the programme may require the project to take a lead with certain stakeholder groups with which it has good engagement.

7.3.4 Projects operating in a commercial environment

There are numerous ways to structure the project management team roles in a commercial customer/supplier context. The aim is to ensure that both organizations establish and maintain sound business justification for their work and that their individual governance is respected. It is important that the project manager has a good understanding of their obligations under any contract with the supplier organization. In PRINCE2, the project manager will normally come from the customer organization. The supplier's staff may fulfil some of the team manager roles for the project, and they may even be called 'project managers' in the supplier's organization.

There may be projects where the project manager comes from the supplier's organization. The customer may choose to stay at a distance from the working level and expect the supplier to provide the management of the project. The customer is likely to increase the rigour in project assurance (and indeed may choose to appoint one of its own staff to fulfil the role of project assurance).

 Tip

Be careful not to confuse job titles and PRINCE2 roles. A person with the job title 'project manager' may not be undertaking the PRINCE2 project manager role. For example, a person from a supplier organization may have the title of 'project manager', but might be undertaking the team manager role for a specific project.

It helps to ensure that job titles are mapped to PRINCE2 roles, and that responsibilities for each role are clear and recorded in the PID.

Ensure that every member of the project team understands their project responsibilities regardless of their job title and description.

There may be a joint project board with representatives from the customer and all the suppliers that the customer has engaged. The executive on this joint project board may be supplied by the customer and the senior suppliers will represent each of the suppliers.

The supplier may treat their work package(s) within the customer's project as a project within the supplier's organization. This may mean establishing a separate 'supplier project board'. The relationship between any such boards and the customer's project board should be defined.

If there are multiple suppliers, all of them may be represented on the project board as it provides a forum for them to integrate direction and decision-making. If there are more than three or four suppliers, however, then it will be typically more effective for the contracts manager responsible for the performance of all the supplier contracts to sit on the project board on their behalf, or it may be appropriate to appoint a prime contractor.

During procurement, the project may need a temporary appointment from within the customer organization (say, from its procurement team) for the senior supplier role until a supplier has been appointed.

7.3.5 Projects using an agile approach

Understanding of the additional delivery-level roles may be needed, and these agile roles should be mapped, as appropriate, to the roles of the project management team structure. The project manager will need to understand:

- how a self-organizing delivery team operates and how this relates to the team manager and change authority roles
- the responsibilities of roles in the agile approach being used
- that, in an agile environment, the user is often represented by a single person, often referred to as the product owner. However, in the context of a project, a wider view of the customer is likely to be needed due to the cross-functional nature of projects
- how agile team leaders liaise with the project manager when more than one team is involved.

The use of management by exception is essential to enable PRINCE2 and agile to be combined in the most effective way. This empowers the project management team and enables it to self-organize within clearly defined boundaries.

More details about how to combine PRINCE2 with agile can be found in *PRINCE2 Agile* (AXELOS, 2015).

7.3.6 Alternative names for PRINCE2 project roles

Role and job title names vary from organization to organization. It does not matter what a role or job is called as long as all the responsibilities outlined in Appendix C are fulfilled on each project.

The responsibilities of the jobs and roles may also vary; for example, a senior project manager in one organization may actually be performing portfolio management activities or overseeing project managers. Some examples of commonly used alternative terminology are:

- 'sponsor' or 'senior responsible owner (SRO)' instead of executive
- 'business change manager' instead of senior user
- 'PMO' instead of project support
- 'work package manager' instead of team manager.

 What is a PMO?

This is a commonly used abbreviation for the office an organization may set up to provide support and other services for its programmes and projects. It is variously called the programme management office, portfolio management office or project management office. It may also be viewed by progressive organizations as a centre of excellence. For more information, see *Portfolio, Programme and Project Offices* (Cabinet Office, 2013).

7.3.7 Creating an effective project board

A good project board should display four key characteristics:

- **Authority** The members of the project board should be senior enough within the corporate, programme management or customer organization to make strategic decisions about the project. As the project board is accountable for the project, the individuals chosen must have sufficient authority to make these decisions and to provide resources to the project, such as personnel, cash and equipment. The managerial level required to fill the roles will depend on factors such as the budget, scope and importance of the project.

- **Credibility** The credibility of the project board members within the corporate, programme management or customer organization will affect their ability to direct the project.

- **Ability to delegate** A key part of the project board's role is to ensure that the project manager is given enough 'space' to manage the project by keeping project board activity at the right level. Project board members should not be involved in the detail of how the project is managed.

- **Availability** Project board members who meet all the above characteristics are of little value to the project if they are not available to make decisions and provide direction to the project manager.

The executive, supported by the project manager, is responsible for agreeing a suitable team structure and tailoring it to the project's size, risk and complexity. The project board needs to represent all the interested parties in the corporate, programme management or customer organization, and involve any suppliers (internal or external) that have been identified.

On a complex project, tailoring the project management team could mean breaking the PRINCE2 roles into multiple appointments; for example, several senior users or senior suppliers could be appointed. However, it is good practice to keep the size of the project board as small as possible while still representing all business, user and supplier interests.

Producing a matrix of stakeholders against the project product also helps split the project stakeholders (who need to be engaged as part of the communication management approach) from the project decision makers (who need to be on the project board).

The decision on whether to include external suppliers on the project board may be a cultural one based on fear of divulging commercial or financial information. Leaving them out of the directing a project process could cause delays due to the lack of supplier resources to deal with change and to address specialist issues. It is the executive's decision as to how this dilemma is solved practically.

7.3.8 Creating an effective project team

7.3.8.1 Balancing the project, team and individual

People are crucial to the success of a project. It is not enough to have the required processes and systems in place: if the people on a project do not work effectively together, then the chances of the project's success are severely restricted. Knowledge of different types of personalities and how they affect each other can help the project manager to structure balanced teams that can work together effectively during a project.

Different people have different characteristics and a preference for certain types of work and team roles. There are a number of ways of assessing these preferences (e.g. Belbin team role inventory).

Example of team building using different personalities

Some people are very sociable and enthusiastic, generating many different ideas. Others are more analytical, skilled in detailed work and ensuring no tasks get missed. Although it is not usually possible to change people's characteristics, it is possible to balance a team so that it has an appropriate mix of personality types to enable tasks to be completed effectively.

Project managers who know the natural roles of the team members can use that knowledge to build effective teams during the starting up a project process for the management team and the initiating a project process when identifying team members.

It is important to achieve the correct balance; for example, a team consisting of only 'ideas' people risks losing focus on the detail of tasks which need to be performed. Conversely, a team made up of only 'details' people may lack a strategic overview of a solution.

7.3.8.2 Line management/functional management

In a strongly functional environment, project managers can find difficulties when managing cross-functional projects due to the inability to agree overall leadership from within the various groups. As a result, the project board may need to be involved more closely to lead, direct and prioritize work and resolve issues. Whatever the environment, the project manager will have to adapt to, and work within, the corporate organization and this will affect the level of management required for the team members.

Example of a project manager's responsibilities to line/functional management

The project manager may be responsible for carrying out performance appraisals as part of a project, or may provide input to the appraisal undertaken by the functional area of the corporate organization responsible for the team member.

Understanding and working within the wider corporate organization can be challenging for the project manager, particularly if working part-time or on a contract basis. Setting up clear project controls at the start of the project, and agreeing these with the project board, will help to ensure that the project manager understands the level of interaction and support to expect during the project and is given appropriate exposure to other areas of the corporate organization.

7.3.8.3 Training needs for project teams

Project team members may need training to enable them to complete their assigned tasks. This might include training on PRINCE2, specialist training related to their role, or training on the specific processes and standards used on the project.

Project board members may also need training on their roles, including what is expected of them and the procedures needed to carry out their responsibilities. The project manager should ensure that training needs are assessed and built into the appropriate plans.

7.3.8.4 Dealing with changes to the project management team

Ideally, the project manager and project board members should stay with the project throughout its life. In practice, however, this may not always be possible and the project management team and suppliers may change during the project. A clearly defined team structure, together with comprehensive role descriptions outlining the responsibilities for each role, should help to alleviate disruption caused by project management team changes.

The use of management stages also allows a smooth transition for changes to the project management team. Project roles should be reviewed for the next management stage during the managing a stage boundary process. The use of end stage reports and stage plans can help to ensure that any handover procedure is thorough and well documented. Although ideally the executive and project manager should stay with the project throughout its lifecycle, a management stage boundary provides an opportunity to hand over the role during the project if this is necessary.

Example of changes to the project management team

A project may include a procurement step, during which a supplier is selected to develop some of the components of the project product. Before the supplier has been selected, a senior representative from the procurement department may be appointed as the senior supplier on the project. After the supplier has been selected and the project moves to the design step, a senior representative from the selected supplier's organization could be included on the team as a senior supplier.

7.3.8.5 Part-time teams

Project teams are brought together for the duration of a project and then return to their routine work. The manager of a small project is therefore likely to find that team members are working on the project on a part-time basis. Part-time team members suffer more absences and diversions, as a percentage of their working time, than full-time team members. The project manager should allow for this when designing a plan, either by negotiating guaranteed availability or greater tolerance.

If individuals are tasked with working on too many projects, they may simply stand still on all the projects, expending a lot of effort but making no forward progress. Solutions include undertaking fewer projects in parallel or, if possible, allocating staff full time to projects for limited periods.

7.3.9 Stakeholder engagement

Stakeholder engagement is the process of identifying and communicating effectively with those people or groups who have an interest in or influence on the project's outcome. It is usually carried out at the programme level. All projects need to have some level of stakeholder engagement, particularly if not part of a programme.

Parties external to the project management team can exert a powerful influence on a project. Effective communication with key stakeholders, both internal and external to the corporate, programme management or customer organization, is essential to the project's success.

Example of stakeholder engagement

Managing Successful Programmes (Cabinet Office, 2011) identifies the following six-step procedure for stakeholder engagement:

- **Identifying stakeholders (Who?)** Identifying the individual stakeholders involved in, or affected by, the project and perhaps grouping similar stakeholders together so that key messages can be targeted effectively.

- **Creating and analysing stakeholder profiles (Why and What?)** Gaining an understanding of the influences, interests and attitudes of the stakeholders towards the project and the importance and power of each stakeholder. For instance, is a particular group likely to be negative, irrespective of the message, and therefore require particular care? Stakeholders' influence and interests, whether rational or emotional, must all be taken into account. They have the potential to affect the success of the project. Perceptions may be mistaken, but they must be addressed. The stakeholders' perceptions of the benefits should be quantified where possible.

- **Defining the stakeholder engagement approach (How?)** Defining how the project can effectively engage with the stakeholders, including defining the responsibilities for communication and the key messages that need to be conveyed. For each interested party, agree the:

  - information the party needs from the project
  - information the party needs to provide to the project
  - method, format and frequency of communication
  - sender and recipient of the communication.

- **Planning the engagements (When?)** Defining the methods and timings of the communications. These are best planned after defining how the project will engage with the different stakeholders. When selecting the senders of information, it is important to select communicators who have the respect and trust of the audience. Their position in the corporate, programme management or customer organization and expertise in the subject matter will greatly influence their credibility. Many projects have a formal commencement meeting to introduce the project and its aims to the corporate, programme management or customer organization. If this type of meeting is used, it is important that the members of the project board attend to show their support and commitment to the project.

- **Engaging stakeholders (Do)** Carrying out the planned engagements and communications. The first two steps in stakeholder engagement (identifying and analysing) also engage stakeholders to some degree.

- **Measuring effectiveness (Results)** Checking the effectiveness of the engagements. Project assurance could be involved in checking all the key stakeholders, their information needs and that the most appropriate communication channels are covered.

Quality

This chapter covers:

- what quality means in a product-focused method
- customer quality expectations and acceptance criteria
- who is responsible for quality
- the difference between quality assurance and project assurance
- PRINCE2's requirements for the quality theme
- guidance for effective quality management
- a recommended quality review technique

8 Quality

8.1 The quality theme

Key message

The purpose of the quality theme is to define and implement the means by which the project will verify that products are fit for purpose.

Quality is concerned with ensuring that the project product meets business expectations and enables the desired benefits to be realized.

Underestimating or omitting quality management activities is likely to lead to slippages, overspends and/or poor quality results. The quality theme addresses the quality methods and responsibilities not only for the specification, development and approval of the project product, but also for the management of the project.

Terms used to talk about quality are sometimes interpreted differently or interchangeably by various people. This can lead to misunderstandings. PRINCE2 uses specific terminology derived from the ISO 9000 standards, but is aimed specifically at project work.

Definition: Quality

The degree to which a set of inherent characteristics of a product, service, process, person, organization, system or resource fulfils requirements.

Definition: Quality management

The coordinated activities to direct and control an organization with regard to quality.

PRINCE2's focus on products principle is central to its approach to quality. PRINCE2 requires systematic activities to:

- explicitly agree the **customer's quality expectations** and acceptance criteria for the project product
- identify the project's products (i.e. to the level at which the project intends to exert control)
- define the project product and its components in product descriptions, including the quality criteria by which they will be assessed, the quality methods to be used in designing, developing and approving them, and the quality responsibilities of those involved
- implement and track the quality methods employed throughout the project.

 ## Definition: Customer's quality expectations

A statement about the quality expected from the project product, captured in the project product description.

 ## Definition: Acceptance criteria

A prioritized list of criteria that the project product must meet before the customer will accept it (i.e. measurable definitions of the attributes required for the set of products to be acceptable to key stakeholders).

 ## Definition: Quality criteria

A description of the quality specification that the product must meet, and the quality measurements that will be applied by those inspecting the finished product.

8.1.1 Quality planning and control

PRINCE2 explicitly addresses the two activities of quality planning and **quality control**.

Quality planning is about defining the project product and its components, with the respective quality criteria, quality methods (including effort required for quality control and product approval) and quality responsibilities of those involved. The purpose of quality planning is to provide a secure basis:

- to obtain agreement by the project board on the overall quality expectations, the products required with their associated quality criteria (including corporate and other standards to be observed), the means by which quality will be achieved and assessed and, ultimately, the acceptance criteria by which the project product will be judged

- to communicate these agreements unambiguously so that all the project stakeholders have a common understanding of what the project is setting out to achieve
- for control (i.e. establishing an effective baseline for the project's quality controls, including the quality tolerances) and a secure means of achieving products that are fit for purpose.

When these aspects of planning are neglected, the people involved in the project may have conflicting views on:

- the scope of the solution
- what constitutes a successful result
- the approach to be adopted
- the extent of the work required
- who should be involved
- what their roles should be.

Quality control focuses on the operational techniques and activities used by those involved in the project to:

- check that the products meet their quality criteria (e.g. by quality inspections, testing or review)
- identify ways of eliminating causes of unsatisfactory performance (e.g. by introducing process improvements as a result of previous lessons).

Quality control is achieved by implementing, monitoring and recording the quality methods and responsibilities defined in the **quality management approach** and product descriptions (and subsequently agreed to in work packages).

The relationship between products, quality planning and quality control is summarized in Figure 8.1.

It is important not to confuse **quality assurance** with project assurance:

- Quality assurance is a planned and systematic process which provides confidence that outputs will meet their defined quality criteria when tested under quality control. It is carried out independently of the project team. The process must comply with relevant **corporate, programme management or customer standards** and policies.
- Project assurance is the project board's responsibility to assure itself that the project is being conducted correctly. The project board members each have a specific area of focus for project assurance, namely business assurance for the executive, user assurance for the senior user(s) and supplier assurance for the senior supplier(s). Project assurance is therefore independent of the project manager but not independent of the project.

8.2 PRINCE2's requirements for the quality theme

To be following PRINCE2, a project must, as a minimum:

- define its quality management approach. This approach must minimally cover:
  - the project's approach to quality control
  - the project's approach to project assurance
  - how the management of quality is communicated throughout the project lifecycle
  - the roles and responsibilities for quality management (PRINCE2's defined roles and responsibilities principle)
- specify explicit quality criteria for products in their product descriptions (PRINCE2's focus on products principle)

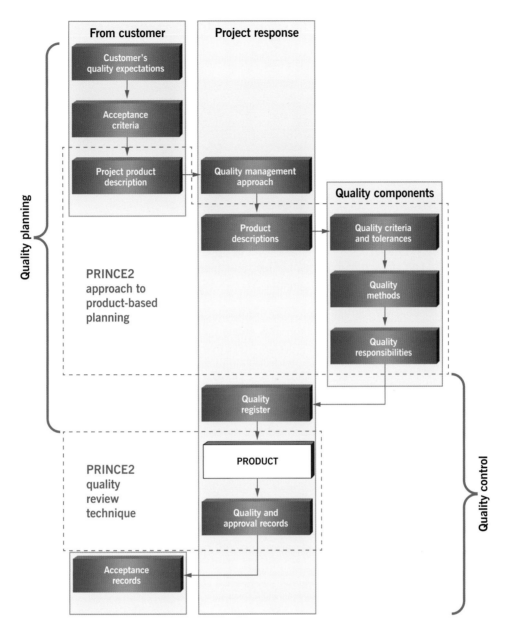

Figure 8.1 The quality audit trail

Chapter 8 – Quality

- maintain **records** to provide evidence that the planned quality activities have been carried out, and summarize those activities that are planned or have taken place in some form of **quality register**
- specify the customer's quality expectations and prioritized acceptance criteria for the project in the project product description (see Appendix A, section A.21)
- use lessons to inform quality planning, the definition of quality expectations and quality criteria (PRINCE2's learn from experience principle).

PRINCE2 requires that two products are produced and maintained:

- Quality management approach A quality management approach describes how quality will be managed on the project.

  This includes the specific processes, procedures, techniques, standards and responsibilities to be applied.

- Quality register A quality register is used to summarize all the quality management activities that are planned or have taken place, and provides information for the end stage reports and end project report.

Refer to Appendix A, sections A.22 and A.23, for more details about the suggested content for these management products.

Key message

PRINCE2 does not prescribe a particular or detailed approach to quality management. Any approach that meets the requirements described can be said to be following PRINCE2.

The quality management approach should be created during the initiating a project process and reviewed, and possibly updated, at the end of each management stage. The quality management approach will define how and when the quality register is reviewed and updated.

The quality register is effectively a diary of the quality events planned and undertaken (e.g. workshops, reviews, inspections, testing, pilots, acceptance and audits). It is created during the initiating a project process as the products and quality control measures are being defined. It is then maintained (in line with the current baseline plans) throughout the project.

As the project progresses and records of the quality activities are received, the quality register is updated to reflect (in summary form) the actual results from the quality activities. The quality register provides key audit and assurance information, relating what was planned and agreed (in the quality management approach and product descriptions) to the quality activities actually performed.

8.2.1 Quality responsibilities in PRINCE2

Responsibilities for managing quality in PRINCE2 are set out in Table 8.1. As described in Chapter 7, even if roles are combined all the responsibilities in this table must still be undertaken.

Tip

A quality management system is the complete set of quality standards, procedures and responsibilities for an organization or specific entity (e.g. site, business unit) within that organization. It is typically the responsibility of a corporate body, programme management team or customer organization.

8.3 Guidance for effective quality management

8.3.1 The cost of correcting quality issues

It is much easier and cheaper to correct quality issues and flaws early in the project lifecycle, rather than when the finished product is being tested or, worse, when the product is already in operational use.

Table 8.1 Responsibilities relevant to the quality theme

Role	Responsibilities
Corporate, programme management or the customer	Provide details of the corporate, programme management or customer **quality management system**. Provide quality assurance.
Executive	Approve the project product description. Approve the quality management approach. Confirm acceptance of the project product.
Senior user	Provide the customer's quality expectations and acceptance criteria. Approve the project product description. Approve the quality management approach. Approve product descriptions for key user products. Provide resources to undertake user quality activities and product approval. Provide acceptance of the project product.
Senior supplier	Approve the project product description (if appropriate). Approve the quality management approach. Approve the quality methods, techniques and tools adopted in product development. Provide resources to undertake supplier quality activities. Approve product descriptions for key specialist products.
Project manager	Document customer's quality expectations and acceptance criteria. Prepare the project product description (with users). Prepare the quality management approach. Prepare and maintain the product descriptions. Ensure that team managers implement the quality control measures agreed in product descriptions and work packages.
Team manager	Assist the project manager with preparing and maintaining the product descriptions. Produce products consistent with product descriptions. Manage quality controls for the products concerned. Assemble **quality records**. Advise the project manager of product quality status.
Project assurance	Advise the project manager on the quality management approach. Assist the project board and project manager by reviewing the product descriptions. Advise the project manager on suitable quality **reviewers/approvers**. Assure project board members on the implementation of the quality management approach (i.e. the proper conduct of the project management and quality procedures).
Project support	Provide administrative support for quality controls. Prepare and maintain the quality register and the quality records. Assist team managers and members with the application of the project's quality processes.

8.3.2 Aligning with corporate and external standards

A starting point for any project in an organization is to identify whether the organization has a mandated quality management system.

It is frequently the case that more than one organization is involved in a project (for example, separate customer and supplier businesses). It follows that each may have its own quality management system. If the project has a single key commissioning organization, or is part of a programme or portfolio, a single established quality management system is more likely to apply.

The project may also be subject to external quality standards (for example, when the project is within a regulated environment). These various circumstances must be addressed when determining the project's approach to quality.

8.3.3 Quality and delivery approaches

It is important that the approach to managing quality works with, and supports, the chosen delivery approach, rather than working against it. For example, when using an agile approach the high frequency of quality checking (in the form of reviews, demos or tests) may have a significant impact on how a project is planned. This will affect the incremental delivery of the project product and how the increments are released. This is especially true in IT situations where continual integration and automated testing are being used.

8.3.4 Quality and projects within a programme or portfolio

Where the project is part of a programme or portfolio, the quality management approach for the programme or portfolio will usually determine the quality management approach for the project.

Where there is already an established quality management system for projects, for example in a programme or portfolio, only the project-specific approaches will need to be documented.

8.3.5 Independent quality assurance

Quality assurance is about independently checking that the organization and processes are in place for quality planning and control (i.e. not actually performing the quality planning or control, which will be undertaken by the project management team). It provides the project's stakeholders with confidence that the quality requirements can be fulfilled. Although PRINCE2 does not address quality assurance, it is good practice to include it in the project's quality management approach.

8.3.6 The customer's quality expectations

The customer's quality expectations should be agreed early in the starting up a project process. The expectations are captured in discussions with the customer and then refined for inclusion in the project product description.

To avoid misinterpretations and inaccurate assumptions about the project's quality requirements, the customer's quality expectations should cover:

- the key quality requirements for the project product
- any standards and processes that will need to be applied to achieve the specified quality requirements, including the extent to which the customer's and/or supplier's quality management system should be used
- any measurements that may be useful to assess whether the project product meets the quality requirements (e.g. existing customer satisfaction measures).

The key quality requirements will drive the choice of solution and, in turn, influence the time, cost, scope, benefits and risk performance targets of the project.

Examples of quality expectation

The quality expectation for a water pump in a remote village is that it is robust enough to 'last a lifetime', whereas because the oil pump in a racing car needs to be as light as possible, it may only need to last the duration of one race.

Chapter 8 – Quality

The customer's quality expectations are often expressed in broad terms as a means to gain common understanding of the general quality requirements. These are then used to identify more detailed acceptance criteria, which should be specific and precise.

Identifying the acceptance methods is crucial because they address the question: How do we prove whether and when the project product has been completed and is it acceptable to the customer? This is particularly relevant in commercial customer/supplier arrangements, where acceptance criteria may be stated as part of a contractual agreement.

Where possible, the customer's quality expectations should be prioritized as they will be used as inputs to define quality tolerances for the project product and its components.

The customer's quality expectations should be reviewed at the end of each management stage in case any external factors have changed them.

Even for a simple project, there must be a shared understanding between the senior user, senior supplier and project manager of the levels of quality required for the project product (including its components). The degree to which these need to be defined will vary depending on the products themselves and must be sufficient to avoid ambiguity.

8.3.7 Quality responsibilities

Be clear as to who is responsible for which aspect of quality. This is particularly important in commercial customer/supplier situations, where the contract needs to make clear what the quality expectations are, what acceptance criteria are to be used and how quality assurance and control will be done.

It is advisable to define the customer's rights of inspection and audit in terms of what can be inspected or audited, how often, and how much notice needs to be given for any inspection or audit. If integrating a supplier's products with those from other parties, care should also be taken that the individual obligations with respect to verification are defined.

8.3.8 Prioritizing acceptance criteria

The project's acceptance criteria form a list of measurable definitions of the attributes required for a set of products to be acceptable to key stakeholders. Examples are ease of use, ease of support, ease of maintenance, appearance, major functions, development costs, running costs, capacity, availability, reliability, security, accuracy and performance. When the project can demonstrate that all the acceptance criteria have been met (according to the priorities set), the project's obligations are fulfilled and the project can be closed.

It should be recognized that it may not be possible to meet all the acceptance criteria and that the criteria may need to be prioritized as described in section 9.4.1.

8.3.9 Evolving acceptance criteria

It is important to recognize that little may be understood about the project's products during the starting up a project process. Consequently, it is often the case that acceptance criteria will be refined and agreed during the initiating a project process, with each management stage providing further information which is incorporated through change control. When finalized, acceptance criteria are subject to change control and can only be changed with the approval of the project board.

When an agile approach is being used, the project product description may be written in the form of an epic or a **user story**, with associated acceptance criteria. As such they can develop iteratively as the project proceeds.

8.3.10 Proxy measures of quality

In considering acceptance criteria, it can be useful to select proxy measures that will be accurate and reliable indicators of whether benefits will subsequently be achieved.

Example of acceptance criteria

If a customer's quality expectation for a water pump is that it 'lasts a lifetime', the acceptance criteria should focus on those measures that provide sufficient indication or confidence that the pump is capable of lasting a lifetime (defined as a specific number of years). This may include complying with certain engineering standards relating to product durability. Another way to give confidence might be for the pump manufacturer to show accelerated life test data as proxy for the 'lasts a lifetime' criterion.

8.3.11 Specifying quality criteria in product descriptions

Quality criteria specified in product descriptions need to be both specific and measurable. For example, 'The user interface is lovely' is neither specific nor measurable. Instead the quality criteria need to be measurable, such as '70 per cent of users agree that the user interface is "easy to use" or better'.

However, care should be taken to write product descriptions in sufficient detail but not in too much detail. Product descriptions that are too detailed can lead to an unnecessary increase in the cost of quality for the project, whereas incomplete or inaccurate product descriptions can lead to acceptance disputes if the delivered results do not match the customer's expectations.

Where necessary, the product description should reference supporting information, such as any applicable standards or specialist design documents.

A product description should include the quality criteria that the product must meet. These must be of sufficient detail and clarity to enable those reviewing a product to unambiguously confirm whether the product meets its requirements.

Example of quality criteria

Consider a project to design and manufacture a new camera. One quality criterion is that the camera and its packaging must weigh no more than 1 kg. The **product breakdown structure** identifies a user guide product. It follows that the size and weight of the user guide is an important factor and not, for example, the number of pages.

Questions to be asked include: What is the target market for the camera? Does this also imply that the manual needs to be written in several languages? Will that mean it gets heavier? Or will a downloadable online manual suffice? This could reduce the weight of the packaging and allow the camera itself to be heavier.

Considering quality criteria often highlights connections and factors such as these which inform the subsequent planning process.

Quality tolerances for a product can be specified in quality criteria by defining an acceptable range of values. For example:

- Is the duration of the presentation 30 minutes (plus or minus 5 minutes)?
- Is temperature maintained in the range of 1–5°C?

The quality methods section of the product description is used to specify the quality activities to be implemented during the development of a product, for review and approval on completion. When specialized skills are implicit in the quality methods, these should also be specified. There are two primary types of quality methods: in-process methods and appraisal methods (see section 8.3.13).

To avoid doubt, the quality responsibilities for a product should be specified. Responsibilities are often described in terms of:

- Producer The person or group responsible for developing a product
- Reviewer(s) A person or group, independent of the **producer**, who assesses whether a product meets its requirements as defined in its product description
- Approver(s) The person or group, for example a project board, who is identified as qualified and authorized to approve a product as being complete and fit for purpose.

8.3.12 The amount of information included in the quality register

The level of detail will often depend on the extent to which quality metrics (e.g. 'defect counts') need to be analysed for process improvement purposes. An example of a quality register is shown in Table 8.2.

Table 8.2 Example of a quality register

Quality activity ID	Product ID	Product	Quality method	Producer	Reviewer(s)	Approver(s)	Target review date	Actual review date	Target approval date	Actual approval date	Result
1	121	Test plan	Inspection	Ali	Paulo	John, Rita	14 Feb	21 Feb	21 Feb	28 Feb	Pass
2	124	Water pump	Performance test	Paulo	Ali, Bob	John	20 Mar	20 Mar	27 Mar	N/A	Fail
3	124	Water pump	Maintenance test	Paulo	Ali, Amir	Rita	21 Mar	21 Mar	27 Mar	27 Mar	Pass
...											
9	124	Water pump	Performance test	Paulo	Ali, Bob	John	14 Jun		21 Jun		

8.3.13 In-process and appraisal quality methods

'In-process' methods are the means by which quality can be 'built into' the products as they are developed.

These might involve the use of specialist methods and/or techniques, including calibrated process controls, automation (e.g. robotics, software tools), piloting exercises, workshops, surveys and consultations. A simpler approach to consider might include the use of quality inspections during the course of product development as well as upon completion.

'Appraisal' methods are used to assess the finished products for completeness and fitness for purpose.

There are, in essence, two types of appraisal methods, depending on the extent to which it is possible to define objective quality criteria:

- testing, if the quality criteria are truly objective and quantifiable
- quality inspection, if some professional judgement is required.

8.3.14 Quality inspections

A quality inspection is a systematic, structured assessment of a product conducted in a planned, documented and organized fashion. A systematic but flexible approach to quality inspection can be used:

- during the development of products, whether formally (i.e. in line with what was agreed during quality planning) or informally (simply as a means of assessing the quality of a 'work in progress')
- to mark the completion and approval of products
- to complement testing (e.g. simply for checking test results).

Quality inspection techniques are particularly applicable when professional judgement is required to assess the product's fitness for purpose. The techniques can be used within the project as quality controls, and by independent experts as part of quality assurance. Peer and gateway reviews are examples of quality assurance activities that can be implemented by using or adapting a generic inspection technique (see section 12.4.2). Used as a project management team control, conducting systematic quality inspections can also have valuable team-building side-benefits.

 Tip

Even when testing is the primary appraisal method, it is often the case that someone has to check that the test results meet the criteria for success and so a simple inspection is still required.

8.3.15 Quality records

The quality records support entries in the quality register by providing the project manager and the project board with assurance that:

- products really are complete (and consequently that the related activities are finished)
- products have met their associated quality criteria and are fit for their intended purposes (alternatively there are records of any quality failures and corrective action)
- the agreed processes have been observed
- approval authorities and key product stakeholders are satisfied
- planned audits have been conducted and reported.

Quality records should include references to the quality inspection documentation, such as a test plan, details of any 'defect' statistics and actions required to correct errors and omissions of the products inspected, and any quality-related reports (e.g. an audit report). When these records are received by project support, the quality register entries for the relevant products can be completed.

During the project and at project closure, the quality records provide a valuable source of information for analysis in accordance with the PRINCE2 principle that projects should learn from experience. For example, quality metrics, such as defect types and trends, can be used as a source of information for lessons and process improvements.

8.3.16 Approval records

Even though quality records provide evidence that each product has met its requirements as specified in its product description, it is good practice to obtain a record that the product has been approved.

PRINCE2 does not specify the format or composition of approval records as these will depend on the level of formality required, the customer/supplier relationship and the quality management system of the organizations involved. The format for approval records could, for example, be a note in the minutes of a meeting, an email, a letter, a signature on a document or a certificate.

8.3.17 Acceptance records

PRINCE2 uses the term 'acceptance' to describe the ultimate approval of the project product. Acceptance is frequently required from more than one set of stakeholders, for instance those using the project product and its components, and those maintaining them (in which case both categories of stakeholder should have been involved in defining the relevant products, participating in quality inspections and granting approval during the course of the project).

Products are approved throughout the life of the project and ownership may even be transferred to the customer as part of a phased handover. However, during the closing a project process, it is important to check that all forms of approval have been obtained and records kept for audit and/or contractual purposes.

Acceptance may be qualified, and documented '**concession**s' can be granted (e.g. if there are faults in the solution or some performance criteria have not been fully achieved). Where concessions have been granted by the project board, it may be necessary to recommend follow-on actions for later improvements or remedies for the products concerned.

8.4 Technique: recommended quality review technique

In the absence of any other approach, PRINCE2 recommends the following quality review technique, which complements the use of product descriptions.

8.4.1 Objectives

The objectives of a PRINCE2 **quality review** are to:

- assess the conformity of a product against the quality criteria documented in the product description
- involve key interested parties in checking the product's quality and in promoting wider acceptance of the product
- provide confirmation that the product is complete and ready for approval
- baseline the product for future change control.

8.4.2 Benefits

The PRINCE2 quality review technique (and other quality inspection techniques) can yield substantial side-benefits, particularly in terms of:

- **Stakeholder engagement** Quality inspections are opportunities for effective cross-functional communication. Many important stakeholders may only have direct contact with the project through these reviews, so they provide a 'window' into the project. This is particularly true for users. Structured quality inspections are among the most effective ways of encouraging buy-in to the project. Generally, the more systematic and effective the reviews, the better the impression for the stakeholders.
- **Leadership** In many circumstances a focus on quality (as in 'fitness for purpose') elicits a better response from review team members (and users) than simply focusing on budgets and schedules. Quality inspection techniques often provide excellent tips and 'soft guidance' on effective behaviour and decision-making in meetings.
- **Team building** Formal and informal quality inspections are opportunities to focus on building an effective project team, where members understand each other's contributions, needs and priorities.
- **Developing individuals** New starters learn from more experienced personnel and spot omissions that others take for granted. Experienced personnel learn from the fresh perspectives brought by newcomers.
- **Quality documentation** Consistent and familiar quality records lead to improvements in communication and in the analysis of quality metrics.
- **Quality culture** The PRINCE2 quality review technique is generic. It can be employed on programmes, projects and services throughout an organization, resulting in a positive and familiar 'quality culture'. For example, the principles also apply to agile delivery approaches with varying degrees of frequency and formality.

8.4.3 Review team roles

The roles of the review team are as follows:

- **Chair** This role is responsible for the overall conduct of the review and to ensure that the review is undertaken properly. The chair reports the results of the review to the approver if they have not attended the review. Chairing quality reviews requires competence in facilitation and independence of the product being reviewed.
- **Presenter** This role introduces the product for review and represents the producer(s) of the product. The presenter also coordinates and tracks the work after the review (i.e. applying the changes to the product agreed by the team).
- **Reviewer** This role reviews the product, submits questions and confirms corrections and/or improvements.
- **Administrator** This role provides administrative support for the chair and records the result and actions.

The minimum form of review (used for simple inspections such as those of test results) involves only two people: one taking the chair and reviewer roles, the other taking the presenter and administrator roles.

The quality review roles have no specific relationship to roles in the project management team structure. However, team-building benefits can be realized where project and team managers regularly chair reviews for products with which they have not been involved.

8.4.4 Preparing for the review

Consider the following tasks when preparing for the review:

- Make the administrative arrangements for the review (chair/administrator).
- Check the product is ready for review and confirm the availability of the reviewers (chair).
- Distribute copies of the product and the relevant product description to the review team, allowing sufficient time for reviewers to prepare (presenter).
- Review the product in line with the quality criteria in the associated product description (reviewers).
- Submit a question list to the chair and presenter ahead of the review (reviewers).
- Identify minor errors that do not require review and advise the presenter (reviewers). For example, if the product is a document, annotate the copy with spelling/grammar errors.
- Produce a consolidated question list and send it to the presenter in advance of the meeting (chair).

8.4.5 Suggested review meeting agenda

The agenda could include the following items:

- **Personal introductions** If necessary (chair)
- **Product introduction** A very brief summary, covering the product's purpose: who needs it, why they need it and what it will do (presenter)
- **Major/global questions** Invite each reviewer to contribute any major or global questions about the product (chair). Global questions relate to issues that appear repeatedly throughout the product. The review team agrees any action on each question as it is raised. The administrator records the actions and responsibilities
- **Product 'talk-through'** Lead the review team through the product (by section or page, as appropriate) by reviewing the consolidated question list and inviting clarification where required (presenter). The review team agrees actions on each question as it is raised. The administrator records the actions and responsibilities
- **Read back actions** Confirm the actions and responsibilities (administrator)
- **Determine the review result** Lead the review team to a collective decision (chair). The options are:
  - complete (the product is fit for purpose, as is)
  - conditionally complete (the product is fit for purpose, subject to the agreed actions)
  - incomplete (the product requires another quality review cycle)
  - Close the review (chair)
- **Inform interested parties of the result** (chair).

Tips

- A review meeting may not be necessary if the remarks/feedback by the reviewers undertaking the preparatory work are sufficient and clear.
- A review meeting is particularly important if not all remarks/feedback are understood by the producer of the product, or if there is contradictory feedback.

8.4.6 Review follow-up

Follow up the review meeting with these action points:

- Coordinate the actions (presenter).
- Sign off individual actions (reviewers, as agreed at the meeting).
- When all actions are complete, sign off that the product is now complete (chair).
- Communicate the quality review outcome to appropriate managers/support personnel (administrator).
- Store the quality records (administrator).
- Request approval for the product (presenter).

 Tips

Reviewers

- Review the product not the person. This means avoid personalizing issues ('You …').
- Operate as a team but defer to specialist areas of expertise. Some reviewers may be selected to address specific aspects of the product and their comments may carry more weight in those areas.
- Do not introduce trivia at reviews (spelling, punctuation, etc.) unless it is a major/global issue (e.g. if the document will be communicated to an important audience, such as the public).

Chair

- Encourage the reviewers to come well prepared to the review meeting.
- Encourage the presenter to maintain a steady pace during the product talk-through. The reviewers must have the opportunity to introduce their issues but allowing too much time invites comments that would not otherwise be made. The presenter should not be opening discussions unnecessarily.
- Resolve each point as it is raised by getting a decision from the review team. Does the product have to be changed or not? Do not allow discussions to drift. Remember, the purpose of the review is to identify defects, not to design solutions to them. Avoid the temptation to formulate and agree solutions. These should be done post-review.
- Focus on this product. Do not allow discussion to drift onto other related products. If it appears that there may be a problem associated with a related product, handle it outside the meeting as an issue.
- Make sure the reviewers contribute effectively. It is your responsibility to approve the product so you must ensure that the reviewers have checked that the product is fit for purpose.
- If a reviewer cannot attend the review, accept their question list and either raise the questions on their behalf or accept a substitute to do so, or replace the reviewer.

Presenter

- It may be that a follow-up action is not feasible to implement or cannot be done within agreed tolerances, in which case an issue should be raised to the project manager.

Approver

- If the person (or group) who will approve the product participates in the quality review, it may be possible to approve the product as part of the review.

9

Plans

This chapter covers:

- the role of planning in effective project management
- different types of plan
- product-based planning
- prioritization, estimation and scheduling
- PRINCE2's requirements for the plans theme
- guidance for effective planning

9 Plans

9.1 The plans theme

Key message

The purpose of the plans theme is to facilitate communication and control by defining the means of delivering the products (the where and how, by whom, and estimating the when and how much).

9.1.1 Plans to enable control

Plans provide the backbone of the management information required for any project; without a plan there can be no control.

Many people think of a plan as just being a chart showing timescales. PRINCE2 takes both a more comprehensive and a more flexible view of plans. A PRINCE2 plan must describe not only timescales but also what will be delivered, how and by whom. Poorly planned projects cause frustration, waste and rework. It is therefore essential to allocate sufficient time for planning to take place.

Definition: Plan

A detailed proposal for doing or achieving something which specifies the what, when, how and by whom it will be achieved. In PRINCE2 there are only the following types of plan: project plan, stage plan, team plan and exception plan.

A plan enables the project team to understand:

- what products need to be delivered
- the risks; both opportunities and threats
- any issues with the definition of scope
- which people, specialist equipment and resources are needed

- when activities and events should happen
- whether targets (for time, cost, quality, scope, benefits and risk) are achievable.

A plan provides a baseline against which progress can be measured and is the basis for securing support for the project, agreeing the scope and gaining commitment to provide the required resources.

Key message

The resources required to deliver a plan need to be committed by those approving that plan to ensure that they are available when needed.

9.1.2 Dealing with the planning horizon

PRINCE2's principle of manage by stages reflects that it is usually not possible to plan the whole project from the outset. Planning becomes more difficult and uncertain the further into the future it extends. There will be a time period over which it is possible to plan with reasonable accuracy; this is called the '**planning horizon**'. It is seldom possible to plan with any degree of accuracy beyond the planning horizon.

A great deal of effort can be wasted on attempts to plan beyond a sensible planning horizon. For example, a detailed plan to show what each team member is doing for the next 12 months will almost certainly be inaccurate after just a few weeks. A detailed team plan for the short term and an outline plan for the long term is a more effective approach.

PRINCE2 addresses the planning horizon issue by requiring that both high-level and detailed plans are created and maintained at the same time, reflecting the relative certainty and uncertainty on either side of the planning horizon. These are:

- a project plan for the project as a whole. This will usually be a high-level plan, providing indicative timescales, **milestone**s, cost and resource requirements based on estimates
- a detailed stage plan for the current management stage, aligned with the overall project plan timescales. This plan is produced before the start of that stage, and must not extend beyond the planning horizon.

Definition: Project plan

A high-level plan showing the major products of the project, when they will be delivered and at what cost. An initial project plan is presented as part of the PID. This is revised as information on actual progress appears. It is a major control document for the project board to measure actual progress against expectations.

Definition: Stage plan

A detailed plan used as the basis for project management control throughout a management stage.

The management stages make up the project lifecycle and are the fundamental building blocks for the plans and governance of a project. See section 9.3.1.1 for further guidance for designing a plan with management stages.

What is the relationship between project lifecycles, phases and stages?

Project lifecycles are often described in terms of project phases, where the term 'phase' is used as an alternative to 'stage' or 'management stage'. For example, BS 6079–1:2010 states:

Most projects, irrespective of size and complexity, will naturally move through a series of distinct phases from conception to completion. This applies as much for sequential development (e.g. analyse, design, build, test) as for iterative and agile development. Generally, the early phases comprise investigative work, which determines the work in the later implementation phases.

In BS 6079 Part 1, there is no assumption regarding the use of the words 'phase' or 'stage' with respect to level in the work breakdown structure; for example, a stage is not assumed to be a sub-part of a phase or vice versa.

9.1.3 Product-based planning

PRINCE2 has a principle to focus on products. The philosophy behind this is that what needs to be delivered (the products) must be identified before deciding what activities, dependencies and resources are required to deliver those products. This approach is called **product-based planning**.

The benefits of product-based planning include:

- clearly and consistently identifying and documenting the products to be produced by the plan and the interdependencies between them: this reduces the risk of important scope aspects being neglected or overlooked
- removing any ambiguity over what the project is expected to produce
- involving users in specifying the product requirements, thus increasing buy-in and reducing approval disputes
- improving communication: the product breakdown structure and **product flow diagram** provide simple and powerful means of sharing and discussing options for the scope and approach to be adopted for the project
- clarifying the scope boundary: defining products that are in and out of the scope for the plan and providing a foundation for change control, thus avoiding uncontrolled change or 'scope creep'

- identifying products that are external to the plan's scope but are necessary for it to proceed, and allocating them to other projects or organizations
- preparing the way for the production of work packages for suppliers
- gaining a clear agreement on production, review and approval responsibilities.

9.2 PRINCE2's requirements for the plans theme

To be following PRINCE2, a project must, as a minimum:

- ensure that plans enable the business case to be realized (PRINCE2's continued business justification principle)
- have at least two management stages: an initiation stage and at least one further management stage. The more complex and risky a project, the more management stages that will be required (PRINCE2's manage by stages principle)
- produce a project plan for the project as a whole and a stage plan for each management stage (PRINCE2's manage by stages principle)
- use product-based planning for the project plan, stage plans and exception plans. It may be optionally used for team plans. PRINCE2 recommends the steps shown in Figure 9.2 for product-based planning although alternative approaches may be used. PRINCE2 recommends the steps shown in Figure 9.6 for defining and analysing the products to produce a product breakdown structure, although alternative approaches may be used
- produce specific plans for managing exceptions (PRINCE2's manage by exception principle)
- define the roles and responsibilities for planning (PRINCE2's defined roles and responsibilities principle)
- use lessons to inform planning (PRINCE2's learn from experience principle).

 Key message

PRINCE2 requires a product-oriented approach to decomposing the project product description into a product breakdown structure or a product-oriented work breakdown structure. Where an agile delivery approach is being used, the product breakdown structure could be represented by epics or user stories.

PRINCE2 requires that four products are produced and maintained:

- **Project product description** A description of the overall project's output, including the customer's quality expectations, together with the acceptance criteria and acceptance methods for the project. As such it applies to a project plan only.
- **Product description** A description of each product's purpose, composition, derivation and quality criteria.
- **Product breakdown structure** A hierarchy of all the products to be produced during a plan.
- **Plan** Provides a statement of how and when objectives are to be achieved, by showing the major products, activities and resources required for the scope of the plan. In PRINCE2, there are three levels of plan: project, stage and team. In addition, PRINCE2 has exception plans, which are created at the same level as the plan they are replacing.

Tip

The terms 'product breakdown structure' and 'work breakdown structure' can be confusing as definitions of the terminology vary according to different project management professional bodies across the world.

PRINCE2 uses the terminology in the following way:

● A product breakdown structure is a hierarchical breakdown of the products to be produced during a plan; in PRINCE2 a product breakdown structure contains just products.

● A work breakdown structure is a hierarchical breakdown of the entire work that needs to be completed during a plan; in PRINCE2 a work breakdown structure contains just activities.

The PMI's *PMBOK® Guide* (Project Management Institute, 2013) defines a work breakdown structure as: 'A deliverable-oriented hierarchical decomposition of the work to be executed by the project team to accomplish the project objectives and create the required deliverables. It organizes and defines the total scope of work.'

Users of PRINCE2 from a PMI background might find it useful to substitute the phrase 'product-oriented work breakdown structure' when they see the term 'product breakdown structure' in this manual.

Importantly, both uses of the terminology agree that project managers need to plan by breaking down the products or outputs of the project first and, only then, break down the activity needed to produce the products.

PRINCE2 recommends, but does not require, that an additional product is created and maintained: the product flow diagram. This is a diagram showing the sequence of production and interdependencies of the products listed in a product breakdown structure.

Tip

Although a sequence is implied when defining and analysing products, in practice the product breakdown structure, product descriptions and product flow diagram are often created in parallel.

9.2.1 The relationship between the PRINCE2 plans

All PRINCE2 plans have the same fundamental structure and contents; it is the purpose, scope and level of detail in the plans that vary. For this reason, PRINCE2 provides a single 'plan' product covering all these plans and Appendix A, section A.16, provides the product description and suggested content.

The relationship between these plans is illustrated in Figure 9.1 and each is described below.

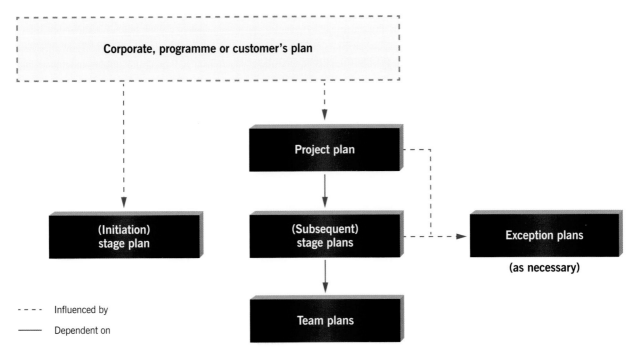

Figure 9.1 How PRINCE2's plans relate to each other

9.2.1.1 Project plan

The project plan provides a statement of how and when a project's time, cost, quality and scope performance targets are to be achieved. It shows the major products, activities and resources required for the project and:

- provides the planned project costs and timescales for the business case, and identifies the major control points, such as management stages and milestones
- is used by the project board as a baseline against which to monitor project progress management stage by management stage
- should align with the corporate, programme management or customer plan as appropriate.

The project plan is created during the initiating a project process and updated towards the end of each management stage during the managing a stage boundary process.

9.2.1.2 Stage plans

A stage plan is required for each management stage. The stage plan is similar to the project plan in content, but each element is broken down to the level of detail required for day-to-day control by the project manager.

A product description is required for all products identified in a stage plan.

The initiation stage plan is created during the starting up a project process, prior to the project plan in the initiating a project process. It is influenced by the corporate, programme management or customer plan (or equivalent) from the organization commissioning the project. All subsequent stage plans are produced near the end of the current management stage when preparing for the next management stage. This approach allows the stage plan to:

- be produced close to the time when the planned events will take place
- exist for a much shorter duration than the project plan, overcoming the planning horizon issue
- be produced with the knowledge of the performance of earlier management stages.

9.2.1.3 Exception plans

PRINCE2 requires that exception plans are produced where appropriate.

 Definition: Exception plan

A plan that often follows an **exception report**. For a stage plan exception, it covers the period from the present to the end of the current management stage. If the exception is at project level, the project plan will be replaced.

Exception plans must be produced to show the actions required to recover from or avoid a forecast deviation from agreed tolerances in the project plan or a stage plan. See Chapter 12 for more explanation of the use of tolerance in PRINCE2. Exception plans are prepared to the same level of detail as the plan they replace. If approved, the exception plan replaces the plan that is in exception and becomes the new baselined plan.

If a stage plan is being replaced, this needs the approval of the project board. Replacement of a project plan should be referred by the project board to corporate, programme management or the customer if it is beyond the authority of the project board.

Exception plans are not produced for team plans used to manage the delivery of work packages (see section 9.2.1.4).

9.2.1.4 Team plans

Each management stage may comprise a number of work packages, each of which may have a detailed team plan.

 Definition: Work package

The set of information relevant to the creation of one or more products. It will contain a description of the work, the product description(s), details of any constraints on production, and confirmation of the agreement between the project manager and the person or team manager who is to implement the work package that the work can be done within the constraints.

 Definition: Team plan

An optional level of plan used as the basis for team management control when executing work packages.

A team plan is produced by a team manager to facilitate the execution of one or more work packages. These plans are optional and their need and number will be determined by the size and complexity of the project and the number of resources involved. Team plans are created in the managing product delivery process.

Chapter 9 – Plans

There may be more than one team on a project and each team may come from separate organizations following different project management methods (not necessarily PRINCE2). In some customer/supplier contexts it could even be inappropriate for the project manager to see the details of a supplier's team plan; instead, sufficient, summary information would be provided to enable the project manager to exercise control. The formality of the team plan could vary from simply appending a schedule to the work package to a fully formed plan in similar style to a stage plan.

Should a team manager forecast that the assigned work package may exceed tolerances, they should notify the project manager by raising an issue. If the issue can be resolved within management stage tolerances, the project manager will authorize corrective action by updating the work package or issuing a new work package(s) and instructing the team manager(s) accordingly.

Team managers may create their team plans in parallel with the project manager creating the stage plan for the management stage.

9.2.2 Planning responsibilities in PRINCE2

Responsibilities for planning in PRINCE2 are set out in Table 9.1. As described in Chapter 7, if roles are combined then all the responsibilities in this table must still be covered.

Table 9.1 Responsibilities relevant to the plans theme

Role	Responsibilities
Corporate, programme management or the customer	Set project tolerances and document them in the project mandate or confirm them to the project board for inclusion in the project brief.
	Approve exception plans when project-level tolerances are forecast to be exceeded.
	Provide the corporate, programme management or customer planning standards.
Executive	Approve the project plan.
	Define tolerances for each management stage and approve stage plans.
	Approve exception plans when management-stage-level tolerances are forecast to be exceeded.
	Commit business resources to stage plans (e.g. finance).
Senior user	Assist the project manager in preparing project and stage plans.
	Ensure that project plans and stage plans remain consistent from the user perspective.
	Commit user resources to stage plans.
Senior supplier	Assist the project manager in preparing project and stage plans.
	Ensure that project plans and stage plans remain consistent from the supplier perspective.
	Commit supplier resources to stage plans.
Project manager	Design the plans.
	Prepare the project plan and stage plans.
	Decide how management stages and delivery steps are to be applied.
	Instruct corrective action when work-package-level tolerances are forecast to be exceeded.
	Prepare an exception plan to implement corporate management, programme management or the project board's decision in response to exception reports.
Team manager	Prepare team plans.
	Prepare schedules for each work package.
Project assurance	Review changes to the project plan to see whether there is any impact on the needs of the business or the project business case.
	Review the management stage and review project progress against agreed tolerances.
Project support	Assist with the compilation of project plans, stage plans and team plans.
	Contribute specialist expertise (e.g. planning tools).
	Baseline, store and distribute project plans, stage plans and team plans.

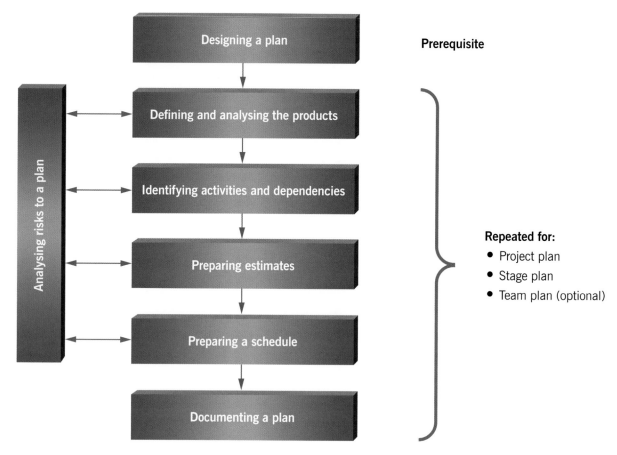

Figure 9.2 PRINCE2's recommended approach to product-based planning

9.3 Guidance for effective planning

9.3.1 PRINCE2's recommended approach to planning

In the absence of any other approach, PRINCE2 recommends the approach to planning shown in Figure 9.2 and described in the following sections.

9.3.1.1 Designing a plan

The number of management stages

Although the use of management stages in a PRINCE2 project is mandatory, the number of management stages is flexible and depends on the scale, duration and risk of the project. A simple project may only need two stages, the first including initiating the project and the second for undertaking the planned work and closing the project. Larger projects may need additional management stages to enable the project management team to have an optimal level of planning and control.

Defining management stages is fundamentally a process of balancing:

- how far ahead in the project it is sensible to plan
- where the key decision points need to be on the project

- the amount of risk within the project
- too many short management stages (increasing the project management overhead) versus too few lengthy ones (reducing the level of control)
- how confident the project board and project manager are in proceeding.

The length of management stages

PRINCE2 does not define how long a management stage should be. Management stages should be shorter when there is greater risk, uncertainty or complexity (for example, at the beginning of projects). They can be longer when risk is lower, typically in the middle of projects. Factors that will influence this decision include:

- **The planning horizon at any point in time** The planning horizon may vary depending on the nature of the work being undertaken. For example, the work involved in installing a computer system during an application migration project may be better understood and less risky than the work involved with migrating the application itself.
- **The delivery steps within the project** The ends of management stages do not necessarily need to occur at the same time as the ends of delivery steps, but there are often benefits if they do. For example, the project board may wish to be able to understand any effects on the business case of the results of a 'proof of concept' before committing to a full-scale deployment.
- **Alignment with programme activities** Programmes may be organized around groups of projects structured around distinct step changes in capability and benefit delivery **tranche**s. It may be a requirement to align the end of a management stage with the end-of-tranche review within the programme. This will allow the project to contribute fully to the assessment of the ongoing viability of the programme itself.
- **The level of risk** Management stages can be very useful as a means of bringing project board control to risky projects. Management stage breaks can be inserted at key points when risks to the project can be reviewed before major commitments of money or resources.

Management stages and delivery approaches

Another method of grouping work is by the set of techniques used or the products created. This results in a delivery approach covering elements such as design, build and implementation, which are included in the plan as work packages or activities described as delivery steps. Delivery steps are a separate concept from the management stages already introduced, and the work comprising delivery steps is always included within a management stage.

Delivery steps often overlap (as in Figures 9.3 and 9.4) but management stages do not. Delivery steps are typified by the use of a particular set of specialist skills. Management stages equate to commitment of resources and authority to spend.

Often the boundary of the management stage and a delivery step will coincide; for instance, when the management decision is based on the output from delivery activities. However, on other occasions management stage and delivery step boundaries will not coincide; for example, there might be more than one delivery step per management stage.

When a delivery step spans a management stage boundary, the extent to which the product(s) of the delivery step should be complete at the stage boundary should be clear in the product description(s) concerned.

Figures 9.3 to 9.5 give examples of the distinction between management stages and delivery steps. Figure 9.3 shows a project with five delivery steps. The numbered management stages in Figures 9.4 and 9.5 show a sequence of stages *within* a project (not from the start of the project).

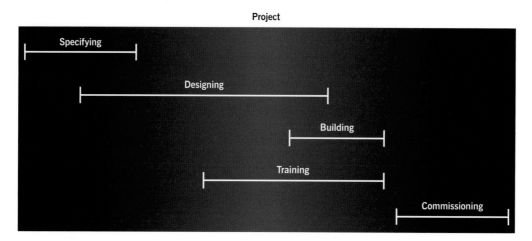

Figure 9.3 Work defined by delivery steps

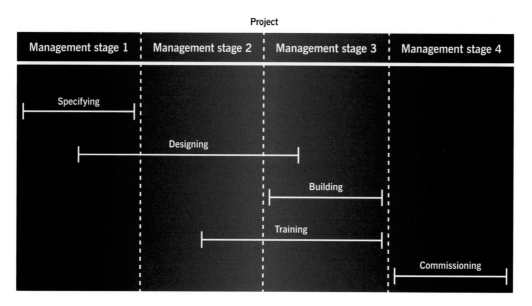

Figure 9.4 Delivery steps crossing management stage boundaries

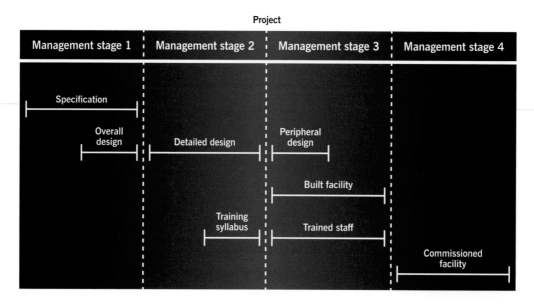

Figure 9.5 Delivery steps aligned with management stages

Figure 9.4 shows the same project as Figure 9.3, but broken down into four management stages. Two of the delivery steps span more than one management stage.

Figure 9.5 shows a 'designing' delivery step that has been broken into three product groups:

● The overall design now falls within management stage 1.

● Detailed design and training syllabus form the second management stage.

● Peripheral design is scheduled for management stage 3, together with the creation of the built facility and trained staff.

The PRINCE2 approach is to concentrate the management of the project on the management stages because these will form the basis of the planning and control processes described throughout the method. To do otherwise runs the risk of the project being driven by the specialist teams instead of the customer's management.

The format and presentation of the plan

Decisions need to be made about how the plan can best be presented, depending on the audience for the plan and how it will be used, together with the presentation and layout of the plan, planning tools, estimating methods, levels of plan and monitoring methods to be used for the project.

PRINCE2 does not prescribe a format for a plan. Charts, documents, spreadsheets and plans on whiteboards are all equally valid if they are fit for purpose and appropriate to the scale, planning horizon and complexity of the project.

If the project is part of a programme or portfolio, the programme or portfolio may have developed a common approach to project planning. This may cover standards (e.g. level of planning) and tools. These will be the starting point for designing any project plan. Any project-specific variations should be highlighted and the agreement of programme or portfolio management sought. There may also be a company standard for planning and control aids, or the customer may stipulate the use of a particular set of tools. The choice of planning tool may depend on the complexity of the project and so the choice may need to be deferred until the level of complexity is known.

The estimating methods to be used in the plan may affect the plan design, so decisions on the methods should be made as part of the plan design itself.

The use of planning tools is not obligatory, but it can save a great deal of time if the plan is to be regularly updated and changed. A good tool can also validate that the correct dependencies have been built in and have not been affected by any plan updates.

 Tip

The plan for a simple project may be very simple, such as a **product checklist** or a diagram on a whiteboard in the workroom, which can be photographed from time to time.

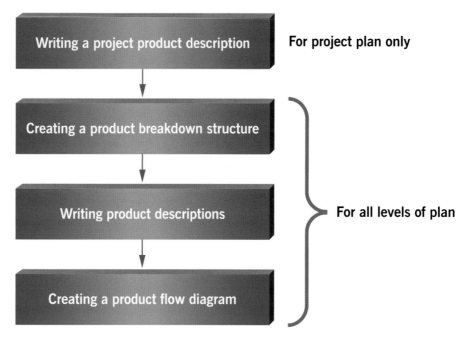

Figure 9.6 PRINCE2's recommended approach to defining and analysing the products

9.3.1.2 Defining and analysing the products

PRINCE2 recommends, but does not mandate, the following approach (summarized in Figure 9.6).

Writing a project product description

The project product description is created in the starting up a project process as part of the initial scoping activity. It may be refined during the initiating a project process when creating the project plan. It is subject to formal change control and should be checked at management stage boundaries (during the managing a stage boundary process) to see if any changes are required. It is used in the closing a project process as part of the verification that the project has delivered what was expected of it and that the acceptance criteria have been met.

Although the senior user is responsible for specifying the project product, in practice the project product description is often written by the project manager in consultation with the senior user and executive. The project product description is included as a component of the project brief and is used to help select the project approach defined within the project brief. The project product description defines what the customer is expecting the project to deliver and the project approach defines the solution or method to be used by the supplier to create the project product.

Every effort should be made to make the project product description as complete as possible at the outset. See Appendix A, section A.21, for the suggested composition of the project product description.

 Tip

If the project's scope includes any transition or business change (necessary to deliver outcomes), these should also be defined as specialist products and explicitly covered in the plan.

Creating a product breakdown structure

The plan is broken down into its major products, which are then further broken down until an appropriate level of detail for the plan is reached. A lower-level product can be a component of only one higher-level product. The resultant hierarchy of products is known as a product breakdown structure.

The format and presentation of the product breakdown structure and product flow diagram are determined by personal preference. See Appendix D for examples.

When creating a product breakdown structure, consider the following:

- It is usual to involve a team of people in the creation of a product breakdown structure, perhaps representing the different interests and various skill sets involved in the plan's output.

- It is common to identify products by running a structured brainstorming session (e.g. using sticky notes or a whiteboard) to capture each product as it is identified.

- When a team is creating a product breakdown structure, there are likely to be different opinions on how to break down the products. For example, if the output of the plan is accounting software, users may want separate modules for accounts payable, accounts receivable, general ledger, etc. The suppliers, however, may prefer screens, reports, databases, etc. Neither breakdown is wrong, but the project management team must agree on which approach will be used in the product breakdown structure (and hence the plan).

- It is useful to identify any products that are required to be created by other projects, or purchased or hired directly from a supplier; these are externally sourced products. The project manager is not responsible for the creation of externally sourced products as they will be supplied by parties outside the project team. The project team will, however, be responsible for the specification of the externally sourced products that are created. Consideration should be given to identifying threats to the plan should the externally sourced products be late or not to the required specification.

- When using product-based planning, it is important to consider whether to include different states of a particular product. An example of product states is 'dismantled machinery, moved machinery and reassembled machinery'. It could be appropriate to identify the different states as separate products, where each state would require its own product description with different quality criteria and quality controls. This may be particularly useful when the responsibility for creating each state will pass from one team to another. Alternatively, a single product description could be used with a set of quality criteria that the product needs to meet in order to gain approval for each state.

- When presenting the product breakdown structure, consider the use of different shapes, styles or colours for different types of product. For example, a rectangle could be used in a product breakdown structure to represent most types of product, but it may be helpful to use different shapes (such as ellipses or circles) to distinguish externally sourced products. Colours could be used to indicate which team is responsible for the product or in which management stage the product will be created.

- If the project is broken down into several stages, the products for each management stage are extracted from the project product breakdown structure to form the management stage product breakdown structure. These may be expanded to more levels of detail and thus 'extra products' may be added to give the detail required of the stage plan. Care must be taken to use the same names in the stage plans as were used in the project plan. The creation of stage plans may cause rethinking that requires further modification of the project plan in order to retain consistency.

- In some cases, the organization's lifecycle model may have a preset product breakdown structure and product flow diagram for common types of projects and a library of product description outlines for common products. In such cases the steps in the PRINCE2 approach to product-based planning should not be skipped but used to verify the completeness of any library material. As every project is unique, there may be additional product requirements for the project or subtle differences in the quality criteria; the locations may be different, or the people and responsibilities involved may be different. Moreover, lifecycle models frequently address only one aspect of a project's scope.

Writing product descriptions

A product description is used to understand the detailed nature, purpose, function and appearance of a product. It is produced as soon as the need for the product is identified.

When creating a product description, consider the following:

- Product descriptions should be written as soon as possible after the need for the product has been identified. Initially, these may only be 'skeletons' with little more than the title and identifier as information. They will be refined and amended as the product becomes better understood and the later planning steps are done. Therefore, early in planning 'write' (as in write a product description) can mean 'start to write and complete as soon as information becomes available'.

- A product description should be baselined when the plan containing the creation of that product is baselined. If the product is later changed, the product description must also pass through change control.

- Although the responsibility for writing product descriptions rests officially with the project or team manager, it is wise to involve representatives from the area with expertise in the product and those who will use the product in question. The latter should certainly be consulted when defining the quality criteria for the product.

- Successful product descriptions may be reused for other projects within that programme or organization. For this to happen, a library of product descriptions for reuse will need to be established and a mechanism for product descriptions to be placed in the library will also need to be implemented. The project manager should therefore refer to the library in order to see if any of the product descriptions within it are suitable for reuse and/or modification for the project.

- If a detailed requirements specification for a product is already available, this may be used as a substitute for the product description as long as the requirements specification covers the components and meets the quality criteria expected of a product description. Alternatively, a product description should be created referencing the requirements specification contents where appropriate.

- For a small project, it may only be necessary to write the project product description and product descriptions for the major/most important products.

- Quality criteria, aimed at separating an acceptable product from an unacceptable one, need careful thought. One way of testing quality criteria is by asking the question: How will I know when work on this product is finished as opposed to stopped?

- When using an agile approach it is important to remember that the initial versions of product descriptions are likely to only address the purpose and quality criteria for the product, with the rest developed during the execution of the work package.

Creating a product flow diagram

A product flow diagram may be helpful in identifying and defining the sequence in which the products of the plan will be developed and any dependencies between them (see Figure D.4 in Appendix D for an example of a product flow diagram).

The product flow diagram also helps to identify dependencies on any products outside the scope of the plan. It leads naturally to the consideration of the activities required, and provides the information for other planning techniques, such as estimating and scheduling.

When creating a product flow diagram, consider the following:

- Although the project or team manager is responsible for the creation of the product flow diagram, it is sensible to involve those who are to develop or contribute to the products contained in the plan.

- Rather than preparing the product flow diagram after the product breakdown structure has been drawn, some planners prefer to create the product flow diagram in parallel with the product breakdown structure.

- A product flow diagram needs very few symbols. Each product to be developed within the plan in question is identified (e.g. it may be enclosed in a rectangle), and the sequence in which they are to be created is shown (e.g. the rectangles may be connected by arrows). Any products that already exist or that come from work outside the scope of the project plan should be clearly identified as products to be sourced externally to the project (e.g. they may be enclosed in a different shape, such as an ellipse).

- It may be useful to add a starting point in the product flow diagram to which all entry points are attached. There is always one exit on a product flow diagram, but when there are many entrances such a place marker prevents any from being overlooked. The symbol becomes the predecessor for all entry points and would be the only symbol on a product flow diagram that is not on the product breakdown structure.

- The product flow diagram may be derived from a benefits map (linking outputs, outcomes and benefits), thereby ensuring the project product will deliver the outputs and outcomes required in order to realize the benefits.

9.3.1.3 Identifying activities and dependencies

Simply identifying products is not sufficient for scheduling and control purposes. The activities required to create or change each of the planned products need to be identified to give a fuller picture of the plan's workload.

There are several ways to identify activities, including:

- making a separate list of the activities, while still using the product flow diagram as the source of the information

- taking the products from the product breakdown structure and creating a work breakdown structure to define the activities required.

The activities should include management and quality checking activities as well as the activities needed to develop the specialist products. The activities should include any that are required to interact with external parties; for example, obtaining a product from an external source or converting such externally sourced products into something that the plan requires.

 Tip

Avoid a proliferation of activities beyond the detail appropriate to the level of the plan.

After the activities have been identified, any dependencies between activities (and products) should also be identified. It is important that dependencies are captured (e.g. on the product flow diagram or some form of register) and that someone responsible for managing the **dependency** is identified (the project manager or some other nominated person). Key dependencies should be noted in the project plan. Consideration should be given to identifying threats to the plan related to dependencies.

Definition: Dependency

A dependency means that one activity is dependent on another. There are at least two types of dependency relevant to a project: internal and external.

An internal dependency is one between two project activities. In these circumstances the project team has control over the dependency.

An external dependency is one between a project activity and a non-project activity, where non-project activities are undertaken by people who are not part of the project team. In these circumstances the project team does not have complete control over the dependency.

9.3.1.4 Preparing estimates

A decision about how much time and resource are required to carry out a piece of work to acceptable standards of performance must be made by:

- identifying the type of resource required. Specific skills may be required depending on the type and complexity of the plan. Requirements may include non-human resources, such as equipment, travel or money
- estimating the effort required for each activity by resource type. At this point, the estimates will be approximate and therefore provisional.

Tip

Basic rules for estimating

Many books and software packages include some basic rules to help ensure that an accurate and realistic estimate is produced. Examples of such planning rules include the following:

- Assume that resources will only be productive for, say, 80 per cent of their time.
- Resources working on multiple projects take longer to complete tasks because of time lost switching between them.
- People are generally optimistic and often underestimate how long tasks will take.
- Make use of other people's experiences and your own.
- Ensure that the person responsible for creating the product is also responsible for creating the effort estimates.
- Always make provision for problem-solving, meetings and other unexpected events.
- Cost each activity rather than trying to cost the plan as a whole.
- Communicate any assumptions, exclusions or constraints you have to the user(s).

Estimating cannot guarantee accuracy but, when applied, provides a view about the overall cost and time required to complete the plan. Estimates will inevitably change as more is discovered about the project.

Estimates should be challenged, as the same work under the same conditions can be estimated differently by various estimators or by the same estimator at different times.

9.3.1.5 Preparing a schedule

A plan can only show the ultimate feasibility of achieving its objectives when the activities are put together in a schedule that defines when each activity will be carried out.

There are many different approaches to scheduling. Scheduling can either be done manually or by using a computer-based planning and control tool.

Defining an activity sequence

Having identified the activities and their dependencies, and estimated their duration and effort, the next task is to determine the optimal sequence in which they can be performed.

This is an iterative task as the assignment of actual resources may affect the estimated effort and duration.

The amount of time that an activity can be delayed without affecting the completion time of the overall plan is known as the float (sometimes referred to as the slack). The float can either be regarded as a provision within the plan, or as spare time.

The critical path(s) through the diagram is the sequence of activities that have zero float. Thus, if any activity on the critical path(s) finishes late, then the whole plan will also finish late (e.g. if task 4 in Figure 9.7 is delayed, then completion of the plan will be delayed).

Identifying a plan's critical path enables the project manager to monitor those activities that:

- must be completed on time for the whole plan to be completed to schedule
- can be delayed for a time period if resources need to be re-allocated to catch up on missed activities.

Example of activity-on-node technique

An activity-on-node diagram (sometimes called an arrow diagram) can be used to schedule dependent activities within a plan. It helps a project manager to work out the most efficient sequence of events needed to complete any plan and enables the creation of a realistic schedule.

The activity-on-node diagram displays interdependencies between activities through the use of boxes and arrows. Arrows pointing into an activity box come from its predecessor activities, which must be completed before the activity can start. Arrows pointing out of an activity box go to its successor activities, which cannot start until at least this activity is complete (assuming a finish-to-start relationship between the activities). A simple activity-on-node diagram is shown in Figure 9.7.

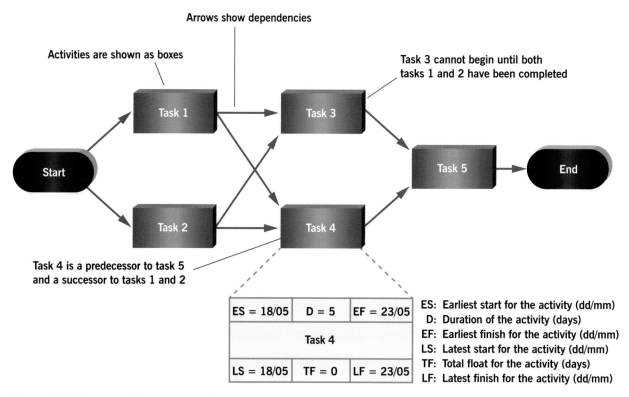

Figure 9.7 Simple activity-on-node diagram

Assessing resource availability

The number of people who will be available to do the work (or the cost of buying in resources) should be established. Any specific information should be noted (e.g. names, levels of experience, percentage availability, available dates).

Assigning resources

Using the resource availability and the information from the activity sequence allows the project manager to assign resources to activities. The result will be a schedule that shows the loading of work on each person, and the use of non-human resources.

A useful approach is to allocate resources to those activities with zero slack first (by definition they are on the critical path). Those activities with the greatest slack are the lowest priority for resource allocation.

It is important that task owners are defined. If a group needs to complete a task, ask one person from the group to be accountable to the group for that task.

If any of the task owners do not participate in creating the schedule, make sure of their availability and willingness to own the task. Do not assume that putting their names on a plan or schedule will automatically get the work done. Collaborate, communicate and follow up with each task owner to make sure that they understand what it means to complete the task.

When assigning resources, it is important to recheck the critical path because the actual resources assigned may be more or less productive than the assumption made when calculating activity effort and duration.

Levelling resource usage

The first allocation of resources may lead to uneven resource usage or over-utilization of some resources. It may therefore be necessary to rearrange resources; this is called levelling.

Activities may be reassigned, or they may have start dates and durations changed within the slack available. The end result is a final schedule with all activities assigned and resource utilization equating to resource availability.

Agreeing control points

The draft schedule enables the control points to be confirmed by the project board.

Activities relating to the end of a management stage (e.g. preparing the end stage report and the next stage plan) should be added to the activity network and the schedule revised.

One common mistake when creating a schedule is not to allow time for approvals of products or releases.

Defining milestones

A milestone is an event on a schedule which marks the completion of key activities. This could be the completion of a work package, a delivery step or a management stage. In a commercial environment, reaching a milestone may be the trigger for a payment to a supplier.

Breaking the plan into intervals associated with a milestone allows the project manager to have an early indication of issues associated with the schedule itself, and also a better view of the activities whose completion is critical to the timeline of the plan.

Although there is no 'correct' number of milestones or duration between them, they lose their value when there are too many or too few. There should be far fewer milestones than deliverables or work packages, but there should be enough milestones at major intervals to gauge whether or not the plan is proceeding as expected.

Calculating total resource requirements and costs

The resource requirements can be tabulated, and the cost of the resources and other costs calculated to produce the plan's budget. The budget should include:

- costs of the activities (including people, equipment and materials) to develop and verify the specialist products, and the cost of the project management activities
- risk budget (see section 10.3.7)
- **change budget** (see section 11.3.6)
- **cost tolerance**s.

The use of risk budgets and change budgets is optional.

9.3.1.6 Documenting a plan

Having completed the schedule satisfactorily, the plan, its costs, the required controls and its supporting text need to be consolidated in accordance with the plan design. Some examples of schedule presentation techniques are provided in section 9.4.3.

Narrative needs to be added to explain the plan, any constraints on it, external dependencies, assumptions made, any monitoring and control required, the risks identified and their required responses. This initial plan will be reviewed and updated throughout the life of the project as further information clarifies any assumptions made.

Tip

It is a good discipline to keep plans as simple as is appropriate. Consider summary diagrams if the plan is to be presented to the project board.

It may be sensible to have one plan format for presentation in submissions seeking approval, and a more detailed format for day-to-day control purposes. Also consider different levels of presentation of the plan for the different levels of readership. Most planning software offers such options.

9.3.1.7 Analysing risks to a plan

This planning activity will typically run in parallel with the other planning steps, as risks may be identified at any point in the creation or revision of a plan.

Each resource and activity, and all the planning information, should be examined for its potential risk content. All identified risks should be entered into the **risk register** (or the daily log when planning the initiation stage).

After the plan has been produced, it should still be considered a draft until the inherent risks in the plan have been identified and assessed, and the plan possibly modified.

See Chapter 10 for more details on identifying and analysing risks.

Examples of planning risks

- Omission of plans at the appropriate management level(s).
- Lots of resources joining the project at the same time can slow progress and cause communication issues. For example, plotting an S-curve (see section 12.4.1) for the resource profile over time can identify this; steep curves should be avoided.
- The plan includes unnamed resources, causing the productivity of the actual resource to differ from the estimated productivity in the plan.
- The plan contains a high proportion of external dependencies.
- The plan uses untested suppliers or is dependent on new technologies.
- There is a high proportion of activities on the critical path; a delay to any one of them will delay the plan.
- The plan does not allow for sufficient management decision points such as management stage boundaries.
- There is not much float in the plan (creating a histogram showing the number of activities by amount of float is a useful way of identifying this risk).
- A large number of products are to be completed at the same time.
- The plan is time-bound by fiscal boundaries (e.g. the budget cannot be transferred from this year to the next) or by calendar boundaries (e.g. preparation for a major sporting event).
- The schedule shows that many paths running closely in parallel with the critical path are likely to become critical themselves if there is a minor slip.

9.3.2 Plans for projects within a programme

Any specific standards that the project planners should work to will be described in the programme's monitoring and control strategy (the document that describes how a programme will apply internal controls to itself).

The programme may have dedicated planners that can help the project manager prepare and maintain the project plan and stage plans.

The programme dependency network will detail which of the project's deliverables are being used by other projects within the programme. Any such dependencies to or from the project should be incorporated into the project's plans.

The number and length of management stages will be influenced by the programme plan. It may be desirable or necessary to align stage reviews to programme milestones (e.g. the end of a tranche). The programme may even define a set of standard management stages with which all projects within the programme comply.

9.3.3 Plans when using an agile approach

Product-based planning can be applied very easily to agile delivery and it is important to plan around the requirements being delivered. Many agile techniques and concepts exist in this area. They focus on how much can be delivered over a fixed period of time (e.g. a sprint or a timebox) and often appear in an informal, low-tech, visible format such as a simple list or **backlog**.

When agile is being used, a common approach would consist of:

- the starting up a project process, producing the vision and product roadmap
- a management stage for the initiating a project process, producing the product backlog
- then a series of delivery management stages containing releases of (groups of) requirements/features.

The first two items could be combined.

There may be other equally valid ways to construct plans for projects using agile delivery approaches.

9.3.4 Plans from a supplier perspective

When tailoring the plans theme for a customer/supplier situation it must be clear, through the contract, how the plans are to be produced and what rights of inspection and audit the customer has. A supplier's plan should have sufficient activities and/or milestones for the customer's project manager to maintain their plans.

Plans need to include procurement-related milestones such as purchase orders and milestone payments aligned with each management stage.

Both the customer's and supplier's plans may be confidential to the other party as they may contain other information such as dependencies to or from other client projects, subcontractor costs, etc. It is therefore beneficial to prepare non-confidential versions of the plan that can be shared, omitting private information.

Chapter 9 – Plans

9.4 Techniques: prioritization, estimation and scheduling

9.4.1 The MoSCoW prioritization technique

Projects seldom have the money, time or resources to deliver everything wanted by the business, users or suppliers, even if delivery of everything has a business justification.

This means that on most projects acceptance criteria and quality criteria need to be prioritized, with the project attempting to deliver as much as is possible and for which there is a business justification.

In the absence of any other approach, PRINCE2 recommends the use of a technique called MoSCoW as a general prioritization technique. MoSCoW stands for:

- Must have
- Should have
- Could have
- Won't have.

Only those things identified as 'must have' are guaranteed to be delivered by a project.

MoSCoW can be used in a range of prioritization contexts, such as prioritizing issues and changes. In the context of acceptance criteria and quality criteria the following definitions apply:

- **Must have** The acceptance criteria or quality criteria define what is essential and critical to the business justification of the project. This would include failing to meet a legal or regulatory requirement.

  If the business justification for the project is viable without the criteria, even if it would involve undesirable workarounds, then the criteria are not 'must haves'.

- **Should have** The acceptance or quality criteria define what is important, but not critical, to the business justification of the project. Their absence materially weakens the business justification.

- **Could have** The acceptance or quality criteria define what is useful, but not critical, to the business justification of the project. Their absence does not weaken the business justification.

  In practical terms the distinction between should have and could have can be difficult to make. In practice it is often determined by:

  - a level of impact on the business justification. For example, a criterion might be considered 'should have' if it has greater than 1 per cent impact on benefits

  - an assessment of the actual or perceived impact of not having satisfied the requirement. For example, a 'no manual workarounds' restriction might be the difference between should have and could have.

- **Won't have** The acceptance criteria or quality criteria define what has been considered but will not be delivered. Even though it might appear strange to record what is not going to be delivered by a project, doing so is often powerful as it formalizes an agreement to not deliver something. This acts as a reminder that something has been consciously considered and can avoid the requirements being reintroduced at a later date.

MoSCoW can be used for other types of prioritization, such as prioritizing changes, by adapting the criteria as necessary. When MoSCoW is used in this way, the criteria for must have, should have and could have should always be based on the impact on business justification, in line with PRINCE2's continued business justification principle.

The MoSCoW technique can also help to define **scope tolerance**s, supporting the manage by exception principle.

9.4.2 Estimating techniques

Examples of estimating techniques

Top-down estimating

When a good overall estimate has been arrived at for the plan (by whatever means), it can be subdivided through the levels of the product breakdown structure. By way of example, historically development may be 50 per cent of the total resource requirement and testing may be 25 per cent. Subdivide development and testing into their components and apportion the effort accordingly.

Bottom-up estimating

Each individual piece of work is estimated on its own merit. These are then added together to find the estimated efforts for the various summary-level activities and overall plan.

Top-down and bottom-up approach

An overall estimate is calculated for the plan. Individual estimates are then calculated, or drawn from previous plans, to represent the relative weights of the tasks. The overall estimate is then apportioned across the various summary- and detailed-level tasks using the bottom-up figures as weights.

Comparative (reference class) estimating

Much data exists about the effort required and the duration of particular items of work. Over time an organization may build up its own historical data regarding projects that it has undertaken (previous experience and captured lessons). If such data exists, it may be useful to reference it for similar projects and apply that data to the estimates.

Parametric estimating

Basing estimates on measured/empirical data where possible (e.g. estimating models exist in the construction industry that predict materials, effort and duration based on the specification of a building).

Single-point estimating

The use of sample data to calculate a single value which is to serve as a 'best guess' for the duration of an activity.

Three-point estimating

Ask appropriately skilled resource(s) for their best-case, most likely and worst-case estimates. The value that the project manager should choose is the weighted average of these three estimates.

Delphi technique

This relies on obtaining group input for ideas and problem-solving without requiring face-to-face participation. It uses a series of questionnaires interspersed with information summaries and feedback from preceding responses to achieve an estimate.

Planning poker (when using an agile approach)

A group uses specially numbered playing cards to vote for an estimate of an item. Voting repeats with discussion until all votes are unanimous.

Examples of estimating techniques continues

Examples of estimating techniques *continued*

Big/uncertain/small (when using an agile approach)

Items to be estimated are placed by the group in one of three categories: big, uncertain and small. The group starts by discussing a few items together and then uses a divide-and-conquer approach to go through the rest of the items.

9.4.3 Scheduling techniques

Examples of presentation formats for the schedule

Gantt charts

A Gantt chart is a graphical representation of the duration of tasks against the progression of time. It allows the project manager to:

- assess how long a plan should take
- lay out the order in which tasks need to be carried out
- manage the dependencies between tasks
- see what should have been achieved at a certain point in time
- see how remedial action may bring the plan back on course.

Critical path diagram

A critical path diagram highlights those tasks which cannot be delayed without causing the plan to be delayed, and those tasks that can be delayed without affecting the end date of the plan. It helps with monitoring and communication.

Spreadsheets

It is possible to create a list of tasks 'down' the spreadsheet and a timeline 'across' it, then colour in the cells to represent where the tasks will occur in the timeline, and progress to date. For simple projects where the timeline is unlikely to change, this may be adequate. For large or complex projects, the timeline may change frequently. This means that the project manager may spend a significant amount of time changing the schedule while neglecting the day-to-day tasks required to manage the project.

Product checklist

A product checklist is a list of the major products of a plan, plus key dates in their delivery. An example of a product checklist is shown in the product description outline for a plan in Appendix A, section A.16.

Risk

This chapter covers:

- uncertainty as a common aspect of project management
- threats and opportunities, and appropriate responses
- PRINCE2's requirements for the risk theme
- roles and responsibilities
- guidance for effective risk management
- PRINCE2 procedure for managing risk

10 Risk

10.1 The risk theme

Key message

The purpose of the risk theme is to identify, assess and control uncertainty and, as a result, improve the ability of the project to succeed.

All projects encounter uncertainty when trying to achieve their objectives. This uncertainty may arise from events inside or outside the organization. For example, there may be uncertainty about the ability of the organization to agree the scope of the project within certain timescales or the availability of critical resources. There might also be uncertainty about the final scope and shape of legislation with which a project is required to ensure compliance.

Definition: Risk

An uncertain event or set of events that, should it occur, will have an effect on the achievement of objectives. A risk is measured by a combination of the **probability** of a perceived threat or opportunity occurring, and the magnitude of its impact on objectives.

Risks can have either a negative or positive impact on objectives if they occur. PRINCE2 uses the terms:

● **Threat** For uncertain events that would have a negative impact on objectives.
● **Opportunity** For uncertain events that would have a positive impact on objectives.

These can impact the project's objectives of delivering an agreed scope and benefits to an agreed time, cost and quality.

Given that all projects involve some degree of risk-taking, it follows that projects need to manage risk, and they need to do so in a way that supports effective decision-making. This provides a disciplined environment for proactive decision-making.

Definition: Risk management

The systematic application of principles, approaches and processes to the tasks of identifying and assessing risks, planning and implementing **risk response**s and communicating risk management activities with stakeholders.

For risk management to be effective:

- risks that might affect the project achieving its objectives need to be identified, captured and described
- each risk needs to be assessed to understand its probability, impact and timing (**proximity**) so that it can be prioritized. The overall **risk exposure** needs to be kept under review, together with the impact of risk on the overall business justification for the project
- responses to each risk need to be planned, and assigned to people to action and to own
- risk responses need to be implemented, monitored and controlled.

Throughout the process, information about risks must be communicated within the project and to stakeholders.

Effective risk management provides confidence that the project is able to meet its objectives and that the business justification continues to be valid. It supports decision-making by ensuring that the project team understand not only individual risks but also the overall risk exposure that exists at a particular time.

Definition: Risk exposure

The extent of risk borne by the organization at the time.

10.2 PRINCE2's requirements for the risk theme

To be following PRINCE2, a project must, as a minimum:

- define its **risk management approach**, which must minimally cover:
  - how risks are identified and assessed, how risk management responses are planned and implemented and how the management of risk is communicated throughout the project lifecycle
  - assessing whether identified risks might have a material impact on the business justification of the project (PRINCE2's continued business justification principle)
  - the roles and responsibilities for risk management (PRINCE2's defined roles and responsibilities principle)
- maintain some form of risk register to record identified risks and decisions relating to their analysis, management and review
- ensure that project risks are identified, assessed, managed and reviewed throughout the project lifecycle
- use lessons to inform risk identification and management (PRINCE2's learn from experience principle).

PRINCE2 requires that two products are produced and maintained:

- **Risk management approach** Describes how risk will be managed on the project. This includes the specific processes, procedures, techniques, standards and responsibilities to be applied.
- **Risk register** Provides a record of identified risks relating to the project, including their status and history. It is used to capture and maintain information on all the identified threats and opportunities relating to the project.

Both of these products should be created during the initiating a project process. The risk management approach should be reviewed and possibly updated at the end of each management stage. The risk management approach will define how and when the risk register is reviewed and updated.

Appendix A (sections A.24 and A.25) provides product descriptions and suggested content for these products.

PRINCE2 recommends an approach to risk management based on *Management of Risk: Guidance for Practitioners* (Office of Government Commerce, 2010).

 Key message

PRINCE2 does not prescribe a particular or detailed approach to risk management. Any approach that meets the requirements described can be said to be following PRINCE2.

10.2.1 Risk responsibilities in PRINCE2

Responsibilities for managing risk in PRINCE2 are set out in Table 10.1. As described in Chapter 7, if roles are combined then all the responsibilities in this table must still be undertaken.

Table 10.1 Responsibilities relevant to the risk theme

Role	Responsibilities
Corporate, programme management or the customer	Provide the corporate, programme management or customer risk management policy and risk management process guide (or similar documents).
Executive	Ensure that the risk management approach is appropriate.
	Ensure that risks associated with the business case are identified, assessed and controlled.
	Escalate risks to corporate, programme management or the customer as necessary.
Senior user	Ensure that risks to the users are identified, assessed and controlled (such as the impact on benefits, operational use and maintenance).
Senior supplier	Ensure that risks relating to the supplier aspects are identified, assessed and controlled (such as the creation of the project product).
Project manager	Create the risk management approach.
	Create and maintain the risk register.
	Ensure that project risks are being identified, assessed and controlled throughout the project lifecycle.
Team manager	Participate in the identification, assessment and control of risks.
Project assurance	Review risk management practices to ensure that they are performed in line with the project's risk management approach.
Project support	Assist the project manager in maintaining the project's risk register.

10.3 Guidance for effective risk management

10.3.1 Align with organizational and other policies and processes

A project may need to align its risk management approach with organizational, programme or portfolio policies, standards or processes. This might include:

● aligning with any centrally defined risk management policies, standards and approaches

● using any centrally defined risk management techniques

● adopting any centrally deployed tools

● aligning with any centrally defined risk management roles or competency frameworks.

Organizations will often require that a consistent, mandated process is used across different projects, typically to ensure they can assess the overall risk exposure of the organization across projects. This will also be the case when organizations are seeking to develop their project management maturity using a maturity model such as P3M3 (see section 21.1.1.3).

10.3.2 Recommended risk management procedure

PRINCE2 recommends, but does not mandate, a risk management procedure based on *Management of Risk: Guidance for Practitioners* (Office of Government Commerce, 2010).

Figure 10.1 shows the elements of the risk management procedure described in section 10.4.

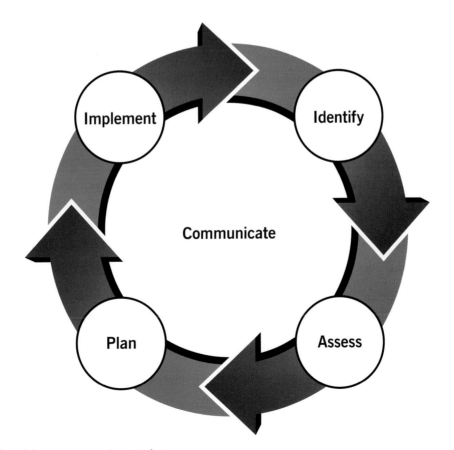

Figure 10.1 The risk management procedure

The procedure consists of five steps, the first four of which are sequential:

- identify: context and risks
- assess: estimate and evaluate
- plan
- implement.

'Communicate', the fifth step, operates in parallel as the outputs of any of the other steps may need to be communicated to stakeholders at any point in the process.

All the steps are repeatable. When additional information becomes available, it is often necessary to repeat earlier steps based on the new information.

10.3.3 Understand the project board's attitude to risk

A key decision that needs to be recorded within the risk management approach is the project board's attitude towards risk-taking. This will determine the amount of risk that is acceptable and will, in turn, help set **risk tolerance**s.

Example of risk tolerance

A large electrical retailer would not tolerate any disruption to its core retail or warehouse systems during the peak trading period extending from November through to January. During this period, it does not allow changes to these systems unless they are needed to keep the company running.

A project would need to escalate to the project board any risk that might impact these systems during this period.

10.3.4 Project size, scale and complexity, and risk impact

Ensure that the risk management approach is appropriate not only to the project's size, scale and complexity but also to the project's likely risk impact. It is important that the risk management approach for a project supports effective decision-making on the project and does not create an undue burden or bureaucracy. In general, smaller, simpler projects will need correspondingly simpler risk management arrangements.

For example, on a less complex project the project manager would typically directly undertake most risk management activities. However, on more complex projects these activities might be delegated to a dedicated risk manager or risk management team. Similarly, a risk register might be held in a simple list on a whiteboard, in a spreadsheet or in a dedicated IT system. What is important is that the risk management approach is appropriate.

In determining the appropriateness of the risk management approach it is critical to consider not just the project's cost, size, scale and complexity but also the potential scale of risk impact from the project. It is possible for projects to create impacts that far outweigh their apparent size, scale and complexity. For example, a small, simple project to replace core IT network infrastructure has the ability to stop an organization working if it goes wrong.

10.3.5 Project delivery approach

It is important that the approach to managing risk works with and supports the project's chosen delivery approach. For example, a risk management approach that includes monthly risk review meetings is unlikely to effectively support an agile project delivery approach where deliveries may be happening every 2 weeks.

PRINCE2 does not mandate a particular format for risk management products, nor does it mandate specific timings for risk management activities. What is important is that they are appropriate for the format and pace of the project. A risk register may be written on a whiteboard and reviewed as part of a daily stand-up meeting (see section 17.5.4.2) as part of an agile delivery approach. In this context it is just as valid as risks stored in a dedicated IT system that is reviewed at a monthly meeting.

It is also important to recognize that the project's delivery approach might work to mitigate or reinforce specific risks. For example, an agile way of working inherently ensures that customers do not inappropriately constrain and over-specify requirements at the beginning of a project, which can be a risk in a more traditional 'waterfall' approach. Similarly, even though agile is characterized by a high level of engagement with customers directly involved in the project, it can lead to uncontrolled changes to the agreed baseline if not managed correctly. More traditional approaches tend to reinforce the impression of 'controlled change', but at a risk of appearing unresponsive. What is important is that the risk management approach recognizes these inherent differences.

10.3.6 Commercial considerations

In a commercial context there may be a need for more than one risk register as some project risks could be unique to only one party, with good reasons for them not to be visible to the other party. Where a joint risk register is used, care should be taken to establish whose risk it really is, and the **risk owner** appointed accordingly. For example, on a fixed-price contract any cost overruns will impact the supplier's business case, but timescale overruns will typically impact the customer's business case.

10.3.7 Establishing a risk budget

It might be appropriate to identify and ring-fence an explicit risk budget within the project's budget. This is a sum of money to fund specific management responses to the project's threats and opportunities (e.g. to cover the costs of any **contingent plan**s should a risk materialize).

The risk budget is based on the aggregate cost of all the project's planned risk responses. For simpler projects it will usually be enough to add up the cost of all risk responses. However, for more complex projects care needs to be taken that the aggregation of the factored costs is not skewed by a small number of large risks. This is where analytical techniques, such as Monte Carlo simulation (see section 10.4.2.2) and associated software tools, can help.

As the project progresses, some of the risks previously identified will occur and others will not. New risks may be identified during the life of the project whose response costs will not have been included within the risk budget. This means that it is prudent to include a provision for unknown risks (yet to be identified) in the risk budget.

 Key message

As the risk budget is part of the project budget, there may be a tendency to treat it as just another sum of money that the project manager can spend. This culture should be discouraged in favour of the risk management approach defining the mechanisms for control of, and access to, this budget.

10.4 Technique: recommended risk management procedure

In the absence of any other approach, PRINCE2 recommends the following risk management procedure, which is based on *Management of Risk: Guidance for Practitioners* (Office of Government Commerce, 2010); see also section 10.3.2 and Figure 10.1.

10.4.1 Identify

10.4.1.1 Identify context

This step obtains information about the project in order to understand the specific objectives that are at risk and to formulate an appropriate risk management approach. The following will have an influence on the project's risk management approach:

- customer's quality expectations
- number of organizations involved and the relationships between them
- the needs of the stakeholders involved with the project
- the importance, complexity and scale of the project
- the delivery approach being used
- what assumptions have been made
- the organization's own environment (e.g. legislative or governance requirements)
- corporate policies, standards, processes and procedures
- whether the project is part of a programme or corporate portfolio.

This information will be derived from the project mandate, the project brief and the project product description.

Appendix A, section A.24, provides the typical contents of a risk management approach.

10.4.1.2 Identify the risks

Risks can, and should, be identified at any time during the management and delivery of the project. Any member of the project, corporate or programme management, the customer, or other stakeholder may raise an issue or risk. PRINCE2 recommends that risks are captured in the risk register as soon as they are identified.

An important aspect of identifying risks is being able to provide a clear and unambiguous expression of each one. A useful way of expressing risk is to consider the following aspects of each risk:

- **Risk cause** This should describe the source of the risk (i.e. the event or situation that gives rise to the risk). These are often referred to as risk drivers. They are not risks in themselves, but the potential trigger points for risk. These may be either internal or external to the project.
- **Risk event** This should describe the area of uncertainty in terms of the threat or the opportunity.
- **Risk effect** This should describe the impact(s) that the risk would have on the project objectives should the risk materialize.

The cause, event and effect relationship could also be expressed in a sentence, for example:

- **Threat** There is a threat that insufficient staffing capacity (risk cause) could lead to the business being unable to provide enough staff to complete user training in the planned timescales (risk event), resulting in the project taking longer than planned (risk effect).
- **Opportunity** If allowable under data regulations, the company could include a discount code in the email (risk event) when it renews customer details every year (risk cause), generating income to offset the cost of the regulatory requirement (risk effect).

There are various techniques that can be used to identify risks, including review lessons, risk checklists, risk prompt lists, brainstorming and risk breakdown structures.

Figure 10.2 shows a risk breakdown structure relating to financial risk. Such a structure will help to identify the appropriate risk owners to develop responses.

Examples of risk identification techniques

Review lessons

Risks are driven by uncertainty, so one of the most effective ways to reduce uncertainty is to review similar previous projects to see what threats and opportunities affected them.

Risk checklists

These are in-house lists of risks that have either been identified or have occurred on previous similar projects. Risk checklists are useful aids to ensure that risks identified on previous projects are not overlooked.

Risk prompt lists

These are publicly available lists that categorize risks into types or areas and are normally relevant to a wide range of projects. Risk prompt lists are useful aids to help stimulate thinking about sources of risk in the widest context.

Brainstorming

This enables group thinking, which can be more productive than individual thinking. However, it is important to avoid criticism during the brainstorm as this can stop people contributing. In addition to identifying risks, brainstorming can also be used to understand the stakeholders' views of the risks identified.

Risk breakdown structure

This is a hierarchical decomposition of the potential sources of risk. Each descending level represents an increasingly detailed definition of sources of risk to the project. The structure acts as a prompt and an aid to support the project management team in thinking through the potential sources of risk to the objectives. There are numerous ways to break down risk and it may be useful to do more than one list.

For example, a risk breakdown structure could be broken down by PESTLE (political, economic, social, technological, legal/legislative, environmental), product breakdown structure, management stage, delivery step, benefits/objectives, etc.

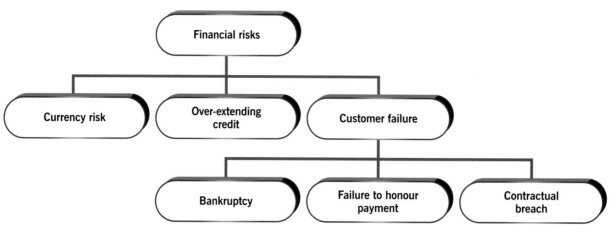

Figure 10.2 Example of a risk breakdown structure

10.4.2 Assess

10.4.2.1 Estimate

The next step is to assess the probability of each risk and its impact. PRINCE2 recommends assessing:

- the probability of the threats and opportunities in terms of how likely they are to occur
- the impact of each risk in terms of the project objectives (e.g. if the objectives are measured in time and cost, the impact should also be measured in units of time and cost)
- the impact of the risk on the stage plan, project plan and business case
- how quickly the risk is likely to materialize if no action were taken (i.e. its 'risk proximity')
- how the impact of the threats and opportunities may change over the life of the project
- whether the project team is best placed to manage the risk or whether the risk needs to be escalated to the project board, any overarching programme or to a corporate body.

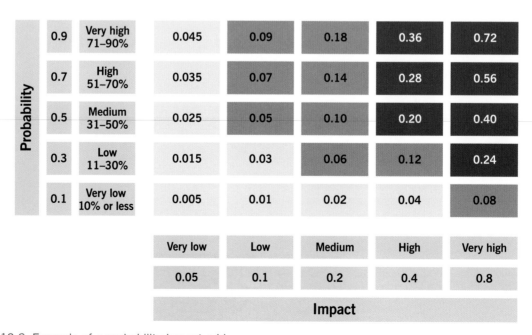

Figure 10.3 Example of a probability impact grid

There are a number of techniques that can be used for **risk estimation**s. These include probability impact grids, the expected value technique, probability trees and Pareto analysis.

Examples of risk estimation techniques

Probability impact grid

This grid contains ranking values that may be used to rank threats and opportunities qualitatively. The probability scales are measures of probability derived from percentages, and the impact scales are selected to reflect the level of impact on project objectives. The values within the grid cells are the combination of a particular probability and impact, and are determined by multiplying the probability by the impact.

A probability impact grid can be used to provide an assessment of the severity of a risk and enable risks to be ranked so that management time and effort can be prioritized. For example, the project board may set its risk tolerance at any risk with a value greater than 0.18, and it may require a proactive response for any risk with a value greater than 0.045, as depicted by the dark and medium shadings shown in Figure 10.3.

Expected value

This technique quantifies risk by combining the cost of the risk impact with the probability of the risk occurring. Expected value is useful when a tangible measure of risk is required to enable risks to be prioritized. For example, if the cost of a risk was £160 000 and its likelihood of occurrence was estimated at 25 per cent, then the expected value would be £40 000.

Probability trees

These are graphical representations of possible events resulting from given circumstances. A probability tree can be used to predict an outcome in a qualitative way when historical data is used to populate the likelihood of each circumstance happening. Probability trees assist in communicating to project participants or decision makers the likelihood of the different possible outcomes to a set of circumstances.

Pareto analysis

This technique ranks or orders risks after they have been assessed to determine the order in which they should be addressed. Pareto analysis can be used to focus management effort on those risks that have the potential to have the greatest impact on the project objectives.

A useful way of summarizing the set of risks and their estimations is to plot them onto a summary **risk profile**, an example of which is shown in Figure 10.4. This profile represents a situation at a specific point in time (i.e. a snapshot of the risk environment). The numbered markers in the matrix represent unique risk identifiers used in

Tip

If using a three-by-three or five-by-five probability impact grid results in too many risks clustering around medium probability and medium impact, consider using a four-by-four grid to force high/low risk assessments.

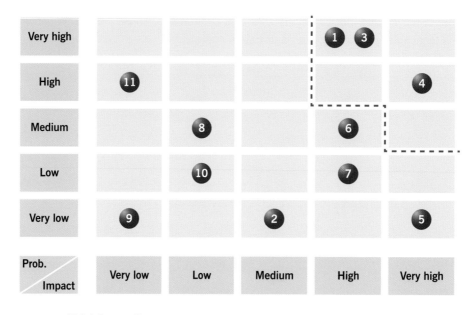

Figure 10.4 Example of a summary risk profile

the risk register on which this is based. The risks above and to the right of the dashed **risk tolerance line** represent those that the organization will not tolerate except under special circumstances. In the depicted case, the project manager would refer risks 1, 3 and 4 to the project board.

The summary risk profile can also be used to show trends. For example, risk 6 may have previously been recorded as 'low probability, high impact', indicating that its likelihood of occurring is increasing.

10.4.2.2 Evaluate

The combined effect of the individual risks needs to be understood to determine if the overall 'risk exposure' of the project remains within the risk appetite determined by the organization and as interpreted and applied by the project board. If the risk exposure is greater than the organization's risk appetite, then control actions will need to be planned in response.

In line with PRINCE2's continued business justification principle, the justification of the project should be evaluated in the context of the risk exposure. There is no such thing as a risk-free project and understanding how risk exposure compares with the risk tolerance informs how much effort is put into risk responses. The risk tolerance will be set by the project board based on the organization's overall risk appetite. Risk exposure can, and should, be assessed both before and after any planned risk responses.

 Definition: Risk appetite

An organization's unique attitude towards risk-taking that in turn dictates the amount of risk that it considers acceptable.

Chapter 10 – Risk

Definition: Risk tolerance

The threshold levels of risk exposure that, with appropriate approvals, can be exceeded, but which when exceeded will trigger some form of response (e.g. reporting the situation to senior management for action).

Tip

Remember that risk appetite, risk exposure and risk tolerance are related to each other, but are not the same.

There are two main **risk evaluation** techniques: risk models (such as Monte Carlo simulation) and expected monetary value.

Examples of risk evaluation techniques

Risk models

Risk models, such as Monte Carlo simulation, enable 'what if' scenarios to be run using random numbers to determine whether each risk within a given range occurs. The simulations are repeatedly run to predict the 'average' level of risk to the project's timescale or cost. The scenarios can also be used to model extreme cases (e.g. if nearly all the risks occur).

Expected monetary value

This technique takes the expected values of a number of risks and sums them to arrive at an overall value. It provides a quick and easy assessment of a group of risks to understand their combined effect. Threats are represented as a negative impact and opportunities as a positive impact. An example is shown in Table 10.2.

Table 10.2 Example of the expected monetary value technique

Risk ID	Likelihood (%)	Impact (£)	Expected value (£)
1	60	-20 000	-12 000
2	30	+13 000	+3 900
3	10	-4 000	-400
4	5	-10 000	-500
Expected monetary value			-9 000

Chapter 10 – Risk

Table 10.3 Risk responses

Response options	Use
Avoid a threat **Exploit** an opportunity	This option is about making the uncertain situation certain by removing the risk. This can often be achieved by removing the cause of a threat, or by implementing the cause of an opportunity.
	This option may be adopted for no extra cost by changing the way the work is planned. More often though, costs will be incurred in order to remove all **residual risk** for threats and opportunities. Where costs are incurred these must be justified (i.e. the cost of response is warranted to make the situation certain).
Reduce a threat **Enhance** an opportunity	This option involves definite action now to change the probability and/or the impact of the risk. The term 'mitigate' is relevant when discussing reduction of a threat (i.e. making the threat less likely to occur and/or reducing the impact if it did).
	Enhancing an opportunity is the reverse process (i.e. making the opportunity more likely to occur and/or increasing the impact if it did). Again, because this option commits the organization to costs for reduction/enhancement now, response costs must be justified in terms of the change to residual risk.
Transfer the risk (threat or opportunity)	Transfer is an option that aims to pass part of the risk to a third party. Insurance is the classic form of transfer, where the insurer picks up the risk cost, but where the insured retains the impact on other objectives (e.g. time delay).
	Transfer can apply to opportunities, where a third party gains a cost benefit but the primary risk taker gains another benefit, but this is not a commonly used option whereas transfer of threats is commonly used.
	Once again, the cost of transference must be justified in terms of the change to residual risk; is the premium to be paid worth it? It is important to note that some elements of risk cannot be transferred, although an organization may choose to delegate the management of the risks to a third party.
Share the risk (threat or opportunity)	Share is an option that is different in nature from the transfer response. It seeks multiple parties, typically within a supply chain, to share the risk on a pain/gain share basis.
	Rarely can risks be entirely shared in this way (for example, the primary risk taker will always need to protect its brand and reputation), but this can be a successful way of encouraging collaboration on risk management activities, particularly in programmes and projects.
Accept the risk (threat or opportunity)	The accept option means that the organization 'takes the chance' that the risk will occur, with its full impact if it did.
	There is no change to residual risk with the accept option, but neither are any costs incurred now to manage the risk, or to prepare to manage the risk in future. An example would be the risk to profitability as a result of currency fluctuations. An organization may decide to take the chance and not engage in any hedging or other provision to protect margins from wide variation in rates. This option would not be appropriate if the risk exposure exceeded the risk tolerance threshold for the organizational activity in question.
	Note that in a case such as currency fluctuations where the impact could be positive or negative, this is actually two risks, because a risk is the relationship between the uncertain event and the impact of that event. There is a risk leading to loss (threat) and a risk leading to gain (opportunity). Framing the uncertainty as two risks allows for different responses to each part.
Prepare contingent plans (threat or opportunity)	This option involves preparing plans now, but not taking action now.
	Most usually associated with the accept option, preparing contingent plans in this instance is saying: 'We will accept the risk for now, but we'll make a plan for what we'll do if the situation changes.' This option applies equally to other responses and is often referred to as a 'fallback' plan (i.e. what we will do if the original response does not work). Fallback plans apply to all other strategies, even avoiding a threat and exploiting an opportunity, because the plan to avoid/exploit may not be successful despite good intentions.
	This option is important because it incorporates future managerial flexibility for a committed cost that is smaller than investing in more proactive strategies. This does not mean that investing now to respond to a risk is wrong, but such investments do need to be cost-justified as previously mentioned.

10.4.3 Plan

The plan step involves identifying and evaluating the appropriate risk response to remove or reduce threats, and to maximize opportunities. Typical risk responses are summarized in Table 10.3. If the risk falls within the tolerances set for the project, the project manager decides on the appropriate response; otherwise the decision is escalated to the project board (see Figure 10.4 for an example of risks exceeding set tolerances).

If a threat is reduced rather than removed, the remaining risk is called the 'residual' risk. If the residual risk is significant then it may be appropriate to select more than one risk response.

In some cases, implementing a risk response will reduce or remove other related risks. It is also possible that the responses to risks, after they have been implemented, will change some aspect of the project. This in turn may lead to secondary risks (i.e. risks that occur as a result of invoking a risk response). It is essential that these are identified, assessed and controlled in the same way as the initially identified risk.

Tip

Review lessons from previous similar projects when planning risk responses. This will help in identifying the range of responses available and in evaluating how effective they are likely to be.

Key message

It is important that the risk response is proportional to the risk and that it offers value for money.

It is important that risk responses balance the cost of implementing the response against the probability and impact of allowing the risk to occur. One way of assessing this is to compare the cost of the risk response with the difference in the expected monetary value of the risk before and after the risk response. If the cost of the risk response is lower than the reduction in the expected monetary value then it is worth undertaking the risk response. However, it is always worth bearing in mind the overall effect of all risk response activities on the project team in terms of moving their focus away from delivering the project on to risk response actions.

Any chosen response needs to be built into the appropriate level of plan. For more significant risks it may be appropriate to put in place not only early-warning indicators to identify whether the risk is likely to materialize, but also plans for managing the risk should it occur.

Consideration should also be given to the effect the possible responses could have on:

● the project plan, management stage plan and work packages

● the business case

● corporate, programme management or the customer.

The risk response needs to identify the most appropriate body to manage a risk (or issue). This may not be the project team, especially if:

● the project team do not have within their scope of influence the ability to implement an appropriate risk response

● realization of risk will materially impact the project's business justification

● the project is part of an overarching programme and it would be more appropriate for the risk to be managed at programme level (e.g. if a specific project identifies a risk that is common across projects within the programme)

● implementation of a risk response will cause the project to exceed agreed tolerances, either within a particular management stage or overall

- reporting of the risk to a corporate body is required by the corporate risk policies or procedures. This might typically occur in a regulated organization where certain risks might either be reportable by the organization, or where realization of the risk might cause a breach of a regulatory condition.

Escalation would first be to the project board. Depending on the risk tolerance, escalation might also be to the overarching programme, corporate body or customer.

Escalating risks is good practice and should not be seen as failure. The earlier that risks are escalated, the more time is available to implement any corrective actions. The types of response are explained further in Table 10.3.

Tip

Do not forget that an opportunity can be rejected. Not all opportunities may be taken up as there could be circumstances such as timing or cost which would have a negative impact on the project goals.

10.4.4 Implement

Planned risk responses need to be actioned, their effectiveness monitored and corrective action taken where responses do not match expectations.

It is critical to ensure that the owner and actionee are identified and agreed for each risk:

- **Risk owner** A named individual who is responsible for the management, monitoring and control of all aspects of a particular risk assigned to them, including the implementation of the selected responses to address the threats or to maximize the opportunities.
- **Risk actionee** A nominated owner of an action to address a risk. Some actions may not be within the remit of the risk owner to control explicitly; in that situation there should be a nominated owner of the action to address the risk. He or she will need to keep the risk owner apprised of the situation.

In many cases, the risk owner and risk actionee are likely to be the same person. The risk owner should be the person most capable of managing the risk. Allocating too many risks to any one individual should be avoided.

Examples of a risk owner and risk actionee

Risk owner

There is a threat that a key supplier may fail, which might impact a project's ability to deliver on time to a customer. The commercial director has been appointed as the risk owner.

Risk actionee

A number of risk responses have been identified and selected. One of the risk responses (prepare contingent plans) is to identify possible alternative suppliers who have the capacity to undertake the affected work packages at short notice, and to obtain some quotes from them. The procurement manager is the **risk actionee** for this particular risk response.

10.4.5 Communicate

Communication should be undertaken continually. The 'communicate' step ensures that information related to the threats and opportunities faced by the project is communicated both within the project and externally to stakeholders. Risks are communicated as part of the following management products:

- **checkpoint report**s
- highlight reports
- end stage reports
- end project report
- exception reports.

Care should be taken in using these reports to communicate risks with external stakeholders and reference should be made to the communication management approach for the most appropriate method.

There are numerous other communication methods (e.g. bulletins, notice boards, dashboards, **information radiator**s, discussion threads, briefings) that could be considered alongside the PRINCE2 management products.

A number of aspects of communication should be recognized and addressed if risk management is to be effective:

- A project's exposure to risk is never static: effective communication is key to the identification of new risks or changes in existing risks. This depends on the maintenance of a good communications network, including relevant contacts and sources of information, to facilitate the identification of changes that may affect the project's overall risk exposure.
- Effective risk management is dependent on participation, which is dependent on effective communication.

Change

This chapter covers:

- why projects need a systemic approach
- types of issue and how to handle them
- PRINCE2's requirements for the change theme
- making change control appropriate for different environments
- guidance for effective change control
- a recommended issue and change control procedure

11 Change

11.1 The change theme

Key message

The purpose of the change theme is to identify, assess and control any potential and approved changes to the project baselines.

Projects take place in their organizational environment and wider context, both of which change over time. It is rare that a project closes having delivered exactly what was envisaged when the project was initiated. It is often said that change is inevitable and this is certainly the case for long and more complex projects.

This means that projects need a systemic approach to the identification, assessment and control of issues that may result in change. Issue and change control is a continual activity, performed throughout the life of the project. Without an ongoing and effective issue and change control procedure, a project will either become unresponsive to its stakeholders or drift out of control.

In PRINCE2, changes are identified as 'issues'. PRINCE2 uses the term 'issue' to cover any relevant event that has happened, was not planned and requires management action during the project. Issues may be raised at any time during the project by anyone with an interest in the project or its outcome.

Table 11.1 provides a summary of the different types of issue that need to be dealt with during a project.

Table 11.1 Types of issue

Types of issue	Definition	Examples
Request for change	A proposal for a change to a baseline.	The senior user would like to increase the capacity of a product from 100 to 150 users.
Off-specification	Something that should be provided by the project, but currently is not (or is forecast not to be). It might be a missing product or a product not meeting its specifications.	Advice from a supplier that they can no longer deliver one of the products specified by the customer.
Problem/concern	Any other issue that the project manager needs to resolve or escalate.	Advice from a team manager that a team member has been taken ill and as a result the target end date for a work package will slip by a week.
		Notification that one of the suppliers has gone bankrupt, resulting in the need to identify and engage a new supplier.

After an issue has been identified and captured, there needs to be a controlled process for assessing the issue and determining what action to take in response. The response to an issue might be to change some dimension of the project's time, cost or scope. However, it is important to understand that the appropriate response to the issue might be to reject it and do nothing; it is not necessarily the case that something has to be done just because an issue has been identified and captured. There are only two reasons to implement a change: to introduce a new benefit or to protect an existing benefit.

Change can only be assessed in terms of its impact on an agreed 'current situation'. In PRINCE2, the 'current situation' at any point in time is represented by a snapshot of all the management and specialist products produced during the project lifecycle (e.g. the project brief, PID and business case).

At a point in time, each of these items will be in a known state or 'baseline'.

 Definition: Baseline

Reference levels against which an entity is monitored and controlled.

In practice, baselines are created at a point in time for a purpose. For example, a baseline might be created when a product is ready to be reviewed or when it has been approved. Making changes to a baselined product creates a new version of the product, with the original baseline being kept unchanged.

A prerequisite of effective issue and change control is to define a way of creating baselines of products and allowing appropriately controlled changes to those baselines. The complexity of doing this depends on the project size, complexity and, usually, sector:

- A simple project to make some limited changes to a process in an organization might just use shared network drives and maintain baselines by following an agreed file naming scheme (e.g. using the suffixes 'Draft', 'For review' and 'Approved' at the end of file names).
- A more complex process re-engineering project might use a formal document management system with appropriate policies, procedures and access rights.
- IT projects will often have complex interdependencies between individually baselined items and manage these interdependencies using a **configuration management system**.
- In more engineering-focused organizations, the process of managing changes is called asset management or product management.

Whatever name is given to the process of preventing unauthorized change, PRINCE2 calls the things that need to be controlled and baselined '**configuration item**s'. Information on their state and status should be collected and may be held in '**configuration item record**s'. See Appendix A, section A.6, for an outline description of a configuration item record.

 Definition: Configuration item record

A record that describes the status, version and **variant** of a configuration item, and any details of important relationships between them.

Definition: Product status account

A report on the status of products. The required products can be specified by identifier or the part of the project in which they were developed.

PRINCE2 also has the concept of a **product status account**, which can be used to provide more detail about the status of products. See Appendix A, section A.18, for an outline description of a product status account.

11.2 PRINCE2's requirements for the change theme

To be following PRINCE2, a project must, as a minimum:

- define its **change control approach**. This approach must minimally cover:
    - how issues are identified and managed
    - assessing whether identified issues might have a material impact on the business justification of the project (PRINCE2's continued business justification principle)
    - the roles and responsibilities for change control (PRINCE2's defined roles and responsibilities principle), including a defined change authority
- define how product baselines are created, maintained and controlled
- maintain some form of **issue register** to record identified issues and decisions relating to their analysis, management and review
- ensure that project issues are captured, assessed, managed and reviewed throughout the project lifecycle
- use lessons to inform issue identification and management (PRINCE2's learn from experience principle).

PRINCE2 requires that the following products are produced and maintained:

- Issue register Captures and maintains information on all the issues that are being formally managed.
- Change control approach Identifies how, and by whom, the project's products will be controlled and protected.

If the issue register does not contain sufficient detail (e.g. for the options appraisal, recommendation and decision), then a separate issue report, as described in Appendix A, section A.13, can be used but this is an optional management product.

The project's controls for issues and change will be defined and established during the initiating a project process, then reviewed and (if necessary) updated towards the end of each management stage by the managing a stage boundary process. Appendix A (sections A.3 and A.12) provides product descriptions and suggested content for these products.

Key message

PRINCE2 recommends an approach to issue management and change control but this is not prescriptive. Any approach that meets the requirements described in section 11.2 can be said to be following PRINCE2.

11.2.1 Change control responsibilities in PRINCE2

Responsibilities for managing change in PRINCE2 are set out in Table 11.2. As described in Chapter 7, if roles are combined then all the responsibilities in this table must still be undertaken.

Table 11.2 Responsibilities relevant to the change theme

Role	Responsibilities
Corporate, programme management or the customer	Provide the corporate, programme management or customer strategies for issue resolution and change control.
Executive	Determine the change authority and change budget.
	Set the scale for rating the severity of issues.
	Set the scale for priority ratings for requests for change and off-specifications.
	Respond to requests for advice from the project manager.
	Make decisions on escalated issues, with particular focus on continued business justification.
Senior user	Respond to requests for advice from the project manager.
	Make decisions on escalated issues, with particular focus on safeguarding the expected benefits.
Senior supplier	Respond to requests for advice from the project manager.
	Make decisions on escalated issues, with particular focus on safeguarding the integrity of the complete solution.
Project manager	Create and maintain the change control approach.
	Manage the issue and change control procedures, assisted by project support where possible.
	Create and maintain the issue register, assisted by project support where possible.
	Implement corrective actions.
Team manager	Implement corrective actions.
Project assurance	Advise on assessing and resolving issues.
Project support	Administer the change control and issue procedures by:
	● maintaining configuration item records, if used
	● producing product status accounts
	● assisting the project manager in maintaining the issue register.

11.3 Guidance for effective change control

11.3.1 General tailoring considerations

The starting point for all projects will be to identify whether there are any corporate, programme management or customer policies and processes that need to be applied, and incorporate them into the project's own change control approach. If the project is within a programme or portfolio, there may be a requirement that the project uses their defined policies and processes.

In a commercial environment the project may be required to adopt change control procedures and processes defined in the contract.

Issue management and change control may be treated as separate processes or procedures provided the relationship between them is defined. The approach may be tailored to reflect any tools used, in terms of roles, work flow and terminology.

11.3.2 Project size, scale and complexity

Ensure that the change control approach is appropriate to project size, scale and complexity. It is important to ensure that the change control approach to a project provides support for effective decision-making on the project and does not create undue burden or bureaucracy. In general, smaller, simpler projects will need correspondingly simpler issue management and change control arrangements.

11.3.3 Managing product baselines

All projects need an appropriate approach to creating, maintaining and controlling product baselines for both management and specialist products. For simpler projects, document management procedures will generally suffice. More complex projects will usually need some form of formal **configuration management**, asset management or product management process, often supported by specific tools.

Regardless of size, scale and complexity, the project team needs to determine:

- the appropriate level at which products need to be baselined. This is generally determined by breaking down the project's products until the level is reached at which a component can be independently released, installed, replaced or modified. However, the level of control exercised will be influenced by the importance of the project and the complexity of the relationships between its products
- how configuration items are identified. Generally, a coding system of some type will need to be established, providing a unique identifier for each configuration item
- the specific authorities and authorizations needed to approve and baseline configuration items
- what information about configuration items needs to be captured and maintained in configuration item records, if used.

It is good practice to periodically verify that the actual status of products reflects the authorized state of products (e.g. if they are registered in configuration item records), looking for any discrepancies. This is usually through reviews or audits, typically undertaken at the end of each stage and at the end of the project.

11.3.4 The project's delivery approach

It is important that the approach to managing issues and change works with, and supports, the project's chosen delivery approach, rather than working against it. For example, a change control approach that defines that there will be a monthly review of proposed changes is unlikely to effectively support an agile delivery approach where delivery may be happening every week or 2 weeks.

The appropriate definition of product descriptions, quality criteria, quality tolerances and work packages is important. They can be defined in such a way as to allow for change at the detailed level, while at the same time creating a clearly defined baseline that can prevent a change to the purpose of a product going undetected.

11.3.5 Delegating to a change authority

The project board is responsible for reviewing and approving requests for change and off-specifications. In a project where few changes are envisaged, it may be reasonable to leave this authority in the hands of the project board. But for projects where there are likely to be many changes, the project board may choose to delegate some decisions to a person or group, called the change authority.

The project manager and/or the people with delegated project assurance responsibilities may act as the change authority. In practice the majority of changes will be generated at work package level. It is important to ensure that the change authority for work packages has sufficient delegated authority so that changes can be made without always having to escalate decisions to the project board for approval.

11.3.6 Establishing a change budget

A change budget is a sum of money that the customer and supplier agree will be used to fund the cost of requests for change, and possibly also their analysis costs.

Unless the anticipated level of change on a project is low, it is advisable for a budget to be set up to pay for changes. This arrangement can reduce the number of trivial exceptions arising in projects where the frequency of requests for change is forecast to be high. Including a change budget provides for a more realistic expectation of the overall costs/timeframe of the project.

Where a change budget is given to a change authority, the project board may wish to put a limit on (a) the cost of any single change, and (b) the amount spent on change in any one stage without reference to the project board. The change control procedure would then be defined in such a way as to control access to the change budget. If used, the change budget is documented in the relevant plan.

The project board should decide the need for a change budget.

11.4 Technique: recommended issue and change control procedure

In the absence of any other approach, PRINCE2 recommends the following issue and change control procedure, shown in Figure 11.1.

11.4.1 Capturing issues

The first step in the procedure is to undertake an initial analysis to determine the type of issue that has been raised and whether it should be managed informally or formally. The project manager makes an initial assessment of the issue's severity and priority.

The project manager is likely to receive many issues that can be handled without having to treat them formally, particularly if the issue can be resolved immediately (e.g. a team member raising an issue that their site access pass is about to expire). In such cases, the project manager should decide on the best course of corrective action.

The purpose of distinguishing between those issues that can be managed informally and those that need to be managed formally is to:

- ensure decisions are made at an appropriate level within the project management team
- avoid the project board being inundated with too many issues and therefore diluting the time it has available to deal with the key issues affecting the project
- reduce the administrative burden on the project manager when dealing with the day-to-day issues that may arise.

Issues being managed formally should be entered in the issue register and given a unique identifier. The daily log can be used to record issues being managed informally.

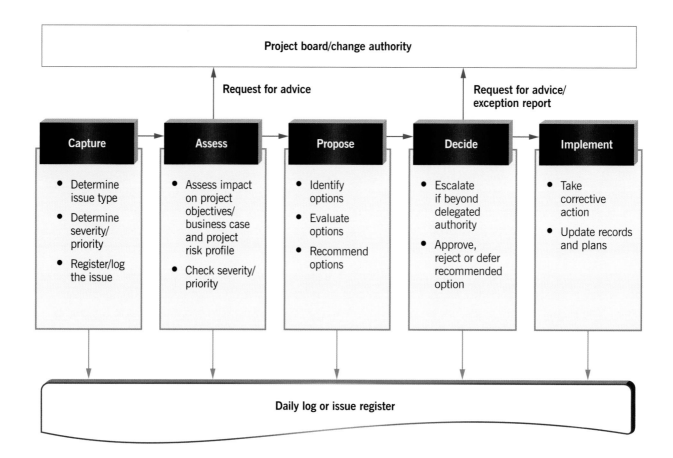

Figure 11.1 Issue and change control procedure

11.4.2 Assessing issues

The next step is to assess the issue by undertaking an impact analysis.

However, the project manager needs to consider whether it is worthwhile doing a detailed impact analysis as the duration and effort required to undertake one may itself cause a deviation from the plan.

The impact analysis should consider the impact the issue has (or will have) on:

- the project performance targets in terms of time, cost, quality and scope, including whether there are any other products that are within the project's scope that will also be impacted by this issue
- the project business case, especially in terms of the impact on benefits
- any other dependent products produced by the project
- the project risk profile (i.e. the impact on the overall risk exposure of the project).

If the project is part of a programme, the impact of the change on the programme as a whole should be considered. There may also be effects on other projects that are not necessarily part of the programme.

Assessing the impact of issues can be wrongly taken to mean only the impact on the customer. Impact analysis must cover the three areas of business, user and supplier (e.g. including the supplier's cost and effort required to implement a change and what products would have to be changed). Having undertaken the impact analysis, the severity or priority of the issue should be re-evaluated.

The issue register should be updated to include the above information and the person who raised the issue should be kept informed of its status.

It may be necessary to request advice from the project board to check its understanding of the issue's priority or severity before proposing resolutions.

11.4.3 Proposing corrective actions

After a full understanding of the impact of the issue has been gained, the next step is to consider alternative options for responding to it and proposing a course of action to take.

Consideration should be given to the effect each of the options will have on the project's time, cost, quality, scope, benefits and risk performance targets. There must be a balance between the advantage to be gained by implementing the option and the time, cost and risk of implementing it, as illustrated in Figure 11.2.

The risk considerations should include both project risks (i.e. of not completing within tolerances) and risks to operational performance when the project product is in use.

If any of the proposed options would take the stage or project beyond any tolerances, seek advice from the project board. The project manager should execute any decision by the project board in response.

11.4.4 Deciding on corrective actions

The project manager may be able to resolve issues without the need to escalate them to the project board. For example, a minor change to an approved detailed design document that does not affect any other products could be handled by the project manager (if allowed in the change control approach), as long as it is formally recorded.

Other issues may need to be escalated to the project board (or its delegated change authority) for a decision.

For escalated issues and exceptions, the likely project board responses are shown in Table 11.3.

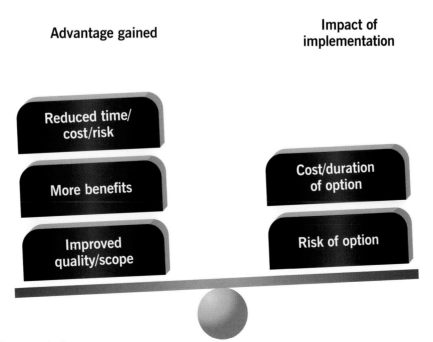

Figure 11.2 Options analysis

145

Table 11.3 Project board decisions

Request	Project board (or change authority) response	Considerations
Request for change	Approve the change. Reject the change. Defer decision. Request more information. Ask for an exception plan (if the request for change cannot be implemented within the limits delegated to the change authority).	If a request for change involves extra cost, there are three principal ways to fund it: ● use the change budget (if being used and of sufficient size) ● request that corporate, programme management or the customer increase the project budget ● de-scope other elements of the project. Tolerance should not be used to fund requests for change.
Off-specification	Grant a concession. Instruct that the off-specification be resolved. Defer decision. Request more information. Ask for an exception plan (if the concession cannot be granted within the limits delegated to the change authority).	The project board may decide to accept the off-specification without immediate corrective action. This is referred to as a concession. When a product is granted a concession, the product description will need to be revised before the product is handed over to the user.
Problem/concern	Provide guidance to enable the project manager to solve the problem. Ask for an exception plan.	Could the problem/concern be resolved by relaxing the stage tolerances?

11.4.5 Implementing corrective actions

The project manager will either:

● take the necessary corrective action, which might include updating affected products, work packages, plans and **registers**, or

● create an exception plan for approval by the project board.

In both cases, the project manager will update the issue register with the decision and inform all interested parties.

Implementation of the corrective action must ensure that baselined products are updated in a controlled manner and with appropriate authorizations. If a product that has been baselined is to be changed, a new version should be created to accommodate the change and the baseline version is kept unchanged. Old baseline versions should be archived where possible, not discarded.

After an issue has been closed, the project manager should update the issue register.

Progress

This chapter covers:

- measuring progress and the achievement of objectives
- PRINCE2's requirements for the progress theme
- tolerances, controls and management by exception
- progress evaluation and peer review

12 Progress

12.1 The progress theme

Key message

The purpose of the progress theme is to:

- establish mechanisms to monitor and compare actual achievements against those planned
- provide a forecast for the project's objectives and continued viability
- control any unacceptable deviations.

Progress is the measure of the achievement of the objectives of a plan. Controlling progress is central to project management, ensuring that the project remains viable against its approved business case. Progress control involves measuring actual progress against the performance targets of time, cost, quality, scope, benefits and risk. This information is used to make decisions such as whether to approve a management stage or work package, whether to escalate deviations and whether to prematurely close the project, and to take actions as required. Progress can be monitored at work package, management stage and project level.

Of PRINCE2's seven principles, manage by exception is particularly important to the progress theme. An exception is a situation where a deviation beyond agreed tolerance levels can be forecast.

Tolerances are the permissible deviation above and below a plan's target for cost and time without escalating the deviation to the next level of management. There may also be tolerances for quality, scope, benefits and risk.

12.2 PRINCE2's requirements for the progress theme

To be following PRINCE2, a project must, as a minimum:

- define its approach to controlling progress in the PID
- be managed by stages (PRINCE2's manage by stages principle)
- set tolerances and be managed by exception against them (PRINCE2's manage by exception principle)
- review the business justification when exceptions are raised (PRINCE2's continued business justification principle)
- learn lessons (PRINCE2's learn from experience principle).

Key message

PRINCE2 does not prescribe a particular or detailed approach to managing progress. Any approach that meets the requirements described can be said to be following PRINCE2.

PRINCE2 provides progress control through:

- delegating authority from one level of management to the level below it
- dividing the project into management stages and authorizing the project one management stage at a time (PRINCE2's manage by stages principle)
- time-driven and event-driven progress reporting and reviews
- raising exceptions (PRINCE2's manage by exception principle).

The project's controls should be documented in the PID.

12.2.1 Tolerances

In PRINCE2, the project is managed by exception against six types of tolerance, as shown in Table 12.1.

Table 12.1 The six tolerance types by level

Tolerance areas	Project-level tolerances	Stage-level tolerances	Work-package-level tolerances	Product-level tolerances
Time ± amounts of time on target completion dates	Project plan	Stage plan	Work package	N/A
Cost ± amounts of planned budget	Project plan	Stage plan	Work package	N/A
Quality Defining quality targets in terms of ranges (e.g. a product that weighs 300 g ± 10 g)	Project product description	N/A[a]	N/A[a]	Product description
Scope Permitted variation of the scope of a project solution (e.g. MoSCoW prioritization of requirements)	Project plan[b]	Stage plan[b]	Work package[b]	N/A
Benefits Defining target benefits in terms of ranges (e.g. to achieve minimum cost savings of 5% per branch, with an average of 7% across all branches)	Business case	N/A	N/A	N/A
Risk Limit on the aggregated value of threats (e.g. expected monetary value to remain less than 10% of the plan's budget), and on any individual threat (e.g. threat to operational service)	Risk management approach	Stage plan[c]	Work package[c]	N/A

a Quality tolerances are not summarily defined at the stage or work-package level but are defined per product description within the scope of the plan.

b The scope of a plan is defined by the set of products to be delivered. Scope tolerance (if used) should be in the form of a note on or reference to the product breakdown structure for the plan. Scope tolerance at the stage or work-package level is of particular use if applying a time-bound iterative development method such as agile.

c More specific stage-level risk tolerances may be set by the project board when authorizing a stage or by the project manager when commissioning work packages, especially from external suppliers.

The allocation of tolerances is outlined in Figure 12.1 and should be in line with the following:

- Corporate, programme management or the customer sits outside the project but sets the overall requirements and tolerance levels for the project. The three levels of management within the project (responsible for directing, managing and delivering) will manage and implement within these tolerances and escalate any forecast breaches of project tolerance.

- The project board has overall control at a project level, as long as forecasts remain within project tolerance, and will allocate tolerances for each management stage to the project manager. The project board has the ability to review progress and decide whether to continue, change or stop the project. During execution of the project plan, if any forecasts indicate that the project is likely to exceed the agreed project tolerances, then the deviation should be referred to corporate, programme management or the customer by the project board in order to get a decision on corrective action.

- The project manager has day-to-day control for a management stage within the tolerance limits laid down by the project board. During execution of a stage plan, if any forecasts indicate that the management stage is likely to exceed the agreed management stage tolerances, then the deviation should be referred to the project board by the project manager in order to get a decision on corrective action. This would be done by raising an issue and an exception report.

- The team manager has control for a work package, but only within the work package tolerances agreed with the project manager. During execution of the work package, if any forecasts indicate that it is likely that the agreed tolerances will be exceeded, then the deviation should be referred to the project manager by the team manager in order to get a decision on corrective action. This would be done by raising an issue.

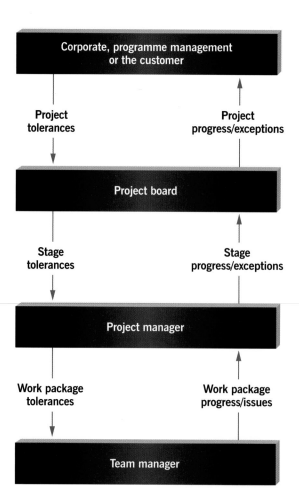

Figure 12.1 Delegating tolerance and reporting actual and forecast progress

12.2.2 Types of control

PRINCE2 provides two types of progress control throughout the life of a project:

● **Event-driven controls** These take place when a specific event occurs. This could be, for example, the end stage assessment at the end of a management stage, the completion of the PID or the creation of an exception report. It could also include organizational events that might affect the project, such as the end of the financial year.

● **Time-driven controls** These take place at predefined periodic intervals. This could be, for example, producing monthly highlight reports for the project board or weekly checkpoint reports showing the progress of a work package.

Monitoring and reporting requires a time-based approach, whereas control (decision-making) is an event-based activity.

The following sections describe the management products that are used to establish and execute event-driven and **time-driven control**s.

12.2.2.1 Baselines for progress control

It is only possible to control progress at the level of detail in the plans; for example, if weekly checkpoint reports are required, the stage plan will have to include what is to be achieved week by week.

The following management products assist the project manager in establishing baselines for progress control:

● **Project plan** Includes the project-level performance targets and tolerances. Threats to the project-level tolerances need to be escalated to the project board, which will seek advice from corporate, programme management or the customer for corrective action.

● **Stage plan** Forms the basis of the day-to-day control of the management stage and detail stage-level tolerances.

● **Exception plan** May be requested by the project board after considering an exception report during the directing a project process.

● **Work package** Forms an agreement between the project manager and team manager as to the work to be completed within defined tolerances.

Appendix A (sections A.16 and A.26) provides product descriptions and suggested content for these products.

12.2.2.2 Reviewing progress

As part of controlling a stage, the project manager will regularly review the progress of work through checkpoint reports and maintain the project registers and **log**s. The project manager will use this information to update the stage plan with actual progress achieved. The format and frequency of checkpoint reporting will depend on the needs of individual work packages.

It is also useful to look at trends to get a view of the overall 'health' of the management stage. For example, the management stage may seem to be progressing well in terms of the products being completed against the schedule. However, the issue register may reveal an increasing number of issues which are not being resolved and which may be a cause for concern. Similarly, a high number of outstanding items against a product in the quality register may show design issues with that product.

The following management products assist in reviewing progress:

- Issue register Contains details of all formal issues raised during the project.
- Product status account Provides a snapshot of the status of products within the project, management stage or a particular area of the project.
- Quality register Records all planned and implemented quality activities.
- Risk register Records identified risks.

Appendix A (sections A.12, A.18, A.23 and A.25) provides product descriptions and suggested content for these products.

In addition, a daily log is a useful tool for recording actions. Project actions may arise from many sources and small actions may simply be recorded on the daily log and marked off when completed. The daily log can also be used to record informal issues and any other notes or observations that are not captured by any other registers or logs. The daily log is a useful way of recording individual observations that on their own may seem insignificant, but when collated may alert the project manager to a new issue or risk.

12.2.2.3 Capturing and reporting lessons

The **lessons log** is used for capturing and reporting lessons when reviewing progress. One of the principles of a PRINCE2 project is that the project management team learns from experience, which means that lessons are sought, recorded and actioned throughout. It is often in the reviewing of progress that lessons are identified. Lessons could include information about management or specialist processes, products, techniques or procedures that either made a contribution to the project's achievements or caused a problem. Examples might include the performance of the project management team, the success of tailoring PRINCE2 to the project, or the analysis of quality statistics and measurements. Larger projects are more likely to make use of a lessons report as part of this process, where more detail would be helpful.

 Tip

Although lessons may be identified and recorded during a project, learning lessons involves taking action to implement improvements. These actions may apply to the current project, in which case they should be incorporated into the appropriate plans and work packages, or they may be relevant to different projects.

Appendix A (sections A.14 and A.15) provides product descriptions and suggested content for the lessons log and lessons report.

12.2.2.4 Reporting progress

The frequency of reporting should reflect the level of control required, and this is likely to vary during the project. For example, if the team is highly experienced then less frequent reporting may be appropriate, whereas for an inexperienced team the project manager may wish to increase the frequency of reporting until sufficient confidence has been gained on the capability of the team.

The following management products are used for progress reporting:

- **Checkpoint report** Provides the project manager with details of progress against the work package and is typically produced by the team manager.
- **Highlight report** Provides the project board with details of progress for the whole project and/or management stage. The project manager produces this report.
- **End stage report** Provides the project board with details of progress towards the end of each management stage (except the final stage), including information on the progress to date, the overall project situation and (together with the next stage plan) sufficient information to ask for a project board decision on what to do next with the project. The report is produced by the project manager.
- **End project report** Provides the project board with information needed to evaluate the project and authorize closure. It is produced by the project manager towards the end of the project.

Appendix A (sections A.4, A.8, A.9 and A.11) provides product descriptions and suggested content for these products.

12.2.3 Raising exceptions

The output from reviewing progress is a decision as to whether the work package, stage plan or project plan remain, or are forecast to remain, within agreed tolerances:

- **Work-package-level exceptions** Having agreed work package tolerances with the team manager, the project manager should be kept informed of progress through regular checkpoint reports. If a work package is forecast to exceed its tolerances, the team manager should inform the project manager by raising an issue. The project manager will advise of any corrective actions required.
- **Stage-level exceptions** If the stage is forecast to exceed its tolerances, the project manager should produce an issue report to capture and analyse the details of the deviation and then provide an exception report for the project board. Based on information in this report, the project board may request that the project manager produces an exception plan to replace the plan that was forecast to exceed tolerance. The project board may also remove the cause, accept and adjust tolerance, or request more time to consider or reject the recommendations. If an exception plan is requested, the project board will conduct an **exception assessment**, similar to the end stage assessment, to review and approve the exception plan.
- **Project-level exceptions** If the forecast is for project tolerances to be exceeded, the project board no longer has the authority to direct the project and must refer the matter to corporate, programme management or the customer for a decision. The project board may request the project manager to produce an exception plan for the project.

12.2.4 Progress responsibilities in PRINCE2

Responsibilities for managing progress in PRINCE2 are set out in Table 12.2. As described in Chapter 7, if roles are combined then all the responsibilities in this table must still be undertaken.

Table 12.2 Responsibilities relevant to the progress theme

Role	Responsibilities
Corporate, programme management or the customer	Provide project tolerances and document them in the project mandate.
	Make decisions on exception plans when project-level tolerances are forecast to be exceeded.
Executive	Provide management stage tolerances.
	Ensure that progress towards the outcome remains consistent from the business perspective.
	Make decisions on exception plans when management-stage-level tolerances are forecast to be exceeded.
	Recommend future action on the project to corporate, programme management or the customer if the project tolerance is forecast to be exceeded.
Senior user	Ensure that progress towards the outcome remains consistent from the user perspective.
Senior supplier	Ensure that progress towards the outcome remains consistent from the supplier perspective.
Project manager	Authorize work packages.
	Monitor progress against stage plans.
	Produce highlight reports, end stage reports and the end project report.
	Produce exception plans and reports for the project board when management-stage-level or project-level tolerances are forecast to be exceeded.
	Maintain the project's registers and logs.
Team manager	Agree work packages with the project manager.
	Inform project support of completed quality activities.
	Produce checkpoint reports.
	Notify the project manager of any forecast deviation from work package tolerances.
Project assurance	Verify the business case against external events and project progress.
	Verify changes to the project plan to see whether there is any impact on the needs of the business or the business case.
	Confirm management stage and project progress against agreed tolerances.
Project support	Assist with the compilation of reports.
	Contribute specialist tool expertise (e.g. planning and control tools).
	Number, record, store and distribute issue reports and exception reports.
	Assist the project manager in maintaining the issue register and risk register.
	Maintain the quality register on behalf of the project manager.

12.3 Guidance for effective progress management

12.3.1 Aligning with corporate governance processes

A starting point for any project in an organization will be to identify the timing of corporate, programme management or the customer **governance** processes from which the project will require decisions or authority. It is usually advisable to design the project's control processes to align with corporate, programme management or the customer timings.

12.3.2 Programme and portfolio controls

If the project is part of a programme or portfolio, then the programme or portfolio will usually mandate the progress controls for the project. This will typically include defining common controls, processes, tolerances and timings.

12.3.3 The project's delivery approach

It is important that the approach to managing progress works with, and supports, the project's chosen delivery approach rather than against it. For example, in agile it will typically be more appropriate to focus on tracking how much of the requirement is being delivered as opposed to time and cost overruns as tolerances would have been set in accordance with this. In agile, the frequent delivery of products that meet their acceptance/quality criteria is a primary source of progress information and provides the basis for forecasting future progress.

12.4 Techniques: progress evaluation and peer review

12.4.1 Progress evaluation techniques

Examples of progress evaluation techniques

Milestone chart

This is a graphical chart showing key planned and actual milestones in a management stage.

S-curve

This is a graph showing cumulative actual figures (e.g. costs or hours) plotted against time. The curve is usually shaped like the letter 'S', reflecting the fact that a project typically consumes fewer resources and costs at the start and end of the project, and more in the middle. The steeper the curve, the more resources are required. When planned and actual figures are shown on the same chart, this can be used to identify potential overspend or forecast areas where tolerances may be exceeded.

Earned value management

This is a technique to measure the scope, schedule and cost performance compared with plans, by comparing the completed products and the actual cost and time taken against their schedule and cost estimates. PRINCE2's approach to product-based planning provides information to support earned value management.

Burn charts

This is a technique for showing progress (e.g. such as during a timebox) where work that is completed and work still to be done are shown with one or more lines, and the chart is updated regularly/daily. This is one of the most popular techniques when using an agile approach and **burn chart**s come in two forms: burn-down charts and burn-up charts. Burn-down charts are the most well-known and they show how much work remains whereas burn-up charts are slightly more complex and they show how much work has been done.

Kanban board

Kanban is a term that covers the use of Kanban systems, which are visual management systems that limit the number of work items in circulation. A Kanban board is a tool used in Kanban to visually display the work in the system (or timebox). It is usually made up of a series of columns and possibly rows where work items move from left to right as they move through various states in order to be completed. A Kanban board acts like a dashboard and enables the team to see blockers and areas where the flow is not smooth.

Measuring the progress of a management stage involves looking backward at the progress made against plans, and forward at what still needs to be completed with what time and resources. There are many techniques available to measure project progress.

12.4.2 Peer review

A peer review is where people experienced in project management but outside the project management team are asked to evaluate the project. There are many peer review techniques and the quality management approach should identify the technique(s) appropriate to the project.

Example of a peer review technique

The OGC Gateway™ Process

OGC Gateway reviews examine projects prior to key decision points in their lifecycle to provide assurance that they can progress successfully to the next stage. The process is used in UK central government, the health sector, local government and defence, and has been adopted by numerous other countries.

OGC Gateway reviews are 'peer reviews' in which independent practitioners from outside the project use their experience and expertise to examine the progress and likelihood of the successful delivery of the project.

The reviews take place at different points in a project's lifecycle and are as follows:

- OGC Gateway review 0: strategic assessment
- OGC Gateway review 1: business justification
- OGC Gateway review 2: delivery strategy
- OGC Gateway review 3: investment decision
- OGC Gateway review 4: readiness for service
- OGC Gateway review 5: operations review and benefits evaluation.

OGC Gateway reviews 0 and 1 happen prior to the project being authorized to start. Reviews 2 and 3 happen during the investigative stages prior to a full business case being approved. Review 4 happens prior to any new operations or services being launched. Review 5 is equivalent to a PRINCE2 post-project benefits review.

An OGC Gateway review is not the same as a 'gate' or decision point (such as the end stage assessment), but a means of providing added assurance as input to the decision on whether the project is likely to meet its objectives. The cost and time of conducting gateway reviews should be included in the project plan and stage plans.

13

Introduction to processes

This chapter covers:

- PRINCE2 as a process-based method
- the PRINCE2 journey
- the seven PRINCE2 processes in an overall model
- a key to the process and activity models
- the structure of the process chapters
- tailoring the processes

13 Introduction to processes

PRINCE2 is a process-based approach for project management. A process is a structured set of activities designed to accomplish a specific objective. It takes one or more defined inputs and turns them into defined outputs.

There are seven processes in PRINCE2, which provide the set of activities required to direct, manage and deliver a project successfully.

Figure 13.1 shows how each process is used throughout a project's lifecycle. The lifecycle shown has three management stages: an initiation stage, subsequent stage(s), and the final stage. Note that on a simple project, there may only be two stages: an initiation stage and one delivery stage (the final stage).

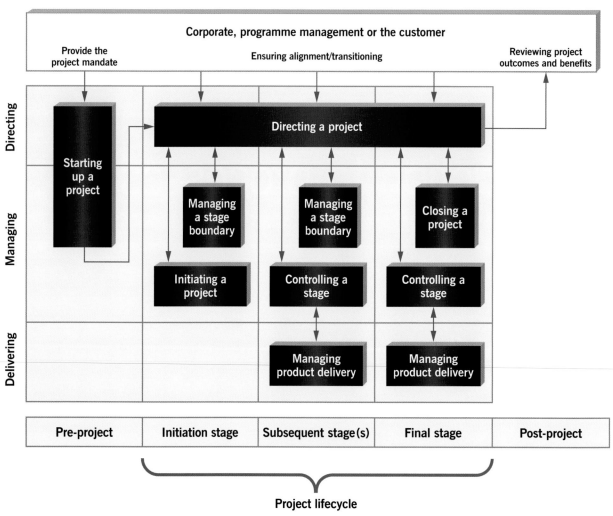

Figure 13.1 The PRINCE2 processes

158

13.1 The PRINCE2 journey

The project board sets direction and makes key decisions throughout the life of the project. The project board's activities are covered by the directing a project process (see Chapter 15), which runs from pre-project through to, and including, the final management stage.

13.1.1 Pre-project

In the beginning, someone has an idea or a need. The **trigger** for the project may come from new business objectives, responding to competitive pressures, changes in legislation or a recommendation in a report or an audit. In PRINCE2, this trigger is called a project mandate. The project mandate is provided by the commissioning organization (corporate, programme management or the customer) and can vary in form from a verbal instruction to a well-defined and justified project definition.

Prior to the activity to scope the project fully, it is important to verify that the project is worthwhile and viable. Such activities are covered by the starting up a project process (see Chapter 14), which culminates in the production of a project brief and a stage plan for project initiation.

The project board reviews the project brief and decides whether to initiate the project, and states the levels of authority to be delegated to the project manager for the initiation stage.

13.1.2 Initiation stage

When a decision has been made to go ahead with the project, it needs to be planned at an appropriate level of detail. Funding needs to be obtained and appropriate controls should be defined to ensure that the project proceeds in accordance with the wishes of those people paying for the project and those who will make use of what the project delivers. The planning, establishment of the project management approaches and controls, development of a robust business case and a means of reviewing benefits are covered by the initiating a project process (see Chapter 16). Also, during the initiation stage, the managing a stage boundary process (see Chapter 19) is used to plan the next management stage in detail.

The initiation stage culminates in the production of the PID, which is reviewed by the project board to decide whether to authorize the project. As the contents of the PID are likely to change throughout the project (under change control), this version of the PID is preserved as input for later performance reviews.

13.1.3 Subsequent stages

The project board delegates day-to-day control to the project manager management stage by management stage. The project manager needs to assign work to be done, ensure that the outputs of such work (products) meet relevant specifications, and gain suitable approval where appropriate. At this point, products may be transitioned into operational use by corporate, programme management or the customer.

The project manager also needs to ensure that progress is in line with the approved plan and that the forecasts for the project's performance targets are within agreed tolerances. The project manager ensures that a set of project records are maintained to assist with progress control. The project manager informs the project board of progress through regular highlight reports. The activities to control each management stage are covered by the controlling a stage process (see Chapter 17).

In the managing product delivery process (see Chapter 18), the team manager(s) or team members execute assigned work packages (that will deliver one or more products) and keep the project manager appraised of progress via checkpoint reports.

Towards the end of each management stage, the project manager requests permission to proceed to the next management stage by reporting how the management stage performed, providing an update to the business case and planning the next management stage in detail. The project manager provides the information needed by the project board in order for it to assess the continuing viability of the project and to make a decision to authorize the next management stage. At all times, the project board must ensure that the project remains aligned with the strategy of corporate, programme management or the customer. The activities to manage each management stage boundary are covered in the managing a stage boundary process (see Chapter 19).

13.1.4 Final stage

As a project is a temporary undertaking, towards the end of the final management stage (when the project manager has gained approval for the project product) it is time to start the closing a project process. The project board needs to be satisfied that the recipients of the project product are in a position to own and use it on an ongoing basis. Should this be the case, the product can be transitioned into operational use and the project can close. The project documentation should be tidied up and archived, the project should be assessed for performance against its original plan and the resources assigned to the project need to be released. Closure activities include planning post-project benefits reviews to take place for those benefits that can only be assessed after the product has been in use (and therefore after the project has closed). The activities to decommission a project are covered by the closing a project process (see Chapter 20).

13.1.5 Post-project

The project is typically contributing towards the benefits defined by corporate, programme management or the customer. Even though some of these benefits may be realized during the project, it is likely that many or all of the benefits will be realized post-project. Corporate, programme management or the customer therefore needs to be satisfied that the project has contributed towards benefits realization, and is therefore likely to hold one or more post-project benefits reviews. The reviews will be signposted in the project's benefits management approach. If the project is part of a programme, then the post-project benefits reviews need to be covered by the programme's benefits management activities.

A post-project benefits review will focus on:

● confirming that the planned benefits have been achieved
● identifying which planned benefits have not been achieved and agreeing a follow-up action plan
● identifying any unexpected benefits that have been achieved and any dis-benefits that resulted
● providing lessons for future projects.

13.2 The PRINCE2 process model

The PRINCE2 process model is shown in Figure 13.2.

The processes are aligned with the management levels of corporate, programme management or the customer, directing, managing and delivering. The triggers between the processes are shown.

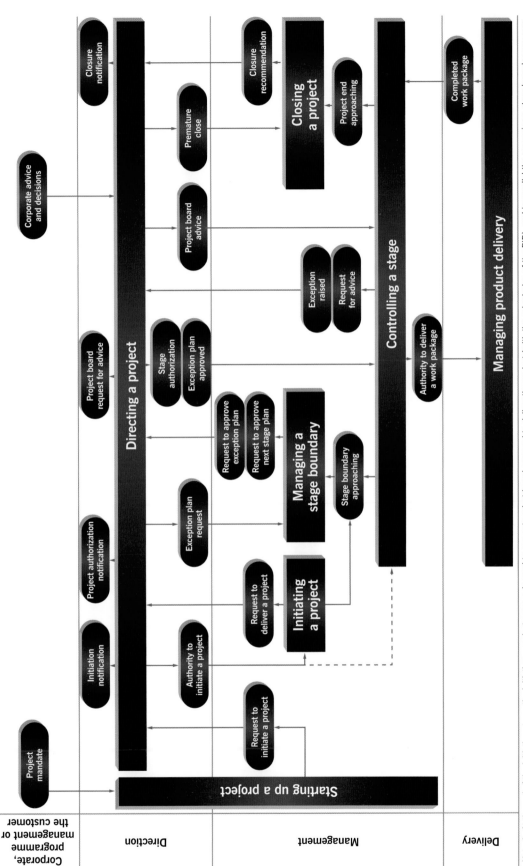

Figure 13.2 PRINCE2 process model

Note 1: At the end of the initiation stage, the initiating a project process is used to request project board approval to deliver the project (with the submission of the PID), and in parallel the managing a stage boundary process is used to request project board approval of the stage plan for the second management stage.

Note 2: The closure activities are planned and approved as part of the stage approval for the final stage, therefore the closing a project process takes place in the final stage.

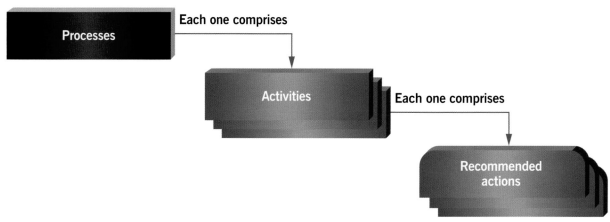

Figure 13.3 Relationship between processes, activities and actions

13.3 Structure of the process chapters

Each process within PRINCE2 is described using the following structure and format:

- **Purpose** Describes the reason for the process.
- **Objective** Describes the specific objectives to be achieved by the process.
- **Context** Puts each process in context with the other processes and activities going on within the project and from corporate, programme management or the customer.
- **Activities** Each PRINCE2 process comprises a set of activities, which may be run in series or in parallel. PRINCE2 activities comprise a set of recommended actions designed to achieve a particular result. The relationship between processes, activities and actions is shown in Figure 13.3.
- **Tailoring guidelines** Describes the approaches that can be used to tailor a process.

A diagram is provided for each activity showing the inputs and outputs, including those products that are created or updated by that activity. The recommended actions to be taken to achieve the objectives of the activity are described. A key to the symbols used in the process and activity diagrams is shown in Figure 13.4.

Each activity is concluded by a table showing the responsibilities (P, R or A) for each product created or updated during the activity, as illustrated in Table 13.1. Note that management products created during one process may be approved in another (e.g. a stage plan is created in the managing a stage boundary process but is approved in the directing a project process). However, the complete set of responsibilities is shown, and those covered by another process are shown in parentheses, as in (P), (R) or (A).

Table 13.1 An example of a table of responsibilities

Product	Action	Corporate/ programme/ customer	Executive	Senior user	Senior supplier	Project manager	Team manager	Project assurance	Project support	Product description available
Stage plan	Create		(A)	(A)	(A)	P		R		A.16

Key: P (producer) – responsible for product's production; R (reviewer) – ideally independent of production; A (approver) – confirms approval. Note that 'Corporate/programme/customer' means corporate or programme management, or the customer.

Symbol	Key
Starting up a project	This is a PRINCE2 process.
Authorize initiation	This is an activity. Each process comprises a number of activities.
Exception plan request / **Corrective action**	This is an event or decision that triggers another process or is used to notify corporate, programme management or the customer. The arrow shows which process is triggered by the event. Double triggers indicate where there are alternative triggers from one process to another (i.e. a request to approve the next stage plan or a request to approve an exception plan). Those with dashed lines are triggers internal to a process (e.g. corrective action is a trigger from one activity in the controlling a stage process to another).
Business case / **Follow-on action recommendations**	These are management products that are created or updated by a process's activities. Those with solid lines are defined management products, as set out in Appendix A. Those with dashed lines are components of a management product or are management products that are not described in Appendix A.

Figure 13.4 Key to process diagrams

13.4 Tailoring the processes

PRINCE2 requires that project management processes are as simple as possible and that they reflect the needs of the project. There may be some activities, however, especially relating to governance which may need to be prescriptive. This happens especially where they interface to a higher-level organization's process, such as for procurement or finance (e.g. when allocating funds at the start of a new stage).

Tailoring enables flexibility in how the processes should be followed. This may range from being rigid and prescriptive, to allowing the project management team a large degree of freedom as to how they undertake an activity and the format of the products. Processes can be tailored 'up' or 'down' (i.e. additional detailed documentation and discipline can be introduced for high-risk projects, whereas concise bullet-point presentations and more informal processes may be adequate for low-risk projects).

A tailored PRINCE2 process should reflect any tailoring of the roles, products, themes (as implemented through management approaches, procedures and controls) and terminology. As terminology can be tailored, so can the names of the processes.

Usually, all processes remain relevant even for simple projects; what changes is the way in which they are undertaken, the activities and the degree of formality. Informality, with the right mindset, does not necessarily mean less rigour.

Key message

Tailoring allows the PRINCE2 process model to be adapted, revising the processes, activities, their sequencing and how the role responsibilities are allocated, provided that:

- the PRINCE2 principles are upheld
- the purpose and objectives of the process are not compromised.

Each PRINCE2 process chapter contains a section suggesting different tailoring options for implementing the process in practice. The general points for consideration are:

- amending the PRINCE2 process model to reflect the organization's project management method or alternative ways of working
- adopting methods or ways of working required by the commissioning organization (corporate, programme management or the customer)
- combining some activities which fulfil related purposes, to simplify the process
- splitting some activities into smaller parts for clarity or to re-assign different roles to the activities
- changing which role is responsible for the activity
- combining, splitting or amending management products
- increasing the granularity of the process model, to include more detailed activities, where needed.

PRINCE2 does not prescribe the format in which a process is documented or published; processes on a web site or in documents are just as valid. If using documents, however, ensure that they are subject to change control so that users know which version is current.

Tip

PRINCE2 defines the project management processes, not the delivery approach related to creating each specialist product. Consider showing how these processes relate in a project lifecycle view.

Starting up a project

This chapter covers:

- developing the outline business case
- building the project management team
- defining the right approach
- preparing for project initiation (creating the project brief and plan)
- guidelines for tailoring products and roles

14 Starting up a project

14.1 Purpose

The purpose of the starting up a project process is to ensure that the prerequisites for initiating a project are in place by answering the question: Do we have a viable and worthwhile project? The decision to start the project must be explicit; the activities from starting up a project happen before this decision.

Nothing should be done until certain base information needed to make rational decisions about the commissioning of the project is defined, key roles and responsibilities are resourced and allocated, and a foundation for detailed planning is available.

The purpose of the starting up a project process is as much about preventing poorly conceived projects from ever being initiated as it is about approving the initiation of viable projects. As such, starting up a project is a lighter process compared to the more detailed and thorough initiating a project process. The aim is to do the minimum necessary in order to decide whether it is worthwhile to even initiate the project.

14.2 Objective

The objective of the starting up a project process is to ensure that:

- there is a business justification for initiating the project (documented in an outline business case)
- all the necessary authorities exist for initiating the project
- sufficient information is available to define and confirm the scope of the project (in the form of a project brief)
- the various ways the project can be delivered are evaluated and a project approach selected
- individuals are appointed who will undertake the work required in project initiation and/or will take significant project management roles in the project
- the work required for project initiation is planned (documented in a stage plan)
- time is not wasted initiating a project based on unsound assumptions regarding the project's scope, timescales, acceptance criteria and constraints.

14.3 Context

Figure 14.1 provides an overview of starting up a project.

Projects can be identified in a variety of ways and thus have a wide variation in the information available at the time of **start-up**. In PRINCE2, the trigger for the project is referred to as the project mandate. This is provided by the **responsible authority** that is commissioning the project, typically corporate, programme management or the customer. The term 'project mandate' applies to whatever information is used to trigger the project, be it a feasibility study or the receipt of a 'request for proposal' in a supplier environment. The project mandate should provide the terms of reference for the project and should contain sufficient information to identify at least the prospective executive of the project board. The mandate is refined to develop the project brief.

The project board must be provided with sufficient information to make the decision to initiate the project. The project brief is prepared for this purpose.

The effort involved in starting up a project will vary enormously from project to project. If the project is part of a programme, the programme itself should provide the project brief and will appoint some, if not all, members of the project board, thus eliminating much of the work required in this process. In such cases, the project manager should validate what is provided by the programme and, if necessary, recommend modifications.

The preparation of the outline business case and the assembling of the project brief (which are parallel and iterative activities) require regular and frequent interaction and consultation between the project manager, the project board members and other stakeholders. The more time spent on getting the requirements clearly captured during the starting up a project process, the more time will be saved during project delivery by avoiding issues, exceptions and replanning.

The contents of the project brief are later extended and refined into the PID via the initiating a project process.

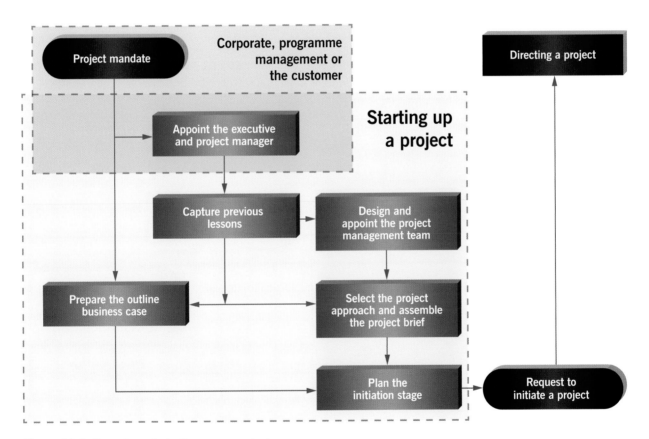

Figure 14.1 Overview of starting up a project

14.4 Activities

The activities within the starting up a project process are likely to be shared between corporate, programme management or the customer, the executive and the project manager. The activities are to:

- appoint the executive and the project manager
- capture previous lessons
- design and appoint the project management team
- prepare the outline business case
- select the project approach and assemble the project brief
- plan the initiation stage.

14.4.1 Appoint the executive and the project manager

To get anything done in the project, a decision maker with appropriate authority is needed (the executive) who represents the interests of the business stakeholder(s). The appointment of the executive is a prerequisite to ensuring that the project is justified.

The appointment of a project manager allows for the project to be managed on a day-to-day basis on behalf of the executive. The executive may need to consult with, and gain agreement from, corporate, programme management or the customer when appointing a project manager.

Figure 14.2 shows the inputs to, and outputs from, this activity. For more details on project organization, see Chapter 7.

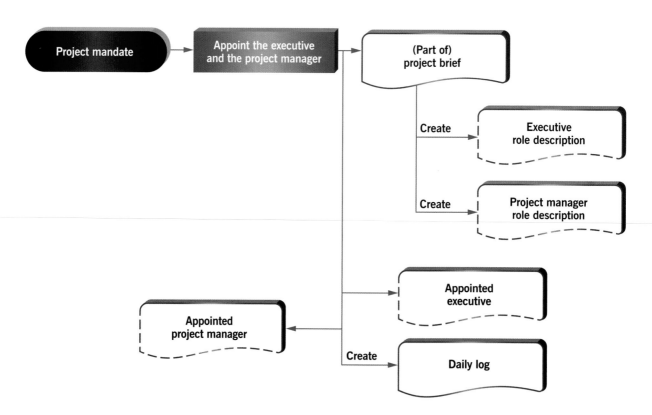

Figure 14.2 Appoint the executive and the project manager: activity summary

PRINCE2 recommends the following actions:

- Review the project mandate and check understanding.
- Appoint the executive. To do this, the commissioning organization needs to:
  - establish the responsibilities for the executive
  - prepare the role description for the executive based on the role description in Appendix C
  - estimate the time and effort required for the executive role (this will be refined later)
  - identify candidates for the executive from the project's stakeholders and select the most appropriate person for the role
  - confirm the selected person's availability, their acceptance of the role and their commitment to carry it out
  - assign the selected person to the role of executive.
- Appoint the project manager. To do this the executive needs to:
  - establish the responsibilities for the project manager
  - prepare a role description for the project manager, based on the role description in Appendix C, and gain agreement from corporate, programme management or the customer
  - estimate the time and effort required for the project manager role (this will be refined later)
  - identify candidates for the project manager and select the most appropriate person for the role
  - confirm the selected person's availability, their acceptance of the role and their commitment to carry it out
  - assign the selected person to the role of project manager
  - confirm the appointment with corporate, programme management or the customer.
- Create the daily log as a repository for project information that is not yet being captured elsewhere.

Table 14.1 shows the responsibilities for this activity.

Table 14.1 Appoint the executive and the project manager: responsibilities

Product	Action	Corporate/ programme/ customer	Executive	Senior user	Senior supplier	Project manager	Team manager	Project assurance	Project support	Product description available
Project mandate	Provide	P								
Appointed executive	Confirm	P								
Executive role description	Create	P								
Project manager role description	Create	A	P							
Appointed project manager	Confirm	A	P							
Daily log	Create					P				A.7

Key: P (producer) – responsible for product's production; R (reviewer) – ideally independent of production; A (approver) – confirms approval.

14.4.2 Capture previous lessons

A number of lessons may have been provided by other projects, corporate, programme management or the customer, and external organizations. These lessons may include weaknesses or strengths of the processes, and procedures, techniques and tools used, when they were used, how they were used and by whom.

The design of the project management team, the outline business case, the contents of the project brief and the stage plan for the initiation stage can be influenced by lessons from previous projects.

Figure 14.3 Capture previous lessons: activity summary

It may be useful to hold a workshop as a means to capture relevant lessons. Attendees could include any interested parties and people who have worked on previous similar projects. If the organization has not done this type of project before, it may be helpful to include people external to the organization who have the relevant experience.

When moving from the general view in the starting up a project process to the detailed view in initiating a project and the updated view in managing a stage boundary, it may be necessary to look beyond the lessons log by repeating this activity to capture any further relevant external lessons.

Figure 14.3 shows the inputs to, and outputs from, this activity.

PRINCE2 recommends the following actions:

- Create the lessons log.
- Review related lessons from similar previous projects to identify lessons that can be applied to this project. This may include, for example, the results of audits and project reviews.
- Review any lessons from corporate, programme management or the customer and external organizations.
- Consult with individuals or teams with previous experience of similar projects.
- If appropriate, record any lessons identified in the lessons log.

Table 14.2 shows the responsibilities for this activity.

Table 14.2 Capture previous lessons: responsibilities

Product	Action	Corporate/ programme/ customer	Executive	Senior user	Senior supplier	Project manager	Team manager	Project assurance	Project support	Product description available
Lessons log	Create		R			P				A.14

Key: P (producer) – responsible for product's production; R (reviewer) – ideally independent of production; A (approver) – confirms approval.

14.4.3 Design and appoint the project management team

The project needs the right people in place, with the authority, responsibility and knowledge to make decisions in a timely manner. The project management team needs to reflect the interests of all parties who will be involved, including business, user and supplier interests.

It is essential for a well-run project that every individual involved in the management of the project understands and agrees who is accountable to whom for what, who is responsible for what, and what the reporting and communication lines are.

Figure 14.4 shows the inputs to, and outputs from, this activity. For more details on project organization, see Chapter 7.

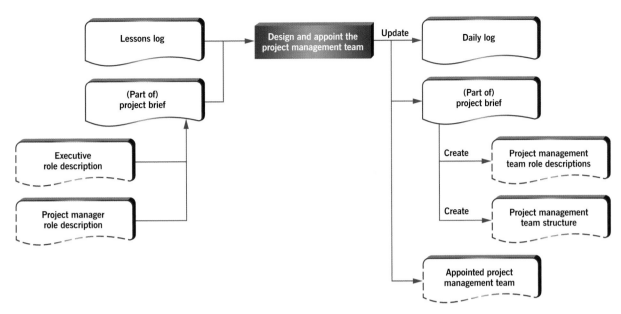

Figure 14.4 Design and appoint the project management team: activity summary

PRINCE2 recommends the following actions:

- Review the lessons log for lessons related to the project management team structure.
- Design the project management team:
  - prepare the project management team structure
  - create role descriptions for the remaining project board roles based on the role descriptions in Appendix C
  - assess whether any members of the project board are likely to delegate any of their assurance responsibilities, and create the role description(s) for project assurance (where appropriate) based on the role description in Appendix C
  - consider whether separate individuals are likely to be needed as team manager(s) or whether the project manager will be filling this role. If appropriate, create role descriptions for the team manager(s) based on the role description in Appendix C
  - consider whether the project manager will be performing the project support role or whether a separate individual(s) will be required. If this role is to be delegated, create the role description for the project support role based on the role description in Appendix C
  - if appropriate, consider how the project management team structure will work if an agile approach is being used (e.g. how the team manager role will relate to agile roles such as that of the **Scrum master**)
  - confirm the reporting and communication lines within the role descriptions.
- Appoint the project management team:
  - estimate the time and effort required by each of the roles identified (this will be refined later)
  - identify candidates for each of the roles, and propose the most appropriate people for them:
    - it may be appropriate to undertake an analysis of the stakeholders (see section 7.3.9) in order to identify suitable candidates for the roles
    - it is possible that candidates may not be known at this time, in which case they will need to be selected later (see sections 16.4.6 and 19.4.1). This is particularly true if team managers are to be sourced from subcontractors
    - consider whether identified candidates match the competencies required of the role and, if not, whether any training or support (e.g. coaching) is required

- confirm the selected people's availability (if they are known), their understanding and acceptance of the roles, and their commitment to carry them out
- assign the selected people to each of the roles identified and confirm the appointment with corporate, programme management or the customer.
- If any risks are identified, add them to the daily log.

Table 14.3 shows the responsibilities for this activity.

Table 14.3 Design and appoint the project management team: responsibilities

Product	Action	Corporate/ programme/ customer	Executive	Senior user	Senior supplier	Project manager	Team manager	Project assurance	Project support	Product description available
Daily log	Update					P				A.7
Project management team role descriptions	Create		A			P				
Project management team structure	Create		A			P				
Appointed project management team	Confirm	A	P							

Key: P (producer) – responsible for product's production; R (reviewer) – ideally independent of production; A (approver) – confirms approval.

14.4.4 Prepare the outline business case

When setting up, and particularly while running the project, it is all too easy to concentrate on what is being done and how it is to be done, while ignoring why it needs to be done. Given the information available, the outline business case is likely to be only a high-level view at this time. It provides an agreed foundation for a more detailed business case developed in the initiating a project process.

Figure 14.5 shows the inputs to, and outputs from, this activity. For more on the business case, see Chapter 6.

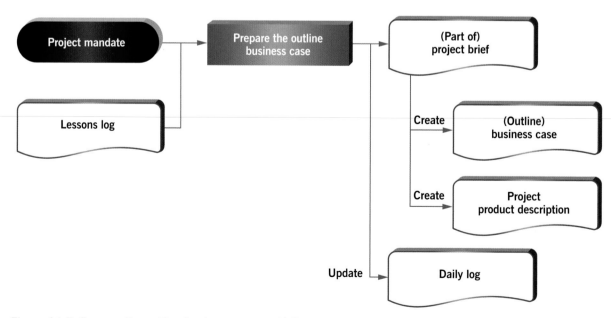

Figure 14.5 Prepare the outline business case: activity summary

PRINCE2 recommends the following actions:

- The executive (in consultation with the senior user if appointed at this time) to draft the outline business case based on what is currently known about the project. They will need to:
  - understand the objectives of, and the reasons for, the project as defined in the project mandate
  - understand how the project will contribute towards corporate, programme management or customer objectives
  - understand how the project will be funded
  - review the lessons log for lessons related to business justification
  - check for any standards mandated for the format and presentation of the business case (e.g. templates, cost metrics)
  - assemble any relevant background information (e.g. contracts, feasibility reports, service-level agreements)
  - if necessary, seek approval of the outline business case from corporate, programme management or the customer.
- Project manager to consult with the senior user, senior supplier and executive to define what the project is to deliver, and create the project product description (see Chapter 8). This action should:
  - capture the customer's quality expectations
  - capture and agree the project's acceptance criteria
  - check feasibility of the timescale from the project mandate or as required by the outline business case
  - determine any key milestones
  - capture any new risks in the daily log.
- Review the risks captured in the daily log and summarize the key risks affecting viability of the project in the outline business case.

Table 14.4 shows the responsibilities for this activity.

Table 14.4 Prepare the outline business case: responsibilities

Product	Action	Corporate/ programme/ customer	Executive	Senior user	Senior supplier	Project manager	Team manager	Project assurance	Project support	Product description available
Outline business case	Create	A	P	R	R	R		R		A.2
Project product description	Create		(A)	(A)	(A)	P		R		A.21
Daily log	Update					P				A.7

Key: P (producer) – responsible for product's production; R (reviewer) – ideally independent of production; A (approver) – confirms approval.

The complete list of responsibilities for each product is shown. Where a product is produced, reviewed or approved in another process, the responsibility is shown in parentheses, as in (P), (R) or (A).

14.4.5 Select the project approach and assemble the project brief

Before any planning of the project can be done, decisions must be made regarding how the work of the project is going to be approached. For example, will the solution be developed in-house or contracted to third parties? Will the solution be a modification to an existing product or built from scratch? Will the solution be based on a commercial off-the-shelf product (often referred to as a COTS) or something that is custom-designed? What delivery approaches should be used? Will the delivery approach use agile working methods?

The way in which the work is to be conducted will depend on any customer or supplier standards, practices and guidelines; for example, any specific delivery approaches that may apply. These should be captured in the project brief as part of the project approach, as they will influence the project approaches to be created in the initiating a project process. It also ensures that the project approach is clearly understood between customer and supplier, and does not jeopardize the project in any way.

An agreed project brief ensures that the project has a commonly understood and well-defined start point.

Figure 14.6 shows the inputs to, and outputs from, this activity.

PRINCE2 recommends the following actions:

- Evaluate the possible delivery solutions and decide upon the project approach appropriate to delivering the project product and achieving the outline business case:
  - review the lessons log for lessons related to the project approach
  - consider any corporate, programme management or customer strategies that are relevant, and put the project in context with any other work or initiatives by establishing external dependencies and prerequisites
  - consider any corporate, programme management or customer standards or practices that should apply (in a commercial customer/supplier context there are likely to be different standards and practices which need to be accommodated)
  - consider the current thinking about the provision of solutions within the industry sectors and specialist skill areas involved (including any options for the delivery approach for the project product)
  - define the operational environment into which the solution must fit (including operational or maintenance implications and constraints) and how the project product can be brought into that environment
  - consider possible delivery approaches and their suitability for use by the project
  - consider any security constraints that apply to the project or the operation of its products
  - consider any training needs for user personnel.

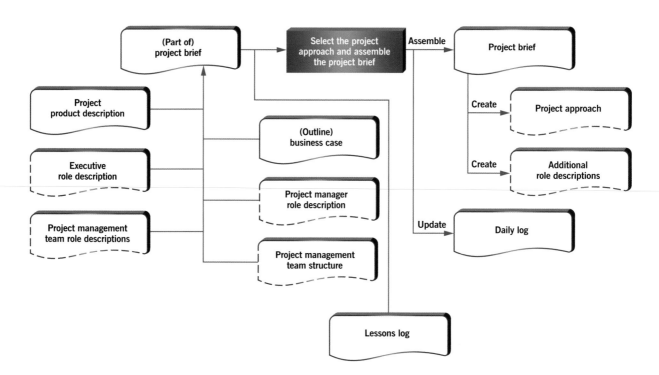

Figure 14.6 Select the project approach and assemble the project brief: activity summary

- Define any tailoring requirements known at this time.
- Assemble the project brief:
  - define the project:
    - confirm the current status of the project (e.g. project background and any preparation work carried out to date)
    - confirm the objectives and desired outcomes
    - confirm the project scope and exclusions
    - identify any constraints and assumptions
    - identify the project tolerances
    - identify the user(s) and any other known interested parties
    - identify the interfaces that the project must maintain
  - incorporate the outline business case
  - incorporate the project product description
  - incorporate the project approach
  - review the project management team structure and role descriptions to identify any additional roles or skills required to conduct the work. Prepare additional role descriptions as necessary
  - incorporate the project management team structure and role descriptions.
- Use the daily log to record any new issues or risks.

Tip

Document what is known at this time, but do not spend time trying to get details not required yet. Details and precision can be added in the PID.

Table 14.5 shows the responsibilities for this activity.

Table 14.5 Select the project approach and assemble the project brief: responsibilities

Product	Action	Corporate/ programme/ customer	Executive	Senior user	Senior supplier	Project manager	Team manager	Project assurance	Project support	Product description available
Project approach	Create/ select		(A)	(R)	(R)	P		R		
Additional role descriptions	Create		(A)	(R)	(R)	P		R		
Project brief	Assemble		(A)	(R)	(R)	P		R		A.19
Daily log	Update					P				A.7

Key: P (producer) – responsible for product's production; R (reviewer) – ideally independent of production; A (approver) – confirms approval.

The complete list of responsibilities for each product is shown. Where a product is produced, reviewed or approved in another process, the responsibility is shown in parentheses, as in (P), (R) or (A).

14.4.6 Plan the initiation stage

Initiating a project takes time and consumes resources. The work should be planned and approved to ensure that initiation is not aimless and unstructured. If the project is part of a programme, the end date for the initiation stage should be checked against that held in the programme's plans. The stage plan for the initiation stage will also give the programme management team warning of any requirements from the programme.

The application of PRINCE2 processes during initiating a project needs to be considered as part of the starting up a project process. For example, the project may choose to apply the controlling a stage and managing product delivery processes during the initiating a project process.

Figure 14.7 shows the inputs to, and outputs from, this activity. For more details on planning, see Chapter 9.

PRINCE2 recommends the following actions:

- Based on the project approach, decide upon suitable management controls for the project sufficient for it to be initiated:
  - review the lessons log for lessons related to project controls
  - define the reporting and control arrangements for the initiation stage.
- Identify any constraints on time and costs for the initiation stage and produce the stage plan for this management stage according to the principles and techniques in Chapter 9.
- Review any risks in the daily log and assess their impact on the stage plan for the initiation stage.
- If any new risks are identified (or existing ones have changed), update the daily log.
- Request authorization to initiate the project.

Table 14.6 shows the responsibilities for this activity.

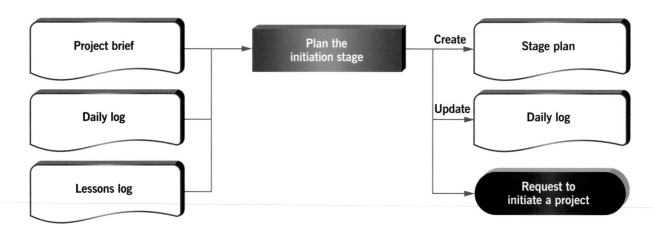

Figure 14.7 Plan the initiation stage: activity summary

Table 14.6 Plan the initiation stage: responsibilities

Product	Action	Corporate/ programme/ customer	Executive	Senior user	Senior supplier	Project manager	Team manager	Project assurance	Project support	Product description available
Stage plan	Create		(A)	(A)	(A)	P		R		A.16
Daily log	Update					P				A.7

Key: P (producer) – responsible for product's production; R (reviewer) – ideally independent of production; A (approver) – confirms approval.

The complete list of responsibilities for each product is shown. Where a product is produced, reviewed or approved in another process, the responsibility is shown in parentheses, as in (P), (R) or (A).

14.5 Tailoring guidelines

14.5.1 General considerations

The activities in this process may be combined, split or run concurrently to suit the context, but care should be taken to ensure the integrity of the interface with the directing a project process when a request to initiate a project is submitted.

At this point in the project lifecycle, it may not always be clear what output the project is intended to create; if this is the case, it should at least be clear what business problem is to be solved or what outcome is required.

14.5.2 Tailoring products in starting up a project

Table 14.7 provides tailoring guidelines for management products in starting up a project.

Table 14.7 Guidelines for tailoring products in starting up a project

Management product	Tailoring guidelines
Lessons log	Capturing of previous lessons is required as part of the PRINCE2 principle of learn from experience, although it may vary in respect of the formality used.
Project brief, comprising: ● outline business case ● project product description	The project brief may be a single document and it may reference corporate, portfolio, programme or customer documentation or reports, such as a feasibility report. It may range from being a simple statement describing the project to a fuller description. The team structure may only be partially complete at this point in time. Any management team structure is allowable as long as organization constraints are respected (see Chapter 7). The options and solutions may not yet be defined, in which case the project approach should describe how these will be determined. Role descriptions may be in any form. If formal role descriptions exist (e.g. as part of an organization's method) only a summary may be needed together with a reference to where the detail is. Alternatively the role description may itself be amended to suit the needs of the project. The outline business case may range from being a simple statement of why the project is needed to a more detailed analysis and description. The project product description may include a statement of desired outcomes, relating to solving a business problem, if the solution products have not yet been identified.
Stage plan (initiation stage)	The plan may include components in any format commensurate with the complexity of the project, with views such as a simple list of accountabilities, products, activities and dates or Gantt chart. The plan may be held totally or partially within a planning tool(s). The management product descriptions within a stage plan can themselves be tailored to suit the project.

14.5.3 Tailoring the roles in starting up a project

If a project manager has not been appointed at the start of this process, the required management products may be created by the executive or anyone appointed by them. Similarly the executive does not need to create the outline business case personally but may have another person create this. The single point of accountability for each role's duty should be maintained.

For more guidance on roles, see Chapter 7.

14.5.4 Common situations

14.5.4.1 Starting up a simple project

If the risks are acceptable, the starting up a project process may be handled in a less formal manner than for larger, more risky projects. The executive and project manager should, however, not bypass it altogether. The project brief, and its component parts, may simply be an elaboration of the mandate, with confirmation of the business problem to be addressed, roles, and an initiation stage plan, outlining expectations for the duration and effort for undertaking the first stage of the project.

14.5.4.2 Starting up projects using an agile delivery approach

The suitability of using an agile way of working needs to be assessed by looking at what agile ways of working exist or need to exist, and their respective advantages and disadvantages; for example, is co-locating the team a good idea or will it be too expensive and undermine the business case?

The impact of frequent releases should be assessed with respect to areas such as how quality will be managed and how the frequent delivery of products (or products in differing states) will take place (e.g. whether they will always go directly into operational use).

14.5.4.3 Starting up projects from a supplier perspective

From a supplier perspective, the starting up a project process will take place pre-contract and is typically in response to the customer's request for information or a proposal.

14.5.4.4 Starting up projects within a programme

The PRINCE2 process most affected by working in a programme will be starting up a project. For example, this process could be undertaken almost entirely by the programme manager under the 'start projects' activity within the delivering the capability process described in *Managing Successful Programmes* (Cabinet Office, 2011). In any case, the programme manager should ensure the appointment of the executive and project manager, prepare the project brief, alert the project manager to any relevant previous lessons and ensure an initial project management team is appointed.

Directing a project

This chapter covers:

- empowering the project board with decision-making authority
- providing direction and control over the life of the project
- communicating with the project management team and interested parties
- dealing with project issues
- authorizing project closure
- guidelines for tailoring roles

15 Directing a project

15.1 Purpose

The purpose of the directing a project process is to enable the project board to be accountable for the project's success by making key decisions and exercising overall control while delegating day-to-day management of the project to the project manager.

15.2 Objective

The objective of the directing a project process is to ensure that:

- there is authority to initiate the project
- there is authority to deliver the project product
- management direction and control are provided throughout the project's life
- the project remains viable
- corporate, programme management or the customer has an interface to the project
- there is authority to close the project
- plans for realizing the post-project benefits are managed and reviewed.

15.3 Context

Figure 15.1 provides an overview of directing a project. The directing a project process starts on completion of the starting up a project process and is triggered by the request to initiate a project.

The directing a project process covers the activities of the project board and is not concerned with the day-to-day activities of the project manager. The project board manages by exception: it monitors via reports and controls through a small number of decision points. There should be no need for other 'progress meetings' for the project board. The project manager will inform the board of any exception situation. It is also important that levels of authority and decision-making processes are clearly identified.

There needs to be a two-way flow of information between the project board and corporate, programme management or the customer during the project. At all times, the project board must ensure that the project remains aligned with the strategy of corporate, programme management or the customer.

It is a key role of the project board to engage with corporate, programme management or the customer and to act as a communication channel. The requirement for the project board to act as a communication channel, and how it is going to do it, should be documented in the communication management approach.

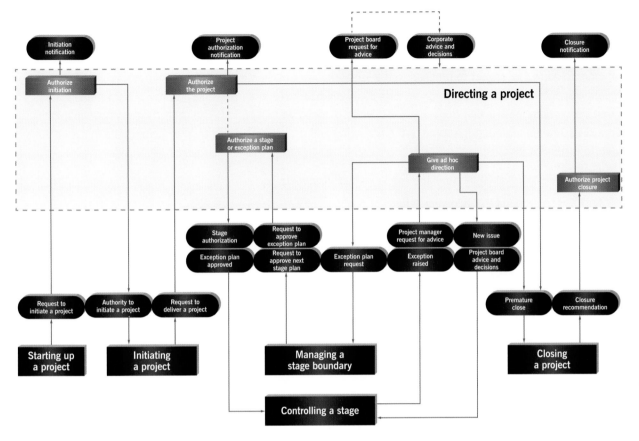

Figure 15.1 Overview of directing a project

The project board should provide unified direction and guidance to the project manager. If the project board is unable to provide a single view, or if independent, possibly contradictory, advice is given, then the risk of project failure significantly increases. In such cases, the project manager should defer to the executive.

The directing a project process provides a mechanism for the project board to meet its responsibility for ensuring that there is continued business justification without being overburdened by project activity.

One of the functions of the project board is to provide informal advice and guidance to the project manager as well as formal direction. The project manager should seek advice whenever necessary during the course of the project.

15.4 Activities

The activities within the directing a project process are project board oriented and are to:

- authorize initiation
- authorize the project
- authorize a stage or exception plan
- give ad hoc direction
- authorize project closure.

15.4.1 Authorize initiation

Projects take time and cost money to initiate, so the activities for initiation should be planned, monitored and controlled. The project board activity to authorize initiation ensures that such investment is worthwhile.

When a request to initiate a project is received from starting up a project, the project board must decide whether to allow the project to proceed to the initiation stage. This may be done at a formal project board meeting or without a formal meeting, as long as all members are in agreement, and the project manager is given documented instruction from the executive to proceed with initiation. The project board may appoint project assurance to undertake some of the reviewing and assessing actions (e.g. inspecting the initiation stage plan to confirm it is viable).

Figure 15.2 shows the inputs to, and outputs from, this activity.

PRINCE2 recommends the following actions:

- Review and approve the project brief:
  - confirm the project definition (including key milestones)
  - confirm the project approach
  - formally confirm the appointments to the project management team, and confirm that all members have agreed their roles.
- Review and approve the project product description:
  - confirm the customer's quality expectations
  - confirm the acceptance criteria.
- Verify that the outline business case demonstrates a viable project.
- Review and approve the stage plan for the initiation stage:
  - understand any risks that affect the decision to authorize the initiation stage
  - obtain or commit the resources needed by the stage plan for the initiation stage
  - ensure that adequate reporting and control mechanisms are in place for the initiation stage and set tolerances for it.

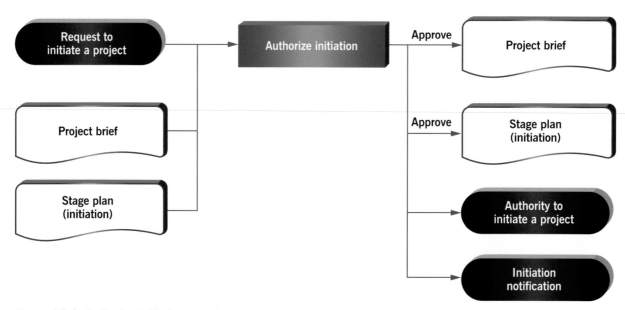

Figure 15.2 Authorize initiation: activity summary

- Inform all stakeholders and the **host site**s that the project is being initiated and request any necessary logistical support (e.g. communication facilities, equipment and any project support) sufficient for the initiation stage.
- Authorize the project manager to proceed with the initiation stage.

Table 15.1 shows the responsibilities for this activity.

Table 15.1 Authorize initiation: responsibilities

Product	Action	Corporate/ programme/ customer	Executive	Senior user	Senior supplier	Project manager	Team manager	Project assurance	Project support	Product description available
Project brief	Approve	(R)	A	A	A	(P)		R		A.19
Stage plan (initiation)	Approve		A	A	A	(P)		R		A.16

Key: P (producer) – responsible for product's production; R (reviewer) – ideally independent of production; A (approver) – confirms approval.

The complete list of responsibilities for each product is shown. Where a product is produced, reviewed or approved in another process, the responsibility is shown in parentheses, as in (P), (R) or (A).

15.4.2 Authorize the project

This activity will be triggered by a request from the project manager for authorization to deliver the project, and may be undertaken in parallel with authorizing a stage or exception plan (see section 15.4.3).

The objective of authorizing the project is to decide whether to proceed with the rest of the project. The project board has to confirm that:

- an adequate and suitable business case exists and that it shows a viable project
- the project plan and the benefits management approach are adequate to deliver the business case
- the project's approaches and controls support delivery of the project plan
- the mechanisms for measuring and reviewing the projected benefits are established and planned.

If the project is not authorized by the project board, then it should be prematurely closed (see Chapter 20).

The project board may appoint project assurance to undertake some of the reviewing and assessing actions (e.g. inspecting the communication management approach to confirm all stakeholders are covered).

Figure 15.3 shows the inputs to, and outputs from, this activity.

PRINCE2 recommends the following actions:

- Review and approve the PID:
  - confirm that the project definition is accurate and complete and that the project approach is achievable
  - confirm that lessons from previous similar projects have been reviewed and incorporated
  - confirm that the quality management approach is sufficient to ensure that the quality expectations will be met, and approve it
  - confirm that the procedures defined in the risk management approach are sufficient to keep the risks under control, and approve it. Confirm that there has been a review of the risks, and that risk responses for both threats and opportunities are appropriate and planned

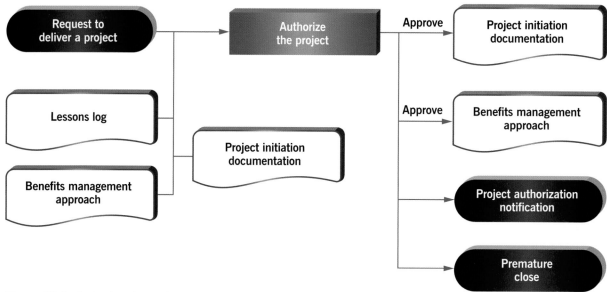

Figure 15.3 Authorize the project: activity summary

- confirm that the change control approach will adequately control the status (versions and variants) of the project's products, and approve it
- ensure that the stakeholder information needs and timing of communications, as defined in the communication management approach, are adequate, and approve it
- confirm that all members of the project management team have agreed their roles and agree any delegations of, and limits to, project board authority (e.g. to a change authority)
- ensure that the project controls are adequate for the nature of the project
- confirm the validity and achievability of the project plan (including any key milestones and proposed management stage structure), and approve it
- review and approve the product description(s)
- review the tolerances for the project provided by corporate, programme management or the customer to ensure they are appropriate and realistic
- obtain or commit the resources needed by the project (these will be released to the project manager management stage by management stage)
- confirm the proposals to tailor the corporate, programme management or customer project management method and any tailoring of PRINCE2
- verify that the business case demonstrates a viable project, and approve it
- confirm that the project remains aligned with the strategy of corporate, programme management or the customer.
- Review and approve the benefits management approach. Confirm it addresses all the expected benefits and meets the needs of corporate, programme management or the customer.
- Notify corporate, programme management or the customer and other interested parties that the project has been authorized.
- Authorize the project manager to deliver the project or instruct the project manager to close the project prematurely if it is decided not to proceed.

Table 15.2 shows the responsibilities for this activity.

Table 15.2 Authorize the project: responsibilities

Product	Action	Corporate/ programme/ customer	Executive	Senior user	Senior supplier	Project manager	Team manager	Project assurance	Project support	Product description available
Lessons log	Review		R	R	R	(P)		R		A.14
Project initiation documentation	Approve	R	A	A	A	(P)		R		A.20
Benefits management approach	Approve	A	A	A	A	(P)		R		A.1

Key: P (producer) – responsible for product's production; R (reviewer) – ideally independent of production; A (approver) – confirms approval.

The complete list of responsibilities for each product is shown. Where a product is produced, reviewed or approved in another process, the responsibility is shown in parentheses, as in (P), (R) or (A).

15.4.3 Authorize a stage or exception plan

It is important that a management stage starts only when the project board says it should. The project board authorizes a management stage by reviewing the performance of the current stage and approving the stage plan for the next stage. Approval of stage plans occurs at the end of every management stage except the last one.

If an exception has occurred during the management stage, the project board may request that the project manager produces an exception plan for project board approval. Only exceptions to stage plans or project plans need to be escalated for approval. Deviations from the project plan may need corporate, programme management or customer approval. Work package exceptions are managed by the project manager using the controlling a stage process (see Chapter 17). If approved, the exception plan will replace the plan that is in exception and will become the new baselined plan.

The project board may appoint project assurance to undertake some of the reviewing and assessing actions (e.g. inspecting the stage plan to confirm it is viable).

Figure 15.4 shows the inputs to, and outputs from, this activity.

PRINCE2 recommends the following end stage and exception assessment actions:

- Review and approve the end stage report:
  - ascertain the performance of the project to date, asking the project manager to explain any deviations from the approved plans and to provide a forecast of project performance for the remainder of the project
  - if required, include lessons from the lessons log. Ensure that the appropriate groups (e.g. corporate, programme management or the customer, or a centre of excellence) have been made aware of their responsibility for taking any recommendations forward
  - check the risk summary to ensure the exposure is still acceptable and that risk responses for both opportunities and threats are appropriate and planned
  - if there has been a phased handover of products during the management stage:
    - verify that **user acceptance** (including operations and maintenance) exists for each product
    - ensure that, where appropriate, the resulting changes in the business are supported and sustainable
    - confirm who should receive which follow-on action recommendation, if any, as summarized in the end stage report (in some instances it may be necessary to review the detailed recommendation for some of the follow-on action recommendations). Ensure that the appropriate groups (e.g. operations or maintenance) have been made aware of their responsibility for taking any recommendations forward.

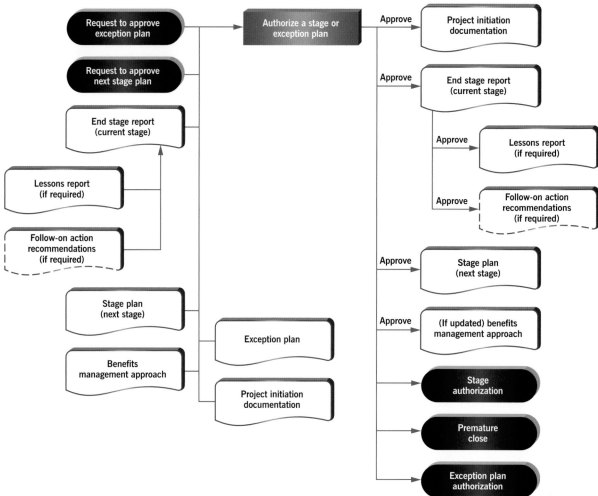

Figure 15.4 Authorize a stage or exception plan: activity summary

- Review the stage plan or exception plan for which the project manager is seeking approval:
  - confirm the validity and achievability of the stage plan or exception plan
  - review and approve any new product description(s)
  - confirm the validity and achievability of the project plan. If necessary, secure appropriate approvals from corporate, programme management or the customer
  - confirm the approaches and project controls in the (updated) PID are adequate for the remainder of the project
  - verify that the (updated) business case continues to demonstrate a viable project
  - review and approve the (updated) benefits management approach to ensure that any benefits planned to be achieved within the next management stage will be measured and reviewed
  - confirm that the project remains aligned with the strategy of corporate, programme management or the customer.
- Make a decision:
  - approve the plan(s) and authorize the project manager to proceed with the submitted plan(s):
    - obtain or commit the resources needed by the plan(s)
    - set tolerances for the plan being approved (for the final management stage, the project board should consider whether any residual tolerances from the previous management stages could be assigned to the plan or whether they are better held back in reserve)

- or ask the project manager to revise the rejected plan, giving guidance about the changes required to make it acceptable
- or instruct the project manager to initiate **premature closure** of the project.
- Communicate the status of the project to corporate, programme management or the customer and keep other interested parties informed about project progress (in accordance with the communication management approach).

Table 15.3 shows the responsibilities for this activity.

Table 15.3 Authorize a stage or exception plan: responsibilities

Product	Action	Corporate/ programme/ customer	Executive	Senior user	Senior supplier	Project manager	Team manager	Project assurance	Project support	Product description available
Specialist products	Confirm approval		A	A	A	(R)	(P)	(R)		
End stage report	Approve		A	A	A	(P)		R		A.9
Lessons report	Approve/distribute		A	R	R	(P)		R		A.15
Follow-on action recommendations	Approve/distribute		A	A	A	(P)		R		
Stage plan for the next stage	Approve		A	A	A	(P)		R		A.16
Exception plan	Approve		A	A	A	(P)		R		A.16
(Updated) project initiation documentation	Approve	(R)	A	A	A	(P)		R		A.20
(Updated) benefits management approach	Approve	A	A	R	R	(P)		R		A.1

Key: P (producer) – responsible for product's production; R (reviewer) – ideally independent of production; A (approver) – confirms approval.

The complete list of responsibilities for each product is shown. Where a product is produced, reviewed or approved in another process, the responsibility is shown in parentheses, as in (P), (R) or (A).

15.4.4 Give ad hoc direction

Project board members may offer informal guidance or respond to requests for advice at any time during a project. The need for consultation between the project manager and project board is likely to be particularly frequent during the initiation stage and when approaching management stage boundaries.

Ad hoc direction may be given collectively or by individual project board members. There are a variety of circumstances that might prompt ad hoc direction, including:

- responding to requests (e.g. when options need clarifying or where areas of conflict need resolving)
- responding to reports (e.g. highlight report, exception report, issue report)
- responding to external influences (e.g. changes in corporate priorities)
- project board members' individual concerns
- responding to changes in project board composition (which may also require corporate, programme management or customer approval).

It is also possible that corporate, programme management or the customer revises the project mandate in response to events external to the project, or instructs the project board to close the project. The project board has two primary options should corporate, programme management or the customer decide to change the project mandate.

The two options for the project board are to:

● treat it as a request for change (see Chapter 11), asking the project manager to replan the management stage and/or project

● stop, and restart the project by triggering premature closure (see Chapter 20). This may result in additional costs compared with the request-for-change option.

The project board may appoint project assurance to undertake some of the reviewing and assessing actions (e.g. inspecting a request for change to confirm that the impact has been adequately assessed). When making decisions, it is important to consider the impact on all stakeholders (as identified in the communication management approach).

Figure 15.5 shows the inputs to, and outputs from, this activity.

PRINCE2 recommends the following actions:

● In response to informal requests for advice and guidance:

  ● seek advice from corporate, programme management or the customer if necessary

  ● assist the project manager as required (this may include asking the project manager to produce an issue report and/or an exception report).

● In response to an escalated issue (see Chapter 11):

  ● seek advice from corporate, programme management or the customer if necessary

  ● make a decision within the project board's delegated limits of authority. This decision could be regarding:

    – a problem/concern Ask for an exception plan or provide guidance

    – a request for change Approve, defer, reject or ask for more information. Consider whether an exception plan is required

    – an off-specification Grant a concession, defer, reject or ask for more information. Consider whether an exception plan is required.

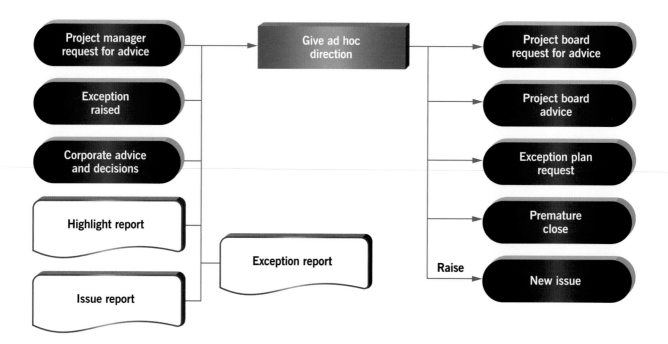

Figure 15.5 Give ad hoc direction: activity summary

- In response to an exception report (see Chapter 12):
  - seek advice from corporate, programme management or the customer if necessary
  - make a decision, within the project board's delegated limits of authority, to:
    - increase the tolerances that are forecast to be breached
    - instruct the project manager to produce an exception plan (stating what will be acceptable)
    - instruct the project manager to close the project prematurely
    - defer the exception for a fixed period of time. This is a useful response if there is low confidence in the forecast (that tolerances will be exceeded) or if the exception is contingent on a risk occurring.
- In response to the receipt of a highlight report (see Chapter 12):
  - review the highlight report to understand the status of the project
  - ensure that the project remains focused on the corporate, programme management or customer objectives set, and remains justified in accordance with its business case
  - ensure that the management stage is progressing according to plan
  - keep corporate, programme management or the customer and other interested parties informed about project progress, as defined by the communication management approach
  - take actions as necessary (e.g. ask the project manager to produce an issue report and/or an exception report).
- In response to advice and decisions from corporate, programme management or the customer:
  - ensure that the project management team is kept informed of external events that may affect it (e.g. advising the project manager of a change of project board personnel)
  - notify the project manager of any changes in the corporate, programme management or customer environment that may impact on the project, and ensure appropriate action is taken. This may involve:
    - raising an issue to the project manager
    - instructing the project manager to produce an exception plan
    - instructing the project manager to close the project prematurely.

Table 15.4 shows the responsibilities for this activity.

Table 15.4 Give ad hoc direction: responsibilities

Product	Action	Corporate/ programme/ customer	Executive	Senior user	Senior supplier	Project manager	Team manager	Project assurance	Project support	Product description available
Highlight report	Review		R	R	R	(P)		R		A.11
Exception report	Respond		R	R	R	(P)		R		A.10
New issue	Raise	P	P	P	P					

Key: P (producer) – responsible for product's production; R (reviewer) – ideally independent of production; A (approver) – confirms approval.

The complete list of responsibilities for each product is shown. Where a product is produced, reviewed or approved in another process, the responsibility is shown in parentheses, as in (P), (R) or (A).

15.4.5 Authorize project closure

The controlled close of a project is as important as the controlled start. There must be a point when the objectives in the original and current versions of the PID and project plan are assessed in order to understand:

- whether the objectives have been achieved
- how the project has deviated from its initial basis
- that the project has nothing more to contribute.

Without this approach, the project may never end; a project can become business as usual and the original focus on benefits will be lost.

Authorizing closure of the project is the last activity undertaken by the project board, prior to its own disbandment, and may require endorsement from corporate, programme management or the customer. The project board may appoint project assurance to undertake some of the reviewing and assessing actions (e.g. inspecting the end project report to confirm it is accurate).

Figure 15.6 shows the inputs to, and outputs from, this activity.

PRINCE2 recommends the following actions:

- Review the original and current versions of the PID to understand the project's initial baseline, and current approaches and controls.
- Review and approve the end project report to:
  - understand the project's actual performance against its initial basis, including a summary of any deviations from the approved plans

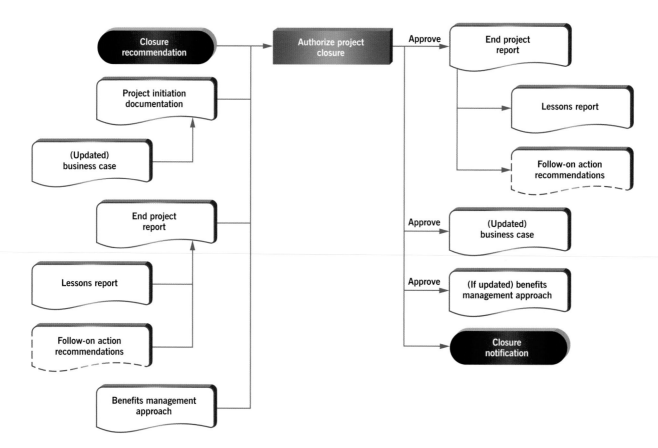

Figure 15.6 Authorize project closure: activity summary

- assess the choice of project approach

- confirm who should receive which follow-on action recommendation as summarized in the end project report (in some instances it may be necessary to review the detailed recommendation for some of the follow-on actions). Ensure that the appropriate groups (e.g. operations or maintenance) have been made aware of their responsibility for taking any recommended actions forward

- review the lessons log and agree lessons to include in the report. Ensure that the appropriate groups (e.g. corporate, programme management or the customer, or a centre of excellence) have been made aware of their responsibility for taking any recommendations forward

- verify that the handover of the project product was in accordance with user acceptance and **operational and maintenance acceptance** procedures. Ensure that, where appropriate, the resulting changes in the business are properly supported and sustainable.

- Ensure that post-project benefits reviews defined by the updated benefits management approach cover the performance of the project product in operational use in order to identify whether there have been any side-effects (beneficial or adverse).

- Review and gain approval for the updated benefits management approach, ensuring that it addresses the expected benefits that cannot yet be confirmed. As the benefits management approach includes resources beyond the life of the project, responsibility for the approach needs to transfer to corporate, programme management or the customer.

- Confirm the updated business case by comparing actual and forecast benefits, costs and risks against the outline business case that was used to justify the project (it may not be possible to confirm all the benefits as some will not be realized until after the project is closed).

- Review and issue a **project closure notification** in accordance with the communication management approach. The project board advises those who have provided the support infrastructure and resources for the project that these can be withdrawn. This should indicate a closing date for costs being charged to the project.

Table 15.5 shows the responsibilities for this activity.

Table 15.5 Authorize project closure: responsibilities

Product	Action	Corporate/ programme/ customer	Executive	Senior user	Senior supplier	Project manager	Team manager	Project assurance	Project support	Product description available
End project report	Approve		A	A	A	(P)		R		A.8
Lessons report	Distribute		A	A	A	(P)		R		A.15
Follow-on action recommendations	Distribute		A	A	A	(P)		R		
(Updated) business case	Confirm	R	A	R	R	(P)		R		A.2
(Updated) benefits management approach	Approve	A	A	R	R	(P)		R		A.1

Key: P (producer) – responsible for product's production; R (reviewer) – ideally independent of production; A (approver) – confirms approval.

The complete list of responsibilities for each product is shown. Where a product is produced, reviewed or approved in another process, the responsibility is shown in parentheses, as in (P), (R) or (A).

15.5 Tailoring guidelines

15.5.1 General considerations

After approval to initiate the project has been confirmed, care should be taken to ensure the integrity of the interface to the initiating a project, managing a stage boundary and closing a project processes when the formal decision to start the next management stage or close the project is made.

The degree of formality may differ in different circumstances provided decisions are explicit and traceable, ranging from verbal advice and decisions to those which are formally documented in email, meeting minutes or other traceable formats.

15.5.2 Tailoring the roles in directing a project

All the activities in this process are the accountability of the executive but the actual work may be done by others. It should, however, be noted that the project manager should not take any decisions or give approval or direction on matters which are the responsibility of the executive; the roles of executive and project manager must be kept separate.

In some contexts the decision at stage boundaries, particularly when funds are released for the next stage, may be taken by a role at a higher level than the executive, such as in a programme, portfolio or organization context. For this reason the 'authorize stage or exception plan' activity may be treated as a separate process in a tailored PRINCE2 process model.

For more guidance on roles, see Chapter 7.

15.5.3 Common situations

15.5.3.1 Directing a simple project

Directing a simple project is likely to be less formal than for a larger project. If the project is a two-stage project, there will be no decisions requested from managing stage boundaries except when an exception plan is needed.

15.5.3.2 Directing projects when using an agile approach

When using an agile approach, direction and decisions need to happen quickly. It is vital to ensure that management by exception is operating effectively for the whole project team as this creates an environment conducive to the agile way of working where people are empowered and self-organized. In terms of progress reporting, the project board should expect emphasis to be placed on the quality and amount of the requirement being delivered as, for agile delivery, times and cost are fixed. Information flows may be frequent and informal; for example, the project board may attend reviews and demos so that decision-making can be based more on information gathered from the team as opposed to formally reported.

15.5.3.3 Directing a project from a supplier perspective

If a supplier manages their contracted work as a PRINCE2 project, the executive for this project looks after the interests of the supplier organization. In this case, the supplier's project board might comprise the senior manager within the supplier's organization whose remit covers the bid/work (acting as the executive); the customer account manager (acting as the senior user); and a resource manager (acting as senior supplier).

The supplier might also provide a person to act as senior supplier on the project board of the customer's project (e.g. the account manager).

In the early stages of a project, it may not be possible to appoint a contractor or supplier representative to the role of senior supplier on the project board, simply because no supplier or contractor has been selected. In such circumstances a person should be appointed to look after their interests until such an appointment can be made.

Some projects have a number of suppliers and so there may be more than one senior supplier role and/or a person nominated to look after the interests of a number of suppliers.

15.5.3.4 Directing a project within a programme

The choice of individuals to undertake the project board roles is open. For example, the executive may be the same person as the programme manager. The key is that each role holder has no conflicts of interest and it is clear who they report to in the respective programme and project organization structures; accountabilities with respect to governance should be explicit.

Initiating a project

This chapter covers:

- reviewing and confirming the business justification
- defining the approaches for managing risk, quality, benefits and communication
- setting up the project controls
- setting up the first stage (agreeing the PID and plan)
- guidelines for tailoring products and roles

16 Initiating a project

16.1 Purpose

The purpose of the initiating a project process is to establish solid foundations for the project, enabling the organization to understand the work that needs to be done to deliver the project product before committing to a significant spend.

16.2 Objective

The objective of the initiating a project process is to ensure that there is a common understanding of:

- the reasons for doing the project, the benefits expected and the associated risks
- the scope of what is to be done and the products to be delivered
- how and when the project product will be delivered and at what cost
- who is to be involved in the project decision-making
- how the quality required will be achieved
- how baselines will be established and controlled
- how risks, issues and changes will be identified, assessed and controlled
- how progress will be monitored and controlled
- who needs information, in what format and at what time
- how the corporate, programme management or customer method will be tailored to suit the project.

16.3 Context

Figure 16.1 provides an overview of initiating a project.

Initiating a project is aimed at laying down the foundations in order to achieve a successful project. Specifically, all parties must be clear on what the project is intended to achieve, why it is needed, how the outcome is to be achieved and what their responsibilities are, so that there can be genuine commitment to it.

The initiating a project process enables the project board, via the directing a project process (see Chapter 15), to decide whether or not the project is sufficiently aligned with corporate, programme management or customer objectives to authorize its continuation.

If, instead, the organization proceeds directly from starting up a project (see Chapter 14) to controlling a stage (see Chapter 17), then it may risk committing significant financial resources to a project without fully understanding how its objectives will be achieved.

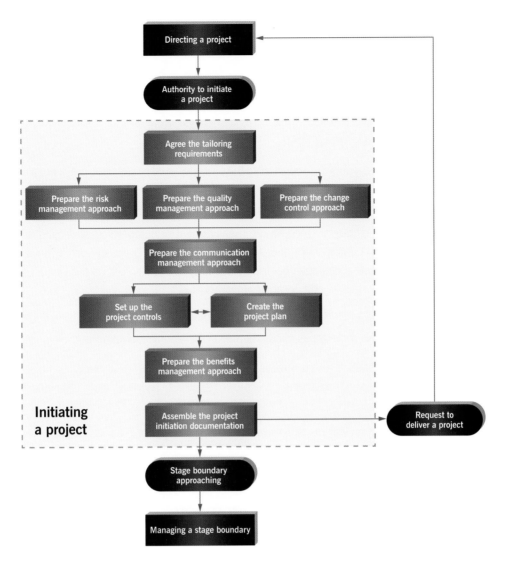

Figure 16.1 Overview of initiating a project

All activities within the initiating a project process need further consideration if the relationship between the customer and the supplier is a commercial one (e.g. the reasons for undertaking the project as defined in the supplier's business case may be different from those defined in the customer's business case).

During the initiating a project process the project manager will be creating the suite of management products required for the level of control specified by the project board. The project manager should have agreed (as part of the initiation stage plan) the means by which the project board will review and approve the management products; the two extremes are one at a time or all at once.

16.4 Activities

The activities within the initiating a project process are project manager oriented and are to:

- agree the tailoring requirements
- prepare the risk management approach
- prepare the change control approach

- prepare the quality management approach
- prepare the communication management approach
- set up the project controls
- create the project plan
- prepare the benefits management approach
- assemble the project initiation documentation.

The activities to establish the approaches for the project may be executed in parallel, but it is recommended that the communication management approach is completed last as it will need to include any communications required by the other approaches.

The approaches are derived from corporate, programme management or customer strategies, standards or practices that the project needs to comply with, and the customer's quality expectations captured in the project product description. When the approaches have been defined, it is possible to set up the project controls and create the project plan. These are parallel and iterative activities as:

- each control will need time and resources to operate, which will need to be documented in the project plan
- there may be additional controls required as products and activities are identified in the project plan.

After the controls have been established and a project plan created, it is then possible to complete the business case because forecast time and costs of developing the project product, and managing the project, are now fully understood.

The final activity in the initiating a project process is to assemble the project initiation documentation. This is a compilation of all the documentation developed during initiation that will be used to gain project board approval to proceed.

16.4.1 Agree the tailoring requirements

The project manager may need to tailor how the project is directed and managed in order to recognize internal and external factors that affect the way in which the project is delivered. Any deviations from the organization's standard project management approach must be documented and agreed.

Figure 16.2 shows the inputs to, and outputs from, this activity. For more details on tailoring, see sections 4.1 and 4.3.

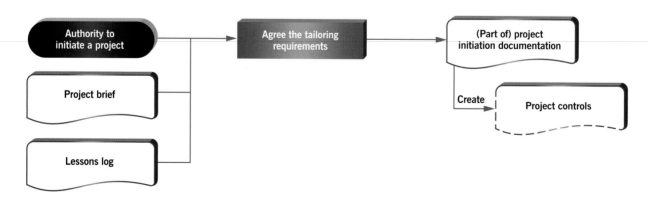

Figure 16.2 Agree the tailoring requirements: activity summary

PRINCE2 recommends the following actions:

- Review the project brief to understand the outline tailoring approach (if defined).
- Seek lessons from similar previous projects, corporate, programme management or the customer, and external organizations, related to how tailoring was applied.
- Define the tailoring as part of the PID and create initial project controls.
- Consult with project assurance to check that any proposed tailoring will meet the needs of the project board and/or corporate, programme management or the customer.
- Seek project board approval for any tailoring (although they may prefer to review it later as part of the PID).

Table 16.1 shows the responsibilities for this activity.

Table 16.1 Agree the tailoring requirements: responsibilities

Product	Action	Corporate/ programme/ customer	Executive	Senior user	Senior supplier	Project manager	Team manager	Project assurance	Project support	Product description available
Project brief	Approve	(R)	(A)	(A)	(A)	(P)		R		A.19
Lessons log	Review		R	R	R	R		R		A.14
Proposed tailoring requirements	Approve		A	A	A	P		R		
(Part of) project initiation documentation	Assemble		(A)	(A)	(A)	P		R		A.20
Project controls	Create		(A)	(A)	(A)	P		R		

Key: P (producer) – responsible for product's production; R (reviewer) – ideally independent of production; A (approver) – confirms approval.

The complete list of responsibilities for each product is shown. Where a product is produced, reviewed or approved in another process, the responsibility is shown in parentheses, as in (P), (R) or (A).

16.4.2 Prepare the risk management approach

The risk management approach describes the goals of applying risk management, the procedure that will be adopted, the roles and responsibilities, the risk tolerances, the timing of risk management activities, the tools and techniques that will be used and the reporting requirements. For more on risk management, see Chapter 10.

Figure 16.3 shows the inputs to, and outputs from, this activity.

PRINCE2 recommends the following actions:

- Review the tailoring approach included in the PID and its implications for risk management.
- Review the project brief to understand whether any corporate, programme management or customer strategies, standards or practices relating to risk management need to be applied by the project.
- Seek lessons from similar previous projects, corporate, programme management or the customer, and external organizations related to risk management. Some of these may already have been captured in the lessons log.
- Review the daily log for any issues and risks related to risk management.
- Define the risk management approach.
- Consult with project assurance to check that the proposed risk management approach meets the needs of the project board and/or corporate, programme management or the customer.

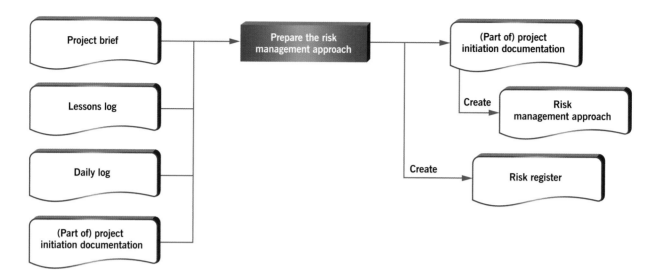

Figure 16.3 Prepare the risk management approach: activity summary

- Create the risk register in accordance with the risk management approach, and populate it with any risks from the daily log.
- Seek project board approval for the risk management approach (although the project board may prefer to review it later as part of the PID).

Table 16.2 shows the responsibilities for this activity.

Table 16.2 Prepare the risk management approach: responsibilities

Product	Action	Corporate/ programme/ customer	Executive	Senior user	Senior supplier	Project manager	Team manager	Project assurance	Project support	Product description available
Risk management approach	Create		(A)	(A)	(A)	P		R		A.24
Risk register	Create and populate					A		R	P	A.25

Key: P (producer) – responsible for product's production; R (reviewer) – ideally independent of production; A (approver) – confirms approval.

The complete list of responsibilities for each product is shown. Where a product is produced, reviewed or approved in another process, the responsibility is shown in parentheses, as in (P), (R) or (A).

16.4.3 Prepare the change control approach

Change control is essential for the project to maintain control over its management and specialist products.

The level of control required will vary from project to project. The maximum level of control possible is determined by breaking down the project's products until the level is reached at which a component can be independently installed, replaced or modified. However, the level of control exercised will be influenced by the importance of the project and the complexity of the relationship between its products.

The change control approach will define the format and composition of the records that need to be maintained (see Appendix A, section A.3). For more details on change control, see Chapter 11.

Figure 16.4 shows the inputs to, and outputs from, this activity.

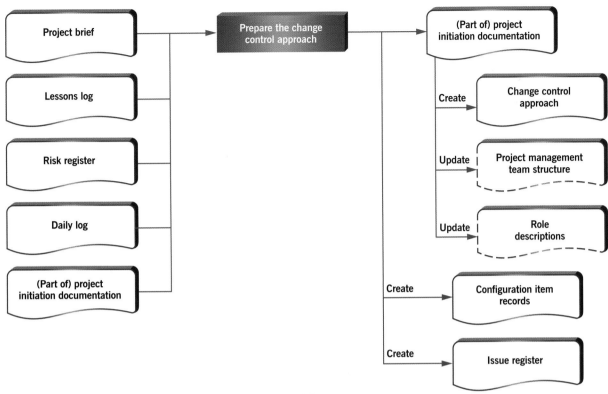

Figure 16.4 Prepare the change control approach: activity summary

PRINCE2 recommends the following actions:

- Review the tailoring approach included in the PID and its implications for change control.
- Review the project brief to understand whether any corporate, programme management or customer strategies, standards or practices relating to change control need to be applied (including any that are contractual requirements).
- Seek lessons from similar previous projects, corporate, programme management or the customer, and external organizations related to change control. Some of these may already have been captured in the lessons log.
- Review the risk register and daily log for risks and issues associated with change control.
- Define the change control approach.
- Consult with project assurance to check that the proposed change control approach meets the needs of the project board and/or corporate, programme management or the customer.
- Create the initial configuration item records, if used.
- Create the issue register and consider whether any issues already captured in the daily log need to be managed formally and therefore transferred.
- If any new risks or issues are identified (or existing ones have changed), update the risk register, issue register and/or daily log.
- Seek project board approval for the change control approach (the project board may prefer to review it later as part of the PID).

Table 16.3 shows the responsibilities for this activity.

Table 16.3 Prepare the change control approach: responsibilities

Product	Action	Corporate/ programme/ customer	Executive	Senior user	Senior supplier	Project manager	Team manager	Project assurance	Project support	Product description available
Change control approach	Create		(A)	(A)	(A)	P		R		A.3
(Initial) configuration item records	Create					A		R	P	A.6
Issue register	Create and populate					A				A.12

Key: P (producer) – responsible for product's production; R (reviewer) – ideally independent of production; A (approver) – confirms approval.

The complete list of responsibilities for each product is shown. Where a product is produced, reviewed or approved in another process, the responsibility is shown in parentheses, as in (P), (R) or (A).

16.4.4 Prepare the quality management approach

A key success factor of any project is that it delivers what the user expects and finds acceptable. This will only happen if these expectations are both stated and agreed at the beginning of the project, together with the standards to be used and the means of assessing their achievement. The purpose of the quality management approach is to ensure such agreements are captured and maintained. For more details on quality management, see Chapter 8.

Figure 16.5 shows the inputs to, and outputs from, this activity.

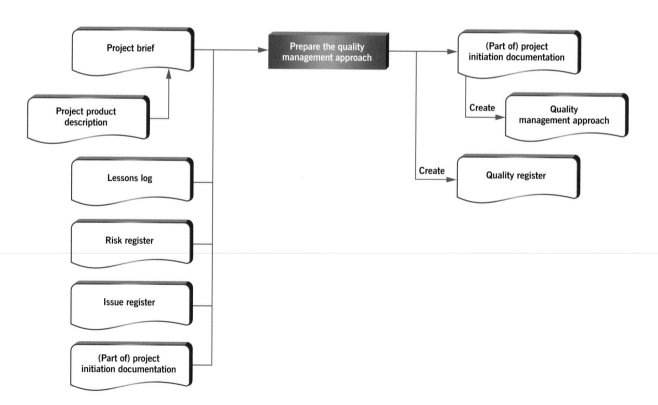

Figure 16.5 Prepare the quality management approach: activity summary

PRINCE2 recommends the following actions:

- Review the tailoring approach included in the PID and its implications for quality management.

- Review the project product description to understand the customer's quality expectations and to check that the project's acceptance criteria are sufficiently defined.

- Review the project brief to understand whether any corporate, programme management or customer strategies, standards or practices relating to quality management need to be applied by the project (in particular whether the customer and/or supplier has an existing quality management system that should be applied to aspects of the project).

- Seek lessons from similar previous projects, corporate, programme management or the customer, and external organizations related to quality management. Some of these may already have been captured in the lessons log.

- Review the risk register and issue register for issues and risks associated with quality management.

- Define the quality management approach.

- Consult with project assurance to check that the proposed quality management approach meets the needs of the project board and/or corporate, programme management or the customer.

- Create a quality register in readiness to record details of all quality activities.

- If any new risks or issues are identified (or existing ones have changed), update the risk register, issue register and/or daily log.

- Seek project board approval for the quality management approach (although the project board may prefer to review it later as part of the PID).

Table 16.4 shows the responsibilities for this activity.

Table 16.4 Prepare the quality management approach: responsibilities

Product	Action	Corporate/ programme/ customer	Executive	Senior user	Senior supplier	Project manager	Team manager	Project assurance	Project support	Product description available
Quality management approach	Create		(A)	(A)	(A)	P		R		A.22
Quality register	Create					A		R	P	A.23

Key: P (producer) – responsible for product's production; R (reviewer) – ideally independent of production; A (approver) – confirms approval.

The complete list of responsibilities for each product is shown. Where a product is produced, reviewed or approved in another process, the responsibility is shown in parentheses, as in (P), (R) or (A).

16.4.5 Prepare the communication management approach

The communication management approach addresses both internal and external communications. It should contain details of how the project management team will send information to, and receive information from, the wider organization(s) involved with, or affected by, the project. In particular, if the project is part of a programme, details should be given on how information is to be fed to the programme.

If a formal stakeholder engagement procedure is needed (such as that described in section 7.3.9), this should also be documented as part of the communication management approach and should record the types of stakeholder, desired relationships and key messages, approaches for communication, and methods for evaluating the success of communications.

Figure 16.6 shows the inputs to, and outputs from, this activity.

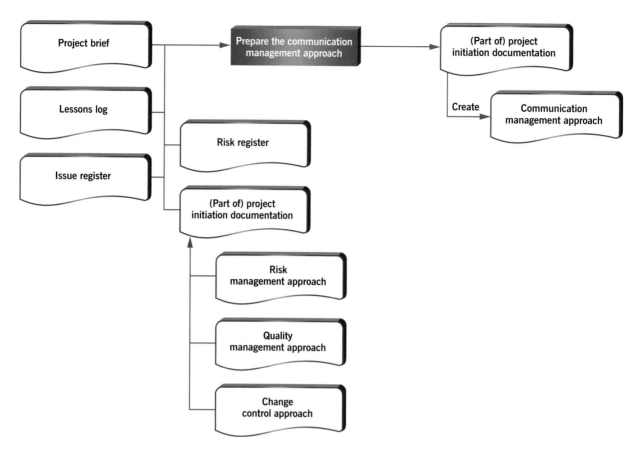

Figure 16.6 Prepare the communication management approach: activity summary

PRINCE2 recommends the following actions:

- Review the tailoring approach included in the PID and its implications for communication management.
- Review the project brief to understand whether any corporate, programme management or customer strategies, standards or practices relating to communication management need to be applied by the project.
- Seek communication management lessons from previous projects, corporate, programme management or the customer, and external organizations. Some may already have been captured in the lessons log.
- Review the risk register and issue register for risks and issues associated with communication management.
- Identify and/or review stakeholders, and consult them for their information needs:
  - identify desired relationships
  - clarify key communication messages
  - determine desired outcomes from successful communications.
- Establish the information needs associated with the quality management approach, the risk management approach and the change control approach.
- Define the communication management approach.
- Consult with project assurance to check that the proposed communication management approach meets the needs of the project board and/or corporate, programme management or the customer.
- If any new risks or issues are identified (or existing ones have changed), update the risk register, issue register and/or daily log.
- Seek project board approval for the communication management approach (although the project board may prefer to review it later as part of the PID).

Table 16.5 Prepare the communication management approach: responsibilities

Product	Action	Corporate/ programme/ customer	Executive	Senior user	Senior supplier	Project manager	Team manager	Project assurance	Project support	Product description available
Communication management approach	Create		(A)	(A)	(A)	P		R		A.5

Key: P (producer) – responsible for product's production; R (reviewer) – ideally independent of production; A (approver) – confirms approval.

The complete list of responsibilities for each product is shown. Where a product is produced, reviewed or approved in another process, the responsibility is shown in parentheses, as in (P), (R) or (A).

Table 16.5 shows the responsibilities for this activity.

16.4.6 Set up the project controls

The level of control required by the project board after initiation needs to be agreed and the mechanism for such controls needs to be established, as does the level of control required by the project manager of the work to be undertaken by team managers. Project controls enable the project to be managed in an effective and efficient manner that is consistent with the scale, risks, complexity and importance of the project. Effective project controls are a prerequisite for managing by exception. Project controls can include:

● the frequency and format of communication between the project management levels (see Chapter 7)

● the number of management stages and hence end stage assessments (see Chapter 9)

● mechanisms to capture and analyse issues and changes (see Chapter 11)

● mechanisms to monitor tolerances and escalate exceptions (see Chapter 12)

● tolerances for delegated authority (see Chapter 12)

● how delegated authority from one level of management to another will be monitored (see Chapter 12).

Many of these controls will have been defined in the project's approaches but not necessarily set up. The focus of this activity is to establish such controls and to make sure that they make sense as a coherent set. Figure 16.7 shows the inputs to, and outputs from, this activity.

PRINCE2 recommends the following actions:

● Review the tailoring approach included in the PID and its implications for project controls.

● Review the quality management approach, change control approach, risk management approach and communication management approach to identify which controls need to be established.

● Actively seek lessons from similar previous projects, corporate, programme management or the customer, and external organizations related to project controls. Some may have been captured in the lessons log.

● Review the risk register and issue register for risks and issues associated with project controls. The aggregated set of risks will have an impact on the scale and rigour of control activities.

● Confirm and document the management stage boundaries required to provide the appropriate level of control.

● Allocate the various levels of decision-making required within the project to the most appropriate project management level. Establish any decision-making procedures that may be appropriate, possibly by tailoring procedures within an existing quality management system or other standard procedures.

● Incorporate the agreed decision-making authority and responsibility into the project management team structure and role descriptions where appropriate; this may include finalizing any roles not previously allocated, re-allocating roles previously filled and, if necessary, redesigning the project management team.

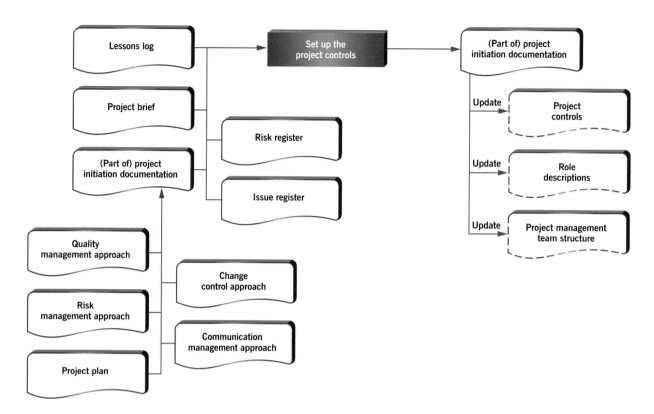

Figure 16.7 Set up the project controls: activity summary

- Confirm the tolerances for the project and the escalation procedures (from team managers to project manager, project manager to project board, and project board to corporate, programme management or the customer).
- Summarize the project controls in the PID.
- Consult with project assurance to check that the proposed project controls are consistent with the nature of the project and meet the needs of the project board and/or corporate, programme management or the customer.
- If any new risks or issues are identified (or existing ones have changed), update the risk register, issue register and/or daily log.
- Seek project board approval for the project controls (the board may review them later as part of the PID).

Table 16.6 shows the responsibilities for this activity.

Table 16.6 Set up the project controls: responsibilities

Product	Action	Corporate/ programme/ customer	Executive	Senior user	Senior supplier	Project manager	Team manager	Project assurance	Project support	Product description available
Project controls	Update		(A)	(A)	(A)	P		R		
Role descriptions	Update		(A)	(A)	(A)	P		R		
Project management team structure	Update		(A)	(A)	(A)	P				

Key: P (producer) – responsible for product's production; R (reviewer) – ideally independent of production; A (approver) – confirms approval.

The complete list of responsibilities for each product is shown. Where a product is produced, reviewed or approved in another process, the responsibility is shown in parentheses, as in (P), (R) or (A).

16.4.7 Create the project plan

Before committing to major expenditure on the project, the timescale and resource requirements must be established. This information is held in the project plan and is needed so that the benefits management approach can be prepared and the project board can control the project.

Planning is not an activity that the project manager performs in isolation but, rather, something that should be done with close involvement of the user(s) and supplier(s). It is often useful to hold planning workshops to help identify all the products required, their details and the dependencies between them.

For more details on planning, see Chapter 9.

Figure 16.8 shows the inputs to, and outputs from, this activity.

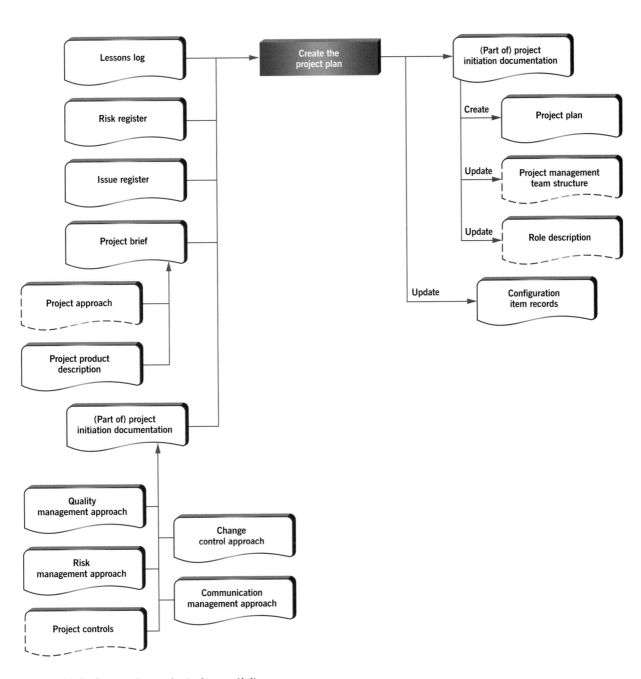

Figure 16.8 Create the project plan: activity summary

PRINCE2 recommends the following actions:

- Review the project brief to:
  - understand what the project is to deliver and check for any predetermined milestones as defined in the project brief
  - check whether there are any corporate, programme management or customer strategies, standards or practices relating to planning that the project needs to follow
  - check understanding of any prerequisites, external dependencies, constraints and assumptions documented in the project brief
  - check understanding of the selected solution.
- Review the tailoring approach included in the PID and its implications for planning.
- Seek lessons from similar previous projects, corporate, programme management or the customer, and external organizations related to planning. Some of these may already have been captured in the lessons log.
- Review the risk register and issue register for risks and issues associated with planning.
- Decide on the format and presentation of the project plan, given the audience for the plan and how it will be used (e.g. is it sufficient to use a product checklist for presenting the plan to the project board?). See the product description for a plan in Appendix A, section A.16, for more information.
- Identify any planning and control tools to be used by the project.
- Choose the method(s) of estimating for the project's plans.
- Review the quality management approach, risk management approach, change control approach and communication management approach to understand the resources, standards, methods and costs for the work to be carried out.
- Create a product breakdown structure for the project product and its major components, write product descriptions for these, and devise a product flow diagram; include them all in the project plan. Identify the arrangements for the transition of the project product into operational use. If the project product is likely to require maintenance when operational, then plan for a suitable service agreement or contract to be drawn up between the support group and the user. In such instances, it will be necessary to include any agreement as a product in the project plan.
- Consider whether the project product description needs to be updated (e.g. if the understanding of the acceptance criteria has changed or been refined in the course of initiating the project).
- Create or update the configuration item records, if used, for each product to be delivered by the plan.
- Identify and confirm resources required. Confirm the selected people's availability, their acceptance of these roles and their commitment to carry them out. See Chapter 7 for more details.
- Identify the activities, resources and timings for the project controls and include them in the plan.
- Document the project plan.
- Consult with project assurance to check that the proposed project plan meets the needs of the project board and/or corporate, programme management or the customer.
- If any new risks or issues are identified (or existing ones have changed), update the risk register, issue register and/or daily log.
- Seek project board approval for the project plan (although the project board may prefer to review it later as part of the PID).

Table 16.7 shows the responsibilities for this activity.

Table 16.7 Create the project plan: responsibilities

Product	Action	Corporate/ programme/ customer	Executive	Senior user	Senior supplier	Project manager	Team manager	Project assurance	Project support	Product description available
Project plan	Create		(A)	(A)	(A)	P		R		A.16
Product descriptions	Create		(A)	(A)	(A)	P		R		A.17
Configuration item records	Create/ update					A		R	P	A.6
Project management team structure	Update		(A)	(A)	(A)	P		R		
Role descriptions	Update		(A)	(A)	(A)	P		R		

Key: P (producer) – responsible for product's production; R (reviewer) – ideally independent of production; A (approver) – confirms approval.

The complete list of responsibilities for each product is shown. Where a product is produced, reviewed or approved in another process, the responsibility is shown in parentheses, as in (P), (R) or (A).

16.4.8 Prepare the benefits management approach

The outline business case produced during starting up a project needs to be updated to reflect the estimated time and costs, as determined by the project plan, and the aggregated risks from the updated risk register.

The detailed business case will be used by the project board to authorize the project and provides the basis of the ongoing check that the project remains viable. For more details on business justification, see Chapter 6.

Figure 16.9 shows the inputs to, and outputs from, this activity.

PRINCE2 recommends the following actions:

● Review the project brief to check whether there are any corporate, programme management or customer requirements for the format and content of a business case.

● Seek lessons from similar previous projects, corporate, programme management or the customer, and external organizations related to business case development. Some of these may already have been captured in the lessons log.

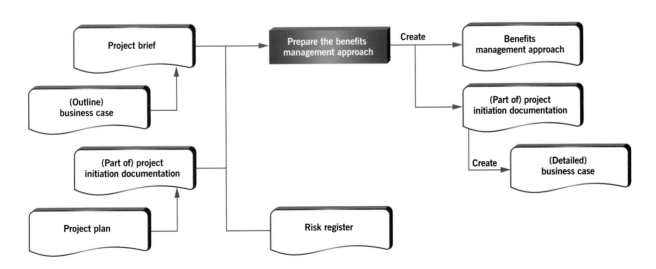

Figure 16.9 Prepare the benefits management approach: activity summary

- Create a more detailed business case with the additional detail gained, namely:
  - the costs and timescale as calculated in the project plan
  - the major risks that affect the viability and achievability of the project (from the risk register)
  - the benefits to be gained
  - the tolerances permitted for each of the benefits.
- Create the benefits management approach:
  - review the tailoring approach, as included in the PID, and its implications for benefits management
  - review the business case and check understanding of the benefits expected of the project
  - identify the management actions required to ensure that outcomes are likely to be achieved
  - identify how the realization of each benefit/dis-benefit is to be measured and capture the current baseline measures
  - identify the timing of benefits reviews (most likely to align with management stage boundaries)
  - if the project is part of a programme, the benefits management approach may be created, maintained and executed at the programme level.
- If any new risks or issues are identified (or existing ones have changed), update the risk register, issue register and/or daily log.
- Consult with project assurance to check that the proposed business case and benefits management approach meet the needs of the project board and/or corporate, programme management or the customer.
- Seek project board approval for the business case and benefits management approach (although the project board may prefer to review them later as part of the PID).

Table 16.8 shows the responsibilities for this activity.

Table 16.8 Prepare the benefits management approach: responsibilities

Product	Action	Corporate/ programme/ customer	Executive	Senior user	Senior supplier	Project manager	Team manager	Project assurance	Project support	Product description available
Benefits management approach	Create	(A)	(A)	(A)	(A)	P		R		A.1
(Detailed) business case	Create	(R)	(A)	(A)	(A)	P		R		A.2

Key: P (producer) – responsible for product's production; R (reviewer) – ideally independent of production; A (approver) – confirms approval.

The complete list of responsibilities for each product is shown. Where a product is produced, reviewed or approved in another process, the responsibility is shown in parentheses, as in (P), (R) or (A).

16.4.9 Assemble the project initiation documentation (PID)

There needs to be a focal point at which all information relating to the 'what, why, who, how, where, when and how much' of the project is:

- gathered for agreement by the key stakeholders
- available for guidance and information for those involved in the project.

This information is collated into the PID. The PID is an aggregation of many of the management products created during initiation and used to gain authorization for the project to proceed. It is not necessarily (and rarely) a single document, but a collection of documents or other forms of information (such as flip-charts, data in software tools, etc.).

The version of the PID created during the initiating a project process, and used to gain authorization for the project to proceed, should be placed under change control. It will be used later as a means to compare the project's actual performance against the original forecasts that formed the basis of approval.

Figure 16.10 shows the inputs to, and outputs from, this activity.

PRINCE2 recommends the following actions:

- Extract and, if necessary, revise information from the project brief.
- Include or reference information in the:
  - project's management team structure and role descriptions
  - business case
  - quality management approach
  - change control approach
  - risk management approach
  - communication management approach
  - project plan.

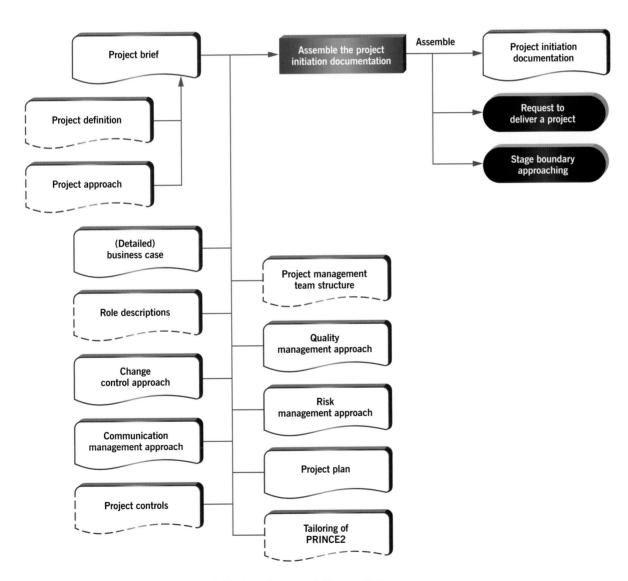

Figure 16.10 Assemble the project initiation documentation: activity summary

- Include or reference the project controls and summarize how the project has tailored PRINCE2.
- Assemble the project initiation documentation.
- Carry out a cross-check of the information in the various elements to ensure that they are compatible.
- Consult with project assurance to check that the assembled PID meets the needs of the project board and/or corporate, programme management or the customer.
- Prepare for the next management stage (which triggers the managing a stage boundary process).
- Request authority from the project board to deliver the project.

Table 16.9 shows the responsibilities for this activity.

Table 16.9 Assemble the project initiation documentation: responsibilities

Product	Action	Corporate/ programme/ customer	Executive	Senior user	Senior supplier	Project manager	Team manager	Project assurance	Project support	Product description available
Project initiation documentation	Assemble		(A)	(A)	(A)	P		R		A.20

Key: P (producer) – responsible for product's production; R (reviewer) – ideally independent of production; A (approver) – confirms approval.

The complete list of responsibilities for each product is shown. Where a product is produced, reviewed or approved in another process, the responsibility is shown in parentheses, as in (P), (R) or (A).

16.5 Tailoring guidelines

16.5.1 General considerations

The activities in this process may be combined, split or run concurrently to suit the project's circumstances.

The number of management products created in this process can look daunting and, together, may imply a level of detail that is not always needed. This process lays the foundation and it is here that tailoring for the project is primarily decided.

Tailoring is needed to suit a project's circumstances but it may not always be obvious, at the start of initiation, what the relevant factors are. At such an early stage in the project, there may not be enough information; tailoring needs will emerge as the initiation work progresses. For this reason, it is better to start 'simple' and then elaborate if needed, rather than create a management environment suitable for a hypothetical major project.

Some projects are too complex to have a full definition of the project's output (and hence a project's final products) agreed by the end of this process. In such cases, it is common to have a project lifecycle with a number of investigative stages to look at options and choose a solution. In these cases, the initiating a project process is only used at the start of the first stage, to set up the management and control environment.

16.5.2 Tailoring products in initiating a project

Just because PRINCE2 has separate management products in this process, it does not mean each management product is reflected in a discrete and separate document or even as a document at all, where information and collaborative systems are used.

Table 16.10 relates to the **baseline management product**s which are created in this process, whereas Table 16.11 relates to the records management products.

Table 16.10 Guidelines for tailoring baseline management products in initiating a project

Management product	Tailoring guidelines
PID, comprising: ● detailed business case ● risk management ● quality management ● change control ● communication management ● project plan ● project controls ● tailoring of PRINCE2	The PID may be a single document which includes all the components, a set of separate documents or any combination of documents and data. Change control may be known by other names in some industries/environments (e.g. asset management or parts management). The project plan may be informal or formal, depending on the context. It may be a single document which includes the project product description, product descriptions and benefits management approach. The project plan may include components in any format commensurate with the complexity of the project, with views ranging from a simple list of accountabilities, products, activities and dates, Gantt charts or product backlog. The plan may be held totally or partially within a planning tool(s).
Benefits management approach	The benefits management approach may be combined with the detailed business case, either in the body of the document or as an appendix.

Table 16.11 Guidelines for tailoring records management products in initiating a project

Management product	Tailoring guidelines
Risk register	The risk register may be a part of a workbook containing issues, assumptions and decisions.
Issue register	The issue register may be a part of a workbook containing issues, assumptions and decisions. As issues do not all result in changes, the issue register may be split into a change register (for recording and tracking change requests) and an issue register for all other issues, such as suggestions, concerns or queries. Similarly, 'off-specification' issues may also be held in a separate log.
Quality register	The amount of information included in the quality register can vary considerably, depending on the extent to which quality metrics (e.g. 'defect counts') need to be analysed for process improvement purposes.

16.5.3 Tailoring roles in initiating a project

This manual shows the creation of these management products as the responsibility of the project manager. Project support may be responsible for some supporting products, but in all cases the project manager is responsible to the executive for how the project is run. The project manager may therefore assign whoever is appropriate to the tasks. Often support may be provided by a higher-level programme office or similar.

For more guidance on roles, see Chapter 7.

16.5.4 Common situations

16.5.4.1 Initiating a simple project

Initiating a simple project is likely to be less formal than for a larger project, with management products combined into a small number of documents. The project manager may also be acting as a team manager for one or more work packages.

16.5.4.2 Initiating projects when using an agile approach

At the start of the project it may not be certain that an agile delivery approach is appropriate for some or all of the specialist products. It is during the initiating a project process that the decision is likely to be made on what parts of a project are best approached using agile and which not. Agile is more likely to be appropriate when the end product needs to be developed iteratively, provided the project management team understand the approach and implement a control system which deals with a more volatile environment.

The project product description (and the business case) should be defined with more focus on how the outcome can be described so that the outputs can evolve during the project. If the project product description is based only on the solution, there is more likely to be a focus on this rather than the value to be delivered.

Product descriptions can be written in the form of epics or user stories as long as they meet the requirements of the product description outline. These then represent the project's 'requirements'.

The mapping of existing agile roles to the PRINCE2 roles should be defined and understood (e.g. how the team manager role will be fulfilled).

Levels of uncertainty need to be explicitly stated as these may affect the choice of agile techniques such as the use of prototyping, spikes or experiments and the choice of how long to make the management stages and the timeboxes within them.

16.5.4.3 Initiating a project from a supplier perspective

Some of the initiating a project process activities will be undertaken pre-contract as the supplier will need to formulate the approaches, plans and controls in order to assess the viability and desirability of the proposed contract, together with the costs and prices of the proposed solution. The initiating a project process is not completed, however, until contract negotiation has concluded and the customer's project board authorizes the project.

On large projects, some suppliers may be identified during the course of the project and their contracts negotiated subsequently. The project board will have to allocate a budget, with defined tolerances, to account for these contracts.

16.5.4.4 Initiating a project within a programme

All the guidance provided above is applicable to a project within a programme. The main difference is that the programme manager may prescribe or constrain the project manager's choices. In some cases, the PID (or parts of it, such as the detailed business case) might be produced by a member of the programme team, and may even exist in detail prior to initiating the project or be included in the programme's business case.

Controlling a stage

This chapter covers:

- authorizing, receiving and reviewing work packages
- reviewing the stage status
- using reports to manage progress
- managing risks and issues that may impact the plan
- guidelines for tailoring products and roles

17 Controlling a stage

17.1 Purpose

The purpose of the controlling a stage process is to assign work to be done, monitor such work, deal with issues, report progress to the project board, and take corrective actions to ensure that the management stage remains within tolerance.

17.2 Objective

The objective of the controlling a stage process is to ensure that:

● attention is focused on delivery of the management stage's products. Any movement away from the direction and products agreed at the start of the management stage is monitored to avoid uncontrolled change and loss of focus

● risks and issues are kept under control

● the business case is kept under review

● the agreed products for the management stage are delivered to stated quality standards, within cost, effort and time agreed, and ultimately in support of the achievement of the defined benefits

● the project management team is focused on delivery within the tolerances laid down.

17.3 Context

Figure 17.1 provides an overview of controlling a stage.

The controlling a stage process describes the work of the project manager in handling the day-to-day management of the management stage. This process will be used for each delivery stage of a project. Towards the end of each management stage, except the final one, the activities within the managing a stage boundary process (see Chapter 19) will occur.

The controlling a stage process is normally first used after the project board authorizes the project, but it may also be used during the initiation stage, especially for large or complex projects.

Work packages are used to define and control the work to be done, and also to set tolerances for the team manager(s). If the project manager is fulfilling the team manager role, work packages should still be used to define and control the work of the individual team members being assigned work. When this is the case, references to the team manager throughout the controlling a stage process should be regarded as references to the individual team member being assigned work.

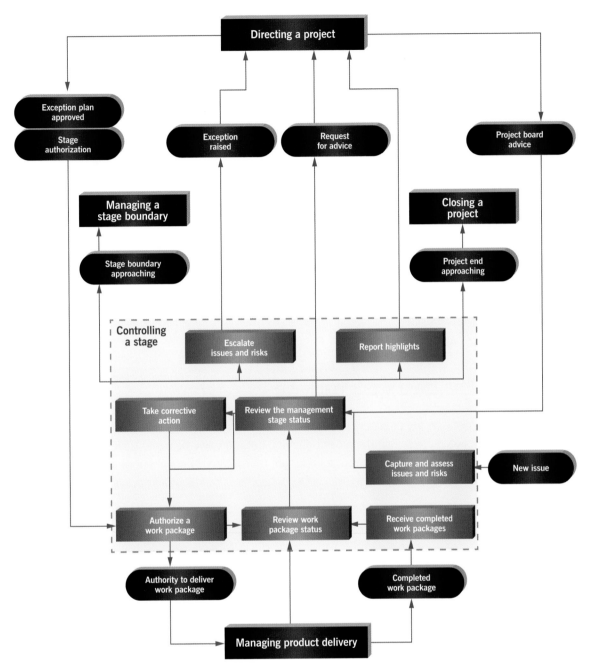

Figure 17.1 Overview of controlling a stage

Central to the ultimate success of the project is the day-to-day control of the work that is being conducted. Throughout a management stage, this will consist of a cycle of:

- authorizing work to be done
- monitoring progress information about that work, including signing off completed work packages
- reviewing the situation (including that for product quality) and triggering new work packages
- reporting highlights
- watching for, assessing and dealing with issues and risks
- taking any necessary corrective action.

Towards the end of the last management stage, the closing a project process (see Chapter 20) will be invoked.

17.4 Activities

Controlling a stage activities are project manager oriented and comprise:

- Work packages:
    - authorize a work package
    - review work package status
    - receive completed work packages.
- Monitoring and reporting:
    - review the management stage status
    - report highlights.
- Issues and risks:
    - capture and assess issues and risks
    - escalate issues and risks
    - take corrective action.

17.4.1 Authorize a work package

If the people who are working on the project were to start activities whenever they thought fit, it would be chaotic. There must be a level of autonomy within the project team(s), but there will be wider issues involved of which they cannot be expected to be aware. It is therefore important that work only commences and continues with the consent of the project manager. The vehicle for this is the production, execution and delivery of a work package.

A work package may include extracts from, or simply make cross-reference to elements of, the project plan, stage plan or PID.

A work package should cover the work to create one or more products. If a product requires more than one work package to create it, then it should be broken down into further products with their supporting product descriptions.

The triggers for the project manager to authorize a work package include:

- stage authorization: the project board gives authority to execute a stage plan
- exception plan approved: the project board gives authority to execute an exception plan
- new work package required: an output from reviewing the management stage status (see section 17.4.4)
- corrective action: in response to an issue or risk.

This activity is used to authorize new work packages or to authorize amendments to existing ones.

Figure 17.2 shows the inputs to, and outputs from, this activity.

PRINCE2 recommends the following actions:

- Examine the stage plan for the current management stage to understand the:
    - products to be produced
    - cost and effort that the work is expected to consume
    - tolerances available.

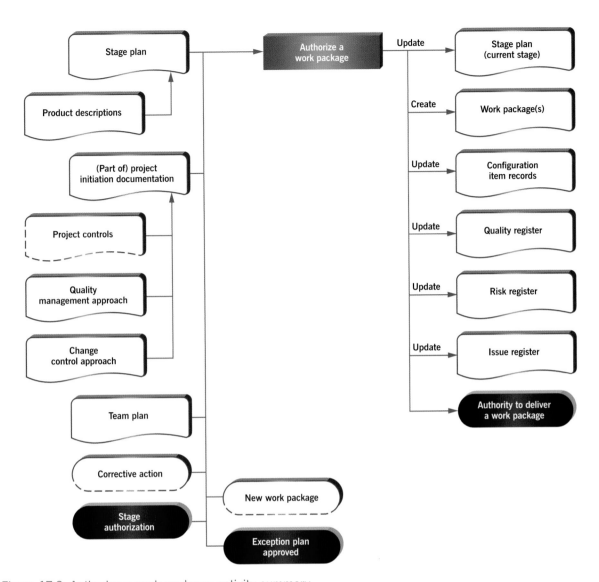

Figure 17.2 Authorize a work package: activity summary

- Examine the PID to understand:
  - the project controls required (e.g. progress reporting arrangements)
  - the quality standards required, as defined in the quality management approach
  - if any products are to be handed over, how this will be done (as defined in the change control approach).
- Define each work package to be authorized (or amended):
  - obtain the relevant product descriptions for inclusion in the work package
  - if an agile approach is being used, prioritize the products and features to be delivered
  - define the techniques, processes and procedures to be used
  - define the development interfaces to be maintained
  - define the operational and maintenance interfaces to be maintained
  - define the change control requirements
  - define the joint agreements on effort, cost, start and end dates, key milestones and tolerances
  - define any constraints that may apply
  - define the reporting, problem handling and escalation arrangements

- define the approval method
- provide relevant references (e.g. stage plan, product descriptions).

● Review the work package with the team manager, ensure that they have accepted it, and authorize them to begin work (see Chapter 18).

● Review the team manager's team plan (or the milestone extract from it if the commercial environment means it is inappropriate for the project manager to see its contents) and update the stage plan to reflect the timing of the work package(s) authorized.

● Update any configuration item records, if used, to reflect the content of the work package(s) authorized.

● Update the quality register for planned quality management activities. Consult with project assurance that the identified and selected quality reviewers are acceptable.

● If necessary, update the risk register in accordance with the risk management approach.

● If necessary, update the issue register in accordance with the change control approach.

Table 17.1 shows the responsibilities for this activity.

Table 17.1 Authorize a work package: responsibilities

Product	Action	Corporate/ programme/ customer	Executive	Senior user	Senior supplier	Project manager	Team manager	Project assurance	Project support	Product description available
Work package	Create					P	(A)	R		A.26
Configuration item records	Create/update					A	(R)	R	P	A.6
Quality register	Update					R	(R)	R	P	A.23
Risk register	Update					P				A.25
Issue register	Update					P				A.12
Team plan	Review					R	(P)			A.16
Stage plan	Update					P	(R)	R		A.16

Key: P (producer) – responsible for product's production; R (reviewer) – ideally independent of production; A (approver) – confirms approval.

The complete list of responsibilities for each product is shown. Where a product is produced, reviewed or approved in another process, the responsibility is shown in parentheses, as in (P), (R) or (A).

17.4.2 Review work package status

This activity provides the means for a regular assessment of the status of the work package(s). The frequency and formality of this activity will usually be aligned with the frequency of reporting defined in the work package(s) and supported by the stage plan for the current management stage.

Figure 17.3 shows the inputs to, and outputs from, this activity.

PRINCE2 recommends the following actions for each work package in progress:

● Collect and review progress information from the checkpoint report for the work package being executed:
  - assess the estimated time and effort to complete any unfinished work (including that not yet started)
  - review the team plan with the team manager (or the milestone extract from it if the commercial environment means it is inappropriate for the project manager to see its contents) to ascertain whether work will be completed on time and to budget

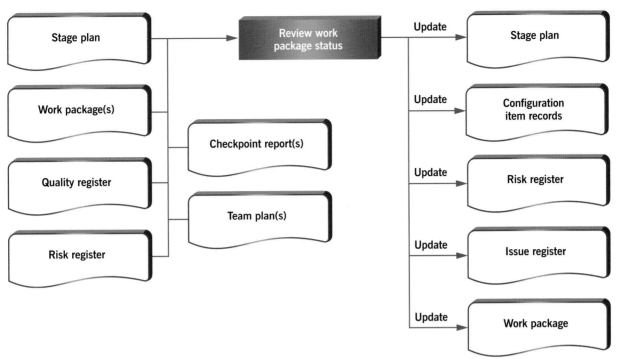

Figure 17.3 Review work package status: activity summary

- review entries in the quality register to understand the current status of quality management activities
- if used, confirm that the configuration item record for each product in the work package matches its status.
- If necessary, update the risk register and issue register.
- Update the stage plan for the current management stage with actuals to date, forecasts and adjustments.

Table 17.2 shows the responsibilities for this activity.

Table 17.2 Review work package status: responsibilities

Product	Action	Corporate/ programme/ customer	Executive	Senior user	Senior supplier	Project manager	Team manager	Project assurance	Project support	Product description available
Checkpoint report	Review					R	(P)			A.4
Team plan	Review					R	(P)			A.16
Stage plan	Update					P		R		A.16
Configuration item records	Update					A	(R)	R	P	A.6
Risk register	Update					P				A.25
Issue register	Update					P				A.12
Work package	Update					P	(A)	R		A.26

Key: P (producer) – responsible for product's production; R (reviewer) – ideally independent of production; A (approver) – confirms approval.

The complete list of responsibilities for each product is shown. Where a product is produced, reviewed or approved in another process, the responsibility is shown in parentheses, as in (P), (R) or (A).

17.4.3 Receive completed work packages

When work has been allocated to individuals or teams, there should be a matching confirmation that the work has been completed and approved.

When approved, any subsequent changes to the product(s) must pass through change control (see Chapter 11). This should be an automatic part of any change control method being used.

Figure 17.4 shows the inputs to, and outputs from, this activity.

PRINCE2 recommends the following actions:

● Ensure that the team manager has completed the work defined by the work package or, if an agile approach is being used, has delivered the features agreed for the timebox.

● Check that the quality register entries relating to the product(s) are complete.

● Ensure that each product in the work package has gained its requisite approval (as defined in the quality responsibilities in its product description).

● If used, confirm that the configuration item record for each approved product has been updated.

● Update the stage plan to show the work package as completed.

Table 17.3 shows the responsibilities for this activity.

Table 17.3 Receive completed work packages: responsibilities

Product	Action	Corporate/ programme/ customer	Executive	Senior user	Senior supplier	Project manager	Team manager	Project assurance	Project support	Product description available
Configuration item records	Update					A	(R)	R	P	A.6
Stage plan	Update					P		R		A.16

Key: P (producer) – responsible for product's production; R (reviewer) – ideally independent of production; A (approver) – confirms approval.

The complete list of responsibilities for each product is shown. Where a product is produced, reviewed or approved in another process, the responsibility is shown in parentheses, as in (P), (R) or (A).

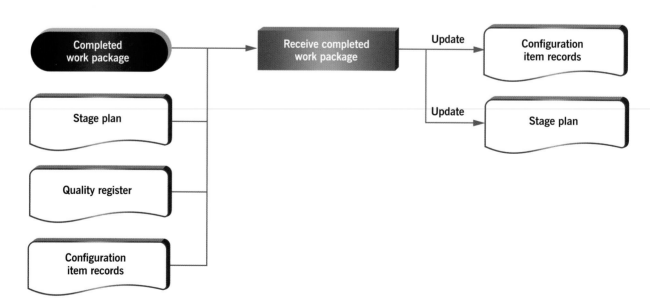

Figure 17.4 Receive completed work packages: activity summary

17.4.4 Review the management stage status

If the project is not checked on a timely basis, there is a danger that it will get out of control. There needs to be a balance between planning ahead and reacting to events.

In order to make informed decisions and exercise rational control, it is necessary to compare what has actually happened with what was expected to happen and what might happen next (including any issues and risks). It is therefore essential to have a steady flow of information that provides an overall view of progress and simple, robust monitoring systems to supply that information.

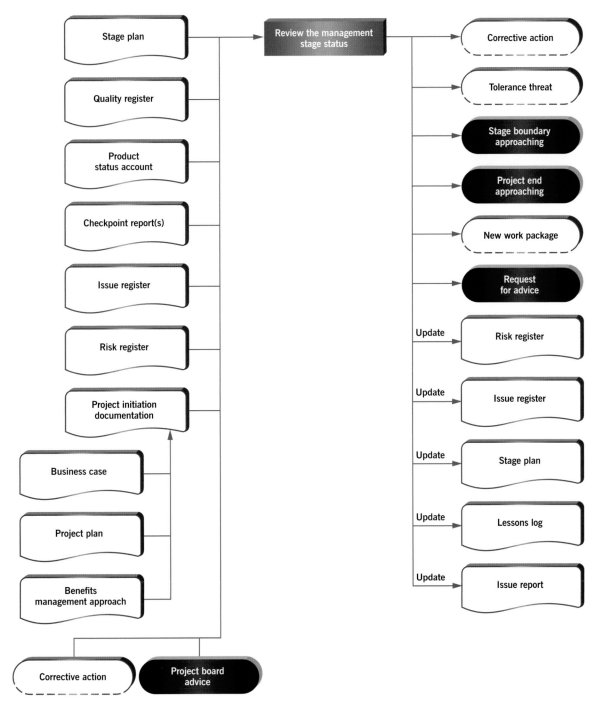

Figure 17.5 Review the management stage status: activity summary

The objective of this activity, therefore, is to maintain an accurate and current picture of progress on the work being carried out and the status of resources.

This activity occurs at a frequency defined in the stage plan, may be triggered by project board advice, or forms part of the analysis of new issues and risks.

Figure 17.5 shows the inputs to, and outputs from, this activity.

PRINCE2 recommends the following actions:

- Review progress for the management stage:
  - review checkpoint reports for the period
  - review the current stage plan forecast and actuals
  - request a product status account from project support to identify any variation between planned progress, reported progress and actual progress
  - check for any quality issues shown in the quality register
  - check the risk register for any new or revised risks and assess their impact on the business case, stage plan or project plan
  - check the issue register to see whether anything has happened within the project or externally that will impact on the business case, stage plan or project plan
  - check the status of any corrective actions
  - assess the utilization of resources in the period under review and their availability for the remainder of the management stage (or project). Check for any variation in the expected future resource availability
  - check the benefits management approach to see whether any benefits management actions are due, and execute them as necessary.
- Based on the above analysis, decide whether any actions are required. For example, whether to:
  - authorize a work package (section 17.4.1)
  - report highlights (section 17.4.5) in accordance with the communication management approach
  - capture and assess issues and risks (section 17.4.6)
  - escalate issues and risks (section 17.4.7) if tolerances are threatened
  - take corrective action (section 17.4.8)
  - seek project board advice (and if necessary provide the project board with the issue report)
  - log any lessons that have been identified
  - continue as planned.
- Revise the risk register and issue register as necessary.
- Update the stage plan if the aggregated assessment changes any forecasts.
- If ownership of any of the products is to be transferred to the customer as part of a phased handover:
  - request a product status account for what is being handed over
  - ensure that the:
    - products have been approved by those specified in its product description
    - products meet all the quality criteria, or are covered by approved concessions
    - operation and maintenance organizations are ready to take responsibility for the products
  - hand over the products (see Chapter 20). Note that there may be multiple handovers throughout the project lifecycle.

- Consider whether to review lessons now or wait until either a later review of management stage status or when approaching a management stage end.
- If the end of the current management stage is approaching (as indicated by, for example, the stage plan, the contents of the quality register, a milestone etc.), prepare for the next management stage (see Chapter 19).
- If the end of the final management stage is approaching, prepare to close the project (see Chapter 20).

Table 17.4 shows the responsibilities for this activity.

Table 17.4 Review the management stage status: responsibilities

Product	Action	Corporate/ programme/ customer	Executive	Senior user	Senior supplier	Project manager	Team manager	Project assurance	Project support	Product description available
Risk register	Update					P				A.25
Issue register	Update					P				A.12
Stage plan	Update					P		R		A.16
Lessons log	Update					P				A.14
Issue report	Update					P				A.13

Key: P (producer) – responsible for product's production; R (reviewer) – ideally independent of production; A (approver) – confirms approval.

17.4.5 Report highlights

The project manager must provide the project board with summary information about the status of the management stage and project, and distribute other information to stakeholders at a frequency documented in the communication management approach (as defined by the project board). For more details on progress controls, see Chapter 12.

Figure 17.6 shows the inputs to, and outputs from, this activity.

PRINCE2 recommends the following actions:

- Assemble the information from the checkpoint reports, risk register, issue register, quality register, lessons log, product status account and any significant revisions to the stage plan for the current reporting period (the information is gained from the review of the management stage status; see section 17.4.4).
- Assemble a list of corrective actions (as noted in the daily log and/or recorded in the issue register) undertaken during the reporting period. This will, for example, assure the project board that the project manager is acting within the agreed tolerances (the information is gained from taking corrective action; see section 17.4.8).
- Review the highlight report for the previous reporting period.
- Produce the highlight report for the current reporting period.
- Distribute the highlight report to the project board and any other recipients identified in the communication management approach.

Table 17.5 shows the responsibilities for this activity.

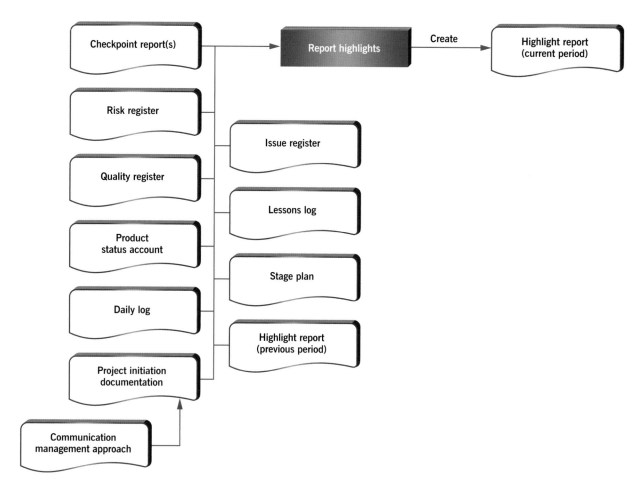

Figure 17.6 Report highlights: activity summary

Table 17.5 Report highlights: responsibilities

Product	Action	Corporate/ programme/ customer	Executive	Senior user	Senior supplier	Project manager	Team manager	Project assurance	Project support	Product description available
Highlight report	Create					P		R		A.11

Key: P (producer) – responsible for product's production; R (reviewer) – ideally independent of production; A (approver) – confirms approval.

17.4.6 Capture and assess issues and risks

In the course of managing the project, various issues will occur and risks may be identified. They will arrive in an ad hoc manner and will need to be captured in a consistent and reliable way. Any member of corporate, programme management or the customer, the project or other stakeholders may raise an issue or risk.

Before making a decision on a course of action, each issue or risk should be registered and then assessed for its impact. For more details on risk management, see Chapter 10. For more details on issue and change control procedures, see Chapter 11.

Figure 17.7 shows the inputs to, and outputs from, this activity.

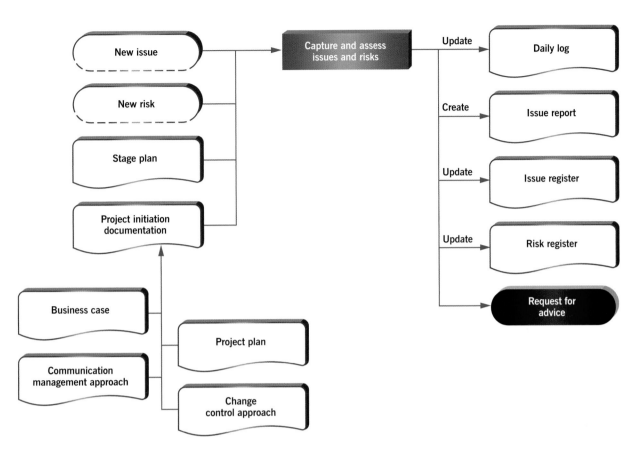

Figure 17.7 Capture and assess issues and risks: activity summary

PRINCE2 recommends the following actions:

- If an issue can be dealt with by the project manager informally, then this should be done, and a note made in the daily log (see section 11.4 for more information).
- For issues that need to be managed formally (see section 11.4 for more information):
  - check the requirements of the issue management and change control procedure in the change control approach
  - manage the issue in accordance with the change control approach
  - report the status of the issue in accordance with the change control approach and check the communication management approach to see whether there are any external parties that need to be informed of the issue.
- For risks (see Chapter 10 for more information):
  - check the requirements of the risk management procedure in the risk management approach
  - manage the risk in accordance with the risk management approach
  - report the status of the risk in accordance with the risk management approach and check the communication management approach to see whether there are any external parties that need to be informed of the risk.
- If it is necessary to take corrective action, seek advice from the project board or escalate an issue or risk, then review the management stage status first so that a full picture can be considered (see section 17.4.4).

Table 17.6 shows the responsibilities for this activity.

Table 17.6 Capture and assess issues and risks: responsibilities

Product	Action	Corporate/ programme/ customer	Executive	Senior user	Senior supplier	Project manager	Team manager	Project assurance	Project support	Product description available
Daily log	Update					P				A.7
Issue report	Create					P				A.13
Issue register	Update					P				A.12
Risk register	Update					P				A.25

Key: P (producer) – responsible for product's production; R (reviewer) – ideally independent of production; A (approver) – confirms approval.

17.4.7 Escalate issues and risks

A management stage should not exceed the tolerances agreed with the project board. The project manager can only take corrective action or maintain the status quo as long as the management stage (or project) is forecast to be completed within the tolerances set by the project board. This activity applies where any corrective action within the project manager's control would not save the management stage (or project) from going beyond the tolerances agreed. This applies to all types of issue and risk (or aggregations of them) that cannot be resolved within the tolerances set by the project board.

As it may take some time to gather the information to create an exception report, it is recommended that the project board be alerted as early as possible. Therefore, the project manager may wish to execute this activity in two steps: an early notification to the project board of the forecast exception situation so that the board is prepared, followed by supporting information in the form of an exception report.

The project manager should execute any decision by the project board in response to the escalation. Escalating issues and risks is good practice and should not be seen as failure. The earlier that issues are escalated, the more time is available to implement any corrective actions.

For more details on management of risk, see Chapter 10. For more details on issue and change control, see Chapter 11. For more details on exception management, see Chapter 12.

Figure 17.8 shows the inputs to, and outputs from, this activity.

PRINCE2 recommends the following actions:

● Examine the stage plan to define the extent of the deviation and the unfinished products, and to extrapolate what would happen if the deviation were allowed to continue.

● Examine the project plan for the project status and overall effect of any deviation (using the current baseline of the PID).

● Determine the options for recovery and assess them against the business case.

● Assess the impact of the options for recovery against the stage plan for the current management stage. Consideration should be given to the availability of individuals or groups with the skills or experience to assess the impact.

● Put the situation, options and the recommendation for a course of action to the project board in an exception report. The project board will then decide on an appropriate course of action (which may support or otherwise the project manager's recommendation). This may include:

  ● requesting more information or more time to consider its response

  ● approving, deferring or rejecting a request for change

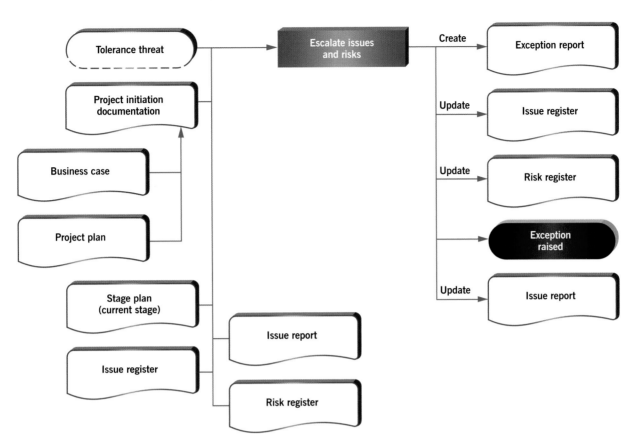

Figure 17.8 Escalate issues and risks: activity summary

- granting a concession for an off-specification, or deferring or rejecting it
- increasing the tolerances that are forecast to be breached
- instructing the project manager to produce an exception plan, stating what will be acceptable (see section 19.4.5)
- instructing the project manager to close the project prematurely (see Chapter 20).

Table 17.7 shows the responsibilities for this activity.

Table 17.7 Escalate issues and risks: responsibilities

Product	Action	Corporate/ programme/ customer	Executive	Senior user	Senior supplier	Project manager	Team manager	Project assurance	Project support	Product description available
Exception report	Create		(A)	(R)	(R)	P		R		A.10
Issue register	Update					P				A.12
Risk register	Update					P				A.25
Issue report	Update					P				A.13

Key: P (producer) – responsible for product's production; R (reviewer) – ideally independent of production; A (approver) – confirms approval.

The complete list of responsibilities for each product is shown. Where a product is produced, reviewed or approved in another process, the responsibility is shown in parentheses, as in (P), (R) or (A).

17.4.8 Take corrective action

Changes and adjustments to the project need to be made in a considered and rational way, even when they appear to be easily manageable and within tolerances.

In taking corrective action, the objective is to select and, within the limits of the management stage and project tolerances, implement actions that will resolve deviations from the plan. Corrective action is triggered during the review of the management stage status (section 17.4.4) and typically involves dealing with advice and guidance received from the project board, and with issues raised by team managers.

For more details on planning, see Chapter 9. For more details on issue and change control, see Chapter 11.

Figure 17.9 shows the inputs to, and outputs from, this activity.

PRINCE2 recommends the following actions:

● Collect any relevant information about the deviation.

● Identify the potential ways of dealing with the deviation and select the most appropriate option.

● Trigger corrective action via authorizing a work package (see section 17.4.1).

● If used, update the configuration item records of the affected products.

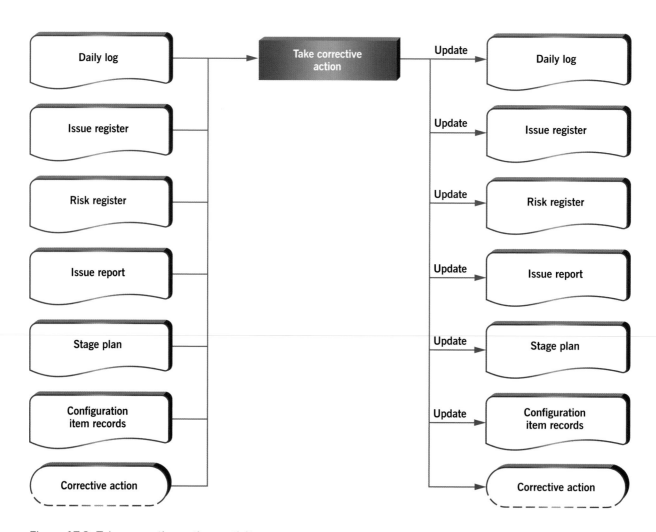

Figure 17.9 Take corrective action: activity summary

- Update the issue report (if necessary) to show the status of the corrective action.
- Update the issue register with any changes resulting from the corrective action (or if being handled informally, update the daily log with the details and status of the corrective action).
- Update the risk register with any changes resulting from the corrective action.
- Update the stage plan for the current management stage.

Table 17.8 shows the responsibilities for this activity.

Table 17.8 Take corrective action: responsibilities

Product	Action	Corporate/ programme/ customer	Executive	Senior user	Senior supplier	Project manager	Team manager	Project assurance	Project support	Product description available
Issue register	Update					P				A.12
Risk register	Update					P				A.25
Issue report	Update					P		R		A.13
Stage plan	Update					P		R		A.16
Configuration item records	Update					P	(R)		R	A.6
Daily log	Update					P				A.7

Key: P (producer) – responsible for product's production; R (reviewer) – ideally independent of production; A (approver) – confirms approval.

The complete list of responsibilities for each product is shown. Where a product is produced, reviewed or approved in another process, the responsibility is shown in parentheses, as in (P), (R) or (A).

17.5 Tailoring guidelines

17.5.1 General considerations

The work packages are fundamentally important to this process as they relate to the PRINCE2 principle to focus on products.

17.5.2 Tailoring products in controlling a stage

Table 17.9 provides tailoring guidelines for management products in controlling a stage.

Tip

As it is within this process that much of the tailoring is used, the project manager should continually monitor the effectiveness of the procedures and controls. Where necessary, the project manager takes corrective action, which might entail further tailoring and an update to the PID. For example, it may be found that the summary risk profile matrix categorizes all risks as 'high' (when they are clearly not) and needs to be adjusted to give a meaningful spread.

Table 17.9 Guidelines for tailoring products in controlling a stage

Management product	Tailoring guidelines
Work package	Work packages can take many forms as specialist disciplines often have their own practices for defining their specialist deliverables. They are also likely to differ if the work is done internally or contracted to a supplier.
	The project manager should use the work package outline as a checklist to ensure that the relevant content is present.
Highlight report	The frequency of highlight reporting may change to suit the risk profile and output being created. This is documented in the communication management approach in the PID.
	Additional information, such as KPIs, may be added or referenced if it provides clarity.
	Highlight reports may be in the form of wall charts or Kanban boards.
Issue report	An issue report is simply a view of the issue register with additional information covering an impact analysis, recommendation and decision. If this additional information is added to the issue register, there is no need for a separate, formally documented report.
Exception report	As the recipients of the report are the project board members, this report may be in any format acceptable to them as long as it includes the information the project board requires.

17.5.3 Tailoring roles in controlling a stage

The project manager is responsible for the creation of all new management products in this process, but may delegate this to others, while retaining accountability. For example, PRINCE2 shows the project manager as responsible for creating work packages. However, in practice they may not have the requisite skills to define specialist products and their role is rather to see that they are defined and reviewed rigorously.

17.5.4 Common situations

17.5.4.1 Controlling a stage on a simple project

For a simple project, when the project manager also acts as the team manager, the project manager may choose to use work packages as a control for individual team members.

The project manager is likely to undertake the project support role personally.

17.5.4.2 Controlling a stage when using an agile approach

When controlling a stage that is using an agile approach, the project manager should empower the teams to deliver in the best way possible. This means being collaborative with work assignment, based around the amount of requirements to be delivered (e.g. in the form of features), and making full use of the most effective visual communication channels. Further to this, the use of regular reviews and retrospectives along with setting the appropriate tolerances (based primarily around scope and quality criteria) creates an environment where creativity and responding to change exist in order to best address the customer's needs.

Team members typically plan their work according to the order decided by the customer (this role is often referred to as a product owner), who is in the delivery team. As a result, work is typically not assigned to specific team members in advance. Work packages are structured flexibly (e.g. through the use of tolerances) to enable teams to self-organize, and their sign-off may be informal. Reviews and demos at the end of a sprint or a release provide transparent and regular feedback to the customer as a means of validating that the acceptance criteria in the product description(s) have been met. A work package may contain several timeboxes (e.g. in the form of sprints) and, although each one will deliver something, they may not necessarily deliver something into operational use.

When using an agile approach, teams track progress during a short meeting called a daily stand-up. The project manager or team managers may be invited to attend/assist stand-up meetings if appropriate, and/or facilitate them. Reporting of progress is typically done via wall charts or information radiators, from which information can be pulled at any time by any project stakeholder.

Forecasting in general is more likely to be in an empirical style (based on evidence), with progress usually shown as a burn chart rather than a Gantt chart. The project manager should focus on flexing the scope and the quality criteria of the defined products and ensuring that those variables stay within agreed tolerances.

The daily stand-up provides the delivery team with the opportunity to identify issues and risks. This approach ensures they are uncovered and escalated quickly to ensure that goals are not compromised. Sprint and release retrospectives also provide an opportunity to improve the underlying processes that the team is using.

17.5.4.3 Controlling a stage from a supplier perspective

For an external supplier, a customer's work package may take the form of a legally binding contract. However, the supplier may decompose the contracted work packages into smaller work packages to manage its part of the work.

The project manager should ensure that they have sufficient information from the supplier to control the work. This may require specific obligations on the supplier to be included in the contract.

17.5.4.4 Controlling a stage of a project within a programme or portfolio

Consider how the project's logs and registers should be maintained and how escalation to programme or portfolio level is to be done in practical terms. For example, there may be a single risk register system (administered by the programme or portfolio and including both the programme- or portfolio-level risks and the risks for each project), or each project could maintain its own risk register. If the latter is chosen, the project's risk management approach should define how programme- or portfolio-level risks that are identified and captured by the project are escalated to the programme or portfolio risk register. Likewise, the programme's or portfolio's risk management approach should define mechanisms for project risks that are identified and captured at the programme or portfolio level to be delegated to the project risk register.

Chapter 17 – Controlling a stage

18

Managing product delivery

This chapter covers:

- defining the team manager's responsibilities
- producing a team plan to deliver the work package
- managing the execution and delivery of work packages
- guidelines for tailoring products and roles

18 Managing product delivery

18.1 Purpose

The purpose of the managing product delivery process is to control the link between the project manager and the team manager(s), by agreeing the requirements for acceptance, execution and delivery.

The role of the team manager(s) is to coordinate an area of work that will deliver one or more of the project product's components. They can be internal or external to the customer's organization.

18.2 Objective

The objective of the managing product delivery process is to ensure that:

- work on products allocated to the team is authorized and agreed
- team managers, team members and suppliers are clear as to what is to be produced and what is the expected effort, cost or timescales
- the planned products are delivered to expectations and within tolerance
- accurate progress information is provided to the project manager at an agreed frequency to ensure that expectations are managed.

18.3 Context

Figure 18.1 provides an overview of managing product delivery.

Managing product delivery views the project from the team manager's perspective, whereas the controlling a stage process views it from the project manager's perspective.

The team manager ensures that products are created and delivered by the team to the project by:

- accepting and checking authorized work packages from the project manager
- ensuring that interfaces identified in the work package are maintained
- creating a team plan for the work packages being assigned (this may be done in parallel with the project manager creating the stage plan for the management stage)
- ensuring that the products are developed in accordance with any development method(s) specified in the work package
- demonstrating that each product meets its quality criteria through the quality method(s) specified in the product description; this may include using the PRINCE2 quality review technique (see Chapter 8)
- obtaining approval for completed products from the authorities identified in the product description
- delivering the products to the project manager in accordance with any procedures specified in the work package.

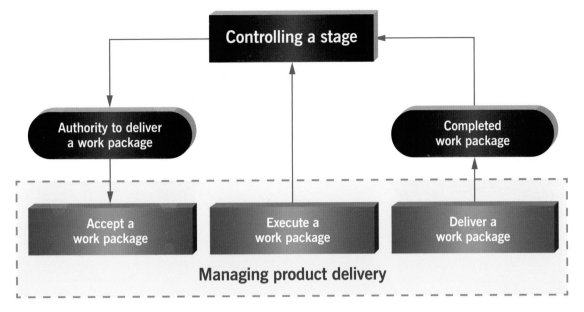

Figure 18.1 Overview of managing product delivery

If the project uses external suppliers that are not using PRINCE2, managing product delivery provides a statement of the required interface between the team manager and the PRINCE2 method being used in the project by the project manager. The work package may be part of a contractual agreement. Therefore, the formality of a team plan could vary from simply appending a schedule to the work package to creating a fully formed plan that is presented in a similar style to a stage plan.

18.4 Activities

The activities within the managing product delivery process are team manager oriented and are to:

- accept a work package
- execute a work package
- deliver a work package.

18.4.1 Accept a work package

The fundamental principle is that before a work package is allocated to a team, there should be agreement between the project manager and the team manager as to what is to be delivered. This should cover the reporting requirements, what constraints apply, any procedures to be applied and whether the requirements of the work package are reasonable and can be achieved.

Figure 18.2 shows the inputs to, and outputs from, this activity.

PRINCE2 recommends the following actions:

- Review the work package:
  - obtain any referenced documentation
  - clarify with the project manager what is to be delivered
  - negotiate with the project manager, on behalf of the team, the constraints within which the work is to be done
  - agree tolerances for the work package

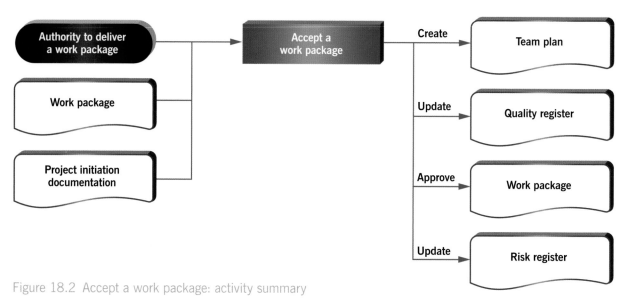

Figure 18.2 Accept a work package: activity summary

- ○ understand the reporting requirements
- ○ understand how, and from whom, approval for the product(s) is to be obtained
- ○ understand how the approved product(s) is to be formally handed over
- ○ confirm how the project manager is to be informed about the completion of the work package.
- ● Produce a team plan to show which product(s) can be completed within the given constraints (e.g. within the timebox when using an agile approach).
- ● Consult with project assurance (supplier) that the team plan is viable and in accordance with relevant supplier standards.
- ● Seek necessary approval for the team plan (although in a commercial customer/supplier relationship it may be inappropriate for the project manager to review and approve the team plan and, in such a context, the senior supplier may review and approve the team plans).
- ● Undertake a review of the risks against the team plan, and advise the project manager of any additional or modified risks (and, if the work package allows the team manager to directly log the risks, the team manager should update the risk register).
- ● Consult with project assurance as to whether any extra reviewers are required and ensure that the quality register is updated accordingly (check the work package for the procedure to update the quality register).
- ● Agree to deliver the work package.

Table 18.1 shows the responsibilities for this activity.

Table 18.1 Accept a work package: responsibilities

Product	Action	Corporate/ programme/ customer	Executive	Senior user	Senior supplier	Project manager	Team manager	Project assurance	Project support	Product description available
Team plan	Create				(A)	(A)	P	R		A.16
Risk register	Update					(R)	P			A.25
Quality register	Update					(R)	R		(P)	A.23
Work package	Approve					(P)	A	R		A.26

Key: P (producer) – responsible for product's production; R (reviewer) – ideally independent of production; A (approver) – confirms approval.

The complete list of responsibilities for each product is shown. Where a product is produced, reviewed or approved in another process, the responsibility is shown in parentheses, as in (P), (R) or (A).

18.4.2 Execute a work package

The work has to be executed and monitored to the requirements defined in the authorized work package.

While developing the products, the team manager should not exceed the work package tolerances agreed with the project manager. The team manager can only proceed with the work package or take corrective action while the work package is forecast to be completed within the tolerances set by the project manager. As soon as work package tolerances are forecast to be exceeded, the team manager should raise an issue to the project manager who will then decide upon a course of action.

Figure 18.3 shows the inputs to, and outputs from, this activity.

PRINCE2 recommends the following actions:

- Manage the development of the required products:
  - develop the products required by the work package to the quality criteria defined in the product descriptions
  - ensure that the work is conducted in accordance with the required techniques, processes and procedures specified in the work package
  - maintain the development and operational and support interfaces as detailed in the work package

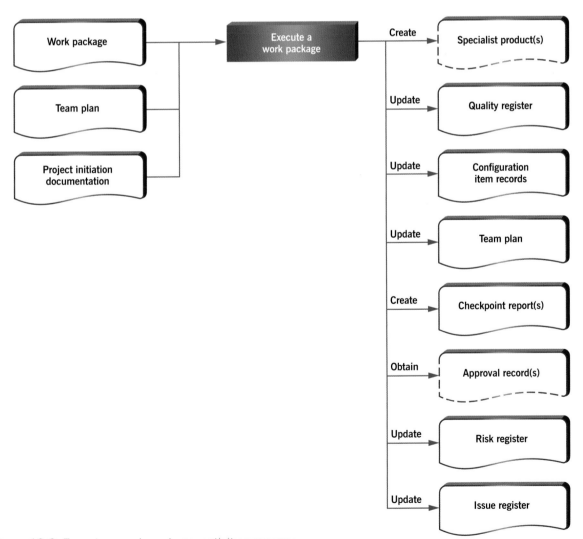

Figure 18.3 Execute a work package: activity summary

- check the work package for the procedure to update the quality register (e.g. to record completed quality management activities)
- capture and record the effort expended
- monitor and control any issues and risks associated with the work package and advise the project manager of their status.

- Notify the project manager of any new issues, risks or lessons. The project manager can then decide on an appropriate course of action.

- Take the action required by the project manager.

- Obtain approvals for completed products:
  - check the work package and follow the method of obtaining and issuing approval records
  - check the work package and follow the procedure to update any configuration item records, if used.

- Review and report the status of the work package to the project manager:
  - determine the status of each product in the work package
  - update the team plan and, if necessary, consult with project assurance (supplier) regarding its viability
  - feed the progress information back to the project manager in checkpoint reports, in the manner and at the frequency defined in the work package
  - if the agreed tolerances for the work package are forecast to be exceeded, notify the project manager by raising an issue.

Table 18.2 shows the responsibilities for this activity.

Table 18.2 Execute a work package: responsibilities

Product	Action	Corporate/ programme/ customer	Executive	Senior user	Senior supplier	Project manager	Team manager	Project assurance	Project support	Product description available
Specialist products	Create		(A)	(A)	(A)	(R)	P	R		
Quality register	Update					(R)	R		(P)	A.23
Configuration item records	Update						P		P	A.6
Team plan	Update						P	R		A.16
Checkpoint report(s)	Create					(R)	P			A.4
Issue register	Update					(R)	P			A.12
Risk register	Update					(R)	P			A.25
Approval record(s)	Obtain					(R)	P	R	R	

Key: P (producer) – responsible for product's production; R (reviewer) – ideally independent of production; A (approver) – confirms approval.

The complete list of responsibilities for each product is shown. Where a product is produced, reviewed or approved in another process, the responsibility is shown in parentheses, as in (P), (R) or (A).

18.4.3 Deliver a work package

Just as the work package was accepted from the project manager, notification of its completion must be returned to the project manager.

Figure 18.4 shows the inputs to, and outputs from, this activity.

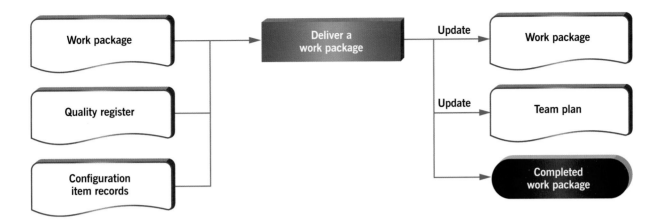

Figure 18.4 Deliver a work package: activity summary

PRINCE2 recommends the following actions:

- Review the quality register to verify that all the quality activities associated with the work package are complete.
- Review the approval records to verify that all the products to be delivered by the work package are approved.
- Update the team plan to show that the work package is complete.
- Check the work package and follow the procedure to deliver the completed products.
- Notify the project manager that the work package is complete.

Table 18.3 shows the responsibilities for this activity.

Table 18.3 Deliver a work package: responsibilities

Product	Action	Corporate/ programme/ customer	Executive	Senior user	Senior supplier	Project manager	Team manager	Project assurance	Project support	Product description available
Work package	Update					(A)	P	R		A.26
Team plan	Update					(R)	P	R		A.16

Key: P (producer) – responsible for product's production; R (reviewer) – ideally independent of production; A (approver) – confirms approval.

The complete list of responsibilities for each product is shown. Where a product is produced, reviewed or approved in another process, the responsibility is shown in parentheses, as in (P), (R) or (A).

18.5 Tailoring guidelines

18.5.1 General considerations

The activities in this process may be combined, split or run concurrently to suit the context, but care should be taken to ensure the integrity of the interface to the controlling a stage process.

As this process is where the specialist work is undertaken, work will be done using practices which are appropriate to the type of work. It is important that monitoring and control of specialist work is done using controls and measures which are appropriate to that work and that the project manager should incorporate them into the appropriate management products.

Work packages are not necessarily small in scale. All the PRINCE2 principles are as applicable to a work package as to a project, requiring appropriate governance and control and often needing a team manager who is skilled in project management. For large work packages, a team manager may create a hierarchy of smaller work packages to allocate to the team members. In this case the process for managing product delivery should be tailored to ensure the work in any lower-level work packages is controlled.

18.5.2 Tailoring products in managing product delivery

Table 18.4 provides tailoring guidelines for management products in managing product delivery.

Table 18.4 Guidelines for tailoring products in managing product delivery

Management product	Tailoring guidelines
Team plan	The team plan may be a subset of the stage plan, and may be informal or formal, depending on the context.
	The team plan may include components in any format commensurate with the complexity of the work package, with views ranging from a simple list of accountabilities, products, activities and dates to Gantt charts. The plan may be held totally or partially within a planning tool(s).
	The team plan should be developed at the same time as the stage plan, not waiting for the work package; this will help ensure commitment and a well-integrated set of plans. In the accept a work package activity there would need to be a confirmation that the team plan is still valid.
Checkpoint report	Checkpoint reports may be informal or formal, depending on the context. If a project manager meets with the team managers regularly, then a verbal update, captured by the project manager in a daily log to be used to create the highlight report, may be sufficient. Additional information, such as KPIs, may be added if it helps understanding of progress.

18.5.3 Tailoring roles in managing product delivery

A project manager may also undertake a team manager role.

The team manager is responsible for all activities but may be supported by team members. If a team manager is responsible for a lower-level work package, they may report to the higher-level team manager who is responsible for the next-higher-level work package.

Although the PRINCE2 processes define who creates, updates and approves a work package, these responsibilities may be changed provided both the team manager and project manager are in agreement on what the work package comprises.

18.5.4 Common situations

18.5.4.1 Managing product delivery on a simple project

For simple projects, the nature of the specialist deliverables is likely to mean that controls can be light or informal (e.g. oral checkpoint reports recorded by the project manager in the daily log). Work packages are likely to comprise only a few specialist products.

If the project manager is also undertaking a team manager role, there may be no need for checkpoint reports. The project manager may, however, request individual team members to provide them. Checkpoint reports may be verbal and noted in a daily log by the project manager.

18.5.4.2 Managing product delivery when using an agile approach

Managing product delivery handles the important interface between the project manager and the delivery team, who will be working in an agile way. The interface would need to be collaborative and transparent where there is a collective agreement on what is to be produced and how this will be achieved (as opposed to a situation where instructions are given and followed). In agile working, delivery is done iteratively.

Progress information would be visible on an information radiator which is frequently updated by way of the daily activities of working in an agile way. This provides the information for the project manager to manage the project at the stage level by having clear and regular information across all the teams at the delivery level.

 Tip

Retrospectives and Kanban boards can provide good progress information to feed into end stage and project closure reports.

18.5.4.3 Managing product delivery from a supplier perspective

From the supplier perspective, all its contracted work (to provide products) is likely to be managed as work packages within the customer's project. Note, however, there may be times when a supplier is providing specialist services within work packages run by others or has part of its own work packages contracted to another supplier (subcontractor). The controls and reporting within the managing product delivery process should be reflected in the relevant supplier contracts to ensure the project manager has visibility of progress and quality.

18.5.4.4 Managing product delivery on a project within a programme

Because all work packages are managed by a team manager through a project manager, managing product delivery has no direct interface with programme management and is therefore free of any direct impact.

Chapter 18 – Managing product delivery

Managing a stage boundary

This chapter covers:

- reviewing the current stage
- planning for the next stage
- updating the project plan and business case
- reporting the stage end
- producing an exception report and exception plan
- guidelines for tailoring products and roles

19 Managing a stage boundary

19.1 Purpose

The purpose of the managing a stage boundary process is to enable the project manager to provide the project board with sufficient information to be able to:

- review the success of the current management stage
- approve the next stage plan
- review the updated project plan
- confirm continued business justification and acceptability of the risks.

Therefore, the process should be executed at, or close to, the end of each management stage.

Projects do not always go to plan and in response to an exception report (if the management stage or project is forecast to exceed its tolerances) the project board may request that the current management stage (and possibly the project) is replanned. The output from replanning is an exception plan which is submitted for project board approval in the same way that a stage plan is submitted for approval.

19.2 Objective

The objective of the managing a stage boundary process is to:

- assure the project board that all products in the stage plan for the current management stage have been completed and approved
- prepare the stage plan for the next management stage
- review and, if necessary, update the PID; in particular the business case, project plan, project approaches, project management team structure and role descriptions
- provide the information needed for the project board to assess the continuing viability of the project
- record any information or lessons that can help later management stages of this project and/or other projects
- request authorization to start the next management stage.

For exceptions, the objectives of the managing a stage boundary process are to:

- review and, if necessary, update the PID; in particular the customer's quality expectations, project approaches and controls, and role descriptions
- provide the information needed for the project board to assess the continuing viability of the project
- prepare an exception plan as directed by the project board
- seek approval to replace the project plan or stage plan for the current management stage with the exception plan.

Managing a stage boundary is not used towards the end of the final management stage unless there is a need to create an exception plan. This is because the activities to review the performance of the whole project, as part of the closing a project process, include reviewing the performance of the final management stage.

19.3 Context

Figure 19.1 provides an overview of managing a stage boundary.

The managing a stage boundary process is predicated on dividing the project into management stages (see Chapter 13).

A project, whether large or small, needs to ensure that the products it creates will deliver the benefits being sought, either in their own right or as part of a larger programme. The continuing correct focus of the project should be confirmed at the end of each management stage. If necessary, the project can be redirected or stopped to avoid wasting time and money.

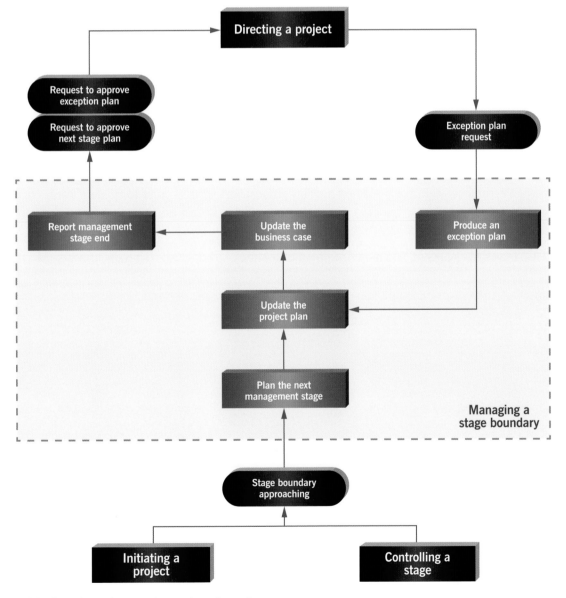

Figure 19.1 Overview of managing a stage boundary

It is also important to recognize that projects can go wrong or can be affected by external factors that invalidate the business justification. An early identifier of potential failure is the project manager's forecast that any of the project or management stage tolerances are likely to be exceeded. In such cases it is important to have a mechanism for corrective action in order to bring the project back into the right direction.

A positive decision not to proceed is not failure. However, providing insufficient information that prevents the project board from making an informed decision is itself a failure as it may lead to a wrong decision.

The managing a stage boundary process provides a means by which an exception process can be implemented.

19.4 Activities

The activities within the managing a stage boundary process are project manager oriented and are to:

- plan the next management stage
- update the project plan
- update the business case
- report management stage end
- produce an exception plan.

19.4.1 Plan the next management stage

The stage plan for the next management stage is produced near the end of the current management stage. Closure activities should be planned as part of the stage plan for the final management stage.

Planning is not an activity undertaken in isolation. The project manager will need to consult with the project board, project assurance, team managers and possibly other stakeholders in order to create a viable plan. The more people involved in planning, the more robust the plan will be (as long as the right people are involved). See Chapter 9 for more details on planning.

Figure 19.2 shows the inputs to, and outputs from, this activity.

 Tip

It is good practice to produce a team plan in parallel with planning the next management stage. It should be reviewed and, if necessary, updated as part of the accept a work package activity. This will ensure that the project manager has sufficient information to plan the stage, with an understanding of what is achievable at a team level.

PRINCE2 recommends the following actions:

- Review the components of the PID. It may be necessary to consult with the project board regarding any required changes. The following should be reviewed and, if necessary, updated:
  - any change to the customer's quality expectations, acceptance criteria or project approach
  - the relevance and suitability of the approaches and controls

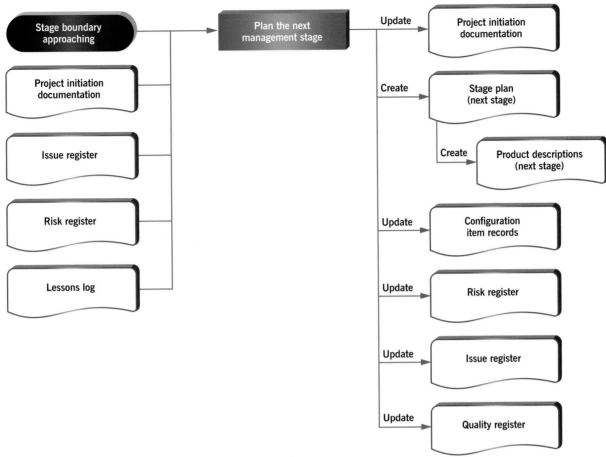

Figure 19.2 Plan the next management stage: activity summary

- any change in the project management team or their role descriptions (in particular the situation with regard to external resources or suppliers as these may affect the stage plan).
- Produce the stage plan for the next management stage:
  - decide how the plan can best be presented given its audience, and how it will be used
  - review the project plan to understand the products required for the next management stage
  - examine the quality management approach for the quality standards and procedures required
  - if used, create (or update) the product breakdown structure, product descriptions and product flow diagram for the products to be delivered by the next management stage
  - review the issue register as it may contain issues marked for assessment at the management stage end or information that affects the next management stage
  - review the risk register for any risks that may affect the stage plan for the next management stage, and check the status of risk responses by consulting with the risk owners.
- Create (or update) configuration item records, if used, for products planned to be produced in the next stage.
- Update the issue register and risk register if any new issues or risks have been identified (or if existing ones need to be modified).
- Update the quality register for planned quality management activities. This should include target review and approval dates for the products.

Table 19.1 shows the responsibilities for this activity.

Table 19.1 Plan the next management stage: responsibilities

Product	Action	Corporate/ programme/ customer	Executive	Senior user	Senior supplier	Project manager	Team manager	Project assurance	Project support	Product description available
Project initiation documentation	Update	(R)	(A)	(A)	(A)	P		R		A.20
Stage plan	Create		(A)	(A)	(A)	P		R		A.16
Configuration item records	Create/ update					P		R	R	A.6
Risk register	Update					P		R		A.25
Issue register	Update					P		R		A.12
Quality register	Update					R		R	P	A.23

Key: P (producer) – responsible for product's production; R (reviewer) – ideally independent of production; A (approver) – confirms approval.

The complete list of responsibilities for each product is shown. Where a product is produced, reviewed or approved in another process, the responsibility is shown in parentheses, as in (P), (R) or (A).

19.4.2 Update the project plan

The project board uses the project plan throughout the project to measure progress.

The project plan is updated to incorporate actual progress from the management stage that is finishing, and to include forecast duration and costs from the exception plan or stage plan for the management stage about to begin. Details of any revised costs or end dates are used when updating the business case. See Chapter 9 for more details on planning.

Figure 19.3 shows the inputs to, and outputs from, this activity.

PRINCE2 recommends the following actions:

● Check that the current stage plan is up to date with actual progress and update it if necessary.
● Revise the project plan to reflect:
  ● actuals from the current stage plan
  ● forecasts from the next stage plan, or the impact of the exception plan

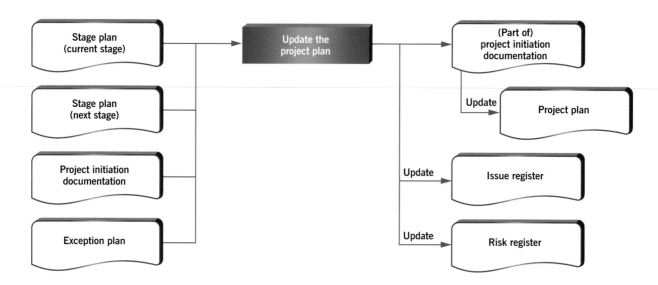

Figure 19.3 Update the project plan: activity summary

- any changes to the project product description

- the implications of any issues or risks

- any new or changed PRINCE2 process-tailoring requirements for the project

- any changed or extra products sanctioned by the project board

- any changes within the PID (e.g. revised project approaches, project controls, project management team structure or role descriptions).

- Update the issue register and risk register if any new issues or risks have been identified (or if existing ones need to be modified).

Table 19.2 shows the responsibilities for this activity.

Table 19.2 Update the project plan: responsibilities

Product	Action	Corporate/ programme/ customer	Executive	Senior user	Senior supplier	Project manager	Team manager	Project assurance	Project support	Product description available
Project plan	Update		(A)	(A)	(A)	P		R		A.16
Issue register	Update					P		R		A.12
Risk register	Update					P		R		A.25

Key: P (producer) – responsible for product's production; R (reviewer) – ideally independent of production; A (approver) – confirms approval.

The complete list of responsibilities for each product is shown. Where a product is produced, reviewed or approved in another process, the responsibility is shown in parentheses, as in (P), (R) or (A).

19.4.3 Update the business case

It is a PRINCE2 principle that projects have continued business justification.

The project board is ordinarily only authorized to continue while the project remains viable (i.e. the benefits will be realized within the time, cost, quality, scope and risk parameters set out in the currently agreed business case).

Projects, however, do not take place in a static environment. The environment external to the project changes, as does the development of the project product. The business case needs to reflect these changes and must be reviewed and amended to keep it relevant to the project. As the executive is responsible for the business case, the project manager should consult with the executive when reviewing and updating the business case in preparation for project board approval. For further details on business justification, see Chapter 6.

Figure 19.4 shows the inputs to, and outputs from, this activity.

PRINCE2 recommends the following actions:

- Check whether there have been any changes to the risk appetite and risk capacity of the organizations involved and whether risk tolerances need to be redefined. Assess the project's risks using the risk register to ascertain the aggregated risk exposure for the project and identify the current key risks that affect the business case. This should include an assessment that the aggregated risk exposure remains within risk tolerances.

- Update the benefits management approach with the results from any benefits management actions undertaken during the management stage.

- Examine and review:
  - the benefits management approach for the results of any benefits management actions undertaken during the management stage compared with the expected results
  - the impact of approved changes as these may affect the projected benefits

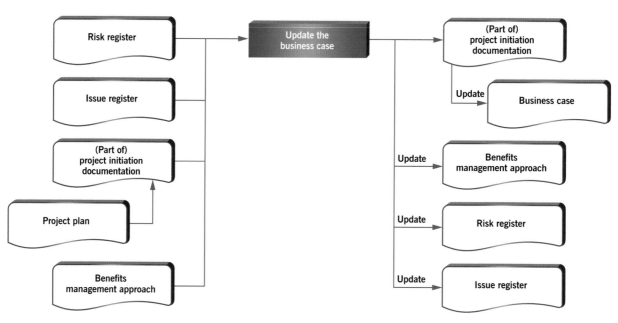

Figure 19.4 Update the business case: activity summary

- the project risk profile and key risks
- the issue register for any issues that may affect the business case
- the project plan to see whether the final implementation date of the project has changed (to earlier or later), which might affect some or all of the projected benefits
- the project plan to see whether the cost of delivering the project product has changed, which may affect the cost–benefit analysis
- the corporate, programme management or customer environment into which the project product will be delivered, as it may have changed
- whether any benefits reviews are required in the next management stage.
- Revise the business case and, if necessary, the benefits management approach, ready for project board approval.
- Update the risk register and issue register as necessary.

Table 19.3 shows the responsibilities for this activity.

Table 19.3 Update the business case: responsibilities

Product	Action	Corporate/ programme/ customer	Executive	Senior user	Senior supplier	Project manager	Team manager	Project assurance	Project support	Product description available
Business case	Update	(R)	(A)	(A)	(A)	P		R		A.2
Benefits management approach	Update	(R)	(A)	(A)	(A)	P		R		A.1
Risk register	Update					P		R		A.25
Issue register	Update					P		R		A.12

Key: P (producer) – responsible for product's production; R (reviewer) – ideally independent of production; A (approver) – confirms approval.

The complete list of responsibilities for each product is shown. Where a product is produced, reviewed or approved in another process, the responsibility is shown in parentheses, as in (P), (R) or (A).

19.4.4 Report management stage end

The results of a management stage should be reported back to the project board so that progress is clearly visible to the project management team.

The project manager gives a view on the continuing ability of the project to meet the project plan and business case, and assesses the overall risk situation. This activity should happen as close as possible to the actual end of a management stage.

Figure 19.5 shows the inputs to, and outputs from, this activity.

PRINCE2 recommends the following actions:

- For an exception plan:
  - depending on the point within the management stage when the exception occurred, it may be appropriate to produce an end stage report for the activities to date. Whether this is required will be advised by the project board in response to the exception report. If an end stage report is required, then follow the guidance for a stage plan below.
- For a stage plan:
  - review the status of the updated business case and, in particular, the achievement of any benefits anticipated for the management stage. Confirm that any activities in the benefits management approach for the current management stage have been completed
  - review the stage plan to ensure that the objectives of the management stage have been met, and the project plan to ensure that the project objectives are still achievable

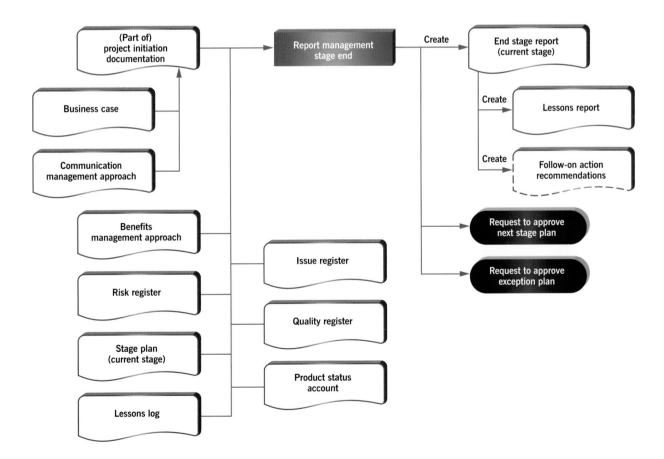

Figure 19.5 Report management stage end: activity summary

- review the team performance for the management stage
- review the product performance for the management stage by reference to the product status account (provided by project support):
  - review the quality management activities for the management stage and their results
  - ensure that all the products planned to be created within the stage plan for the current management stage are complete and approved, or have been carried forward into the next management stage
  - if a phased handover of products (see section 20.4.3) occurred during the management stage, confirm user acceptance and operational and maintenance acceptance of the products transferred to customer ownership. Identify any follow-on action recommendations for the products handed over
- review the issues and risks raised during the stage and any risk response actions taken. Include a summary of the current aggregated risk exposure
- prepare an end stage report for the current management stage.
- If appropriate, review the lessons at this time, particularly for longer projects, where interim reviews of lessons, or the project itself, may benefit corporate, programme management or the customer.
- Seek approval from the project board of the exception plan or stage plan (and, if appropriate, the revised project plan, the revised benefits management approach and the revised business case; see Chapter 15).
- Review the communication management approach to see whether there is a requirement to send copies of the end stage report (and, if appropriate, a lessons report) to external interested parties at this time.

Table 19.4 shows the responsibilities for this activity.

Table 19.4 Report management stage end: responsibilities

Product	Action	Corporate/ programme/ customer	Executive	Senior user	Senior supplier	Project manager	Team manager	Project assurance	Project support	Product description available
End stage report	Create		(A)	(A)	(A)	P		R		A.9
Lessons report	Create		(A)	(A)	(A)	P		R		A.15
Follow-on action recommendations	Create		(A)	(A)	(A)	P		R		

Key: P (producer) – responsible for product's production; R (reviewer) – ideally independent of production; A (approver) – confirms approval.

The complete list of responsibilities for each product is shown. Where a product is produced, reviewed or approved in another process, the responsibility is shown in parentheses, as in (P), (R) or (A).

19.4.5 Produce an exception plan

If a management stage or the project is forecast to deviate beyond its agreed tolerances, it no longer has the approval of the project board.

Exception plans are requested by the project board in response to an exception report. Although an exception plan will be produced prior to the planned management stage boundary, its approval by the project board marks a management stage boundary for the revised management stage.

Planning is not an activity undertaken in isolation. The project manager will need to consult with project board members, project assurance, team managers and possibly other stakeholders in order to create a viable plan. The more people involved in planning, the more robust the plan will be. See Chapter 9 for more details on planning.

Figure 19.6 shows the inputs to, and outputs from, this activity.

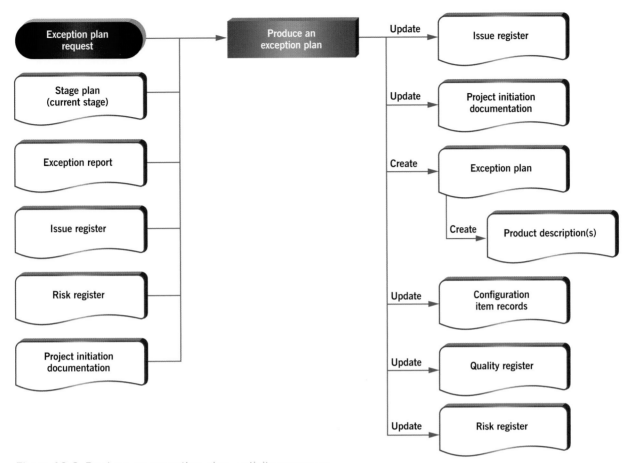

Figure 19.6 Produce an exception plan: activity summary

PRINCE2 recommends the following actions:

- Update the issue register (and, if necessary, the issue report) to record the project board's request for an exception plan.
- Review and, if needed, update the PID. It may be necessary to consult with the project board regarding any required changes. The following should be reviewed:
  - the customer's quality expectations: do they remain unchanged?
  - the relevance and suitability of the project approaches and controls
  - any change in the project management team or their role descriptions (in particular the situation with regard to external resources or suppliers as these may affect the exception plan).
- Produce the exception plan:
  - examine the stage plan to identify the products planned to be created during the management stage
  - examine the exception report for details (such as recommended actions) that will contribute to the exception plan
  - if the exception plan requires new products to be created, then examine the quality management approach for the quality standards and procedures required
  - update the product breakdown structure, product descriptions and product flow diagram for the products to be created by the exception plan
  - update the quality register for planned quality management activities.
- If used, create (or update) configuration item records for products to be produced by the exception plan.

- Update the issue register and risk register if any new issues or risks have been identified (or if existing ones need to be modified).
- Update the quality register for planned quality management activities. This should include target review and approval dates for the products.

Table 19.5 shows the responsibilities for this activity.

Table 19.5 Produce an exception plan: responsibilities

Product	Action	Corporate/ programme/ customer	Executive	Senior user	Senior supplier	Project manager	Team manager	Project assurance	Project support	Product description available
Project initiation documentation	Update	(R)	(A)	(A)	(A)	P		R		A.20
Exception plan	Create		(A)	(A)	(A)	P		R		A.16
Configuration item records	Create/ update					R		R	P	A.6
Risk register	Update					P		R		A.25
Issue register	Update					P		R		A.12
Quality register	Update					R	(R)	R	P	A.23

Key: P (producer) – responsible for product's production; R (reviewer) – ideally independent of production; A (approver) – confirms approval.

The complete list of responsibilities for each product is shown. Where a product is produced, reviewed or approved in another process, the responsibility is shown in parentheses, as in (P), (R) or (A).

19.5 Tailoring guidelines

19.5.1 General considerations

The activities in this process may be combined, split or run concurrently to suit the context, but care should be taken to ensure the integrity of the interfaces with the initiating a project, controlling a stage and directing a project processes.

Although this process is called managing a stage boundary, it also covers the preparation of an exception plan within a stage when tolerances are exceeded. Managing a stage boundary is used when dealing with planned or unplanned activities (such as exceptions).

19.5.2 Tailoring products in managing a stage boundary

Table 19.6 provides tailoring guidelines for management products in managing a stage boundary.

Table 19.6 Guidelines for tailoring products in managing a stage boundary

Management product	Tailoring guidelines
Stage plan	If there are only two management stages (one for initiation and the other for delivery), the stage plan can be included in the project plan.
Product descriptions	The project product description and product descriptions are key as they relate to the PRINCE2 focus on products principle. Although PRINCE2 shows the project manager as responsible for creating product descriptions, in practice they may not have the requisite skills to define specialist products. Their role may be to see that the product descriptions are defined and reviewed rigorously enough to enable planning to be undertaken confidently.
End stage report	If there is only one delivery stage, then the end of that stage is also the end of the project. In this case an end stage report is not needed as its content would be covered in the end project report within the closing a project process. This product may be split into two parts, one covering progress to date in detail, the other forming the basis of the decision to start the next stage.
Lessons log	Lessons from the log or lessons report (if one has been created) may be combined with the end stage report.
Exception plan	The plan may include components in any format commensurate with the complexity of the project, with views ranging from a simple list of accountabilities, products, activities and dates to Gantt charts. The plan may be held totally or partially within a planning tool(s).

19.5.3 Tailoring the roles in managing a stage boundary

The project manager is responsible for the creation of all new management products in this process, but may delegate work to others with the requisite skills, such as project support or a team manager, provided the project manager retains overall responsibility.

19.5.4 Common situations

19.5.4.1 Managing stage boundaries on a simple project

Some projects may only have two management stages: the initiation stage and one delivery stage. In this case, the scope of managing a stage boundary could be reduced to the report management stage end activity.

Plan the next management stage activity would not be needed if the project plan covered the required detail. The project plan and business case would only have just been produced and would not need updating. Exceptions, however, would still need to follow the managing a stage boundary process.

19.5.4.2 Managing stage boundaries when using an agile approach

Ideally the managing stage boundaries process should not interrupt the natural flow of work using agile, with releases and sprints synchronized within each management stage. This process provides an opportunity to assess the ongoing viability of the project as a whole and to decide what the priorities are for the next management stage. This is to ensure that high-value (most beneficial) work from the product backlog is undertaken in preference to lower-value work. Throughout the stage the frequent delivery of products in an iterative and incremental style will mean that it will be clear how many features have been delivered, their level of quality and value added, and which remain to be covered in later management stages.

19.5.4.3 Managing stage boundaries on a project from a supplier perspective

From a supplier perspective when working on work packages for a customer's project, the supplier's input may be to help prepare any plans. From the perspective of the supplier's project, stage boundaries would normally represent its own decision points within its own project lifecycle and delivery of work packages would need to match the stage boundaries in the customer's project.

19.5.4.4 Managing stage boundaries on a project within a programme

All the guidance provided above is applicable to a project within a programme, except that any decisions and plans will be made in the context of the programme. If possible, aligning the programme review points with project management stage boundaries may help keep alignment across the programme.

20

Closing a project

This chapter covers:

- preparing for formal closure
- preparing for premature closure
- handing over the project product
- evaluating the project and recording lessons
- recommending project closure
- guidelines for tailoring products and roles

20 Closing a project

20.1 Purpose

The purpose of the closing a project process is to provide a fixed point at which acceptance of the project product is confirmed, and to recognize that objectives set out in the original PID have been achieved (or approved changes to the objectives have been achieved), or that the project has nothing more to contribute.

20.2 Objective

The objective of the closing a project process is to:

- verify user acceptance of the project product
- ensure that the host site is able to support the products when the project is disbanded
- review the performance of the project against its baselines
- assess any benefits that have already been realized and update the benefits management approach to include any post-project benefit reviews
- ensure that provision has been made to address all open issues and risks, with follow-on action recommendations.

20.3 Context

Figure 20.1 provides an overview of closing a project.

One of the defining features of a PRINCE2 project is that it is finite; it has a start and an end. If the project loses this distinctiveness, it loses some of its advantages over purely operational management approaches.

A clear end to a project:

- is always more successful than a slow drift into use as it is a recognition by all concerned that:
  - the original objectives have been met (subject to any approved changes)
  - the current project has run its course
  - either the operational regime must now take over the products from this project, or the products become inputs into some subsequent project or into some larger programme
  - the project management team can be disbanded
  - project costs should no longer be incurred

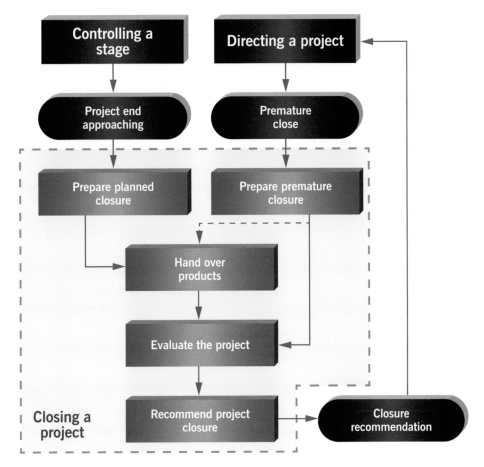

Figure 20.1 Overview of closing a project

- provides an opportunity to ensure that all unachieved goals and objectives are identified so that they can be addressed in the future
- transfers ownership of the products to the customer and terminates the responsibility of the project management team.

Closure activities should be planned as part of the stage plan for the final management stage. When closing a project, work is required to prepare input to the project board in order to obtain its authorization to close the project. Subsequently, the executive should also notify corporate, programme management or the customer that the project has closed (see section 15.4.5).

It is also possible that the project board may wish to trigger a premature closure of the project under some circumstances (e.g. if the business case is no longer valid). If the project is being brought to a premature close, this process will still need to be executed, but may have to be tailored to the actual project situation.

A number of actions specific to the project product may be required after the project, and these should be documented and planned for as follow-on action recommendations. These may have different audiences and therefore may need to be issued individually. The needs of the recipient will determine the format and content; some may want a formal report, some a log entry on a system, and others a meeting.

20.4 Activities

The activities within the closing a project process are project-manager-oriented and are to:

- prepare **planned closure**
- prepare premature closure
- hand over products
- evaluate the project
- recommend project closure.

20.4.1 Prepare planned closure

Before closure of the project can be recommended, the project manager must ensure that the expected results have all been achieved and delivered.

Figure 20.2 shows the inputs to, and outputs from, this activity.

PRINCE2 recommends the following actions:

- Update the project plan with actuals from the final management stage.
- Request a product status account from project support. From the product status account, ensure that the project product:
  - has been approved by the authorities identified in the project product description
  - meets all the quality criteria, or is covered by approved concessions.
- Confirm that the project has delivered what is defined in the project product description, and that the acceptance criteria have been met.
- Seek approval to give notice to corporate, programme management or the customer that resources can be (or are about to be) released.

Table 20.1 shows the responsibilities for this activity.

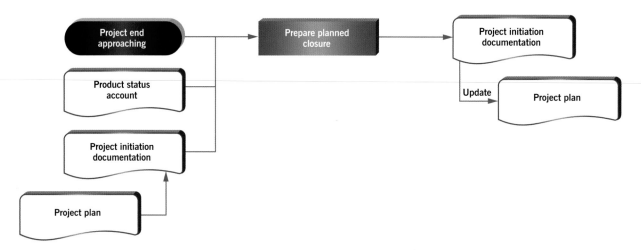

Figure 20.2 Prepare planned closure: activity summary

Table 20.1 Prepare planned closure: responsibilities

Product	Action	Corporate/ programme/ customer	Executive	Senior user	Senior supplier	Project manager	Team manager	Project assurance	Project support	Product description available
Project plan	Update					P		R		A.16
Product status account	Create					R		R	P	A.18

Key: P (producer) – responsible for product's production; R (reviewer) – ideally independent of production; A (approver) – confirms approval.

20.4.2 Prepare premature closure

In some situations, the project board may have instructed the project manager to close the project prematurely. In such circumstances, the project manager must ensure that work in progress is not simply abandoned, but that the project salvages anything of value created to date and checks that any gaps left by the cancellation of the project are raised to corporate, programme management or the customer.

Figure 20.3 shows the inputs to, and outputs from, this activity.

PRINCE2 recommends the following actions:

- Update the issue register (and, if necessary, the issue report) to record the premature closure request.
- Update the project plan with actuals from the final management stage.
- Request a product status account from project support. From this, determine which of the project product's components:
  - have been approved by the authorities identified in their product descriptions
  - are currently in development (and which of those need to be completed)
  - are covered by approved concessions
  - have yet to be started
  - need to be made safe
  - may be useful to other projects.

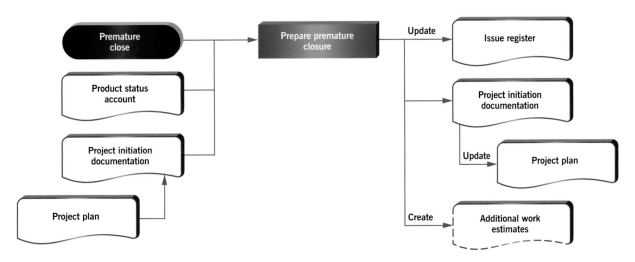

Figure 20.3 Prepare premature closure: activity summary

- Agree the means for recovering products that have been completed or are in progress (if appropriate). This will need project board consultation and may include additional work to create, make safe or complete products that might be useful to other projects (e.g. making an unfinished building safe and weatherproof). In some cases, the additional work may require an exception plan.
- Seek approval to give notice to corporate, programme management or the customer that resources can be (or are about to be) released early.

Table 20.2 shows the responsibilities for this activity.

Table 20.2 Prepare premature closure: responsibilities

Product	Action	Corporate/ programme/ customer	Executive	Senior user	Senior supplier	Project manager	Team manager	Project assurance	Project support	Product description available
Issue register	Update					P				A.12
Project plan	Update					P		R		A.16
Product status account	Create					R		R	P	A.18
Additional work estimates	Create	(A)	(A)	(A)		P		R		

Key: P (producer) – responsible for product's production; R (reviewer) – ideally independent of production; A (approver) – confirms approval.

The complete list of responsibilities for each product is shown. Where a product is produced, reviewed or approved in another process, the responsibility is shown in parentheses, as in (P), (R) or (A).

20.4.3 Hand over products

The project product must be passed to an operational and maintenance environment prior to the project being closed. This may happen as a single release at the end of the project, or the project approach may include phased delivery where products are handed over in a number of releases. In the case of a premature closure, there may be some products that have been approved but not yet handed over and, depending on the project board guidance, the ownership of some or all of those products may need to be transferred to the customer.

When handing over products, the benefits management approach may need to be updated to include the post-project benefits review(s) of the performance of the project product in operational use. Such benefits reviews may identify whether there have been any side-effects (beneficial or adverse) that could provide useful lessons for other projects.

There may be multiple handovers throughout the project lifecycle. It is not a project activity to undertake benefits reviews post-project, only to plan for such benefits reviews to occur. If the project is part of a programme, then the post-project benefits reviews need to be covered by the programme's benefits management activities.

Figure 20.4 shows the inputs to, and outputs from, this activity.

PRINCE2 recommends the following actions:

- In consultation with the project management team, prepare follow-on action recommendations for the project product to include any uncompleted work, issues and risks. There could be separate follow-on action recommendations for the project product (or its components) or for each distinct user group (e.g. human resources, finance, operations).
- Check that the benefits management approach includes post-project activities to confirm benefits that cannot be measured until after the project product has been in operational use for some time (e.g. reliability requirements).

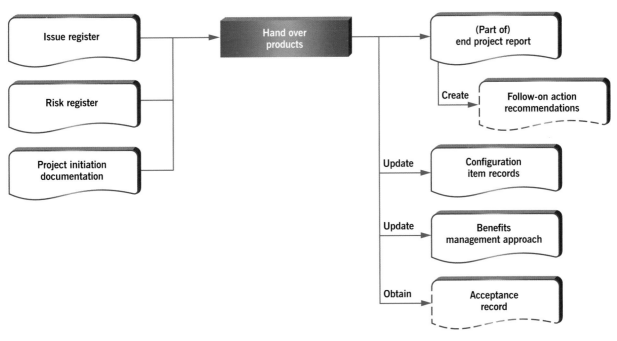

Figure 20.4 Hand over products: activity summary

- Examine the PID to confirm how products are to be handed over to those who will maintain them in their operational life:
  - confirm that the correct operational and maintenance environment is in place
  - consider the early life-support requirements of each product being handed over because the early life of a product is often the period of peak demand on the support organization
  - when a product requires a lot of potentially expensive support and maintenance, ensure that a suitable service agreement or contract has been drawn up between the operations and maintenance organizations and the end-users. Such an agreement should be included as a product to be developed by the project
  - confirm acceptance from the operations and maintenance organizations
  - request and obtain acceptance records
  - transfer the responsibility for the products from the project to the operations and maintenance organizations and update the products' configuration item records, if used.

Table 20.3 shows the responsibilities for this activity.

Table 20.3 Hand over products: responsibilities

Product	Action	Corporate/ programme/ customer	Executive	Senior user	Senior supplier	Project manager	Team manager	Project assurance	Project support	Product description available
Follow-on action recommendations	Create/ update		(A)	(A)	(A)	P		R		
Configuration item records	Update					A		R	P	A.6
Benefits management approach	Update	(A)	(R)	(R)	(R)	P		R		A.1
Acceptance record	Obtain		(A)	(A)	(A)	P		R		

Key: P (producer) – responsible for product's production; R (reviewer) – ideally independent of production; A (approver) – confirms approval.

The complete list of responsibilities for each product is shown. Where a product is produced, reviewed or approved in another process, the responsibility is shown in parentheses, as in (P), (R) or (A).

20.4.4 Evaluate the project

Successful organizations learn from their experiences with projects. When evaluating the project, the objective is to assess how successful or unsuccessful the project has been. It may also be possible to improve the estimation for future projects by analysing the estimates and actual progress metrics for this project.

Figure 20.5 shows the inputs to, and outputs from, this activity.

PRINCE2 recommends the following actions:

- Review the project's original intent as agreed in the initiation stage and defined by the PID, baselined at that time.
- Review the approved changes as defined by the current version of the components of the PID.
- In consultation with the project management team, prepare an end project report to include:
  - the project manager's summary of how the project performed
  - an assessment of the results of the project against the expected benefits in the business case
  - a review of how the project performed against its planned targets and tolerances
  - a review of team performance
  - a review of the project product (which should include a summary of any follow-on action recommendations)
  - if necessary, the documented reasons why a project was brought to a premature close.
- In consultation with the project management team, review the lessons log to identify lessons that could be applied to future projects and incorporate them into the end project report. The report should include:
  - a review of what went well, what went badly and any recommendations for corporate, programme management or customer consideration; in particular, the project management method, any delivery approach(es) used, project approaches and controls, and any abnormal events that caused deviation

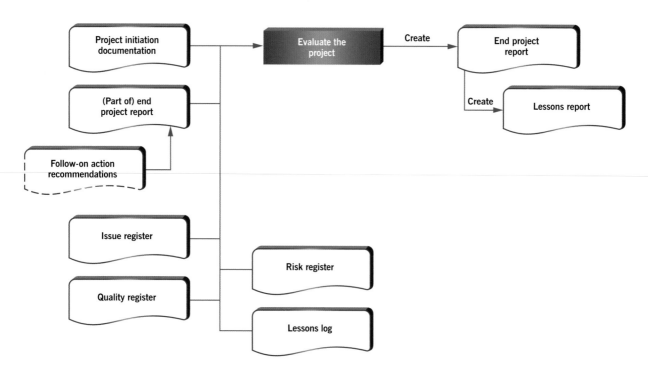

Figure 20.5 Evaluate the project: activity summary

- a review of useful measurements such as: how much effort was required to create the products, how effective the quality management approach was in designing, developing and delivering fit-for-purpose products (e.g. how many errors were found after products had passed quality inspections), and statistics on issues and risks
- any useful knowledge gained regarding the tailoring of PRINCE2 for the project.

Table 20.4 shows the responsibilities for this activity.

Table 20.4 Evaluate the project: responsibilities

Product	Action	Corporate/ programme/ customer	Executive	Senior user	Senior supplier	Project manager	Team manager	Project assurance	Project support	Product description available
End project report	Create		(A)	(A)	(A)	P		R		A.8
Lessons report	Create	(A)	(R)	(R)	(R)	P		R		A.15

Key: P (producer) – responsible for product's production; R (reviewer) – ideally independent of production; A (approver) – confirms approval.

The complete list of responsibilities for each product is shown. Where a product is produced, reviewed or approved in another process, the responsibility is shown in parentheses, as in (P), (R) or (A).

20.4.5 Recommend project closure

After the project manager has confirmed that the project can be closed, a **closure recommendation** should be raised to the project board. Figure 20.6 shows the inputs to, and outputs from, this activity.

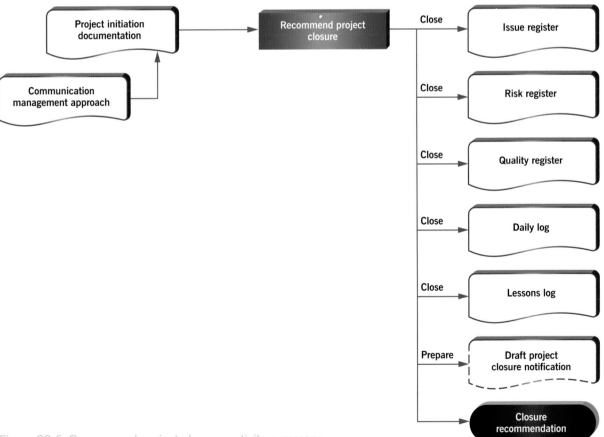

Figure 20.6 Recommend project closure: activity summary

PRINCE2 recommends the following actions:

- Use the communication management approach to identify any organization or interested party who needs to know that the project is closing. Consider also communication activities for public relations and marketing opportunities at this point.
- Close the project's issue register, risk register, quality register, daily log and lessons log.
- Make sure that all project information is secured and archived (in accordance with the change control approach) in order to permit any future audit of the project management team's decisions, actions and performance.
- Prepare and send a draft project closure notification for review by the project board, stating that the project has closed.

Table 20.5 shows the responsibilities for this activity.

Table 20.5 Recommend project closure: responsibilities

Product	Action	Corporate/ programme/ customer	Executive	Senior user	Senior supplier	Project manager	Team manager	Project assurance	Project support	Product description available
Issue register	Close					P				A.12
Risk register	Close					P				A.25
Quality register	Close					P				A.23
Daily log	Close					P				A.7
Lessons log	Close					P				A.14
Draft project closure notification	Prepare		(A)	(A)	(A)	P		R		

Key: P (producer) – responsible for product's production; R (reviewer) – ideally independent of production; A (approver) – confirms approval.

The complete list of responsibilities for each product is shown. Where a product is produced, reviewed or approved in another process, the responsibility is shown in parentheses, as in (P), (R) or (A).

20.5 Tailoring guidelines

20.5.1 General considerations

The activities in this process may be combined, split or run concurrently to suit the context, but care should be taken to ensure the integrity of the interface to the directing a project and controlling a stage processes.

If the final stage(s) of the project includes initial operation of the outputs, the hand over products activity may not be undertaken in the project's final management stage as part of closing the project, but may happen within a number of previous management stages. Closing the project would then only require confirmation that all handovers have been completed.

20.5.2 Tailoring products in closing a project

Table 20.6 provides tailoring guidelines for management products in closing a project.

Table 20.6 Guidelines for tailoring products in closing a project

Management product	Tailoring guidelines
End project report	Any element of the composition may be provided in a separate document or information source, which should be cross-referenced.
	The composition may be adapted to suit the readership; for example, confidential elements, such as the review of the business case or team performance, may be included in separate documents.
Lessons log	Lessons from the log or lessons report (if one has been created) are usually included in the end project report but may be presented in a separate document.

20.5.3 Tailoring roles in closing a project

The project manager is responsible for the creation of all new management products in this process, but may delegate work to others provided overall responsibility is retained.

The checking that post-project benefits reviews are planned to take place may be undertaken by the senior user in the hand over products activity.

20.5.4 Common situations

20.5.4.1 Closing a simple project

All activities may happen in a very short timescale; for example, handover, evaluation and closure approval (from directing a project) could all happen at a single meeting. Closure activities do not need to be formally documented, with a daily log entry, minutes of a meeting or email sufficing, provided it is clear to all stakeholders and the project management team that the project is closed and what the follow-on actions are.

20.5.4.2 Closing a project when using an agile approach

When using agile, project closure is still likely to be a formal event. However, most of the information is already known and most of the work is already done due to the iterative and incremental nature of the agile way of working. Examples of this would be that benefits may already be being realized, most of the project product's functionality is in operational use, and documentation is almost complete and just needs to be finalized. In addition, many lessons will already have been identified during retrospectives at the end of each sprint.

20.5.4.3 Closing a project from a supplier perspective

It should be decided when the project is completed from a supplier perspective. For example, this may be when the work is completed, after any maintenance or warranty period has elapsed, or when the contract is fulfilled.

20.5.4.4 Closing a project within a programme

All the guidance provided above is applicable to a project within a programme, except that any decisions and the plan for the benefits reviews will be made in the context of the programme, whether closure is premature or is on completion of the project.

Considerations for organizational adoption

This chapter covers:

- why an organization-wide method may be wanted
- who should be involved
- assessing the organization's capability
- building and managing the method
- embedding and deploying the method
- consistency of use
- building and sustaining maturity
- examples of tailoring and embedding

21 Considerations for organizational adoption

This chapter builds on section 4.4 to provide more detailed guidance for those organizations which want to adopt PRINCE2 and, in particular, what to consider when:

- tailoring PRINCE2 to create an organization's method (section 21.1)
- embedding the tailored method within the organization's working practices and ensuring its widespread use (section 21.2).

21.1 Tailoring PRINCE2 for an organization

21.1.1 Creating an organization's PRINCE2-based project management method

21.1.1.1 Understanding the drivers and objectives for adopting PRINCE2

Before creating a project management method, it must be understood why an organization wants to do this. By understanding the drivers and objectives, it is more likely that a method will be created that meets the needs of the organization. For example, one typical driver may be to ensure projects comply with external standards, such as ISO 21500 or BS 6079, or bodies of knowledge such as from the APM or PMI (see section 2.6.1). It is possible, through tailoring PRINCE2, to create a method which complies with all these, as each of them also promotes tailoring.

Tip

Few organizations initially aim to build a project method for all their projects but this often becomes a long-term objective. If you are building a method for specific project types, try to write the method so that it could be used on any type of project. This makes adoption of the method by other parts of the business much easier.

Key message

The overriding objective for adopting PRINCE2 should be to improve business performance.

21.1.1.2 Deciding who to involve

The people involved in the development of a new method should have the right skills and experience; they may be in-house experts, consultants or a mix. The method they create must be acceptable to the users (stakeholders). A way of moving to a common method within an organization is to collect together some experienced and respected project managers to compare the way that they do things now, and ask them to agree an approach that appears to be acceptable to all; use recognized experts to facilitate discussions on contentious issues and, if necessary, recommend a solution. This will not only ensure that collective experience is harnessed but will also promote buy-in.

Creating a centre of excellence to manage both the development of a method and its ongoing improvement is a powerful way of ensuring momentum. For more information on creating a centre of excellence, see *Portfolio, Programme and Project Offices* (Cabinet Office, 2013).

21.1.1.3 Using maturity models

The increase in business performance through the effective use of project management methods across organizations has been demonstrated through the use of maturity assessments, which measure an organization's capability to manage projects, programmes and/or portfolios. The higher the maturity an organization attains, the more effective and efficient it is in business terms.

Definition: Maturity

A measure of the reliability, efficiency and effectiveness of a process, function, organization, etc. The most mature processes and functions are formally aligned with business objectives and strategy, and are supported by a framework for continual improvement.

Definition: Maturity model

A method of assessing organizational capability in a given area of skill.

The benefits of using a maturity assessment include, but are not limited to:

- helping organizations decide what maturity level they must achieve to meet their business needs
- creating a reliable capability baseline against which improvements in performance can be objectively measured
- providing an objective assessment of strengths and weaknesses
- justifying investment in project management infrastructure
- providing validation of an organization's maturity
- demonstrating service quality to support proposals to prospective clients
- reducing delivery costs and increasing benefits
- indicating what the next logical improvement steps are to improve project management performance.

One maturity model is AXELOS's Portfolio, Programme and Project Management Maturity Model (P3M3). Table 21.1 shows the characteristics for project management taken from P3M3. At maturity level 2 each project has its own method, whereas at maturity levels 3 and upwards projects are managed using a common method. If an organization seeks to adopt PRINCE2 as its project management method, it needs to aim, in the first instance, for maturity level 3 or its equivalent. The detail in the model describes how the people in an organization would behave over the range of topics which comprise 'project management' at each maturity level. By using such a maturity model, together with PRINCE2, a design can be developed which defines what the organization's method needs to cover.

Table 21.1 Characteristics of P3M3 project maturity levels

Maturity	Characteristics
Level 1: Awareness of process	Does the organization recognize projects and run them differently from its ongoing business? (Projects may be run informally with no standard process or tracking system.)
Level 2: Repeatable process	Does the organization ensure that each project is run with its own processes and procedures to a minimum specified standard? (There may be limited coordination between projects.)
Level 3: Defined process	Does the organization have its own centrally controlled project processes and can individual projects flex within these processes to suit the particular project?
Level 4: Managed process	Does the organization obtain and retain specific measurements on its project management performance and run a quality management organization to better predict future performance?
Level 5: Optimized process	Does the organization run continual process improvement with proactive problem and technology management for projects in order to improve its ability to predict performance over time and optimize processes?

Example: Project management and P3M3

If an organization has no commonly used project management method, each project manager has to define their own approach for each project. PRINCE2 can be used as the basis for this, as PRINCE2 can be tailored directly to suit each project. By taking this approach, an organization being assessed using the P3M3 would be rated as a maturity level 2 organization, in which each project is run with its own processes and procedures.

On the other hand, an organization which has a defined project management method, based on PRINCE2, would become at least a maturity level 3 organization, in which projects are managed to a common set of processes and procedures. Typically, the higher the maturity level, the better projects perform.

21.1.1.4 Pulling the elements of PRINCE2 together

Consistent terminology is important, as using words in a consistent way helps communication and understanding. The organization's method should, as far as is realistic, reflect the terminology used in the organization. Problems will occur when different parts of the business use different terminology, neither of which may be wrong. For this reason, it is helpful to agree, in advance, the definition of key project management terms.

Tip

Make the creation of the glossary an early deliverable in developing the method as this will be a guide for the words to use in the rest of the method. Choose a baseline glossary such as PRINCE2 as the default and use it to create the organization's own glossary. Change individual words if necessary, add to definitions to aid understanding and provide 'also called' alternative names in the glossary to help people relearn any new words. Update the glossary when necessary, amending or adding to it.

Example of changing the glossary

A retailer decided to adopt PRINCE2, but everyone in the organization understood 'product' to mean those items that the organization sells to its customers. Accordingly, the retailer decided to replace the PRINCE2 term 'product' with 'deliverable'. Hence it created 'deliverable descriptions' rather than 'product descriptions'.

Tailoring the processes, roles and product descriptions are closely linked. An activity in a PRINCE2 process is undertaken by a role to create a management product. Change any one relationship and the relationship between the others may also change. For this reason, it is advisable to start by tailoring the processes, changing them to reflect any new terminology and amending the process model and activity flows if necessary to reflect how the organization should operate. Detailed role and product descriptions can then be tailored to reflect the process changes. The processes requiring change will most likely include those related to directing a project and, in particular, relating to authorizing funding for projects or stages of projects; finance departments tend to have prescriptive 'schemes of delegation' defining who has the decisions rights relating to project authorization.

Tip

If the PRINCE2 process map is tailored, maintain a version-controlled copy, showing the inputs and outputs between processes. Link this to tailored versions of each PRINCE2 process. By doing this the integrity of the interfaces in the process model should be retained whenever any changes are made.

PRINCE2's themes are drawn on from particular activities in the processes. Each organization has to decide how each PRINCE2 theme is reflected in its project management method. On individual projects, this is usually described in the PID, the relevant sections being the management approaches (for communications, quality, risk and change control), controls, and roles and structures. Having a defined procedure ensures these aspects are covered in a consistent way and saves each project manager having to define their own as they can refer to the organization's approach.

Tip

Create one-page pocket guides or cards on important topics such as risk management to help people understand the key points.

Consider using checklists (like those in the Appendices to this manual) rather than having document templates for the management products.

21.1.1.5 Project lifecycles

Although PRINCE2 does not prescribe the use of any particular project lifecycle, it does require that one is used. Rather than each project manager designing their own, consider including one in the project management method, describing the purpose of each management stage and linking back to the PRINCE2 processes and themes. Standardizing the project lifecycle gives project managers a basis from which to tailor their own. It also enables the organization to have an overview of the progress of its portfolio of projects. Standardization of project lifecycles can go a step further and, rather than just describing a generic project, can be made to reflect particular types of project by including the specialist activities in the appropriate stages, such as for capability and product development, software development, construction, corporate mergers and complex change. For more on project lifecycle see the plans theme (Chapter 9).

21.1.1.6 Managing the method

After a method has been created, it needs to be managed and maintained. The method should therefore include guide(s), procedures or processes describing how it is managed, together with associated roles and product descriptions. The roles should include one to manage the overall architecture of the method, ensuring that the process model and its component parts work as a whole. Changing one component may impact other components, and so change control should be considered as part of this. Another role would be for the management of each component of the method; this would enable the method architect to have different people manage each component.

Tip

Maturity models often include a requirement to have a defined way of managing a method. For example, *CMMI for Development* (CMMI-DEV; Carnegie Mellon University, 2010) has two process areas at maturity level 3 covering this, called 'organizational process focus' and 'organizational process definition'.

21.1.2 Creating tailoring rules and guidelines

As PRINCE2 has a tailoring principle, any method derived from it should also allow tailoring. This means that the method should include tailoring rules and guidelines. This may be covered in a few pages of text or may involve a lot of detail, describing if and how each element of the method could be tailored.

Key message

An organization may choose to limit the extent to which its project management method can be tailored by defining the following:

- What rules or guidelines are applicable to the organization?
- What degrees of freedom should each role holder have?
- Who 'approves' tailoring?
- Who can advise people on tailoring?

Example

A multinational company defined its project management method in processes. The method's processes reflected the PRINCE2 processes, themes and templates (derived from PRINCE2's product description outlines). Each of the method's processes and product descriptions included guidelines stating how they could be tailored.

See section 21.1.3 for further examples.

As PRINCE2 can be used regardless of the complexity or scale of the project, organizations may consider rating their projects by complexity and providing guidance on how each category should be tailored. Table 21.2 illustrates a simple approach to categorizing projects and provides suggestions about how PRINCE2 could be tailored.

The aim is to help project practitioners decide what is 'just enough' project management in order to ensure project success.

The greater the complexity of the project, the more information that is generated. A project manager should ensure that the means of storing and distributing information is efficient and secure. For simpler projects, a log book and wall display may be sufficient, but for more complex projects, especially with distributed teams, information systems will need to be developed and rolled out.

An approach to complexity modelling may be found in Table 5.5 of *Portfolio, Programme and Project Offices* (Cabinet Office, 2013).

Tip

There are many ways to measure complexity. Most involve scoring a project against a number of criteria to assess the overall complexity of the project and which parts are the greatest source of complexity. One such model is the Delivery Environment Complexity Analytic (DECA), which was developed by the UK's National Audit Office (NAO) to provide a high-level overview of the challenges, complexity and risks to delivery of a project, programme, policy or area of work.

Table 21.2 Examples of projects of different complexity

Complexity		Characteristic	Applying PRINCE2
High ↑↓ **Low**	Programme	Major business transformation Multiple projects	**This is not a project.** A programme management framework such as Managing Successful Programmes (MSP) should be used. PRINCE2 should be used to manage the projects within the programme.
	Daunting project	Essential for strategic objectives High number of influential stakeholders Ambiguous requirements Uncertain context Significant finance needs New or novel outputs and outcomes Multiple parties involved Large range of disciplines needed Significant organizational change needed	Multiple delivery stages Extended project board (e.g. user/supplier groups) Team manager as a separate role likely Project support as a separate role likely Individual management products
	Normal project	Medium priority Moderate number of stakeholders Requirements need elaboration Some novel deliverables Moderate number of parties involved Moderate number of disciplines needed Change to status quo	One or more delivery stages Standard project board Team manager as a separate role optional Project support as a separate role optional Some management products combined
	Simple project	Low priority Few stakeholders Clear requirements Finances not significant Tried and tested deliverables Few parties involved Few disciplines needed Insignificant change to status quo	Single delivery stage Simple project board The project manager fulfils the team manager role The project manager fulfils the project support role Combined management products
	Task	Low risk, cost, importance, visibility Single discipline Single site	**This is not a project.** PRINCE2's managing product delivery process (using work packages, product descriptions, logs/registers and checkpoint reviews) can be used to manage a task. in such a case the team manager would not report to a project manager but to another manager in the organization.

21.1.3 Examples of how organizations have tailored PRINCE2

Example: Multinational company A

Modifying the process model

The company defined a project lifecycle, comprising five management stages, which was applied to all projects, and outlined the project management and specialist activities within each stage. The project management activities, defined in very brief documents, reflected the PRINCE2 processes and themes. PRINCE2's directing a project process was tailored to be three separate processes:

- providing ad hoc direction
- authorizing the start of each stage and project closure
- suspending or terminating projects.

Four guide publications were created to support the method:

- a guide to the stages and gates, which describes the project lifecycle and includes criteria to be met at each gate, prior to starting each stage and to closing the project
- summary notes covering project set-up, benefits, schedule, finance, risk, issues, change control, project reviews, value management, quality and closing the project
- a guide for project sponsors, describing their role (equivalent to the PRINCE2 executive)
- a guide for decision makers, which comprised a board that made the actual decisions at stage boundaries and a supporting board that ensured there were sufficient resources to undertake the work.

Templates, supported by guides, were produced for the commonly used management products. PRINCE2's PID was reflected in a single document which included the business case, project definition and plan.

Project milestones and reporting were via a company-wide web tool which included the risk, issues, change logs, key milestone dates, interdependencies and live financial feeds coming from the company's accounting system for each project, stage and work package. The project tool was also the project register (over 2500 concurrent projects), listing which stage the project is in, the sponsor, the project manager, the RAG (red, amber, green) status and the project status (proposed, in progress, suspended, terminated or completed) as well as the highlight report.

Example: Multinational company B

Aligning with external standards

The company made an explicit decision to ensure its method complied with not only PRINCE2 but also CMMI-DEV, BS 6079 Part 1, ISO 21500 and the APM and PMI bodies of knowledge. Guides were produced to show how each was dealt with and used with customers and auditors as evidence that the method complied.

The PRINCE2 processes were reflected in a 'direct and manage a project' procedure, comprising identify a project, direct a project, initiate a project, control a stage, prepare for next stage and close a project. Authorize a project was a separate process. PRINCE2 'manage product delivery' was reflected in a separate 'manage work package' process as this could also be used outside a project. Each management product had a template and product description with its own tailoring guidelines.

The PRINCE2 themes were dealt with as support procedures comprising benefits realization, planning, reporting, risks, issues, change control, stakeholders, communications, lessons and document management. They also covered areas outside PRINCE2, including induction, training, reviews/assurance, audit, quality, peer reviews, meetings and managing the method.

All procedures had flow charts, role summaries, tables of activities, clear responsibilities and accountabilities, checklists and tailoring guidelines with references (hyperlinks) to additional material (such as guides, standards, videos and tools) against the appropriate activities.

There were guide booklets on each topic as education sources and the most commonly needed were supplemented with single-page 'pocket guides'. By separating out educational material from the procedures, the company was able to keep the procedures to a minimum size.

Example: Major infrastructure company

Ensuring scope integrity and quality

The company's aim was to be 'process light', prescribing what products were needed, but leaving the choice and sequencing of activities to the project manager's professional judgement. There was only one process in the method, which was related to a statutory requirement.

This project management method focused on a defined project lifecycle tailored for the company's infrastructure projects with strong gating between stages. Each stage of the project included a list of the management and specialist products required to be created in that stage. All management and specialist products were predefined, with the product descriptions including applicability criteria which would drive the decision as to whether that product would be needed.

The project management team was supported by a set of directive handbooks which reflected the PRINCE2 themes, such as for risk management, managing gates, stakeholder management and planning. In addition, there were handbooks on sponsorship and the engineering process.

Example: Major communications company

An agile approach to tailoring

A major communications company developed its own PRINCE2-based project management method to replace 20 local methods across the company. The owners of the local methods all became part of the working group for the development of the new method; many had been having problems maintaining their methods due to lack of funds and time. The principles and high-level requirements were agreed by the group and from these a method architecture was developed. The method was designed and delivered using an agile way of working, which started with defining a minimum set of features (which included a glossary) and then agreeing the priority for the remaining features. These priorities were reviewed during regular team meetings and amended if necessary. Progress was measured against a burn chart of over 400 features comprising templates, procedures, guides and other products. After the first release, new features were delivered for use as soon as they became available.

21.2 Embedding PRINCE2 in the organization

21.2.1 Management of change

21.2.1.1 Changing the way people work

The introduction of an organization's project management method involves changing the way that people work, so that the outcome (in this case, widespread use of the project management method) can be realized, leading to a higher project success and enhanced business performance.

Current approaches to change management combine the psychological and engineering views of the world to create repeatable change methods, drawing on a wide range of tools and techniques. The application of different change methods has implications for the way organizations and their leaders regard change, the way they manage change and even the effectiveness of any change initiatives. At the heart of most change models is gaining the support of those who are required to change their ways of working. This involves:

- understanding the current situation (current state)
- identifying what changes are needed in the wider organization (future state)
- understanding the resilience of those who will be impacted by the change and their levels of resistance
- developing the necessary capabilities to meet the organization's needs (roles, processes, systems, culture and behaviours)
- engaging those affected by the change and winning their support.

To gain stakeholder support, change management approaches should not just involve training, but may also include coaching, mentoring, stakeholder engagement, marketing and communications activities to embed a real understanding of the need for the change and the resulting benefits. Change is as much about managing people's expectations and perceptions as managing facts.

Tip

Do not confuse 'change control', as described in the PRINCE2 change theme, with 'change management' as described in this section. Many proprietary methods and standards use the terms interchangeably.

21.2.1.2 Design of the future state

The design of the future state of a project management method should reflect the vision for how project management will work after the method is embedded. It should include the roles, processes, tools and behaviours relating to using the method itself and to any supporting organizational units. Projects should be perceived as part of the organization and therefore any processes, roles or approaches should align with those used in the rest of an organization. As project management is a form of governance it should explicitly link with the overall governance of the organization; embedding project management strengthens corporate governance. Common areas where this is apparent include the allocation of resources, the authorization of funding for projects, procurement of goods and services, audit, accounting and human resources practices.

The design of the future state not only incudes the tailoring of PRINCE2 (as described in section 21.1) but also the design of every other part of the organization which is needed to support project management.

For example, if the use of the method is mandated, an organization may create a special audit team to assess each project manager's degree of compliance with the method; sanctions may be applied to those who do not comply. The auditors may need special training, checklists, knowledge and processes to support their work (see section 21.2.4 for an example). A less directive organization may have mentors and coaches to help the practitioners understand and use the method effectively; such coaches need to be familiar with the project management method, supporting techniques and how to tailor them.

Organizations will often support their project managers by implementing tools and systems to aid communication and reduce the administrative overhead. Such tools may be for planning and tracking, controlling changes, tracking risks and actions, and recording lessons. The PRINCE2 product description outlines include a number of such products. Unfortunately many proprietary tools use their own terminology and work flow which may not match PRINCE2 or an organization's own terminology. Sometimes the terms can be changed but often not. In these cases the choice is to adapt the organization's terminology to match the tool or choose an alternative tool. The decision depends on the value put on maintaining the chosen terminology or work flows. Experienced project managers should be able to cope with different terminology but people new to project management or from disciplines outside project management may have a problem.

The 'future-state design' may also be referred to as the 'blueprint'. See *Managing Successful Programmes* (Cabinet Office, 2011) for more information.

Tip

The POTI model sets a high-level scope of what must be included and integrated in an effective future-state design:

P   Processes, business models of operations and functions including operational costs and performance levels.

O   Organizational structure, staffing levels, roles, skills requirements, organizational culture, supply chain and style.

T   Technology, buildings, IT systems and tools, equipment, machinery and accommodation.

I   Information and data required for the future business operations and performance measurement.

Tip

If embarking on a long-term roll-out of a project management method, do not forget to define what the interim states will be and make sure each is designed to work effectively while work continues towards the next one.

21.2.2 Consistently deploying the method

21.2.2.1 Ensure consistency across all impacted parts of the organization

The deployment of project management throughout an organization involves the roll-out of the project management method and supporting tools, together with the change management activities to promote the use of the method. Section 4.4 has already stated the benefits of the method being written and communicated in a consistent way. Such consistency also has to be applied to every other activity related to the implementation; for example, training content should reflect the concepts and terminology used in the method. Other activities associated with deployment may include communications, assurance, audit, mentoring and coaching.

As a large number of specialist products may need to be created in order to implement a project management method, the deployment strategy needs to be carefully thought through. Two alternatives are the 'big bang' approach and the incremental approach.

21.2.2.2 Big bang approach

In the 'big bang' approach, the project management method and its supporting elements are activated for use on the same day; all plans focus on this go-live date. Such an approach may be suitable in a small or new organization, but the actual go-live date would be constrained by the longest lead element of the project and thus early benefits may be lost. There could also be teething problems on launch, unless full trials have been carried out. Trials would normally need to cover the questions: Does it work in practice? Does it work at scale? As the big bang approach focuses on a single go-live date, this could be managed as a project.

21.2.2.3 Incremental approach

In most cases an incremental approach to rolling out the project management method and its supporting capabilities would be the most flexible and practical. By taking this approach, early benefits can be realized and the amount of change that users have to cope with at any one time reduced. It enables roll-out to be progressive, say geographically, so that deployment resources are not overstretched. In this case, the essential features required for launch would need to be determined, with other features rolled out as they become available. In some cases the plan may show interim states where the capabilities are used and bedded in before new capabilities are rolled out later. As the roll-out would require a number of projects and change activities, this would be better managed as a programme with tranches to reflect any interim operating states.

21.2.2.4 Track progress of the change

Whatever approach is taken, it is helpful to track the progress of the change effort during deployment and in the early operational period. Many change management techniques include change-tracking approaches. Maturity models can be used to assess progress of the roll-out for the whole of the organization or a sub-part.

Tip

If you are implementing a portfolio, programme and project management method, make sure they are designed to work together from the very start, sharing as much as possible in common and using the same glossary of terms. The chain of governance from corporate level through portfolio and programme to project needs to be explicit.

21.2.3 Building and sustaining maturity

If practitioners do not continue to use a project management method after the initial deployment, the effort and cost of creating it are wasted. A method needs ongoing active management if it is to benefit the business and help to continually improve business performance.

The creation of a method should not be an objective in its own right but just one component in a mix of capabilities aimed at improving business performance. Using a method requires people to be skilled and competent at their jobs; a method simply brings consistency in approach, where consistency adds value. The method should remain relevant to its users and so direct engagement should be encouraged through feedback and stakeholder involvement, such as in communities of practice and user groups.

Tip

If used, coaching and mentoring should be continued for as long as the practitioners find them valuable.

Tracking usage of the method can be hard; however, as most methods tend to be published on an organization's intranet site, a simple 'click' count combined with analytics can provide a pattern of usage. Initially the use of the site should increase, but unless momentum is maintained, usage may drop off. Part of this may be because people can find what they need more quickly (fewer clicks) or need to refer to it less as they have learned the content. Tracking the quantity of feedback and any resulting changes to the project management method is indicative of user engagement.

Web site counts may be indicative of a method being used but they are not hard evidence. Evidence of the practices actually being used can be gleaned by quality assurance, project assurance and through audits. If a maturity model is used, the gradual progression of capability through the maturity levels is also evidence of improvement.

Many larger organizations create 'communities of practice', which have the aim of improving performance by knowledge sharing and creating a sense of community. These often have their own web sites, blogs, social media and events to motivate their members to contribute to the development of the profession. Some companies run internal conferences or actively encourage participation in external events and with professional associations. A community of practice can develop subject matter experts who take a leadership role on an aspect of project management and act as a focal point for advice; they may also own the relevant parts of the method, working with the overall method owner.

Just as maturity relates to the capability of an organization, 'competence' relates to an individual. The development of individual skills should be encouraged. This may be by only allowing individuals to manage projects if they have a 'licence' obtained through achieving a prescribed competence level (e.g. through assessment centres). Any gaps in competencies can be dealt with through additional training and development. The skills and competencies should be traceable to parts of the method, so that they can be used together seamlessly.

Training and development should reflect both the competencies and method if they are to be seen as relevant, particularly at lower levels. Experienced practitioners can be encouraged to act as mentors or coaches, ensuring the right behaviours and that use of the method does not become mechanistic.

Tip

Do not expect a project management method to run itself. Someone in the higher levels of the business should continue to sponsor it and someone, with resources, should have the responsibility for managing its ongoing development and use.

Chapter 21 – Considerations for organizational adoption

21.2.4 Examples of how organizations have embedded PRINCE2

Example: Major infrastructure company

Maturity-model-led

A major infrastructure company achieved a low score in a P3M3 maturity assessment, which reflected its actual performance. As a result the company decided to develop and deploy a single project management method, based on PRINCE2, to replace the eight methods currently being used. The new method was developed with the active involvement of the project management community. The method was piloted on one programme and feedback from its use was used to tune the method before further roll-out. Roll-out was then started, with each area deciding its own deployment approach to suit its circumstances; the only requirement was that the area had a plan.

A central implementation and deployment team monitored the roll-out and resulting performance. It held frequent question-and-answer sessions and managed the associated training. The team also attended project meetings and gate events to ensure they were being run in the 'spirit' of the method and not just the written word. This team stayed in place for 18 months until the method had been embedded. This organization achieved P3M3 maturity level 3 as a result.

Example: Major communications company

Incremental release and communications

A major communications company used agile methods to develop its own PRINCE2-based project management method, together with a programme management method (based on Managing Successful Programmes), which was required to replace 20 local methods across the company (see one of the examples in section 21.1.3). Features of the method were made available as soon as they were ready, being published on a platform used specifically for the method. This platform provided the material in both document and online formats. People were welcome to use any of the material and provide feedback to the designers. At the same time, two training courses were developed, one online and the other a workshop, which used the same concepts and language as the method. High-quality videos were also created and made available, as defined in a communications plan, which also included regular newsletters, tele-conferences, face-to-face presentations and blogs. The minimum feature set was available within 6 months with the full method completed within another 9 months, including training. Each area of the business, based around the original 20 local process owners, decided when and how to adopt and roll out the method in their areas, against an agreed plan. Over the first year the web site recorded more than 750 000 hits, progressively rising month on month.

Example: International IT company

Big bang and incremental roll-out

The PRINCE2 method for an international IT company was designed by a central team with some consultation. It was released in its completed state and rolled out on a geographic basis. The central programme management office (PMO) in the head office was accountable for the method, with each location having a local PMO to manage the roll-out and use of the method in their location.

Example: International company

Covert or overt?

The change manager in an international company found that there was a significant level of resistance to PRINCE2 due to perceptions of bureaucracy and, in some areas, a preference for their local standards. Although it was based on PRINCE2, the new method was designed without any explicit reference to PRINCE2 but reflected the features of the standards people wanted. As a result, a method was developed which had the support of the users, with little resistance to its roll-out. Later, guides were produced which explained how the method met the requirements of each of the source methods and standards. These were useful for engaging customers who had requirements to use a particular standard or method and for informing staff and contactors trained in those standards on how they were dealt with in the method.

Example: Major engineering programme

Harnessing success in one area to improve performance in others

A major system engineering programme had sufficient funds and senior support to develop its own programme and project management method, based on publicly available standards, bodies of knowledge and, for projects, PRINCE2. The brief from the programme director was for the method to be written in such a way that it could be used on other programmes and as a focal point for learning and improvement. Furthermore, the web site for the method and supporting materials should be available to anyone with access to the company's intranet. One key benefit of having a standard method was that the PID need only refer to the appropriate part of the method, rather than describe everything in full; this resulted in a slim, single document reflecting PRINCE2's PID, rather than multiple documents. The programme ran for more than 10 years, but within 3 years of it becoming available the method was used as the basis for an enterprise-wide programme and project management method, with very few significant changes.

Example: Organization A

Capturing and acknowledging feedback

The culture in a certain organization was not to provide feedback on anything as people felt that nothing ever happened as a result. When the project management method was launched, ease of feedback was built into the design of its web pages. Every page had a context-sensitive link to a feedback form; feedback appeared on the page, when posted, so the person giving the feedback did not have to say what page or item they were feeding back on. The method owner was able to post a reply, so anyone viewing the page could see all the comments and replies. The method owner, however, chose not to post a response straight away, but rather phone the person who gave the feedback to discuss their issue; often a lot more information was gleaned. The response to be posted on the site was also agreed. In many cases the improvements suggested were implemented within a day. This immediate and personal approach was soon recognized and the volume and quality of feedback gradually rose as direct relationships with users developed. Importantly, the method owner and team did not insist people use the web pages for feedback but accepted it in any form (such as verbal, scribbled note, email), anywhere, thereby helping to dispel the perceptions of 'process' and 'bureaucracy'.

Example: Organization B

Using internal audit as change agents

The internal audit group of a company had always audited projects against its own checklists as the organization had no consistent project management approach. When the new project management method was launched, the method owner requested that internal audit use the method as the audit base. The audit lead was reluctant as use of the new method was not mandated by senior management. He did, however, find that the new method was more rigorous than anything he had and covered the requirements of a range of external methods, standards and bodies of knowledge. He asked that his auditors receive a full-day briefing on the method and created an audit guide. As a result, the company's auditors used the same language and concepts as the method in their reports. Although the auditors could not prescribe how auditees responded to audit points, they were able to be helpful and point them to the relevant parts of the method.

A

Product description outlines

A Product description outlines

This appendix contains product description outlines for PRINCE2's defined management products. These are not full product descriptions as defined in section A.17, as some elements, such as quality method, will vary depending on the project's needs. Format examples are provided, but these are not exhaustive.

Tailoring management product description outlines

Tailoring is described in Chapters 4 and 21. Management products should be tailored to the requirements and environment of each project. This could include the composition, format, quality criteria and naming of the management products. For example:

- Management products can be in other formats and do not necessarily need to be 'text documents'. They could be slides, spreadsheets or data in information systems, which are brought together, either on screen or as outputs to form reports.
- Reports do not need to be documents. They could be emails, notes of meetings, wall charts or an entry in a daily log. Where verbal reports are used, the information would be incorporated in other reports.
- Management products can be combined for simpler projects where the products fulfil related purposes.
- Management products can be split into smaller parts if it makes them easier to use and maintain.
- Parts of the composition that are not relevant to the project can be added to or left out, or elements can be combined. The composition is not a table of contents; rather it is simply a list of what the product should typically cover and therefore the order of the topics may be changed.
- The PRINCE2 principles of focus on products and learn from experience recognize that projects need to retain information about product status and identified lessons. PRINCE2 does not recommend specific record or report formats for the information, and formal management products are not always used in projects unless there is a specific requirement for the additional information they provide. The following document names are used to show when the information is required in some form; they have outline descriptions of purpose but no recommended composition, derivation, format and presentation, nor any quality criteria:
  - configuration item record
  - lessons report
  - product status account.

The product description outlines in this appendix may be tailored to an organization to create its own set of outlines which would form part of its own PRINCE2-based project management method. To be following PRINCE2, the purpose of each management product must be clearly stated and satisfied. More information on creating an organization's project management method is given in Chapters 4 and 21.

Types of management products

There are three types of management product: baselines, records and reports.

Baseline management products are those that define aspects of the project and, when approved, are subject to change control. These are:

- A.1 Benefits management approach
- A.2 Business case
- A.3 Change control approach
- A.5 Communication management approach
- A.16 Plan (covers project plans, stage plans, exception plans and, optionally, team plans)
- A.17 Product description
- A.19 Project brief
- A.20 Project initiation documentation (PID)
- A.21 Project product description
- A.22 Quality management approach
- A.24 Risk management approach
- A.26 Work package.

Records are dynamic management products that maintain information regarding project progress. These are:

- A.6 Configuration item record
- A.7 Daily log
- A.12 Issue register
- A.14 Lessons log
- A.23 Quality register
- A.25 Risk register.

Reports are management products providing a snapshot of the status of certain aspects of the project. These are:

- A.4 Checkpoint report
- A.8 End project report
- A.9 End stage report
- A.10 Exception report
- A.11 Highlight report
- A.13 Issue report
- A.15 Lessons report
- A.18 Product status account.

Most of the baseline products evolve during pre-project and initiation stage activities, as shown in Figure A.1. The baseline products are then reviewed and (possibly) updated at the end of each stage or if an exception occurs.

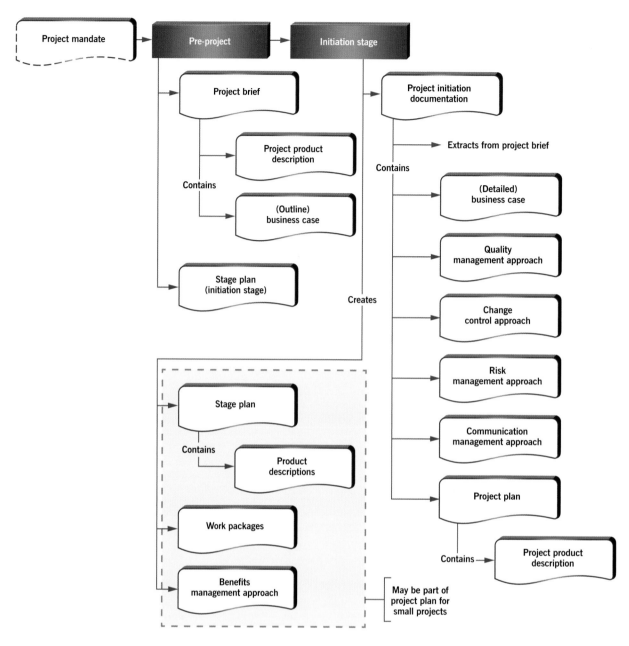

Figure A.1 Evolution of baseline management products

A.1 Benefits management approach

A.1.1 Purpose

A benefits management approach defines the benefits management actions and benefits reviews that will be put in place to ensure that the project's outcomes are achieved and confirm that the project's benefits are realized.

If the project is part of a programme, the benefits management approach may be contained within the programme's benefits realization plan and executed at the programme level. Post-project, the benefits management approach is maintained and executed by corporate, programme management or the customer.

A.1.2 Composition

A benefits management approach includes the following:

- the scope of the benefits management approach covering what benefits are to be managed and measured
- who is accountable for the expected benefits
- what management actions are required in order to ensure that the project's outcomes are achieved
- how to measure achievement of expected benefits, and when they can be measured
- what resources are needed
- baseline measures from which the improvements will be calculated
- how the performance of the project product will be reviewed.

A.1.3 Derivation

The benefits management approach is derived from the following:

- business case
- project product description (and the acceptance criteria in particular)
- the programme's benefits management approach and benefits realization plan (when the project is part of a programme)
- the corporate, programme management or customer performance monitoring function (such as a centre of excellence), if one exists.

A.1.4 Format and presentation

A benefits management approach can take a number of formats, including:

- a document, a spreadsheet or presentation slides
- an entry in a project management tool.

A.1.5 Quality criteria

The following quality criteria apply to a benefits management approach:

- It covers all benefits stated in the business case.
- The benefits are measurable and baseline measures have been recorded.
- It describes suitable timing for measurement of benefits, together with reasons for the timing.
- It identifies the skills or individuals who will be needed to carry out the measurements.
- The effort and cost to undertake the benefits reviews are realistic when compared with the value of the anticipated benefits.
- Consideration is given to whether dis-benefits should be measured and reviewed.

A.2 Business case

A.2.1 Purpose

A business case is used to document the business justification for undertaking a project, based on the estimated costs (of development, implementation and incremental ongoing operations and maintenance costs) against the anticipated benefits to be gained and offset by any associated risks. It should outline how and when the anticipated benefits can be measured.

The outline business case is developed in the starting up a project process and refined by the initiating a project process. The directing a project process covers the approval and reaffirmation of the business case.

The business case is used by the controlling a stage process when assessing impacts of issues and risks. It is reviewed and updated at the end of each management stage by the managing a stage boundary process, and at the end of the project by the closing a project process.

A.2.2 Composition

A business case includes the following:

- **Executive summary** Highlights the key points in the business case, which should include important benefits and the return on investment.
- **Reasons** Defines the reasons for undertaking the project and explains how the project will enable the achievement of corporate, programme management or customer strategies and objectives.
- **Business options** Analysis and reasoned recommendation for the base business options of do nothing, do the minimum or do something. 'Do nothing' should always be the starting option to act as the basis for quantifying the other options. The difference between 'do nothing' and 'do the minimum' or 'do something' is the benefit that the investment will buy.

  The analysis of each option provides the project board and the project's stakeholders with sufficient information to judge which option presents the best value for the organization. It provides the answer to the question: for this level of investment, are the anticipated benefits more desirable, viable and achievable than the other options available?

  The business case for the chosen option should be continually assessed for desirability, viability and achievability as any new risks and/or changes may make one of the other options more justifiable.

- **Expected benefits** These result from the desired outcomes to be achieved through the use of the project outputs. The benefits are expressed in measurable terms against the situation as it exists prior to the project. Benefits should be both qualitative and quantitative. They should be aligned with corporate, programme management or customer benefits. Tolerances should be set for each benefit and for the aggregated benefit. Any benefits realization requirements should be stated.

  The quantification of benefits enables benefits tolerances to be set (e.g. a 10–15 per cent increase in sales) and the measurability of the benefits ensures that they can be proven. If the project includes benefits that cannot be proven, then it is impossible to judge whether the project:

  - has been a success
  - has provided value for money
  - should be (or have been) initiated.

There are many ways to verify the expected benefits. For example, sensitivity analysis can be used to determine whether the business case is heavily dependent on a specific benefit. If it is, this may affect project planning, monitoring and control activities, and risk management, as steps would need to be taken to protect that specific benefit.

- **Expected dis-benefits** The impact of one or more outcomes of the project might be perceived as negative by one or more stakeholders. Dis-benefits are actual consequences of an activity whereas, by definition, a risk is uncertain and may never materialize. For example, a decision to merge two elements of an organization onto a new site may have benefits (e.g. better joint working), costs (e.g. expanding one of the two sites) and dis-benefits (e.g. drop in productivity during the merger). Dis-benefits need to be valued and incorporated into the investment appraisal.

- **Timescale** The period over which the project will run (summary of the project plan) and the period over which the benefits will be realized. This information is subsequently used to help timing decisions when planning (project plan, stage plan and benefits management approach).

- **Costs** A summary of the project costs (taken from the project plan), the ongoing operations and maintenance costs and their funding arrangements.

- **Investment appraisal** Compares the aggregated benefits and dis-benefits with the project costs (extracted from the project plan) and ongoing incremental operations and maintenance costs. The analysis may use techniques such as cash-flow statement, return on investment, net present value, internal rate of return and payback period. The objective is to be able to define the value of a project as an investment. The investment appraisal should address how the project will be funded.

- **Major risks** Gives a summary of the key risks associated with the project, together with the likely impact and plans should they occur.

A.2.3 Derivation

A business case is derived from the following:

- project mandate and project brief: reasons
- project plan: costs and timescales
- senior user(s): expected benefits
- executive: value for money
- risk register
- issue register.

A.2.4 Format and presentation

A business case can take a number of formats, including:

- a document, a spreadsheet or presentation slides
- an entry in a project management tool.

A.2.5 Quality criteria

The following quality criteria apply to a business case:

- The reasons for the project must be consistent with the corporate, programme management or customer strategies.
- The project plan must be aligned with the business case.
- The benefits are clearly identified and justified.
- How the benefits will be realized must be clear.
- What defines a successful outcome is described.
- The preferred business option is stated, along with the reasons why.
- Where external procurement is required, the preferred sourcing option is stated, and why.
- How any necessary funding will be obtained is described.
- The business case includes non-financial, as well as financial, criteria.
- The business case includes operations and maintenance costs and risks, as well as project costs and risks.
- The business case conforms to organizational accounting standards (e.g. break-even analysis and cash-flow conventions).
- The major risks faced by the project are explicitly stated, together with any proposed responses.

A.3 Change control approach

A.3.1 Purpose

A change control approach is used to identify, assess and control any potential and approved changes to the project baselines to protect the project's products. It describes the procedures, techniques and standards to be applied and the responsibilities for achieving an effective issue management and change control procedure.

A.3.2 Composition

A change control approach includes the following:

- **Introduction** States the purpose, objectives and scope, and identifies who is responsible for the approach.
- **Issue management and change control procedure** Describes (or refers to) the issue management and change control procedure to be used. Any variance from corporate, programme management or customer standards should be highlighted, together with a justification for the variances. The procedure should cover activities such as capturing issues, assessing their impact, proposing actions, deciding on actions, and implementing actions.
- **Tools and techniques** Refers to any systems or tools to be used and any preference for techniques that may be used for each step in the issue management and change control procedure.
- **Records** Defines the composition and format of the issue register.
- **Reporting** Describes the composition and format of the reports that are to be produced, their purpose, timing and chosen recipients. This should include reviewing the performance of the procedures.

- **Timing of issue management and change control and issue activities** States when formal activities (e.g. reviews or audits) are to be undertaken.
- **Roles and responsibilities** Describes who will be responsible for what aspects of the procedures, including any corporate, programme management or customer roles involved with the change control of the project's products. Describes whether a change authority and/or change budget will be established.
- **Scales for priority and severity** Describes the scales for prioritizing requests for change and off-specifications and for determining the level of management that can make decisions on the severity of an issue.

A.3.3 Derivation

A change control approach is derived from the following:

- the customer's quality expectations
- the corporate, programme management or customer tools and systems used for change control (e.g. any software in use or mandated by the user)
- the programme quality management strategy and information management strategy (if the project is part of a programme)
- the user's quality management system
- the supplier's quality management system
- specific needs of the project product and environment
- project management team structure (to identify those with change control responsibilities)
- facilitated workshops and informal discussions.

A.3.4 Format and presentation

A change control approach can take a number of formats, including:

- a stand-alone document or a section of the PID
- an entry in a project management tool.

A.3.5 Quality criteria

The following criteria apply to a change control approach:

- Responsibilities are clear and understood by both user and supplier.
- The issue management and change control procedure is clearly documented and can be understood by all parties.
- The chosen change control approach is appropriate for the size and nature of the project.
- Scales are clear and unambiguous.
- The scales are appropriate for the level of control required.
- Reporting requirements are fully defined.
- Resources are in place to administer the chosen method of change control.

A.4 Checkpoint report

A.4.1 Purpose

A checkpoint report is used to report, at a frequency defined in the work package, the status of the work package.

A.4.2 Composition

A checkpoint report includes the following:

- **Date** The date of the checkpoint
- **Period** The reporting period covered by the checkpoint report
- **Follow-ups** The outstanding items from previous reports (e.g. action items completed or unresolved issues)
- **This reporting period**:
  - the products being developed by the team during the reporting period
  - the products completed by the team during the reporting period
  - quality management activities carried out during the period
  - lessons identified
- **Next reporting period**:
  - the products being developed by the team in the next reporting period
  - the products planned to be completed by the team in the next reporting period
  - quality management activities planned for the next reporting period
- **Work package tolerance status** How execution of the work package is performing against its tolerances (e.g. cost/time/scope actuals and forecast)
- **Issues and risks** An update on issues and risks associated with the work package.

A.4.3 Derivation

A checkpoint report is derived from the following:

- work package
- team plan and actuals
- previous checkpoint report.

A.4.4 Format and presentation

A checkpoint report can take a number of formats, including:

- an oral report to the project manager (could be in person or over the phone)
- a presentation at a progress review (physical meeting or conference call)
- a document or email issued to the project manager
- an entry in a project management tool.

A.4.5 Quality criteria

The following quality criteria apply to a checkpoint report:

- The report is prepared at the frequency required by the project manager.
- The level and frequency of progress assessment is right for the management stage and/or work package.
- The information is timely, useful, objective and accurate.
- Every product in the work package, for that period, is covered by the report.
- The report includes an update on any unresolved issues from the previous report.

A.5 Communication management approach

A.5.1 Purpose

A communication management approach contains a description of the means and frequency of communication with parties both internal and external to the project. It facilitates engagement with stakeholders through the establishment of a controlled and bidirectional flow of information.

A.5.2 Composition

A communication management approach includes the following:

- **Introduction** States the purpose, objectives and scope, and identifies who is responsible for the approach.
- **Communication procedure** Describes (or refers to) any communication methods to be used. Any variance from corporate, programme management or customer standards should be highlighted, together with a justification for the variance.
- **Tools and techniques** Refers to any communication tools to be used, and any preference for techniques that may be used, for each step in the communication process.
- **Records** Defines what communication records will be required and where they will be stored (e.g. logging of external correspondence).
- **Reporting** Describes any reports on the communication process that are to be produced, including their purpose, timing and recipients (e.g. performance indicators).
- **Timing of communication activities** States when formal communication activities are to be undertaken (e.g. at the end of a management stage), including performance audits of the communication methods.
- **Roles and responsibilities** Describes who will be responsible for what aspects of the communication process, including any corporate, programme management or customer roles involved with communication.
- **Stakeholder analysis**, including:
  - identification of the interested party (which may include accounts staff, user forum, internal audit, corporate, programme management or customer quality assurance, competitors, etc.)
  - current relationship
  - desired relationship
  - interfaces
  - key messages

- **Information needs for each interested party**, including:
  - information required to be provided from the project
  - information required to be provided to the project
  - information provider and recipient
  - frequency of communication
  - means of communication
  - format of the communication.

A.5.3 Derivation

A communication management approach is derived from the following:

- the corporate, programme management or customer communications policies (e.g. rules for disclosure for publicly listed companies)
- the programme's information management strategy
- other components of the PID; in particular, the project management team structure, risk management approach, quality management approach and change control approach
- facilitated workshops/informal discussions with stakeholders
- stakeholder analysis.

A.5.4 Format and presentation

A communication management approach can take a number of formats, including:

- a stand-alone product or a section of the PID
- a document, spreadsheet or mind map
- an entry in a project management tool.

A.5.5 Quality criteria

The following quality criteria apply to a communication management approach:

- All stakeholders have been identified and consulted with regard to their communication requirements.
- There is agreement from all stakeholders about the content, frequency and method of communication.
- A common standard for communication has been considered.
- The time, effort and resources required to carry out the identified communications have been allowed for in stage plans.
- The formality and frequency of communication is reasonable for the project's importance and complexity.
- For projects that are part of a programme, the lines of communication, and the reporting structure between the project and programme, have been made clear in the communication management approach.
- The communication management approach incorporates corporate, programme management or customer communications facilities where appropriate (e.g. using the marketing communications department for distributing project bulletins).

A.6 Configuration item record

A.6.1 Purpose

Configuration item records are created only if required by the project's change control approach. Their purpose is to provide a record of such information as the history, status, version and variant of each configuration item, and any details of important relationships between them. If configuration item records are not used, then less formal information about the configuration status of products may be part of the product status information.

The set of configuration item records for a project is often referred to as a configuration library. The records may be derived from:

- the change control approach
- the product breakdown structure
- a stage plan and work package
- the quality register, issue register and risk register.

PRINCE2 does not define the composition, format and presentation, nor any quality criteria for this product.

A.7 Daily log

A.7.1 Purpose

A daily log may be used to record informal issues, required actions or significant events not captured by other PRINCE2 registers or logs. It can act as the project diary for the project manager. It can also be used as a repository for issues and risks during the starting up a project process if the other registers have not been set up.

There may be more than one daily log as team managers may elect to have one for their work packages, separate from the project manager's daily log. Entries are made when the project manager or team manager feels it is appropriate to log some event. Often entries are based on thoughts, conversations and observations.

PRINCE2 does not define the composition, format and presentation, nor any quality criteria for this product.

A.8 End project report

A.8.1 Purpose

An end project report is used during project closure to review how the project performed against the version of the PID used to authorize it. It also allows the passing on of:

- any lessons that can be usefully applied to other projects
- details of unfinished work, ongoing risks or potential product modifications to the group charged with future support of the project product in its operational life.

A.8.2 Composition

An end project report includes the following:

- **Project manager's report** Summarizes the project's performance
- **Review of the business case** Summarizes the validity of the project's business case, including:
  - benefits achieved to date
  - residual benefits expected (post-project)
  - expected net benefits
  - deviations from the approved business case
- **Review of project objectives** Review of how the project performed against its planned targets and tolerances for time, cost, quality, scope, benefits and risk. Evaluates the effectiveness of the project's approaches and controls
- **Review of team performance** In particular, provides recognition for good performance
- **Review of products**, including:
  - **Quality records** Listing the quality activities planned and completed
  - **Approval records** Listing the products and their requisite approvals
  - **Off-specifications** Listing any missing products or products that do not meet the original requirements, and confirmation of any concessions granted
  - **Project product handover** Confirmation (in the form of acceptance records) by the customer that operations and maintenance functions are ready to receive the project product
  - **Summary of follow-on action recommendations** Request for project board advice about who should receive each recommended action. The recommended actions are related to unfinished work, ongoing issues and risks, and any other activities needed to take the products to the next phase of their life
- **Lessons** A review of what went well, what went badly, and any recommendations for corporate, programme management or customer consideration (and if the project was prematurely closed, then the reasons should be explained). Sourced from the lessons log (see section A.14) or any lessons reports that may exist.

A.8.3 Derivation

An end project report is derived from the following:

- PID
- business case
- project plan
- benefits management approach
- issue register, quality register and risk register
- lessons log
- end stage reports (and exception reports, if applicable).

A.8.4 Format and presentation

An end project report can take a number of formats, including:

- a presentation to the project board (physical meeting or conference call)
- a document or email issued to the project board
- an entry in a project management tool.

A.8.5 Quality criteria

The following quality criteria apply to an end project report:

- Any abnormal situations are described, together with their impact.
- At the end of the project, all issues should either be closed or become the subject of a follow-on action recommendation.
- Any available useful documentation or evidence should accompany the follow-on action recommendation(s).
- Any appointed project assurance roles should agree with the report.

A.9 End stage report

A.9.1 Purpose

An end stage report is used to give a summary of progress to date, the overall project situation, and sufficient information to ask for a project board decision on what to do next with the project.

The project board uses the information in the end stage report in tandem with the next stage plan to decide what action to take with the project; for example, authorize the next stage, amend the project scope or stop the project.

A.9.2 Composition

An end stage report includes the following:

- **Project manager's report** Summarizes the management stage performance
- **Review of the business case** Summarizes the validity of the project's business case, including:
    - benefits achieved to date
    - residual benefits expected (remaining management stages and post-project)
    - expected net benefits
    - deviations from approved business case
    - aggregated risk exposure
- **Review of project objectives** Review of how the project has performed to date against its planned targets and tolerances for time, cost, quality, scope, benefits and risk. Evaluates the effectiveness of the project's approaches and controls
- **Review of management stage objectives** Review of how the specific management stage performed against its planned targets and tolerances for time, cost, quality, scope, benefits and risk

- **Review of team performance** In particular, provides recognition for good performance
- **Review of products**, including:
  - **Quality records** Listing the quality activities planned and completed in the management stage
  - **Approval records** Listing the products planned for completion in the management stage and their requisite approvals
  - **Off-specifications** Listing any missing products or products that do not meet the original requirements, and confirmation of any concessions granted
  - **Phased handover** (if applicable) Confirmation by the customer that operations and maintenance functions are ready to receive the release
  - **Summary of follow-on action recommendations** (if applicable) Request for project board advice for who should receive each recommended action. The recommended actions are related to unfinished work, ongoing issues and risks, and any other activities needed to take the products handed over to the next phase of their life
- **Lessons** (if appropriate) A review of what went well, what went badly, and any recommendations for corporate, programme management or customer consideration. Sourced from the lessons log (see section A.14) or any lessons reports that may exist
- **Issues and risks** Summary of the current set of issues and risks affecting the project
- **Forecast** The project manager's forecast for the project and next management stage against planned targets and tolerances for time, cost, quality, scope, benefits and risk.

Where the end stage report is being produced at the end of the initiation stage, not all the above content may be appropriate or necessary.

A.9.3 Derivation

An end stage report is derived from the following:

- current management stage plan and actuals
- project plan
- benefits management approach
- risk register, quality register and issue register
- exception report (if applicable)
- lessons log
- completed/slipped work packages
- updated business case.

A.9.4 Format and presentation

An end stage report can take a number of formats, including:

- a presentation to the project board (physical meeting or conference call)
- a document or email issued to the project board
- an entry in a project management tool.

A.9.5 Quality criteria

The following quality criteria apply to an end stage report:

- The report clearly shows management stage performance against the plan.
- Any abnormal situations are described, together with their impact.
- Any appointed project assurance roles agree with the report.

A.10 Exception report

A.10.1 Purpose

An exception report is produced when a stage plan or project plan is forecast to exceed tolerance levels set. It is prepared by the project manager in order to inform the project board of the situation, and to offer options and recommendations for the way to proceed.

A.10.2 Composition

An exception report includes the following:

- **Exception title** An overview of the exception being reported
- **Cause of the exception** A description of the cause of a deviation from the current plan
- **Consequences of the deviation** What the implications are if the deviation is not addressed for:
  - the project
  - corporate, programme management or the customer
- **Options** What options are available to address the deviation and the effect of each option on the business case, risks and tolerances
- **Recommendation** Of the available options, which is recommended, and why?
- **Lessons** What can be learned from the exception, on this project or future projects?

A.10.3 Derivation

An exception report is derived from the following:

- current plan and actuals
- issue register, risk register and quality register
- highlight reports, issue reports (for management stage/project-level deviations) or checkpoint reports (for team-level deviations)
- project board advice of an external event that affects the project.

A.10.4 Format and presentation

An exception report can take a number of formats, including:

- an issue raised at a minuted progress review (physical meeting or conference call)
- a document or email issued to the next higher level of management
- an entry in a project management tool.

For urgent exceptions, it is recommended that the exception report is oral in the first instance, and is then followed up in the agreed format.

A.10.5 Quality criteria

The following quality criteria apply to an exception report:

- The current plan must accurately show the status of time and cost performance.
- The reason(s) for the deviation must be stated, the exception clearly analysed, and any impacts assessed and fully described.
- The implications for the business case have been considered and the impact on the overall project plan has been calculated.
- Options are analysed (including any risks associated with them) and recommendations are made for the most appropriate way to proceed.
- The exception report is given in a timely and appropriate manner.

A.11 Highlight report

A.11.1 Purpose

A highlight report is used to provide the project board (and possibly other stakeholders) with a summary of the management stage status at intervals defined by them. The project board uses the report to monitor management stage and project progress. The project manager also uses it to advise the project board of any potential problems or areas where the project board could help.

A.11.2 Composition

A highlight report includes the following:

- **Date** The date of the report
- **Period** The reporting period covered by the highlight report
- **Status summary** An overview of the status of the management stage at this time
- **This reporting period:**
  - work packages, including those pending authorization, in execution, and completed in the period (if the work packages are being performed by external suppliers, this information may be accompanied by purchase order and invoicing data)
  - products completed in the period

- products planned but not started or completed in the period (providing an early warning indicator or potential breach of **time tolerance**)
- corrective actions taken during the period
- **Next reporting period**:
  - work packages, including those to be authorized, in execution and to be completed during the next period (if the work packages are being performed by external suppliers, this information may be accompanied by purchase order and invoicing data)
  - products to be completed in the next period
  - corrective actions to be completed during the next period
- **Project and management stage tolerance status** How execution of the project and management stage are performing against their tolerances (e.g. cost/time actuals and forecast)
- **Requests for change** Raised, approved/rejected and pending
- **Key issues and risks** Summary of actual or potential problems and risks
- **Lessons** (if appropriate) A review of what went well, what went badly, and any recommendations for corporate, programme management or customer consideration. Sourced from the lessons log (see section A.14) or any lessons reports that may exist.

A.11.3 Derivation

A highlight report is derived from the following:

- PID
- checkpoint reports
- issue register, quality register and risk register
- stage plan and actuals
- communication management approach.

A.11.4 Format and presentation

A highlight report can take a number of formats, including:

- a presentation to the project board (physical meeting or conference call)
- a document or email issued to the project board
- an entry in a project management tool
- a wall chart or Kanban board.

A.11.5 Quality criteria

The following quality criteria apply to a highlight report:

- The level and frequency of progress reporting required by the project board are right for the management stage and/or project.
- The project manager provides the highlight report at the frequency, and with the content, required by the project board.
- The information is timely, useful, accurate and objective.
- The report highlights any potential problem areas.

A.12 Issue register

A.12.1 Purpose

The purpose of the issue register is to capture and maintain information on all the issues that are being formally managed. The issue register should be monitored by the project manager on a regular basis.

A.12.2 Composition

The composition of the issue register will be defined in the change control approach. For each entry in the issue register, the following should be recorded:

- **Issue identifier** Provides a unique reference for every issue entered into the issue register. It will typically be a numeric or alphanumeric value
- **Issue type** Defines the type of issue being recorded, namely:
  - request for change
  - off-specification
  - problem/concern
- **Date raised** The date on which the issue was originally raised
- **Raised by** The name of the individual or team who raised the issue
- **Issue report author** The name of the individual or team who created the issue report
- **Issue description** Describes the issue, its cause and impact
- **Priority** This should be given in terms of the project's chosen categories. Priority should be re-evaluated after impact analysis
- **Severity** This should be given in terms of the project's chosen scale. Severity will indicate what level of management is required to make a decision on the issue
- **Status** The current status of the issue and the date of the last update
- **Closure date** The date the issue was closed.

A.12.3 Derivation

The issue register is derived in the following way:

- Entries are initially made on the issue register when a new issue is raised.
- The issue register is updated as the issue is progressed. When the issue has been resolved, the entry in the issue register is closed.

A.12.4 Format and presentation

The format of the issue register will be defined in the change control approach. It can take a number of formats, including:

- a document, spreadsheet or database
- a stand-alone register or a carry-forward in the minutes of progress review meetings
- an entry in a project management tool
- a part of an integrated project register for all risks, actions, decisions, assumptions, issues, lessons, etc.

A.12.5 Quality criteria

The following quality criteria apply to an issue register:

- The status indicates whether action has been taken.
- The issues are uniquely identified, including information about which product they refer to.
- A process is defined by which the issue register is to be updated.
- Entries on the issue register that, upon examination, are in fact risks, are transferred to the risk register and the entries annotated accordingly.
- Access to the issue register is controlled and the register is kept in a safe place.

A.13 Issue report

A.13.1 Purpose

An issue report is a report containing the description, impact assessment and recommendations for a request for change, off-specification or a problem/concern. It is created only for those issues that need to be handled formally.

The report is initially created when capturing the issue, and updated both after the issue has been assessed and when proposals are identified for issue resolution. The issue report is later amended further in order to record what option was decided upon, and finally updated when the implementation has been verified and the issue is closed.

A.13.2 Composition

The composition of the issue report will be defined in the change control approach. It includes the following:

- **Issue identifier** As shown in the issue register (provides a unique reference for every issue report)
- **Issue type** Defines the type of issue being recorded, namely:
  - request for change
  - off-specification
  - problem/concern
- **Date raised** The date on which the issue was originally raised
- **Raised by** The name of the individual or team who raised the issue

- **Issue report author** The name of the individual or team who created the issue report
- **Issue description** Describes the issue in terms of its cause and impact
- **Impact analysis** A detailed analysis of the likely impact of the issue. This may include, for example, a list of products impacted
- **Recommendation** A description of what the project manager believes should be done to resolve the issue (and why)
- **Priority** This should be given in terms of the project's chosen scale. It should be re-evaluated after impact analysis
- **Severity** This should be given in terms of the project's chosen scale. Severity will indicate what level of management is required to make a decision on the issue
- **Decision** The decision made (accept, reject, defer or grant concession)
- **Approved by** A record of who made the decision
- **Decision date** The date of the decision
- **Closure date** The date that the issue was closed.

A.13.3 Derivation

An issue report is derived from the following:

- highlight report(s), checkpoint report(s) and end stage report(s)
- stage plan, together with actual values and events
- users and supplier teams working on the project
- the application of quality controls
- observation and experience of the processes
- quality register, risk register and lessons log
- completed work packages.

A.13.4 Format and presentation

The format of the issue report will be defined in the change control approach. Its various formats include:

- a document, spreadsheet or database
- an entry in a project management tool.

Not all entries in the issue register will need a separately documented issue report.

A.13.5 Quality criteria

The following quality criteria apply to an issue report:

- The issue stated is clear and unambiguous.
- A detailed impact analysis has occurred.
- All implications have been considered.
- The issue has been assessed for its effect on the tolerances.
- The issue has been correctly registered in the issue register.
- Decisions are accurately and unambiguously described.

A.14 Lessons log

A.14.1 Purpose

The lessons log is a project repository for lessons that apply to this project or future projects. Some lessons may originate from other projects and should be captured on the lessons log for input to the project's approaches and plans. Some lessons may originate from within the project, where new experience (both good and bad) can be passed on to others.

A.14.2 Composition

For each entry in the lessons log, the following should be recorded:

- **Lesson type** Defines the type of lesson being recorded, namely:
  - project (to be applied to this project)
  - corporate, programme management or the customer (to be passed on to corporate, programme management or the customer)
  - both project and corporate, programme management or the customer
- **Lesson detail** The detail may include:
  - event
  - effect (e.g. positive/negative financial impact)
  - causes/trigger
  - whether there were any early warning indicators
  - recommendations
  - whether it was previously identified as a risk (threat or opportunity)
- **Date logged** The date on which the lesson was originally logged
- **Logged by** The name of the person or team who raised the lesson
- **Priority** In terms of the project's chosen categories.

A.14.3 Derivation

The lessons log is derived from the following:

- lessons from other projects
- project mandate or project brief
- daily log, issue register, quality register and risk register
- checkpoint reports and highlight reports
- completed work packages
- stage plans with actuals
- observation and experience of the project's processes.

A.14.4 Format and presentation

A lessons log can take a number of formats, including:

- a document, spreadsheet or database
- a stand-alone log or a carry-forward in the minutes of progress review meetings
- an entry in a project management tool
- a part of an integrated project register for all risks, actions, decisions, assumptions, issues, lessons, etc.

A.14.5 Quality criteria

The following quality criteria apply to the lessons log:

- The status indicates whether action has been taken.
- Lessons are uniquely identified, including to which product they refer.
- A process is defined by which the lessons log is to be updated.
- Access to the lessons log is controlled.
- The lessons log is kept in a safe place.

A.15 Lessons report

A.15.1 Purpose

A lessons report may be produced to support the lessons log if more information is required. It can be used to pass on any lessons that can be usefully applied to other projects.

The purpose of the report is to provoke action so that the positive lessons become embedded in the organization's way of working, and so that the organization is able to avoid any negative lessons on future projects.

A lessons report can be created at any time in a project and should not necessarily be delayed until the end. Typically it can be included as part of the end stage report and end project report. It may be appropriate (and necessary) for there to be several lessons reports specific to the particular organization (e.g. user, supplier, corporate or programme).

The data in the report should be used by the corporate group that is responsible for the quality management system, in order to refine, change and improve the standards. Statistics on how much effort was needed for products can help improve future estimating.

A lessons report may be derived from:

- the PID (for the baseline position)
- the lessons log (for identification of lessons)
- the quality register, issue register and risk register (for statistical analysis)
- quality records (for statistical analysis)
- the communication management approach (for the distribution list).

PRINCE2 does not define the composition, format and presentation, nor any quality criteria for this product.

A.16 Plan

A.16.1 Purpose

A plan provides a statement of how and when objectives are to be achieved, by showing the major products, activities and resources required for the scope of the plan. In PRINCE2, there are three levels of plan: project, stage and team. Team plans are optional and may not need to follow the same composition as a project plan or stage plan.

An exception plan is created at the same level as the plan that it is replacing.

A project plan provides the business case with planned costs, and it identifies the management stages and other major control points. It is used by the project board as a baseline against which to monitor project progress.

Stage plans cover the products, resources, activities and controls specific to the management stage and are used as a baseline against which to monitor management stage progress.

Team plans (if used) could comprise just a schedule appended to the work package(s) assigned to the team manager.

A plan should cover not just the activities to create products but also the activities to manage product creation, including activities for assurance, quality management, risk management, change control, communication and any other project controls required.

A.16.2 Composition

A plan includes the following:

- **Plan description** A brief description of what the plan encompasses (i.e. project, stage, team, exception) and the planning approach
- **Plan prerequisites** Any fundamental aspects that must be in place, and remain in place, for the plan to succeed
- **External dependencies** Dependencies that may influence the plan
- **Planning assumptions** Assumptions upon which the plan is based
- **Delivery approach(es)** A description of the approaches to be used
- **Lessons incorporated** Details of relevant lessons from previous similar projects, which have been reviewed and accommodated within this plan
- **Monitoring and control** Details of how the plan will be monitored and controlled
- **Budgets** Time and cost budgets, including provisions for risks and changes
- **Tolerances** Time, cost and scope tolerances for the level of plan (which may also include more specific management-stage- or team-level risk tolerances)
- **Product descriptions** (see section A.17) Descriptions of the products within the scope of the plan (for the project plan this will include the project's products; for the stage plan this will be the management stage products; and for a team plan this should be a reference to the work package assigned). Quality tolerances will be defined in each product description

- **Schedule** This may include graphical representations as:
  - a Gantt or bar chart
  - a product breakdown structure (see Appendix D for examples)
  - a product flow diagram (see Appendix D for an example)
  - an activity network
  - a table of resource requirements, by resource type (e.g. four engineers, one test manager, one business analyst)
  - a table of requested/assigned specific resources, by name (e.g. Nikki, Jay, Francesca).

A.16.3 Derivation

A plan is derived from the following:

- project brief
- quality management approach (for quality management activities to be included in the plan)
- risk management approach (for risk management activities to be included in the plan)
- communication management approach (for communication management activities to be included in the plan)
- change control approach
- resource availability
- registers and logs.

A.16.4 Format and presentation

A plan can take a number of formats, including:

- a stand-alone document or a section of the PID
- a document, spreadsheet, presentation slides or mind map
- an entry in a project management tool.

The schedule may be in the form of a product checklist (which is a list of the products to be delivered within the scope of the plan, together with key status dates such as draft ready, quality inspected, approved, etc.) or the output from a project planning tool. Table A.1 provides an example of a product checklist.

Table A.1 Example of a product checklist

Product identifier	Product title	Product description approved		Draft ready		Final quality check completed		Approved		Handed over (if applicable)	
		Plan	Actual	Plan	Actual	Plan	Actual	Plan	Actual	Plan	Actual
...											
121	Test plan	02 Jan	02 Jan	07 Jan	07 Jan	14 Feb	21 Feb	21 Feb	28 Feb	N/A	N/A
124	Water pump	02 Jan	02 Jan	13 Mar	13 Mar	14 Jun		30 Jun		14 Jul	
...											

A.16.5 Quality criteria

The following quality criteria apply to a plan:

- The plan is achievable.
- Estimates are based on consultation with those responsible for the people who will undertake the work, and/ or historical data.
- Team managers agree that their part of the plan is achievable.
- It is planned to an appropriate level of detail (not too much, not too little).
- The plan conforms to required corporate, programme management or customer standards.
- The plan incorporates lessons from previous projects.
- The plan incorporates any legal requirements.
- The plan covers management and control activities (such as quality) as well as the activities to create the products in scope.
- The plan supports the quality management approach, change control approach, risk management approach, communication management approach and project approach.
- The plan supports the management controls defined in the PID.

A.17 Product description

A.17.1 Purpose

A product description is used to:

- understand the detailed nature, purpose, function and appearance of the product
- define who will use the product
- identify the sources of information or supply for the product
- identify the level of quality required of the product
- enable identification of activities to produce, review and approve the product
- define the people or skills required to produce, review and approve the product.

A.17.2 Composition

A product description includes the following:

- **Identifier** Unique key, probably allocated by the change control method and likely to include the project name, item name and version number
- **Title** Name by which the product is known
- **Purpose** This defines the purpose that the product will fulfil and who will use it. Is it a means to an end or an end in itself? It is helpful in understanding the product's functions, size, quality, complexity, robustness, etc.
- **Composition** This is a list of the parts of the product. For example, if the product were a report, this would be a list of the expected chapters or sections

- **Derivation** What are the source products from which this product is derived? Examples are:
  - a design is derived from a specification
  - a product is bought in from a supplier
  - a statement of the expected benefits is obtained from the user
  - a product is obtained from another department or team
- **Format and presentation** The characteristics of the product; for example, if the product were a report, this would specify whether the report should be a document, presentation slides or an email
- **Development skills required** An indication of the skills required to develop the product or a pointer to which area(s) should supply the development resources. Identification of the actual people may be left until planning the management stage in which the product is to be created
- **Quality criteria** To what quality specification must the product be produced, and what quality measurements will be applied by those inspecting the finished product? This might be a simple reference to one or more common standards that are documented elsewhere, or it might be a full explanation of some yardstick to be applied. If the product is to be developed and approved in different states (e.g. dismantled machinery, moved machinery and reassembled machinery), then the quality criteria should be grouped into those that apply for each state
- **Quality tolerance** Details of any range in the quality criteria within which the product would be acceptable
- **Quality method** The kinds of quality method (e.g. design verification, pilot, test, inspection or review) that are to be used to check the quality or functionality of the product
- **Quality skills required** An indication of the skills required to undertake the quality method or a pointer to which area(s) should supply the checking resources. Identification of the actual people may be left until planning the management stage in which the quality inspection is to be done
- **Quality responsibilities** These define the producer, reviewer(s) and approver(s) for the product.

A.17.3 Derivation

A product description is derived from the following:

- product breakdown structure
- the end-users of the product
- quality management approach
- change control approach.

A.17.4 Format and presentation

A product description can take a number of formats, including:

- a document, presentation slides or mind map
- an entry in a project management tool.

A.17.5 Quality criteria

The following quality criteria apply to a product description:

- The purpose of the product is clear and is consistent with that of other products.
- The product is described to a level of detail that is sufficient to plan and manage its development.

- The product description is concise yet sufficient enough to enable the product to be produced, reviewed and approved.
- Responsibility for the development of the product is clearly identified.
- Responsibility for the development of the product is consistent with the roles and responsibilities described in the project management team organization and the quality management approach.
- The quality criteria are consistent with the project quality standards, standard checklists and acceptance criteria.
- The quality criteria can be used to determine when the product is fit for purpose.
- The types of quality inspection required are able to verify whether the product meets its stated quality criteria.
- The senior user(s) confirms that their requirements of the product, as defined in the product description, are accurately described.
- The senior supplier(s) confirms that the requirements of the product, as defined in the product description, can be achieved.

A.18 Product status account

A.18.1 Purpose

Information about the status of products should be maintained and may be presented, within defined limits, in a product status account. The limits can vary. For example, the report could cover the entire project, a particular management stage, a particular area of the project or the history of a specific product. It is particularly useful if the project manager wishes to confirm the version number of products.

The product status account may be derived from:

- configuration item records
- a stage plan.

PRINCE2 does not define the composition, format and presentation, nor any quality criteria for this product.

A.19 Project brief

A.19.1 Purpose

A project brief is used to provide a full and firm foundation for the initiation of the project and is created in the starting up a project process.

In the initiating a project process, the contents of the project brief are extended and refined in the PID, after which the project brief is no longer maintained.

A.19.2 Composition

A project brief includes the following:

- **Project definition** Explains what the project needs to achieve. It should include:
  - background
  - project objectives (covering time, cost, quality, scope, benefits and risk performance)
  - desired outcomes
  - project scope and exclusions
  - constraints and assumptions
  - project tolerances
  - the user(s) and any other known interested parties
  - interfaces
- **Outline business case** (see section A.2) Reasons why the project is needed and the business option selected. This will later be developed into a detailed business case during the initiating a project process
- **Project product description** (see section A.21) Includes the customer's quality expectations, user acceptance criteria, and operations and maintenance acceptance criteria
- **Project approach** Defines the choice of solution that will be used within the project to deliver the business option selected from the business case. This will take into consideration the operational environment into which the solution must fit and any tailoring requirements (if known)
- **Project management team structure** A chart showing who will be involved with the project
- **Role descriptions** These describe the roles of those in the project management team and any other key resources identified at this time
- **References** These include references to any associated documents or products.

A.19.3 Derivation

A project brief is derived from the following:

- a project mandate supplied at the start of the project
- programme management: if the project is part of a programme, the project brief is likely to be supplied by the programme, and therefore it will not have to be derived from a project mandate
- discussions with corporate, programme management or the customer regarding corporate, programme management or customer strategies and any policies and standards that apply
- discussions with the project board and users if the project mandate is incomplete or if no project mandate is provided
- discussions with the operations and maintenance organization (if applicable)
- discussion with the (potential) suppliers regarding specialist delivery approaches that could be used
- lessons log.

A.19.4 Format and presentation

A project brief can take a number of formats, including:

- a document or presentation slides
- an entry in a project management tool.

A.19.5 Quality criteria

The following quality criteria apply to a project brief:

- It is brief because its purpose at this point is to provide a firm basis on which to initiate a project. It will later be refined and expanded as part of the PID.
- It accurately reflects the project mandate and the requirements of the business and the users.
- The project approach considers a range of solutions, such as: bespoke or off-the-shelf; contracted-out or developed in-house; or designed from scratch or modified from an existing product.
- The project approach selected maximizes the chance of achieving overall success for the project.
- The project objectives and project approaches are consistent with the organization's social responsibility directive.
- The project objectives are specific, measurable, achievable, relevant and time-bound (SMART).

A.20 Project initiation documentation (PID)

A.20.1 Purpose

The purpose of the PID is to define the project, in order to form the basis for its management and an assessment of its overall success. The PID gives the direction and scope of the project and (along with the stage plan) forms the 'contract' between the project manager and the project board.

The three primary uses of the PID are to:

- ensure that the project has a sound basis before asking the project board to make any major commitment to the project
- act as a base document against which the project board and project manager can assess progress, issues and ongoing viability questions
- provide a single source of reference about the project so that people joining the 'temporary organization' can quickly and easily find out what the project is about, and how it is being managed.

The PID is a living product in that it should always reflect the current status, plans and controls of the project. Its component products will need to be updated and re-baselined, as necessary, at the end of each management stage, to reflect the current status of its constituent parts.

The version of the PID that was used to gain authorization for the project is preserved as the basis against which performance will later be assessed when closing the project.

A.20.2 Composition

There follows a contents list for the PID. Project definition and project approach are extracted from the project brief:

- **Project definition** Explains what the project needs to achieve. It should include:
  - background
  - project objectives and desired outcomes
  - project scope and exclusions
  - constraints and assumptions
  - the user(s) and any other known interested parties
  - interfaces

- **Project approach** Defines the choice of solution and delivery approach that will be used in the project to deliver the business option selected from the business case, taking into consideration the operational environment into which the solution must fit

- **Business case** (see section A.2) Describes the justification for the project based on estimated costs, risks and benefits

- **Project management team structure** A chart showing who will be involved with the project

- **Role descriptions** These describe the roles of those in the project management team and any other key resources

- **Quality management approach** (see section A.22) Describes the quality techniques and standards to be applied, and the responsibilities for achieving the required quality levels. Where the project is subject to the commissioning organization's quality management policies/strategies, the PID should make reference to them rather than duplicate them. Where the project is not subject to the commissioning organization's quality management policies/strategies, appropriate strategies/approaches should be documented

- **Change control approach** (see section A.3) Describes how and by whom the project's products will be controlled and protected. Where the project is subject to the commissioning organization's change control policies/strategies, the PID should make reference to them rather than duplicate them. Where the project is not subject to the commissioning organization's change control policies/strategies, appropriate strategies/approaches should be documented

- **Risk management approach** (see section A.24) Describes the specific risk management techniques and standards to be applied, and the responsibilities for achieving an effective risk management procedure. Where the project is subject to the commissioning organization's risk management policies/strategies, the PID should refer to rather than duplicate them. Where the project is not subject to the commissioning organization's risk management policies/strategies, appropriate strategies/approaches should be documented

- **Communication management approach** (see section A.5) Defines the parties interested in the project and the means and frequency of communication between them and the project. Where the project is subject to the commissioning organization's communication management policies/strategies, the PID should make reference to them rather than duplicate them. Where the project is not subject to the commissioning organization's communication management policies/strategies, appropriate strategies/approaches should be documented

- **Project plan** (see section A.16) Describes how and when the project's objectives are to be achieved, by showing the major products, activities and resources required on the project. It provides a baseline against which to monitor the project's progress, management stage by management stage

- **Project controls** Summarizes the project-level controls such as management stage boundaries, agreed tolerances, monitoring and reporting

- **Tailoring of PRINCE2** A summary of how PRINCE2 will be tailored for the project.

A.20.3 Derivation

The PID is derived from the following:

- project brief
- discussions with user, business and supplier stakeholders for input on methods, standards and controls.

A.20.4 Format and presentation

The PID could be:

- a single document
- an index for a collection of documents
- a document with cross-references to a number of other documents
- a collection of information sources in a project management tool.

A.20.5 Quality criteria

The following quality criteria apply to a PID:

- The PID correctly represents the project.
- It shows a viable, achievable project that is in line with corporate, programme management or customer strategies or overall programme needs.
- The project management team structure is complete, with names and titles. All the roles have been considered and are backed up by agreed role descriptions. The relationships and lines of authority are clear. If necessary, the project management team structure shows to whom the project board reports.
- It clearly shows a control, reporting and direction regime that can be implemented, appropriate to the scale, risk and importance of the project to corporate, programme management or the customer.
- The controls cover the needs of the project board, project manager and team managers and satisfy any delegated assurance requirements.
- It is clear who will administer each control.
- The project objectives and approaches are consistent with the organization's social responsibility directive, and the project controls are adequate to ensure that the project remains compliant with such a directive.
- Consideration has been given to the format of the PID. For small projects a single document is appropriate. For large projects, it is more appropriate for the PID to be a collection of stand-alone documents. The volatility of each element of the PID should be used to assess whether it should be stand-alone (e.g. elements that are likely to change frequently are best separated out).

A.21 Project product description

A.21.1 Purpose

The project product description is a special form of product description that defines what the project must deliver in order to gain acceptance. It is used to:

- gain agreement from the user on the project's scope and requirements
- define the customer's quality expectations
- define the acceptance criteria, method and responsibilities for the project.

The product description for the project product is created in the starting up a project process as part of the initial scoping activity, and is refined during the initiating a project process when creating the project plan. It is subject to formal change control and should be checked at management stage boundaries (during managing a stage boundary) to see if any changes are required. It is used by the closing a project process as part of the verification that the project has delivered what was expected of it, and that the acceptance criteria have been met.

A.21.2 Composition

The project product description includes the following:

- **Title** Name by which the project is known
- **Purpose** This defines the purpose that the project product will fulfil and who will use it. It is helpful in understanding the product's functions, size, quality, complexity, robustness, etc.
- **Composition** A description of the major products and/or outcomes to be delivered by the project
- **Derivation** What are the source products from which this product is derived? Examples are:
  - existing products to be modified
  - design specifications
  - a feasibility report
  - the project mandate
- **Development skills required** An indication of the skills required to develop the product, or a pointer to which area(s) should supply the development resources
- **Customer's quality expectations** A description of the quality expected of the project product and/or outcomes and the standards and processes that will need to be applied to achieve that quality. They will impact on every part of the product development, and thus on time and cost. The quality expectations are captured in discussions with the customer. Where possible, expectations should be prioritized
- **Acceptance criteria** A prioritized list of criteria that the project product and/or outcomes must meet before the customer will accept them. These are measurable definitions of the attributes that must apply to the set of products to be acceptable to key stakeholders and, in particular, the users and the operational and maintenance organizations. Examples are ease of use, ease of support, ease of maintenance, appearance, major functions, development costs, running costs, capacity, availability, reliability, security, accuracy and performance
- **Project-level quality tolerances** Specification of any tolerances that may apply for the acceptance criteria

- **Acceptance method** Statement of the means by which acceptance will be confirmed. This may simply be a case of confirming that the project product and/or outcomes have been approved, or may involve describing complex handover arrangements for the project product, including any phased handover of the project product's components
- **Acceptance responsibilities** Definition of who will be responsible for confirming acceptance.

A.21.3 Derivation

The project product description is derived from the following:

- project mandate
- discussions with the senior user and executive, possibly via scoping workshops
- request for proposal (if in a commercial customer/supplier environment).

A.21.4 Format and presentation

A product description for the project product can take a number of formats, including:

- a document, presentation slides or mind map
- an entry in a project management tool.

A.21.5 Quality criteria

The following quality criteria apply to a project product description:

- The purpose is clear.
- The composition defines the complete scope of the project.
- The acceptance criteria form the complete list against which the project will be assessed.
- The acceptance criteria address the requirements of all the key stakeholders (e.g. operations and maintenance).
- The project product description defines how the users and the operational and maintenance organizations will assess the acceptability of the finished product(s). It should ensure that:
  - all criteria are measurable
  - each individual criterion is realistic
  - the criteria are consistent as a set. For example, high quality, early delivery and low cost may not go together
  - all criteria can be proven within the project life (e.g. the maximum throughput of a water pump) or by proxy measures that provide reasonable indicators as to whether acceptance criteria will be achieved post-project (e.g. a water pump that complies with design and manufacturing standards of reliability)
- The quality expectations have been considered, including:
  - the characteristics of the key quality requirements (e.g. fast/slow, large/small, national/global)
  - the elements of the customer's quality management system that should be used
  - any other standards that should be used
  - the level of customer/staff satisfaction that should be achieved if surveyed.

A.22 Quality management approach

A.22.1 Purpose

A quality management approach describes how quality will be managed on the project. This includes the specific processes, procedures, techniques, standards and responsibilities to be applied.

A.22.2 Composition

A quality management approach includes the following:

- **Introduction** States the purpose, objectives and scope, and identifies who is responsible for the approach
- **Quality management process or procedure** A description of (or reference to) the quality management procedure to be used. Any variance from corporate, programme management or customer quality standards should be highlighted, together with a justification for the variance. The process or procedure should cover:
  - the approach to quality assurance and quality planning
  - quality control: the project's approach to quality control activities. This may include:
    - quality standards
    - templates and forms to be employed (e.g. product description(s), quality register)
    - definitions of types of quality methods (e.g. inspection, pilot)
    - metrics to be employed in support of quality control
  - project assurance: the project's approach to project assurance activities. This may include:
    - responsibilities of the project board
    - compliance audits
    - corporate, programme management or customer reviews
- **Tools and techniques** Refers to any quality management systems or tools to be used, and any preference for techniques which may be used for each step in the quality management procedure
- **Records** Definition of what quality records will be required and where they will be stored, including the composition and format of the quality register
- **Reporting** Describes any quality management reports, including their purpose, timing and recipients
- **Timing of quality management activities** States when formal quality management activities are to be undertaken (e.g. during audits, when this may involve reference to the quality register)
- **Roles and responsibilities** Defines the roles and responsibilities for quality management activities, including those with quality responsibilities from corporate, programme management or the customer.

A.22.3 Derivation

A quality management approach is derived from the following:

- project board
- project brief, including:
  - the project management team structure (for roles and responsibilities)
  - the project product description (for the customer's quality expectations and acceptance criteria)

- organizational standards
- supplier and customer quality management systems
- change control requirements
- corporate, programme management or customer strategies
- facilitated workshops and informal discussions.

A.22.4 Format and presentation

A quality management approach can take a number of formats, including:

- a stand-alone document or a section of the PID
- an entry in a project management tool.

A.22.5 Quality criteria

The following quality criteria apply to a quality management approach:

- The approach clearly defines ways in which the customer's quality expectations will be met.
- The defined ways are sufficient to achieve the required quality.
- Responsibilities for quality are defined up to a level that is independent of the project and project manager.
- The approach conforms to the supplier's and customer's quality management systems.
- The approach conforms to the corporate, programme management or customer quality policy.
- The approaches to assuring quality for the project are appropriate in the light of the standards selected.

A.23 Quality register

A.23.1 Purpose

A quality register is used to summarize all the quality management activities that are planned or have taken place, and provides information for the end stage reports and end project report. Its purpose is to:

- issue a unique reference for each quality activity
- act as a pointer to the quality records for a product
- act as a summary of the number and type of quality activities undertaken.

A.23.2 Composition

The composition of the quality register will be defined in the quality management approach. For each entry in the quality register, the following should be recorded:

- **Quality identifier** Provides a unique reference for every quality activity entered into the quality register. It will typically be a numeric or alphanumeric value
- **Product identifier(s)** Unique identifier(s) for the product(s) that the quality activity relates to
- **Product title(s)** The name(s) by which the product(s) is known
- **Method** The method employed for the quality activity (e.g. pilot, quality review, audit, etc.)

- **Roles and responsibilities** The person or team responsible for the quality management activities (e.g. auditor or, for quality reviews, presenter, reviewer(s), chair, administrator)
- **Dates** Planned, forecast and actual dates for:
  - the quality activity
  - sign-off that the quality activity is complete
- **Result** The result of the quality activity. If a product fails a quality review, then any reassessment should be listed as a separate entry in the register, as the original quality activity has been completed (in deciding that the result is a 'fail')
- **Quality records** The quality inspection documentation, such as a test plan or the details of any actions required to correct errors and omissions of the products being inspected.

A.23.3 Derivation

The quality register is derived in the following way:

- Entries are made when a quality activity is entered on a stage plan for the current management stage. It may be updated when a team plan is created
- The remaining information comes from the actual performance of the quality activity
- The sign-off date is when all corrective action items have been signed off.

A.23.4 Format and presentation

The format of the quality register will be defined in the quality management approach. A quality register can take a number of formats, including:

- a document, spreadsheet or database
- a stand-alone register or a carry-forward in the minutes of progress review meetings
- an entry in a project management tool
- a part of an integrated project register for all risks, actions, decisions, assumptions, issues, lessons, etc.

A.23.5 Quality criteria

The following quality criteria apply to a quality register:

- A procedure is in place that will ensure that every quality activity is entered on the quality register.
- Responsibility for the quality register has been allocated.
- Actions are clearly described and assigned.
- Entries are uniquely identified, including to which product they refer.
- Access to the quality register is controlled.
- The quality register is kept in a safe place.
- All quality activities are at an appropriate level of control.

A.24 Risk management approach

A.24.1 Purpose

A risk management approach describes how risk will be managed on the project. This includes the specific processes, procedures, techniques, standards and responsibilities to be applied.

A.24.2 Composition

The risk management approach includes the following:

- **Introduction** States the purpose, objectives and scope, and identifies who is responsible for the approach
- **Risk management process or procedure** Describes (or refers to) the risk management process or procedure to be used. Any variance from corporate, programme management or customer standards should be highlighted, together with a justification for the variance. The process or procedure must describe how:
  - risks are identified and assessed
  - risk responses are planned and implemented
  - risk management activities are communicated
- **Tools and techniques** Refers to any risk management systems or tools to be used, and any preference for techniques which may be used for each step in the risk management procedure
- **Records** Defines the composition and format of the risk register and any other risk records to be used by the project
- **Reporting** Describes any risk management reports that are to be produced, including their purpose, timing and recipients
- **Timing of risk management activities** States when formal risk management activities are to be undertaken (e.g. at the end of management stages)
- **Roles and responsibilities** Defines the roles and responsibilities for risk management activities
- **Scales** Defines the scales for estimating probability and impact for the project to ensure that the scales for cost and time (for instance) are relevant to the cost and timeframe of the project. These may be shown in the form of probability impact grids giving the criteria for each level within the scale (e.g. for 'very high', 'high', 'medium', 'low' and 'very low')
- **Proximity** Provides guidance on how proximity for risk events is to be assessed. Proximity reflects the fact that risks will occur at particular times and the severity of their impact will vary according to when they occur. Typical proximity categories will be: imminent, within the management stage, within the project, beyond the project
- **Risk categories** Defines the risk categories to be used (if at all). These may be derived from a risk breakdown structure or prompt list. If no risks have been recorded against a category, this may suggest that the risk identification has not been as thorough as it should have been
- **Risk response categories** Defines the risk response categories to be used, which themselves depend on whether a risk is a perceived threat or an opportunity
- **Early warning indicators** Defines any indicators to be used to track critical aspects of the project so that if certain predefined levels are reached corrective action will be triggered. They will be selected for their relevance to the project objectives

- **Risk tolerance** Defines the threshold levels of risk exposure which, when exceeded, require the risk to be escalated to the next level of management. (For example, a project-level risk tolerance could be set as any risk that, should it occur, would result in loss of trading. Such risks would need to be escalated to corporate, programme management or the customer.) The risk tolerance should define the risk expectations of corporate, programme management or customer and the project board

- **Risk budget** Describes whether a risk budget is to be established and, if so, how it will be used.

A.24.3 Derivation

The risk management approach is derived from the following:

- project brief
- business case
- where relevant, any corporate, programme management or customer risk management guides, strategies or policies.

A.24.4 Format and presentation

A risk management approach can take a number of formats, including:

- a stand-alone document
- a section of the PID
- an entry in a project management tool.

A.24.5 Quality criteria

The following quality criteria apply to the risk management approach:

- Responsibilities are clear and understood by both customer and supplier.
- The risk management procedure is clearly documented and can be understood by all parties.
- Scales, expected value and proximity definitions are clear and unambiguous.
- The chosen scales are appropriate for the level of control required.
- Risk reporting requirements are fully defined.

A.25 Risk register

A.25.1 Purpose

A risk register provides a record of identified risks relating to the project, including their status and history. It is used to capture and maintain information on all the identified threats and opportunities relating to the project.

A.25.2 Composition

The composition of the risk register will be derived from the risk management approach. For each entry in the risk register, the following should be recorded:

- **Risk identifier** Provides a unique reference for every risk entered into the risk register. It will typically be a numeric or alphanumeric value
- **Risk author** The person who raised the risk
- **Date registered** The date the risk was identified
- **Risk category** The type of risk in terms of the project's chosen categories (e.g. schedule, quality, legal)
- **Risk description** Describes the risk in terms of the cause, event (threat or opportunity) and effect (in words of the impact)
- **Probability, impact and expected value** It is helpful to estimate the inherent values (pre-response action) and residual values (post-response action). These should be recorded in accordance with the project's chosen scales
- **Proximity** This would typically state how close to the present time the risk event is anticipated to happen (e.g. imminent, within the management stage, within the project, beyond the project). Proximity should be recorded in accordance with the project's chosen scales
- **Risk response categories** How the project will treat the risk in terms of the project's chosen categories. For example:
  - for threats: avoid, reduce, transfer, share, accept, prepare contingent plans
  - for opportunities: exploit, enhance, transfer, share, accept, prepare contingent plans
- **Risk response** Actions to be taken to resolve the risk. These actions should be aligned with the chosen response categories. Note that more than one risk response may apply to a risk
- **Risk status** Typically described in terms of whether the risk is active or closed. Inclusion of a date last amended will help track changes in risk status
- **Risk owner** The person responsible for managing the risk (there should be only one risk owner per risk)
- **Risk actionee** The person(s) who will implement the action(s) described in the risk response. This may or may not be the same person as the risk owner.

A.25.3 Derivation

The risk register is derived in the following way:

- Entries are made on the risk register when a new risk is identified.
- There may be one or more inherent risks in the project mandate.

A.25.4 Format and presentation

The format and presentation of the risk register will be derived from the risk management approach. A risk register can take a number of formats, including:

- a document, spreadsheet or database
- sticky notes on a wall chart
- a stand-alone register or a carry-forward in the minutes of progress review meetings
- an entry in a project management tool
- a part of an integrated project register for all risks, actions, decisions, assumptions, issues, lessons, etc.

A.25.5 Quality criteria

The following quality criteria apply to the risk register:

- The status indicates whether action has been taken.
- Risks are uniquely identified, including information about which product they refer to.
- Access to the risk register is controlled.
- The risk register is kept in a safe place.

A.26 Work package

A.26.1 Purpose

A work package is a set of information about one or more required products collated by the project manager to pass responsibility for work or delivery formally to a team manager or team member.

A.26.2 Composition

Although the content may vary greatly according to the relationship between the project manager and the recipient of the work package, it should cover:

- **Date** The date of the agreement between the project manager and the team manager/person authorized
- **Team manager or person authorized** The name of the team manager or individual with whom the agreement has been made
- **Work package description** A description of the work to be done
- **Techniques, processes and procedures** Any techniques, tools, standards, processes or procedures to be used in the creation of the specialist products
- **Development interfaces** Interfaces that must be maintained while developing the products. These may be people providing information or those who need to receive information
- **Operations and maintenance interfaces** Identification of any specialist products with which the product(s) in the work package will have to interface during their operational life. These may be other products to be produced by the project, existing products, or those to be produced by other projects (e.g. if the project is part of a programme)

- **Change control requirements** A statement of any arrangements that must be made by the producer for:
  - version control of the products in the work package
  - obtaining copies of other products or their product descriptions
  - submission of the product to change control
  - any storage or security requirements
  - who, if anyone, needs to be advised of changes in the status of the work package
- **Joint agreements** Details of the agreements on effort, cost, start and end dates, and key milestones for the work package
- **Tolerances** Details of the tolerances for the work package (the tolerances will be for time and cost but may also include scope and risk)
- **Constraints** Any constraints (apart from the tolerances) on the work, people to be involved, timings, charges, rules to be followed (e.g. security and safety), etc.
- **Reporting arrangements** The expected frequency and content of checkpoint reports
- **Problem handling and escalation** This refers to the procedure for raising issues and risks
- **Extracts or references** Any extracts or references to related documents, specifically:
  - **Stage plan extract** This will be the relevant section of the stage plan for the current management stage or will be a pointer to it
  - **Product description(s)** This would normally be an attachment of the product description(s) for the products identified in the work package (note that the product description contains the quality methods to be used)
- **Approval method** The person, role or group who will approve the completed products within the work package, and how the project manager is to be advised of completion of the products and work package.

There should be space on the work package to record both its initial authorization and its acceptance and return as a completed work package. This can be enhanced to include an assessment of the work and go towards performance appraisal.

Projects with common controls across all work packages may simply cross-reference the controls defined in the project plan or stage plan.

A.26.3 Derivation

The work package is derived from the following:

- existing commercial agreements between the customer and supplier (if any)
- quality management approach
- change control approach
- stage plan.

A.26.4 Format and presentation

A work package can take a number of formats, including:

- a document
- a conversation between the project manager and a team manager
- an entry in a project management tool.

The work package will vary in content and in degree of formality, depending on circumstances. Where the work is being conducted by a team working directly under the project manager, the work package may be an oral instruction, although there are good reasons for putting it in writing, such as avoidance of misunderstanding and providing a link to performance assessment. Where the work is being carried out by a supplier under a contract and the project manager is part of the customer organization, there is a need for a formal written instruction in line with the standards laid down in that contract.

A.26.5 Quality criteria

The following quality criteria apply to the work package:

- The required work package is clearly defined and understood by the assigned resource.
- There is a product description for each required product, with clearly identified and acceptable quality criteria.
- The product description(s) matches up with the other work package documentation.
- Standards for the work are agreed.
- The defined standards are in line with those applied to similar products.
- All necessary interfaces have been defined.
- The reporting arrangements include the provision for raising issues and risks.
- There is agreement between the project manager and the recipient on exactly what is to be done.
- There is agreement on the constraints, including effort, cost and targets.
- The dates and effort are in line with those shown in the stage plan for the current management stage.
- Reporting arrangements are defined.
- Any requirement for independent attendance at, and participation in, quality activities is defined.

B

Standards alignment

B Standards alignment

Project management standards summarize the key concepts and activities that need to be undertaken in order to increase the likelihood of project success.

There is scope for confusion regarding the respective uses of standards and methods, and how they are applied in organizations. In simple terms:

- A standard, such as BS 6079, defines what needs to be done and by whom, but not how activities are done.
- A method, such as PRINCE2, provides not only a set of activities to be done, together with roles, but also techniques for undertaking these activities.

Standards can improve the effectiveness of project management by drawing attention to the key principles and activities required. After they have been established, standards can promote continual improvement by being periodically reviewed and updated. This ensures that the latest consensus on best practice is included and that any omissions or clarifications are dealt with. In this way, all users of standards benefit from the collective experience of all other users.

B.1 How PRINCE2 meets BS 6079

PRINCE2 and BS 6079 (British Standards Institution, 2010) share a core of common practice and both cover 'project management' in its widest sense, notably:

- The roles used map exactly, except that PRINCE2 calls BS 6079's 'project sponsor' the 'executive' and is more prescriptive about the use and constituency of a project board.
- In terms of project lifecycle, PRINCE2 and BS 6079 follow the same concept of phases/stages, with a project having at least two phases/stages.
- BS 6079 describes 'gates', which are decision points to start the next phase/stage of the project and are independent of when a stage actually ends. By contrast, PRINCE2 describes 'stage boundaries'.
- BS 6079 has an activity for managing a project as a whole (managing a project), whereas PRINCE2 manages at stage level (controlling a stage).
- Being a method, PRINCE2 has details of techniques and approaches that are not in BS 6079 (e.g. product-based planning).

Therefore, if an organization is using PRINCE2, it could be said to comply with BS 6079 Part 1 provided that those aspects which are explicitly beyond the scope of PRINCE2 are covered either by its enterprise method or by other corporate processes and methods.

B.2 How PRINCE2 meets ISO 21500

As PRINCE2 and ISO 21500 (International Organization for Standardization, 2012) have different structures and scopes, it is not always possible to make direct comparisons clause by clause.

- ISO 21500 does not cover, in its processes, the roles of what PRINCE2 refers to as the executive or the team manager. However, PRINCE2 and ISO 21500 do share a core of common practice relating to the role and activities of the project manager.

- ISO 21500 does not define the roles of team manager or team member in any detail because they, like the project sponsor, are outside the standard's scope.

- In terms of project lifecycle, PRINCE2 and ISO 21500 have the same concept of phases/stages, with decision points where each phase/stage of the project starts. ISO 21500 provides no detail on best practice relating to such decisions, which are deemed out of scope.

- The actual structure of ISO 21500 in its logical form is very different from that of PRINCE2. In PRINCE2, the stages of a project are explicit and defined within the processes, such that the initiating and closing of a project is done in a different way from the initiating and closing of a phase/stage. ISO 21500 treats a project and a phase/stage within a project identically and has no explicit procedure for starting new stages within a project. How this is done is left to the user of the standard to determine. PRINCE2 provides detail on this in its managing a stage boundary and directing a project processes.

- Being a method, PRINCE2 has details of techniques and approaches which are not in ISO 21500 (e.g. product-based planning).

Therefore, if an organization is using PRINCE2, it could be said to comply with ISO 21500 provided that those aspects which are explicitly beyond the scope of PRINCE2 are covered either by its enterprise method or by other corporate processes and methods.

B.3 Comparative glossary

Table B.1 compares terms used in PRINCE2 with those in BS 6079 and ISO 21500.

Table B.1 PRINCE2 terms compared with those used in BS 6079 and ISO 21500

PRINCE2	BS 6079	ISO 21500
General		
Project	Project	Project
Stage	Phase	Phase
Stage boundary	Gate	
Key roles		
Executive	Sponsor	Sponsor
Project manager	Project manager	Project manager
Team manager	Team manager	
Key products		
Project brief	Project brief	Charter
PID: project definition, project approach, project management team structure, role descriptions, quality management approach, change control approach, risk management approach, communications management approach	Project management plan	Project management plan
Business case (part of PID)	Business case	Business case (treated as an input to the project)
Project plan (part of PID)	Project plan	Project plan
End stage report	Phase closure report	
Issue register	Issues log	Issues log
Highlight report	Project report	Progress report
End project report	Project closure report	Project closure report

C

Roles and responsibilities

C Roles and responsibilities

This appendix includes detailed descriptions of the PRINCE2 roles. In order to meet the needs of different projects, these roles may be tailored as described in Chapter 4 in general and in Chapter 7 in particular. It should be noted, however, that these roles do not necessarily equate to jobs to be allocated to people on a one-to-one basis. Some roles may be undertaken part-time, while many roles may be shared or combined according to the project's needs, provided the minimum requirements set out in section 7.2 are met.

C.1 Project board

The project board is accountable to corporate, programme management or the customer for the success of the project, and has the authority to direct the project within the remit set by corporate, programme management or the customer as documented in the project mandate.

The project board is also responsible for the communications between the project management team and stakeholders external to that team (e.g. corporate, programme management or the customer).

According to the scale, complexity, importance and risk of the project, project board members may delegate some project assurance tasks to separate individuals. The project board may also delegate decisions regarding changes to a change authority.

C.1.1 General responsibilities

During start-up and initiation, the project board should:

- confirm project tolerances with corporate, programme management or the customer
- approve the project brief
- approve the stage plan for the initiation stage
- authorize project initiation
- decide whether to use a change authority and, if so, agree the level of authority to be delegated
- set the scale for severity ratings for issues
- set the scale for priority ratings for requests for change and off-specifications
- approve the supplier contract (if the relationship between the customer and supplier is a commercial one)
- approve the PID, and its components, including any tailoring
- authorize the start of the project.

During the project, the project board should:

- set tolerances for each management stage and approve stage plans
- authorize each management stage and approve the product descriptions for each management stage
- approve exception plans when management-stage-level tolerances are forecast to be exceeded

- communicate with stakeholders as defined in the communication management approach (including briefing corporate, programme management or the customer about project progress)
- provide overall guidance and direction to the project, ensuring it remains viable and within any specified constraints
- respond to requests for advice from the project manager
- ensure that risks are being tracked and managed as effectively as possible
- approve changes (unless delegated to a change authority)
- make decisions on escalated issues
- approve completed products.

At the end of the project, the project board should:

- provide assurance that all products have been delivered satisfactorily
- provide assurance that all acceptance criteria have been met
- confirm acceptance of the project product
- approve the end project report and ensure that any issues, lessons and risks are documented and passed on to the appropriate body
- authorize follow-on action recommendations to be distributed to corporate, programme management or the customer
- transfer responsibility for the updated benefits management approach to corporate, programme management or the customer
- authorize project closure and send project closure notification to corporate, programme management or the customer.

C.1.2 Competencies

To be successful, the project board should:

- have sufficient authority to make decisions, approve plans and authorize any necessary deviation from stage plans
- have sufficient authority to allocate resources to the project
- be capable of adequately representing the business, user and supplier interests
- ideally be able to stay with the project throughout its life.

Key competencies include:

- decision-making
- delegation
- leadership
- negotiation
- conflict resolution.

C.2 Executive

The executive is ultimately accountable for the project, supported by the senior user and senior supplier. The executive's role is to ensure that the project is focused throughout its life on achieving its objectives and delivering a product that will achieve the forecast benefits. The executive has to ensure that the project gives value for money, ensuring a cost-conscious approach to the project, balancing the demands of the business, user and supplier.

Throughout the project, the executive is responsible for the business case.

The project board is not a democracy controlled by votes. The executive is the ultimate decision maker and is supported in the decision-making by the senior user and senior supplier.

C.2.1 Responsibilities

In addition to the project board's collective responsibilities, the executive will:

- design and appoint the project management team (in particular the project manager)
- oversee the development of the project brief and the outline business case, ensuring that the project is aligned with corporate, programme management or customer strategies (and presenting the outline business case to corporate, programme management or the customer for approval where required)
- oversee the development of the detailed business case
- secure the funding for the project
- approve any additional supplier contracts (if the relationship between the user and supplier is a commercial one)
- hold the senior supplier to account for the quality and integrity of the specialist approach and specialist products created for the project
- hold the senior user to account for realizing the benefits defined in the business case, ensuring that benefits reviews take place to monitor the extent to which the business case benefits are achieved
- transfer responsibility for post-project benefits reviews to corporate, programme management or the customer
- monitor and control the progress of the project at a strategic level, in particular reviewing the business case regularly
- escalate issues and risks to corporate, programme management or the customer if project tolerance is forecast to be exceeded
- ensure that risks associated with the business case are identified, assessed and controlled
- make decisions on escalated issues, with particular focus on continued business justification
- organize and chair project board reviews
- ensure overall business assurance of the project so that it remains on target to deliver products that will achieve the expected business benefits, and so that the project will be completed within its agreed tolerances. Where appropriate, delegate some business assurance activities (see section C.7).

C.3 Senior user

The senior user is responsible for specifying the needs of those who will use the project product, for user liaison with the project management team, and for monitoring that the solution will meet those needs within the constraints of the business case in terms of quality, functionality and ease of use.

The role represents the interests of all those who will use the project product (including operations and maintenance services), those for whom the product will achieve an objective or those who will use the product to deliver benefits. The senior user role commits user resources and monitors products against requirements. This role may require more than one person to cover all the user interests. For the sake of effectiveness, the role should not be split between too many people.

The senior user specifies the benefits and is held to account by demonstrating to corporate, programme management or the customer that the forecast benefits which were the basis of project approval have in fact been realized. This is likely to involve a commitment beyond the end of the life of the project.

C.3.1 Responsibilities

In addition to the project board's collective responsibilities, the senior user will:

- provide the customer's quality expectations and define acceptance criteria for the project
- ensure that the desired outcome of the project is specified
- ensure that the project produces products that will deliver the desired outcomes, and meet user requirements
- ensure that the expected benefits (derived from the project's outcomes) are realized
- provide a statement of actual versus forecast benefits at the benefits reviews
- resolve user requirements and priority conflicts
- ensure that any user resources required for the project (e.g. to undertake user quality inspections and product approval) are made available
- make decisions on escalated issues, with particular focus on safeguarding the expected benefits
- brief and advise user management on all matters concerning the project
- maintain business performance stability during transition from the project to business as usual
- provide the user view on follow-on action recommendations
- undertake project assurance from the user perspective (user assurance) and, where appropriate, delegate user assurance activities (see section C.7).

C.4 Senior supplier

The senior supplier represents the interests of those designing, developing, facilitating, procuring and implementing the project product. This role is accountable for the quality of the project product (and its components) delivered by the supplier(s) and is responsible for the technical integrity of the project. If necessary, more than one person may represent the suppliers.

Depending on the particular customer/supplier environment, the customer may also wish to appoint an independent person or group to carry out assurance on the supplier's products (e.g. if the relationship between the customer and supplier is a commercial one).

C.4.1 Responsibilities

In addition to the project board's collective responsibilities, the senior supplier will:

- assess and confirm the viability of the project approach
- ensure that proposals for designing and developing the products are realistic
- advise on the selection of design, development and acceptance methods
- ensure that the supplier resources required for the project are made available
- make decisions on escalated issues, with particular focus on safeguarding the integrity of the complete solution
- resolve supplier requirements and priority conflicts
- brief non-technical management on supplier aspects of the project
- ensure quality procedures are used correctly, so that products adhere to requirements
- undertake project assurance from the supplier perspective (supplier assurance) and, where appropriate, delegate supplier assurance activities (see section C.7).

C.5 Project manager

The project manager is accountable to the project board and ultimately the executive and has the authority to run the project on a day-to-day basis, within the constraints laid down by them.

The project manager's prime responsibility is to ensure that the project produces the required products within the specified tolerances of time, cost, quality, scope, benefits and risk. The project manager is also responsible for the project producing a result capable of achieving the benefits defined in the business case.

C.5.1 Responsibilities

The project manager's responsibilities include the following:

- Prepare the following baseline management products, in conjunction with any project assurance roles, and agree them with the project board:
  - project brief, including the project product description
  - benefits management approach
  - PID, and its components
  - stage/exception plans and their product descriptions
  - work packages.
- Prepare the following reports:
  - highlight reports
  - issue reports
  - end stage reports
  - exception reports
  - end project report.

- Maintain the following records:
  - issue register
  - risk register
  - daily log
  - lessons log.
- Tailor the PRINCE2 method to suit the project's situation, documenting this, as appropriate, in the PID.
- Liaise with corporate, programme management or the customer to ensure that work is neither overlooked nor duplicated by related projects.
- Liaise with any external suppliers or account managers.
- Lead and motivate the project management team.
- Establish behavioural expectations of team members.
- Manage the information flows between the directing and delivering levels of the project.
- Manage the production of the required products, taking responsibility for overall progress and use of resources and initiating corrective action where necessary.
- Establish and manage the project's procedures: risk management, issue management, change control and communication.
- Establish and manage the project controls: monitoring and reporting.
- Authorize work packages.
- Advise the project board of any deviations from the plan.
- Unless appointed to another person(s), perform the team manager role (see section C.6).
- Unless appointed to another person (or corporate, programme management or customer function), perform the project support role (see section C.9).
- Implement the change control approach.
- Ensure project personnel comply with the change control approach.
- Schedule audits to check that the physical products are consistent with the configuration item records and initiate any necessary corrective action.

C.5.2 Competencies

Different types of project will require different types of project management skills. To be successful, the project manager must be able to balance the different aspects of the project manager role for a particular project.

Key competencies include:

- planning
- time management
- people management
- problem-solving
- attention to detail
- communication
- negotiation
- conflict management.

C.6 Team manager

The team manager's prime responsibility is to ensure production of those products defined by the project manager to an appropriate quality, in a set timescale and at a cost acceptable to the project board. The team manager is accountable to, and takes direction from, the project manager.

C.6.1 Responsibilities

The team manager's responsibilities include the following:

- Prepare the team plan and agree it with the project manager.
- Provide the project manager with recommendations on how PRINCE2 may be tailored to suit the management of the work package.
- Produce checkpoint reports as agreed with the project manager.
- Plan, monitor and manage the team's work.
- Take responsibility for the progress of the team's work and use of team resources, and initiate corrective action, where necessary, within the constraints laid down by the project manager.
- Identify, and advise the project manager of, any issues and risks associated with a work package.
- Advise the project manager of any deviations from the plan, recommend corrective action and help to prepare any appropriate exception plans.
- Pass back to the project manager products that have been completed and approved in line with the agreed work package requirements.
- Liaise with any project assurance and project support roles.
- Ensure that quality activities relating to the team's work are planned and performed correctly, and are within tolerance.
- Ensure that the appropriate entries are made in the quality register.
- Manage specific issues and risks as directed by the project manager.
- Assist the project manager in assessing issues and risks.
- Ensure that all assigned issues are properly reported to the person maintaining the issue register.

C.6.2 Competencies

Different types of project will require different types of skills from the team manager. Key competencies are similar to those of a project manager.

C.7 Project assurance

Project assurance covers the primary stakeholder interests (business, user and supplier). The role has to be independent of the project manager; therefore the project board cannot delegate any of its assurance activities to the project manager.

C.7.1 Responsibilities

The implementation of the assurance responsibilities needs to answer the question of what is to be assured. A list of possibilities applicable to the business, user and supplier stakeholder interests would include ensuring that:

- liaison is maintained between the business, user and supplier throughout the project
- risks are controlled
- the right people are involved in writing product descriptions
- the right people are planned to be involved in quality inspection at the correct points in the development of product(s)
- staff are properly trained in the quality methods
- the quality methods are being correctly followed
- tailoring of PRINCE2 is suited to the project's situation
- quality control follow-up actions are dealt with correctly
- an acceptable solution is being developed
- the scope of the project is not changing unnoticed
- internal and external communications are working
- applicable standards are being used
- the needs of specialist interests (e.g. security) are being observed.

Business assurance responsibilities include:

- assisting the project manager to develop the business case and benefits management approach (if it is being prepared by the project manager)
- advising on the selection of project management team members
- advising on the risk management approach
- reviewing the business case for compliance with corporate, programme management or customer standards
- verifying the business case against external events and project progress
- checking that the business case is being adhered to throughout the project
- checking that the project remains aligned with the corporate, programme management or customer strategy
- reviewing project finance on behalf of the customer
- verifying that the solution continues to provide value for money
- periodically checking that the project remains viable
- assessing whether the aggregated risk exposure remains within project tolerance
- checking that any supplier and contractor payments are authorized
- reviewing issues and risks by assessing their impact on the business case

- constraining user and supplier excesses
- informing the project management team of any changes caused by a programme of which the project is part (this responsibility may be transferred if there is other programme representation on the project management team)
- monitoring management stage and project progress against the agreed tolerances.

User assurance responsibilities include:

- advising on stakeholder engagement
- advising on the communication management approach
- ensuring that the specification of the user's needs is accurate, complete and unambiguous
- assessing whether the solution will meet the user's needs and is progressing towards that target
- advising on the impact of potential changes from the user's point of view
- monitoring risks to the user
- ensuring that the quality activities relating to products at all management stages have appropriate user representation
- ensuring that quality control procedures are used correctly to ensure that products meet user requirements
- ensuring that user liaison is functioning effectively.

Supplier assurance responsibilities include:

- reviewing the product descriptions
- advising on the quality management approach and change control approach
- advising on the selection of the development strategy, design and methods
- ensuring that any supplier and operating standards defined for the project are met and used to good effect
- advising on potential changes and their impact on the correctness, completeness and integrity of products against their product description from a supplier perspective
- monitoring any risks in the production aspects of the project
- assessing whether quality control procedures are used correctly, so that products adhere to requirements.

C.7.2 Competencies

To be successful, project assurance should:

- be capable of adequately representing the business, user or supplier stakeholder interests
- have sufficient credibility to ensure that advice and guidance are followed
- have sufficient specialist knowledge of the business, user or supplier stakeholder areas
- ideally be able to stay with the project throughout its lifecycle.

Key competencies include:

- diplomacy
- thoroughness
- attention to detail
- ability to communicate effectively.

C.8 Change authority

The project board may delegate authority for approving responses to requests for change or off-specifications to a separate individual or group, called a change authority. The project manager could be assigned as the change authority for some aspects of the project (e.g. changing baselined work packages if this does not affect management stage tolerances).

C.8.1 Responsibilities

Responsibilities of the change authority include:

- Review and approve or reject all requests for change and off-specifications within the delegated limits of authority and change budget set by the project board.
- Refer to the project board if any delegated limits of authority or allocated change budget are forecast to be exceeded.

C.8.2 Competencies

The change authority should:

- be capable of adequately representing the business, user and supplier stakeholder interests
- have sufficient credibility to ensure that advice and guidance are followed
- have sufficient specialist knowledge of the business, user or supplier stakeholder areas.

Key competencies include:

- decision-making
- planning
- attention to detail
- problem-solving.

C.9 Project support

The provision of any project support on a formal basis is optional. If it is not delegated to a separate person or function, it will need to be undertaken by the project manager.

One support function that must be considered is that of change control. Depending on the project size and environment, there may be a need to formalize this and it may become a task with which the project manager cannot cope without support.

Project support functions may be provided by a project office or by specific resources for the project. For further information on the use of a project office, see *Portfolio, Programme and Project Offices* (Cabinet Office, 2013).

C.9.1 Responsibilities

The following is a suggested list of tasks for project support:

- Set up and maintain project files.
- Establish document control procedures.
- Collect actuals data and forecasts.
- Update plans.
- Administer or assist the quality review process.
- Administer or assist project board meetings.
- Assist with the compilation of reports.
- Contribute expertise in specialist tools and techniques (e.g. planning and control tools, risk analysis), including tailoring recommendations suited to the project's situation.
- Maintain the following records:
  - quality register
  - configuration item records, if used
  - any other registers/logs delegated by the project manager.
- Administer the change control procedure as follows (these responsibilities may be undertaken by a configuration librarian from corporate, programme management or the customer):
  - administer the receipt, identification, versions, storage and issue of all the project's products
  - provide information on the status of all products
  - archive superseded product copies
  - ensure the security and preservation of the master copies of all the project's products
  - maintain a record of all copies issued
  - notify holders of any changes to their copies
  - number, record, store and distribute issue reports
  - conduct reviews or audits.

C.9.2 Competencies

Typical competencies for project support roles will depend on the type of project and organization. Key competencies include:

- administration and organization
- knowledge of specialist tools and techniques
- knowledge of corporate, programme management or customer standards applicable to the project.

D

Product-based planning example

D Product-based planning example

D.1 Scenario

A project is required to organize and run a conference for between 80 and 100 delegates. The date and subject matter are set, and the focus of the conference is to bring members of a particular profession up to date on recent developments in professional procedures and standards. The project team will need to identify a venue, and check its availability, facilities and price before booking it. They will also need to identify suitable speakers and book them, before producing a detailed agenda and programme. A mailing list of delegates is available, and after the venue has been booked, the project team will need to issue a press release based on the agreed programme. Part of the project will involve producing 100 delegate handouts, with a cover reflecting the selected subject matter. These handouts must contain a printed agenda covering the agreed programme, copies of slides and notes used by the speakers, and a feedback form to capture attendee reviews. Booking arrangements for attending the conference, including details of the programme and venue, must be sent out in the bulk email. The team will need to regularly update the attendance list based on responses to the email, and make arrangements to recruit staff to help on the day, based on the final attendance list.

D.2 Product examples

Table D.1 gives an example of a project product description for the conference. Examples of a product breakdown structure for this event are provided as a hierarchical chart (Figure D.1), a mind map (Figure D.2) and an indented list. Note that PRINCE2 does not specify the format in which the product breakdown structure is drawn.

Figure D.3 gives an example of a product description for the bulk email for the conference, whereas Figure D.4 shows a possible product flow diagram.

Note that only the project product, releases and products need to be transferred from the product breakdown structure in Figure D.1 to the product flow diagram in Figure D.4. For example, in this scenario the planner has used 'publicity' in the product breakdown structure but the only publicity products that need to be produced are the bulk email and press release. (Note that 'product groups' in Figure D.1 are not products that require work but a way of identifying products that have some common characteristics or focus. In this case, 'publicity' is a convenient way to describe the products that provide publicity for the conference.) The delegate handout, however, is a product that is created by bringing together the covers, printed agenda, print-outs of the conference slides and notes, and the satisfaction survey form products.

Table D.1 Example of a project product description for the conference

Title	Conference
Purpose	The conference is the annual showcase of the profession and provides its members with an opportunity to learn about the latest developments in professional procedures and standards, and to network with fellow members
Composition	Conference venue Attendees Speakers Publicity Delegate handouts Conference logistics
Derivation	Selected subject matter Email list Previous conference lessons and materials Agreed date
Development skills required	Conference management Marketing Public relations
Customer's quality expectations	**Must have:** ● The conference must be professional in style, be funded by attendees, and address the needs of the range of members (from beginners to experienced professionals). ● The event must provide a forum for networking. ● The conference must generate repeat attendance at future events by satisfied members. **Should have:** ● The speakers will be chosen on the basis of their knowledge, experience and expertise. They are not delivering a 'sales pitch' to the members. ● The conference will be interactive in style. ● The conference will be held at a central location, therefore minimizing travel.
Acceptance criteria and project-level quality tolerances	In priority order: ● The cost of the conference must be covered by the attendance fees. ● A minimum of 80 and a maximum of 100 people must attend the conference. ● More than 50% of the presentations are interactive (tutorials rather than lectures). ● The speakers and programme are approved by the editorial board representing the interests of the members. ● The attendees' satisfaction survey indicates that more than 75% will attend next year's conference and/or recommend it to colleagues. ● The hotel venue is within 3 miles of a main line train station.
Acceptance method	As the conference cannot be rerun should it prove to be unacceptable, the project board will grant: ● **Preliminary acceptance** Based on approval of the agreed programme by the editorial board and independent assurance that the attendee numbers and conference costs are forecast to be acceptable ● **Final acceptance** Based on the end project report providing evidence that the acceptance criteria were met.
Acceptance responsibilities	The senior user and executive are responsible for confirming acceptance.

Appendix D – Product-based planning example

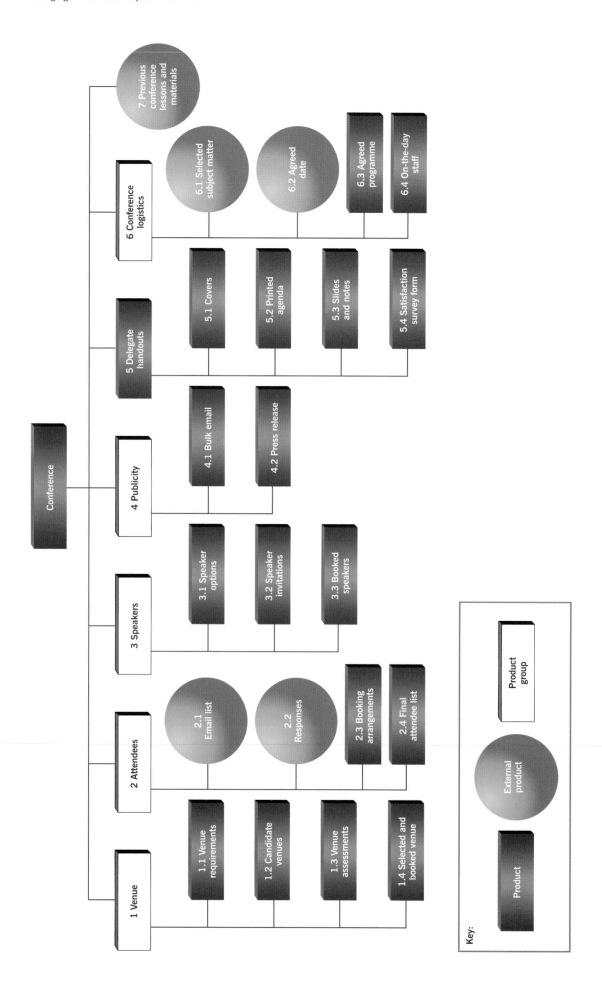

Figure D.1 Product breakdown structure in the form of a hierarchical chart

Appendix D – Product-based planning example

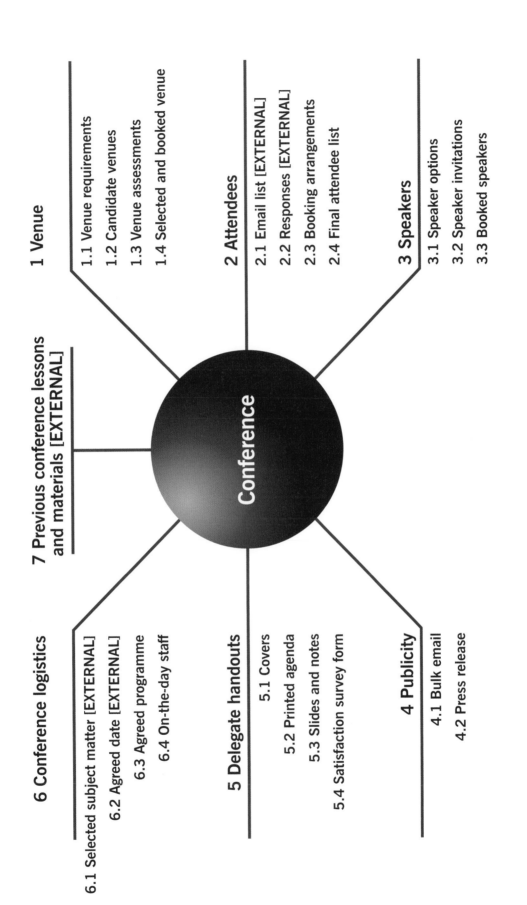

1 Venue

1.1 Venue requirements

1.2 Candidate venues

1.3 Venue assessments

1.4 Selected and booked venue

2 Attendees

2.1 Email list [EXTERNAL]

2.2 Responses [EXTERNAL]

2.3 Booking arrangements

2.4 Final attendee list

3 Speakers

3.1 Speaker options

3.2 Speaker invitations

3.3 Booked speakers

7 Previous conference lessons and materials [EXTERNAL]

Conference

6 Conference logistics

6.1 Selected subject matter [EXTERNAL]

6.2 Agreed date [EXTERNAL]

6.3 Agreed programme

6.4 On-the-day staff

5 Delegate handouts

5.1 Covers

5.2 Printed agenda

5.3 Slides and notes

5.4 Satisfaction survey form

4 Publicity

4.1 Bulk email

4.2 Press release

Figure D.2 Product breakdown structure in the form of a mind map

Product breakdown structure for the conference as an indented list

1 Venue

    1.1 Venue requirements

    1.2 Candidate venues

    1.3 Venue assessments

    1.4 Selected and booked venue

2 Attendees

    2.1 Email list (external)

    2.2 Responses (external)

    2.3 Booking arrangements

    2.4 Final attendee list

3 Speakers

    3.1 Speaker options

    3.2 Speaker invitations

    3.3 Booked speakers

4 Publicity

    4.1 Bulk email

    4.2 Press release

5 Delegate handouts

    5.1 Covers

    5.2 Printed agenda

    5.3 Slides and notes

    5.4 Satisfaction survey form

6 Conference logistics

    6.1 Selected subject matter (external)

    6.2 Agreed date (external)

    6.3 Agreed programme

    6.4 On-the-day staff

7 Previous conference lessons and materials (external)

Identifier	Conference/4.1/version 1.0
Title	Bulk email
Purpose	The bulk email is the primary means of advertising the conference to potential delegates It will be sent to a list of professionals working in the industry
Composition	• An email covering an outline of the conference with a web-link to the conference web site and online booking details • An email attachment with the conference programme, the venue and travel information
Derivation	• Email list • Agreed programme • Booking arrangements • Selected venue
Format and presentation	• Email format and attachment branded with corporate event logo • Contact email address included and link to conference web site with online booking/registration • Email and attachment to comply with corporate style guidelines • Email and attachment to be viewable on tablets and smartphones
Development skills required	• Marketing, design and copywriting skills required • Knowledge of conference necessary
Quality responsibilities	• Producer – event management company • Reviewers – as stated under 'Quality skills required' • Approver – membership secretary

Quality criteria	Quality tolerance	Quality method	Quality skills required
Adheres to corporate identity standards	As defined in corporate identity standards	PRINCE2 quality review	Marketing team
Email and attachment accurately reflect all agreed details of the conference as described in the conference web site	None	Inspection	Conference project manager
No spelling or grammatical errors in any elements of the email and attachment	None	Spell-checker Inspection	Proof reader
When printed, the email attachment fits on one side of A4	May extend to reverse of a single sheet of A4	Inspection	Proof reader

Figure D.3 Example of a product description for the conference bulk email

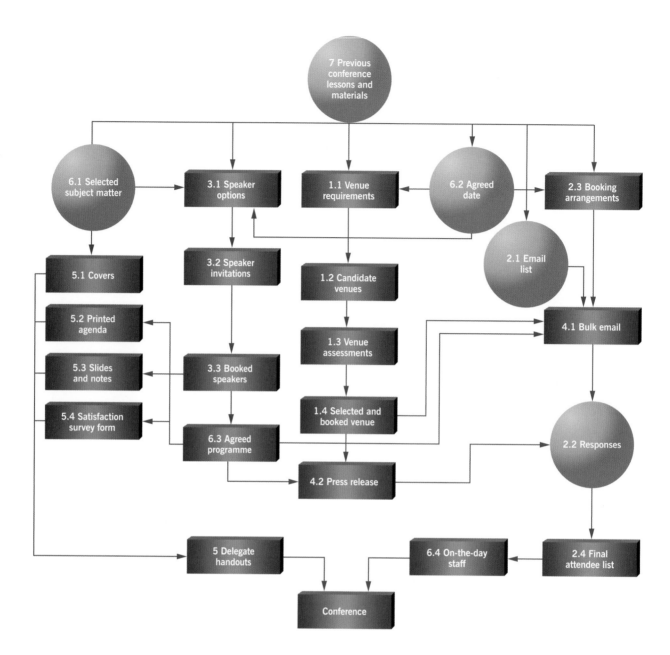

Figure D.4 Example of a product flow diagram for the conference project

E

Health check

E Health check

The following are process-oriented checklists that can be used at various points in the project to assess whether the key aspects of PRINCE2 are adequately addressed. The checklists are not exhaustive but should provide reasonable confidence as to whether a project is being managed in accordance with PRINCE2.

It is important to note that any reference to a management product means 'in accordance with the product description in Appendix A' and in particular the quality criteria for those management products should also be reviewed.

The checklists may need to be adapted to reflect any tailoring of the PRINCE2 method.

E.1 Starting up a project

Question			Yes/No
1	Have project management team roles been allocated for the:		
	a	executive?	
	b	project manager?	
	c	senior user(s)?	
	d	senior supplier(s), if appropriate at this point?	
	e	project support?	
	f	team managers, if appropriate at this point?	
	g	project assurance?	
	h	change authority, if appropriate at this point?	
2	Do the project board members have sufficient authority, availability and credibility to direct the project?		
3	Are the project's stakeholders sufficiently represented by the project board?		
4	Do role descriptions exist for each key appointment?		
5	Have those people appointed confirmed their acceptance?		
6	Has a daily log been set up?		
7	Has the lessons log been set up?		
8	Have lessons from previous similar projects been identified and, where appropriate, applied?		
9	If the organization has not undertaken a project like this before, have lessons been sought from comparable projects external to the organization?		
10	Has the project brief been produced?		
11	Is there an outline business case?		
12	Has the project product description been produced?		
13	Has the project approach been decided upon?		
14	Is there a stage plan for the initiation stage?		

E.2 Directing a project

E2.1 Authorize initiation

Question			Yes/No
15		Has the project board approved the project brief? Specifically, has it:	
	a	confirmed the project definition and approach?	
	b	reviewed and approved the project product description?	
	c	formally confirmed the appointments to the core project management team?	
	d	reviewed and approved the outline business case, particularly the projected benefits?	
16		Has the project board approved the initiation stage plan? Specifically, has it:	
	a	approved the plan to develop the PID?	
	b	obtained or committed the resources needed by the stage plan for the initiation stage?	
	c	ensured that adequate reporting and control mechanisms are in place for the initiation stage?	
	d	set tolerances for the initiation stage?	
	e	requested the necessary logistical support (e.g. accommodation, communication facilities, equipment and any project support) from corporate, programme management or the customer?	
	f	confirmed that it has understood any risks that affect the decision to authorize the initiation stage?	
	g	confirmed to the project manager that the work defined in the initiation stage plan may start?	
17		Has the project board informed corporate, programme management or the customer (and other interested parties) that project initiation has been authorized?	

E.2.2 Authorize the project

Question			Yes/No
18		Has the project board approved the PID? Specifically, has it:	
	a	confirmed that the business case is viable, desirable and achievable and meets corporate, programme management or customer expectations and standards, and approved it?	
	b	confirmed that lessons from previous similar projects have been reviewed and incorporated?	
	c	confirmed that the quality management approach will deliver the quality expectations, and approved it?	
	d	confirmed that the change control approach will deliver the approach expected, and approved it?	
	e	confirmed that the risk management approach will safeguard the project, and approved it?	
	f	confirmed that there has been a risk assessment, and that risk response actions have been planned?	
	g	confirmed the validity and achievability of the project plan and approved it?	
	h	confirmed that the benefits management approach covers all expected benefits, and approved it?	
	i	confirmed that all members of the project management team have agreed their roles (the project management team structure, roles and responsibilities)?	
	j	ensured that the project controls are adequate for the nature of the project?	
	k	ensured that the information needs and timing of communications, as defined in the communication management approach, are adequate for the nature of the project, and approved it?	
	l	reviewed the tolerances for the project provided by corporate, programme management or the customer to ensure that they are appropriate and realistic?	
	m	considered the consistency of the various components and approved the PID overall, including any tailoring?	
19		Has the project board informed corporate, programme management or the customer (and other interested parties) that the project has been authorized?	

E.2.3 Authorize a stage or exception plan

Question			Yes/No
20		Has the project board reviewed the end stage report? Specifically:	
	a	did the board review the performance status of the project using the end stage report for the current management stage?	
	b	has the board reviewed the benefits achieved and lessons captured during the management stage?	
21		Has the project board assessed overall project viability? Specifically, has it:	
	a	reviewed the project plan and the position in relation to project tolerances agreed with corporate, programme management or the customer?	
	b	reviewed the business case to ensure that the project is still justified?	
	c	reviewed the key risks to ensure that the exposure level is still acceptable and that response actions are planned?	
	d	obtained decisions from outside the project for any potential deviations beyond project tolerances? (For example, if this project is part of a programme, then programme management should have examined the impact on the programme, and taken appropriate action.)	
22		Has the project board reviewed and approved the next stage plan (or exception plan)? Specifically, has it:	
	a	reviewed the plan for which the project manager is seeking approval? (This will be a stage plan for the next management stage or an exception plan.)	
	b	authorized the project manager to proceed with the submitted plan (stage plan or exception plan) or instructed the project manager to prematurely close the project?	
	c	set the tolerances for the next management stage or (in the case of an exception plan) revised the current stage tolerances as necessary?	
23		Has the project board informed corporate, programme management or the customer (and other interested parties) that the next management stage has been authorized (or that an exception plan for the current management stage has been approved)?	

E.2.4 Give ad hoc direction

Question			Yes/No
24		Has the project board responded to the project manager's requests? Specifically, has it:	
	a	reviewed the request? (This could be informal or formal, the latter in the form of an issue report.)	
	b	made a decision (e.g. approved, rejected, deferred decision or requested more information)?	
	c	provided guidance to the project manager?	
25		Has the project board responded to reports? Specifically, has it:	
	a	reviewed the latest highlight report in order to understand the status of the project and satisfied itself, through a dialogue with the project manager, that the management stage is progressing according to plan?	
	b	made decisions on exception reports, adjusted tolerances or approved responses to the exception as appropriate?	
	c	made decisions on issue reports within the board's delegated limits of authority or sought advice from corporate, programme management or the customer?	
26		Has the project board responded to external influences? Specifically, has it:	
	a	ensured that the project is kept informed of external events that may affect it?	
	b	ensured that the project remains focused on the corporate, programme management or customer objectives set, and remains justified in business terms?	
	c	ensured that the project manager is notified of any changes in the corporate, programme management or customer environment that may impact on the project and that appropriate action is taken?	
27		Has the project board informed corporate, programme management or the customer (and other interested parties) of the project's progress in accordance with the communication management approach?	

E.2.5 Authorize project closure

Question			Yes/No
28		Has the project board confirmed handover and acceptance? Specifically, has it:	
	a	verified that the handover of the project product was in accordance with the change control approach and in particular that records of all required user acceptance and operational/maintenance acceptance exist?	
	b	ensured that, where appropriate, the resulting changes in the business are supported and sustainable?	
	c	ensured that any customer quality expectations that cannot be confirmed until after the project closes (e.g. performance levels regarding reliability) are included in the benefits management approach as a post-project check?	
29		Has the project board approved the end project report? Specifically, has it:	
	a	used the version of the PID which was approved at project initiation as the baseline to assess how the project has deviated from its initial basis, and to provide information against which the success of the project can be judged?	
	b	ensured follow-on action recommendations have been recorded correctly in the end project report and that the appropriate groups have been made aware of their responsibility for taking them forward?	
	c	approved the end project report for distribution to any interested parties, such as corporate, programme management or the customer?	
30		Has the project board reviewed the lessons log and agreed how the lessons should be disseminated? Has the board ensured that the appropriate groups (e.g. corporate, programme management or the customer, centre of excellence) have been made aware of their responsibility for taking any recommendations forward?	
31		Has the project board confirmed the business case? Specifically, has it confirmed the updated business case by comparing actual and forecast benefits, costs and risks against the approved business case within the PID? (It may not be possible to confirm all the benefits as some will not be realized until after the project is closed.)	
32		Has the project board approved the updated benefits management approach? Specifically, has it:	
	a	reviewed and gained approval for the updated benefits management approach, ensuring that it addresses the expected benefits that cannot yet be confirmed?	
	b	confirmed that the responsibility for the benefits management approach has been transferred to corporate, programme management or the customer?	
33		Has the project board issued the project closure notification? Specifically, has it:	
	a	reviewed and issued a project closure notification in accordance with the communication management approach?	
	b	advised those who have provided the support infrastructure and resources for the project that these can now be withdrawn?	
	c	released the resources provided to the project?	
	d	provided a closing date for costs being charged to the project?	

E.3 Initiating a project

Question		Yes/No
34	Have lessons from previous similar projects been identified and, where appropriate, have they been applied?	
35	Has the risk management approach been defined and documented?	
36	Has the risk register been set up and populated?	
37	Has the change control approach been defined and documented?	
38	Have the initial configuration item records, if used, been set up?	
39	Has the issue register been set up and populated?	
40	Has the quality management approach been defined and documented?	
41	Has the quality register been set up and populated?	
42	Has the communication management approach been defined and documented?	
43	Have the project controls been determined and established?	
44	Has the project plan been created?	
45	Has the project management team structure been updated to reflect any new roles being appointed or any changes to responsibilities of existing roles?	
46	For new appointments, do role descriptions exist and have those people who have been appointed confirmed their acceptance?	
47	Has the outline business case been refined into a detailed business case?	
48	Has the benefits management approach been created (this may have been done by corporate, programme management or the customer)?	
49	Has the PID been assembled, including tailoring?	

E.4 Controlling a stage

Question		Yes/No
50	Have work packages been created and issued?	
51	Have all the team managers agreed all their work packages?	
52	Have completed products been produced in accordance with the work package and product description?	
53	Have the relevant configuration item records, if used, been created/updated?	
54	Has the quality register been maintained?	
55	Were any products handed over as part of a phased delivery? If so, were they handed over in accordance with the change control approach?	
56	Has the risk register been maintained?	
57	Has the issue register been maintained?	
58	Has the stage plan been updated with actuals and revised forecasts?	
59	Has the daily log been maintained?	
60	Have checkpoint reports been received for each issued work package at the frequency and in the format agreed?	
61	Was progress (actual and forecast) checked against agreed tolerances?	
62	If tolerances were forecast to be exceeded, were they escalated to the project board?	
63	If corrective actions were required, were they logged, implemented and tracked?	
64	Was the business case periodically checked for ongoing viability?	
65	Were highlight reports created and issued in accordance with the agreed reporting format and frequency?	
66	Do issue reports exist for all issues being handled formally?	
67	Do exception reports exist for all exceptions raised to the project board?	
68	Has the lessons log been updated with any new lessons?	

E.5 Managing product delivery

	Question	Yes/No
69	Did the work package and product description(s) contain sufficient information, including cross-references, to enable the team manager to produce the products required?	
70	Has a team plan been created that demonstrates that the work package could be completed within agreed tolerances?	
71	Has the team plan been updated with actuals and revised forecasts?	
72	Was progress (actual and forecast) checked against agreed tolerances?	
73	If tolerances were forecast to be exceeded, were they escalated to the project manager?	
74	Were checkpoint reports issued to the project manager at the frequency and in the format agreed?	
75	Did the team manager notify the project manager of any issues and risks?	
76	Do approval records exist for each planned product?	
77	Did the team manager notify project support of any required updates to configuration item records, if used, and the quality register?	
78	Did the team manager notify the project manager that all the products in the work package had been delivered?	

E.6 Managing a stage boundary

	Question	Yes/No
79	Have all products that were planned to be completed within the management stage been approved?	
80	Has a product status account been created to verify the status of the management stage's products?	
81	If there was a product handover during the management stage, were related outstanding issues documented as follow-on action recommendations ready for distribution subject to project board approval?	
82	Has the lessons log been reviewed and updated?	
83	Has the stage plan been updated with actuals?	
84	Has the risk management approach been reviewed and (if necessary) updated?	
85	Has the risk register been reviewed and updated?	
86	Has the change control approach been reviewed and (if necessary) updated?	
87	Have the configuration item records, if used, been reviewed and updated?	
88	Has the issue register been reviewed and updated?	
89	Has the quality management approach been reviewed and (if necessary) updated?	
90	Has the quality register been reviewed and updated?	
91	Has the communication management approach been reviewed and (if necessary) updated?	
92	Have the project controls been reviewed and (if necessary) updated?	
93	Has the project plan been reviewed and (if necessary) updated?	
94	Has the project management team structure been updated to reflect any new roles being appointed or any changes to responsibilities of existing roles?	
95	For new appointments, do role descriptions exist and have those people who have been appointed confirmed their acceptance?	
96	Has the business case been reviewed and (if necessary) updated?	
97	Has the benefits management approach been reviewed and (if necessary) updated?	
98	Has the PID been reviewed and (if necessary) updated?	

Questions continue

E.6 Managing a stage boundary *continued*

Question		Yes/No
99	Has an end stage report been produced showing actual against planned performance, and summarizing lessons and follow-on action recommendations?	
100	Has the end stage report been issued to the project board in accordance with the project controls?	
For the next stage		
101	Has a stage plan for the next management stage been created?	
102	Have product descriptions been created for the next management stage's products?	
103	Has the project board been requested to authorize the next management stage?	
For exceptions		
104	Has an exception plan been created (if requested by the project board)?	
105	Have product descriptions been created/updated for the exception plan?	
106	Has the project board been requested to approve the exception plan?	

E.7 Closing a project

Question		Yes/No
107	Have all products been completed and approved?	
108	Has a product status account been created to verify the status of all the products?	
109	Have all outstanding issues been documented as follow-on action recommendations ready for distribution subject to project board approval?	
110	For premature closure, has the means for recovering products that have been completed or are in progress been approved by the project board? If requested, was an exception plan created and approved?	
111	Is there an acceptance record for the handover of the project product?	
112	Does the acceptance record include operational and maintenance acceptance?	
113	Has the lessons log been reviewed and have relevant lessons been included in the end project report?	
114	Has the project plan been updated with actuals?	
115	Has the business case been updated with actuals?	
116	Has the benefits management approach been updated with actuals?	
117	Has an end project report been produced showing actual against planned performance and summarizing lessons and follow-on action recommendations?	
118	Has the end project report been issued to the project board in accordance with the project controls?	
119	Has a draft project closure notification been created for project board approval and onward distribution?	
120	Have all registers and logs been closed?	
121	Has all project documentation been archived?	

Further research

Further research

AXELOS publications

AXELOS (2014) *Integrating PRINCE2*. The Stationery Office, London.

AXELOS (2014) Portfolio, Programme and Project Management Maturity Model (P3M3): https://www.axelos.com/best-practice-solutions/p3m3 [accessed: 3 February 2017].

AXELOS (2015) *PRINCE2 Agile*. The Stationery Office, London.

AXELOS (2015) *RESILIA: Cyber Resilience Best Practice*. The Stationery Office, London.

AXELOS (2016) *ITIL Practitioner Guidance*. The Stationery Office, London.

Cabinet Office (2011) *ITIL Continual Service Improvement*. The Stationery Office, London.

Cabinet Office (2011) *ITIL Service Design*. The Stationery Office, London.

Cabinet Office (2011) *ITIL Service Operation*. The Stationery Office, London.

Cabinet Office (2011) *ITIL Service Strategy*. The Stationery Office, London.

Cabinet Office (2011) *ITIL Service Transition*. The Stationery Office, London.

Cabinet Office (2011) *Management of Portfolios*. The Stationery Office, London.

Cabinet Office (2011) *Managing Successful Programmes*. The Stationery Office, London.

Cabinet Office (2013) *Portfolio, Programme and Project Offices*. The Stationery Office, London.

Office of Government Commerce (2009) *Directing Successful Projects with PRINCE2*. The Stationery Office, London.

Office of Government Commerce (2010) *Management of Risk: Guidance for Practitioners*. The Stationery Office, London.

Office of Government Commerce (2010) *Management of Value*. The Stationery Office, London.

White Papers

Buttrick, R. (2012) PRINCE2 and the national and international standards [online]. AXELOS, London. https://www.axelos.com/case-studies-and-white-papers/prince2-and-national-and-international-standards [accessed: 3 February 2017].

Other sources

The following is a list of useful references, some of which have been cited by the PRINCE2 authors.

Adair, John (2004) *The John Adair Handbook of Management and Leadership*. Thorogood, London.

The Agile Manifesto (2001): http://agilemanifesto.org [accessed 3 February 2017].

APM (2012) *APM Body of Knowledge* (6th edition). Association for Project Management, Princes Risborough, UK.

APM Governance Specific Interest Group (2011) *Directing Change: A Guide to Governance of Project Management* (2nd edition). Association for Project Management, Princes Risborough, UK.

Belbin team role inventory: http://www.belbin.com [accessed: 3 February 2017].

British Standards Institution (2010) *BS 6079–1:2010 Project Management. Principles and Guidelines for the Management of Projects*. BSI, London.

Buttrick, R. (2009) *The Project Workout: The Ultimate Handbook of Project and Programme Management*. Financial Times/Prentice Hall, Harlow.

Carnegie Mellon University (2010) *CMMI for Development, Version 1.3*. Technical report: CMU/SEI-2010-TR-033.

Franklin, M. (2008) *Communication Skills for Project and Programme Managers*. The Stationery Office, London.

Franklin, M. (2008) *Leadership Skills for Project and Programme Managers*. The Stationery Office, London.

Franklin, M. (2008) *Team Management Skills for Project and Programme Managers*. The Stationery Office, London.

International Organization for Standardization (2012) *ISO 21500:2012 Guidance on Project Management*. ISO, Geneva.

International Organization for Standardization (2015) *ISO 9000:2015 Quality Management Systems – Fundamentals and Vocabulary*. ISO, Geneva.

International Project Management Association (2015) *Individual Competence Baseline for Project, Programme & Portfolio Management* (4th version). International Project Management Association, The Netherlands.

OGC Gateway Review process: https://www.gov.uk/government/publications/major-projects-authority-assurance-toolkit [accessed 3 February 2017].

Project Management Institute (2013) *A Guide to the Project Management Body of Knowledge (PMBOK® Guide)* (5th edition). Project Management Institute, Pennsylvania.

Ries, Eric (2011) *The Lean Startup: How Today's Entrepreneurs Use Continuous Innovation to Create Radically Successful Businesses* (1st edition). Crown Business, New York.

Schwaber, K. and Sutherland, J. (2016) *The Scrum Guide*. http://www.scrumguides.org/ [accessed: 3 February 2017].

Tudor, Dorothy J. (2016) *Agile Project and Service Management – Delivering IT Services Using PRINCE2, ITIL and DSDM Atern* (2nd edition). The Stationery Office, London.

Further research

Glossary

Glossary

accept (risk response)

A risk response that means that the organization takes the chance that the risk will occur, with full impact on objectives if it does.

acceptance

The formal act of acknowledging that the project has met agreed acceptance criteria and thereby met the requirements of its stakeholders.

acceptance criteria

A prioritized list of criteria that the project product must meet before the customer will accept it (i.e. measurable definitions of the attributes required for the set of products to be acceptable to key stakeholders).

accountable

Personally answerable for an activity. Accountability cannot be delegated, unlike responsibility.

activity

A process, function or task that occurs over time, has recognizable results and is managed. It is usually defined as part of a process or plan.

agile and agile methods

A broad term for a collection of behaviours, frameworks, concepts and techniques that go together to enable teams and individuals to work in an agile way that is typified by collaboration, prioritization, iterative and incremental delivery, and timeboxing. There are several specific methods (or frameworks) that are classed as agile, such as Scrum and Kanban. PRINCE2 is completely compatible with working in an agile way.

approval

The formal confirmation that a product is complete and meets its requirements (less any concessions) as defined by its product description.

approver

The person or group (e.g. a project board) who is identified as qualified and authorized to approve a (management or specialist) product as being complete and fit for purpose.

asset

An item, thing or entity that has potential or actual value to an organization [ISO 55000:2014].

assumption

A statement that is taken as being true for the purposes of planning, but which could change later. An assumption is made where some facts are not yet known or decided, and is usually reserved for matters of such significance that, if they change or turn out not to be true, there will need to be considerable replanning.

assurance

All the systematic actions necessary to provide confidence that the target (e.g. system, process, organization, programme, project, outcome, benefit, capability, product output or deliverable) is appropriate. Appropriateness might be defined subjectively or objectively in different circumstances. The implication is that assurance will have a level of independence from that which is being assured. *See also* project assurance; quality assurance.

authority

The right to allocate resources and make decisions (applies to project, management stage and team levels).

authorization

The point at which an authority is granted.

avoid (risk response)

A risk response to a threat where the threat either can no longer have an impact or can no longer happen.

backlog

A list of new features for a product. The list may be made up of user stories which are structured in a way that describes who wants the feature and why.

baseline

Reference levels against which an entity is monitored and controlled.

baseline management product

A type of management product that defines aspects of the project and, when approved, is subject to change control.

benefit

The measurable improvement resulting from an outcome perceived as an advantage by one or more stakeholders.

benefits management approach

An approach that defines the benefits management actions and benefits reviews that will be put in place to ensure that the project's outcomes are achieved and to confirm that the project's benefits are realized.

benefits tolerance

The permissible deviation in the expected benefit that is allowed before the deviation needs to be escalated to the next level of management. Benefits tolerance is documented in the business case. *See also* tolerance.

burn chart

A technique for showing progress (e.g. such as with a timebox), where work that is completed and work still to do are shown with one or more lines that are updated regularly or daily.

business case

The justification for an organizational activity (project), which typically contains timescales, costs, benefits and risks, and against which continuing viability is tested.

centre of excellence

A corporate coordinating function for portfolios, programmes and projects providing standards, consistency of methods and processes, knowledge management, assurance and training.

change authority

A person or group to which the project board may delegate responsibility for the consideration of requests for change or off-specifications. The change authority may be given a change budget and can approve changes within that budget.

change budget

The money allocated to the change authority available to be spent on authorized requests for change.

change control

The procedure that ensures that all changes that may affect the project's agreed objectives are identified, assessed and then approved, rejected or deferred.

change control approach

A description of how and by whom the project's products will be controlled and protected.

checkpoint

A team-level, time-driven review of progress.

checkpoint report

A progress report of the information gathered at a checkpoint, which is given by a team to the project manager and which provides reporting data as defined in the work package.

closure recommendation

A recommendation prepared by the project manager for the project board to send as a project closure notification when the board is satisfied that the project can be closed.

communication management approach

A description of the means and frequency of communication between the project and its stakeholders.

concession

An off-specification that is accepted by the project board without corrective action.

configuration item

An entity that is subject to change control. The entity may be a component of a product, a product or a set of products in a release.

configuration item record

A record that describes the status, version and variant of a configuration item, and any details of important relationships between them.

configuration management

Technical and administrative activities concerned with the controlled change of a product.

configuration management system

The set of processes, tools and databases that are used to manage configuration data. Typically, a project will use the configuration management system of either the customer or supplier organization.

constraints

The restrictions or limitations by which the project is bound.

contingent plan

A plan intended for use only if required (e.g. if a risk response is not successful). Often called a fallback plan.

corporate, programme management or customer standards

These are overarching standards to which the project must adhere. They will influence the four project approaches (communication management, change control, quality management and risk management) and the project controls.

corrective action

A set of actions to resolve a threat to a plan's tolerances or a defect in a product.

cost tolerance

The permissible deviation in a plan's cost that is allowed before it needs to be escalated to the next level of management. Cost tolerance is documented in the respective plan. *See also* tolerance.

customer

The person or group who commissioned the work and will benefit from the end results.

customer's quality expectations

A statement about the quality expected from the project product, captured in the project product description.

daily log

A log used to record problems/concerns that can be handled by the project manager informally.

deliverable

See output.

delivery approach

The specialist approach used to create the products.

delivery step

A step within the delivery approach.

dependency (plan)

A dependency means that one activity is dependent on another. There are at least two types of dependency relevant to a project: internal and external.

An internal dependency is one between two project activities. In these circumstances the project team has control over the dependency.

An external dependency is one between a project activity and a non-project activity, where non-project activities are undertaken by people who are not part of the project team. In these circumstances the project team does not have complete control over the dependency.

dis-benefit

A measurable decline resulting from an outcome perceived as negative by one or more stakeholders, which reduces one or more organizational objective(s).

embedding (PRINCE2)

The act of making something an integral part of a bigger whole.

Embedding is what an organization needs to do to adopt PRINCE2 as its corporate project management method and encourage its widespread use.

end project report

A report given by the project manager to the project board, confirming the handover of all products. It provides an updated business case and an assessment of how well the project has done against the original PID.

end stage assessment

The review by the project board and project manager of the end stage report to decide whether to approve the next stage plan. Depending on the size and criticality of the project, the review may be formal or informal. The authority to proceed should be documented as a formal record.

end stage report

A report given by the project manager to the project board at the end of each management stage of the project. This provides information about the project's performance during the management stage and the project status at the management stage end.

enhance (risk response)

A risk response to an opportunity where proactive actions are taken to enhance both the probability of the event occurring and the impact of the event should it occur.

epic

A high-level definition of a requirement that has not been sufficiently refined or understood yet. Eventually, an epic will be refined and broken down into several user stories or requirements.

event-driven control

A control that takes place when a specific event occurs. This could be, for example, the end of a management stage, the completion of the PID, or the creation of an exception report. It could also include organizational events that may affect the project, such as the end of the financial year.

exception

A situation where it can be forecast that there will be a deviation beyond the tolerance levels agreed between the project manager and the project board (or between the project board and corporate, programme management or the customer).

exception assessment

A review by the project board to approve or reject an exception plan.

exception plan

A plan that often follows an exception report. For a stage plan exception, it covers the period from the present to the end of the current management stage. If the exception were at project level, the project plan would be replaced.

exception report

A description of the exception situation, its impact, options, recommendation and impact of the recommendation. This report is prepared by the project manager for the project board.

executive

The individual with overall responsibility for ensuring that a project meets its objectives and delivers the projected benefits. This individual should ensure that the project maintains its business focus, that it has clear authority, and that the work, including risks, is actively managed. The executive is the chair of the project board. He or she represents the customer and is responsible for the business case.

exploit (risk response)

A risk response to an opportunity. It means seizing the opportunity to ensure that it will happen and that the impact will be realized.

follow-on action recommendations

Recommended actions related to unfinished work, ongoing issues and risks, and any other activities needed to take a product to the next phase of its life. These are summarized and included in the end stage report (for phased handover) and end project report.

governance (corporate)

The ongoing activity of maintaining a sound system of internal control by which the directors and officers of an organization ensure that effective management systems, including financial monitoring and control systems, have been put in place to protect assets, earning capacity and the reputation of the organization.

governance (project)

Those areas of corporate governance that are specifically related to project activities. Effective governance of project management ensures that an organization's project portfolio is aligned with the organization's objectives, is delivered efficiently and is sustainable.

handover

The transfer of ownership of a set of products to the respective user(s). The set of products is known as a release. There may be more than one handover in the life of a project (phased delivery). The final handover takes place in the closing a project process.

highlight report

A time-driven report from the project manager to the project board on management stage progress.

host site

A location where project work is being undertaken (e.g. an office or construction site).

impact (of risk)

The result of a particular threat or opportunity actually occurring, or the anticipation of such a result.

information radiator

A general term used to describe the use of walls or boards containing information that can be readily accessed by people working on the project. It can contain any information, although it would typically show such things as work to do and how work is progressing.

inherent risk

The exposure arising from a specific risk before any action has been taken to manage it.

initiation stage

The period from when the project board authorizes initiation to when it authorizes the project (or decides not to go ahead with it). The detailed planning and establishment of the project management infrastructure is covered by the initiating a project process.

issue

A relevant event that has happened, was not planned, and requires management action. It can be any concern, query, request for change, suggestion or off-specification raised during a project. Project issues can be about anything to do with the project.

issue register

A register used to capture and maintain information on all of the issues that are being managed formally. The issue register should be monitored by the project manager on a regular basis.

issue report

A report containing the description, impact assessment and recommendations for a request for change, off-specification or a problem/concern. It is created only for those issues that need to be handled formally.

key performance indicator (KPI)

A measure of performance that is used to help an organization define and evaluate how successful it is in making progress towards its organizational objectives.

lessons log

An informal repository for lessons that apply to this project or future projects.

log

An informal repository managed by the project manager that does not require any agreement by the project board on its format and composition. PRINCE2 has two logs: the daily log and the lessons log.

management product

A product that will be required as part of managing the project, and establishing and maintaining quality (e.g. highlight report, end stage report). The management products are constant, whatever the type of project, and can be used as described, or with any relevant modifications, for all projects. There are three types of management product: baselines, records and reports.

management stage

The section of a project that the project manager is managing on behalf of the project board at any one time, at the end of which the project board will wish to review progress to date, the state of the project plan, the business case and risks and the next stage plan, in order to decide whether to continue with the project.

maturity

A measure of the reliability, efficiency and effectiveness of a process, function, organization, etc. The most mature processes and functions are formally aligned with business objectives and strategy, and are supported by a framework for continual improvement.

maturity model

A method of assessing organizational capability in a given area of skill.

milestone

A significant event in a plan's schedule, such as completion of key work packages, a development step or a management stage.

off-specification

Something that should be provided by the project, but currently is not (or is forecast not to be). It might be a missing product or a product not meeting its specifications. It is one type of issue.

operational and maintenance acceptance

A specific type of acceptance by the person or group who will support the product after it has been handed over into the operational environment.

outcome

The result of change, normally affecting real-world behaviour and/or circumstances. Outcomes are desired when a change is conceived. They are achieved as a result of the activities undertaken to effect the change.

output

A specialist product that is handed over to a user (or users). Note that management products are not outputs but are created solely for the purpose of managing the project.

performance targets

A plan's goals for time, cost, quality, scope, benefits and risk.

plan

A detailed proposal for doing or achieving something which specifies the what, when, how and by whom it will be achieved. In PRINCE2 there are only the following types of plan: project plan, stage plan, team plan and exception plan.

planned closure

The PRINCE2 activity to close a project.

planning horizon

The period of time for which it is possible to plan accurately.

portfolio

The totality of an organization's investment (or segment thereof) in the changes required to achieve its strategic objectives.

premature closure

The PRINCE2 activity to close a project before its planned closure. The project manager must ensure that work in progress is not simply abandoned, but that the project salvages any value created to date, and checks that any gaps left by the cancellation of the project are raised to corporate, programme management or the customer.

prerequisites (plan)

Any fundamental aspects that must be in place, and remain in place, for a plan to succeed.

PRINCE2 principles

The guiding obligations for good project management practice that form the basis of a project being managed using PRINCE2.

PRINCE2 project

A project that applies the PRINCE2 principles.

probability

This is the evaluated likelihood of a particular threat or opportunity actually happening, including a consideration of the frequency with which this may arise.

problem

A type of issue (other than a request for change or off-specification) that the project manager needs to resolve or escalate. Also known as a concern.

procedure

A series of actions for a particular aspect of project management established specifically for the project (e.g. a risk management procedure).

process

A structured set of activities designed to accomplish a specific objective. A process takes one or more defined inputs and turns them into defined outputs.

producer

The person or group responsible for developing a product.

product

An input or output, whether tangible or intangible, that can be described in advance, created and tested. PRINCE2 has two types of products: management products and specialist products.

product breakdown structure

A hierarchy of all the products to be produced during a plan.

product checklist

A list of the major products of a plan, plus key dates in their delivery.

product description

A description of a product's purpose, composition, derivation and quality criteria. It is produced at planning time, as soon as possible after the need for the product is identified.

product flow diagram

A diagram showing the sequence of production and interdependencies of the products listed in a product breakdown structure.

product status account

A report on the status of products. The required products can be specified by identifier or the part of the project in which they were developed.

product-based planning

An approach for developing a comprehensive plan based on the creation and delivery of required outputs. The approach considers prerequisite products, quality requirements and the dependencies between products.

programme

A temporary, flexible organization structure created to coordinate, direct and oversee the implementation of a set of related projects and activities in order to deliver outcomes and benefits related to the organization's strategic objectives. A programme is likely to have a life that spans several years.

project

A temporary organization that is created for the purpose of delivering one or more business products according to an agreed business case.

project approach

A description of the way in which the work of the project is to be approached. For example, are we building a product from scratch or buying in a product that already exists?

project assurance

The project board's responsibilities to assure itself that the project is being conducted correctly. The project board members each have a specific area of focus for project assurance, namely business assurance for the executive, user assurance for the senior user(s), and supplier assurance for the senior supplier(s).

project brief

A statement that describes the purpose, cost, time and performance requirements, and constraints for a project. It is created before the project begins, during the starting up a project process, and is used during the initiating a project process to create the PID and its components. It is superseded by the PID and not maintained.

project closure notification

Advice from the project board to inform all stakeholders and the host sites that the project resources can be disbanded and support services, such as space, equipment and access, demobilized. It should indicate a closure date for costs to be charged to the project.

project initiation documentation (PID)

A logical set of documents that brings together the key information needed to start the project on a sound basis and that conveys the information to all concerned with the project.

project initiation notification

Advice from the project board to inform all stakeholders and the host sites that the project is being initiated and to request any necessary logistical support (e.g. communication facilities, equipment and any project support) sufficient for the initiation stage.

project lifecycle

The period from initiation of a project to the acceptance of the project product.

project management

The planning, delegating, monitoring and control of all aspects of the project, and the motivation of those involved, to achieve the project objectives within the expected performance targets for time, cost, quality, scope, benefits and risk.

project management team

The entire management structure of the project board, and the project manager, plus any team manager, project assurance and project support roles.

project management team structure

An organization chart showing the people assigned to the project management team roles to be used, and their delegation and reporting relationships.

project manager

The person given the authority and responsibility to manage the project on a day-to-day basis to deliver the required products within the constraints agreed with the project board.

project mandate

An external product generated by the authority commissioning the project that forms the trigger for starting up a project.

project office

A temporary office set up to support the delivery of a specific change initiative being delivered as a project. If used, the project office undertakes the responsibility of the project support role.

project plan

A high-level plan showing the major products of the project, when they will be delivered and at what cost. An initial project plan is presented as part of the PID. This is revised as information on actual progress appears. It is a major control document for the project board to measure actual progress against expectations.

project product

What the project must deliver in order to gain acceptance.

project product description

A special type of product description used to gain agreement from the user on the project's scope and requirements, to define the customer's quality expectations and the acceptance criteria for the project.

project support

An administrative role in the project management team. Project support can be in the form of advice and help with project management tools, guidance, administrative services such as filing, and the collection of actual data.

proximity (of risk)

The time factor of risk (i.e. when the risk may occur). The impact of a risk may vary in severity depending on when the risk occurs.

quality

The degree to which a set of inherent characteristics of a product, service, process, person, organization, system or resource fulfils requirements.

quality assurance

A planned and systematic process that provides confidence that outputs will match their defined quality criteria when tested under quality control. It is carried out independently of the project team.

quality control

The process of monitoring specific project results to determine whether they comply with relevant standards and of identifying ways to eliminate causes of unsatisfactory performance.

quality criteria

A description of the quality specification that the product must meet, and the quality measurements that will be applied by those inspecting the finished product.

quality inspection

A systematic, structured assessment of a product carried out by two or more carefully selected people (the review team) in a planned, documented and organized fashion.

quality management

The coordinated activities to direct and control an organization with regard to quality.

quality management approach

An approach defining the quality techniques and standards to be applied, and the various responsibilities for achieving the required quality levels, during a project.

quality management system

The complete set of quality standards, procedures and responsibilities for an organization or specific entity (site, business unit, etc.) within that organization.

quality records

Evidence kept to demonstrate that the required quality assurance and quality control activities have been carried out.

quality register

A register containing summary details of all planned and completed quality activities. The quality register is used by the project manager and project assurance as part of reviewing progress.

quality review

See quality inspection.

quality review technique

A technique with defined roles and a specific structure, designed to assess whether a product in the form of a document (or similar, such as a presentation) is complete, adheres to standards and meets the quality criteria agreed for it in the relevant product description. The participants are drawn from those with the necessary competence to evaluate its fitness for purpose.

quality tolerance

The tolerance identified for a product for a quality criterion defining an acceptable range of values. Quality tolerance is documented in the project product description (for the project-level quality tolerance) and in the product description for each product to be delivered.

records

Dynamic management products that maintain information regarding project progress.

reduce (risk response)

A response to a risk where proactive actions are taken to reduce the probability of the event occurring by performing some form of control, and/or to reduce the impact of the event should it occur.

registers

Formal repositories managed by the project manager that require agreement by the project board on their format, composition and use. PRINCE2 has three registers: issue register, risk register and quality register.

release

The set of products in a handover. The contents of a release are managed, tested and deployed as a single entity. *See also* handover.

reports

Management products providing a snapshot of the status of certain aspects of the project.

request for change

A proposal for a change to a baseline. It is a type of issue.

Glossary

residual risk

The risk remaining after the risk response has been applied.

responsible

Used to describe the individual who has the authority and is expected to deliver a task or activity; responsibility can be delegated.

responsible authority

The person or group commissioning the project (typically corporate, programme management or the customer) who has the authority to commit resources and funds on behalf of the commissioning organization.

reviewer

A person or group independent of the producer who assesses whether a product meets its requirements as defined in its product description.

risk

An uncertain event or set of events that, should it occur, will have an effect on the achievement of objectives. A risk is measured by a combination of the probability of a perceived threat or opportunity occurring, and the magnitude of its impact on objectives.

risk actionee

A nominated owner of an action to address a risk. Some actions may not be within the remit of the risk owner to control explicitly; in that situation there should be a nominated owner of the action to address the risk. He or she will need to keep the risk owner apprised of the situation.

risk appetite

An organization's unique attitude towards risk-taking that in turn dictates the amount of risk that it considers acceptable.

risk estimation

The estimation of probability and impact of an individual risk, taking into account predetermined standards, target risk levels, interdependencies and other relevant factors.

risk evaluation

The process of understanding the net effect of the identified threats and opportunities on an activity when aggregated together.

risk exposure

The extent of risk borne by the organization at the time.

risk management

The systematic application of principles, approaches and processes to the tasks of identifying and assessing risks, planning and implementing risk responses and communicating risk management activities with stakeholders.

risk management approach

An approach describing the goals of applying risk management, as well as the procedure that will be adopted, roles and responsibilities, risk tolerances, the timing of risk management interventions, the tools and techniques that will be used, and the reporting requirements.

risk owner

A named individual who is responsible for the management, monitoring and control of all aspects of a particular risk assigned to them, including the implementation of the selected responses to address the threats or to maximize the opportunities.

risk profile

A description of the types of risk that are faced by an organization and its exposure to those risks.

risk register

A record of identified risks relating to an initiative, including their status and history.

risk response

Actions that may be taken to bring a situation to a level where exposure to risk is acceptable to the organization. These responses fall into a number of risk response categories.

risk response category

A category of risk response. For threats, the individual risk response category can be to avoid, reduce, transfer, share, accept or prepare contingent plans. For opportunities, the individual risk response category can be to exploit, enhance, transfer, share, accept or prepare contingent plans.

risk tolerance

The threshold levels of risk exposure that, with appropriate approvals, can be exceeded, but which when exceeded will trigger some form of response (e.g. reporting the situation to senior management for action).

risk tolerance line

A line drawn on the summary risk profile. Risks that appear above this line cannot be accepted (lived with) without referring them to a higher authority. For a project, the project manager would refer these risks to the project board.

schedule

A graphical representation of a plan (e.g. a Gantt chart), typically describing a sequence of tasks, together with resource allocations, which collectively deliver the plan. In PRINCE2, project activities should be documented only in the schedules associated with a project plan, stage plan or team plan. Actions that are allocated from day-to-day management may be documented in the relevant project log (i.e. risk register, daily log, issue register or quality register) if they do not require significant activity.

scope

For a plan, the sum total of its products and the extent of their requirements. It is described by the product breakdown structure for the plan and associated product descriptions.

scope tolerance

The permissible deviation in a plan's scope that is allowed before the deviation needs to be escalated to the next level of management. Scope tolerance is documented in the respective plan in the form of a note or reference to the product breakdown structure for that plan. See tolerance.

Scrum

An iterative, timeboxed approach to product delivery that is described as 'a framework within which people can address complex adaptive problems, while productively and creatively delivering products of the highest possible value' (Schwaber and Sutherland, 2016).

Scrum master

A Scrum role that is responsible for ensuring Scrum is understood and enacted and that the Scrum team adheres to Scrum theory, practice and rules.

senior supplier

The project board role that provides knowledge and experience of the main discipline(s) involved in the production of the project's deliverable(s). The senior supplier represents the supplier's interests within the project and provides supplier resources.

senior user

The project board role accountable for ensuring that user needs are specified correctly and that the solution meets those needs.

share (risk response)

A risk response to either a threat or an opportunity through the application of a pain/gain formula: both parties share the gain (within pre-agreed limits) if the cost is less than the cost plan, and both share the pain (again within pre-agreed limits) if the cost plan is exceeded.

specialist product

A product whose development is the subject of the plan. The specialist products are specific to an individual project (e.g. an advertising campaign, a car park ticketing system, foundations for a building or a new business process). Also known as a deliverable. See also output.

sponsor

The main driving force behind a programme or project. PRINCE2 does not define a role for the sponsor, but the sponsor is most likely to be the executive on the project board, or the person who has appointed the executive.

sprint

A fixed timeframe (typically of 2–4 weeks) for creating selected features from the backlog.

stage

See management stage.

stage plan

A detailed plan used as the basis for project management control throughout a management stage.

stakeholder

Any individual, group or organization that can affect, be affected by or perceive itself to be affected by, an initiative (i.e. a programme, project, activity or risk).

start-up

The pre-project activities undertaken by the executive and the project manager to produce the outline business case, project brief and initiation stage plan.

supplier

The person, group or groups responsible for the supply of the project's specialist products.

tailoring

Adapting a method or process to suit the situation in which it will be used.

team manager

The person responsible for the production of products allocated by the project manager (as defined in a work package) to an appropriate quality, timescale and at a cost acceptable to the project board. This role reports to, and takes direction from, the project manager. If a team manager is not assigned, the project manager undertakes the responsibilities of the team manager role.

team plan

An optional level of plan used as the basis for team management control when executing work packages.

theme

An aspect of project management that needs to be continually addressed, and that requires specific treatment for the PRINCE2 processes to be effective.

threat

An uncertain event that could have a negative impact on objectives or benefits.

time tolerance

The permissible deviation in a plan's time that is allowed before the deviation needs to be escalated to the next level of management. Time tolerance is documented in the respective plan. *See also* tolerance.

time-driven control

A management control that is periodic in nature, to enable the next higher authority to monitor progress (e.g. a control that takes place every 2 weeks). PRINCE2 offers two key time-driven progress reports: checkpoint report and highlight report.

timebox

A finite period of time when work is carried out to achieve a goal or meet an objective. The deadline should not be moved, as the method of managing a timebox is to prioritize the work inside it. At a low level a timebox will be a matter of days or weeks (e.g. a sprint). Higher-level timeboxes act as aggregated timeboxes and contain lower-level timeboxes (e.g. stages).

tolerance

The permissible deviation above and below a plan's target for time and cost without escalating the deviation to the next level of management. There may also be tolerance levels for quality, scope, benefits and risk. Tolerance is applied at project, management stage and team levels.

tranche

A programme management term describing a group of projects structured around distinct step changes in capability and benefit delivery.

transfer (risk response)

A response to a threat where a third party takes on responsibility for some of the financial impact of the threat (e.g. through insurance or by means of appropriate clauses in a contract).

transformation

A distinct change to the way an organization conducts all or part of its business.

trigger

An event or decision that triggers a PRINCE2 process to begin.

user

The person or group who will use the project product.

user acceptance

A specific type of acceptance by the person or group who will use the product after it has been handed over into the operational environment.

user story

A tool used to write a requirement in the form of who, what and why.

variant

A variation of a baselined product. For example, an operations manual may have English and Spanish variants.

version

A specific baseline of a product. Versions typically use naming conventions that enable the sequence or date of the baseline to be identified. For example, project plan version 2 is the baseline after project plan version 1.

waterfall method

A development approach that is linear and sequential, with distinct goals for each phase of development. After a phase of development has been completed, the development proceeds to the next phase and earlier phases are not revisited (hence the analogy that water flowing down a mountain cannot go back).

work package

The set of information relevant to the creation of one or more products. It will contain a description of the work, the product description(s), details of any constraints on production, and confirmation of the agreement between the project manager and the person or team manager who is to implement the work package that the work can be done within the constraints.

Glossary

Index

Index

Index

W